The
Sacred Books of the East

translated
by various Oriental scholars
and edited by

F. Max Müller

Vol. XV

The Upaniṣads

Translated by F. Max Müller

in two parts

Part II

Kaṭha Upaniṣad
Muṇḍaka Upaniṣad
Taittirīya Upaniṣad
Bṛhadāraṇyaka Upaniṣad
Śvetāśvatara Upaniṣad
Praśna Upaniṣad
Maitrāyaṇi Upaniṣad

Dover Publications, Inc.
New York   New York

Published in Canada by General Publishing Company, Ltd., 30 Lesmill Road, Don Mills, Toronto,
Ontario.

Published in the United Kingdom by Constable
and Company, Ltd., 10 Orange Street, London WC 2.

This new Dover edition, first published in 1962,
is an unabridged and unaltered republication of the
work first published by the Clarendon Press, Oxford.
The Upanishads, Part I, first published in 1879, is
Volume I of "The Sacred Books of the East" and
Part II, first published in 1884, is Volume XV of the
same series.

For bibliographic ease and accuracy the modern
transliteration of Sanskrit has been adopted for the
title page and cover of this book as have the more
usual names of several of the upaniṣads. Within
the text, however, the older transliteration has been
retained.

Standard Book Number: 486-20993-8

Library of Congress Catalog Card Number:62-53180

Manufactured in the United States of America
Dover Publications, Inc.
180 Varick Street
New York, N. Y. 10014

CONTENTS.

INTRODUCTION.

THIS second volume completes the translation of the principal Upanishads to which Saṅkara appeals in his great commentary on the Vedânta-Sûtras[1], viz. :

1. *Kh*ândogya-upanishad,
2. Talavakâra or Kena-upanishad,
3. Aitareya-upanishad,
4. Kaushîtaki-upanishad,
5. Vâ*g*asaneyi or Îs*â*-upanishad,
6. Ka*th*a-upanishad,
7. Mu*nd*aka-upanishad,
8. Taittirîyaka-upanishad,
9. Br*i*hadâra*n*yaka-upanishad,
10. *S*vetâsvatara-upanishad,
11. Pras*ñ*a-upanishad.

These eleven have sometimes[2] been called the old and genuine Upanishads, though I should be satisfied to call them the eleven classical Upanishads, or the fundamental Upanishads of the Vedânta philosophy.

Vidyâra*n*ya[3], in his ' Elucidation of the meaning of all the Upanishads,' Sarvopanishadarthânubhûti-prakâ*s*a, confines himself likewise to those treatises, dropping, however, the Îsâ, and adding the Maitrâya*n*a-upanishad, of which I have given a translation in this volume, and the N*ri*-sim*h*ottara-tapanîya-upanishad, the translation of which had to be reserved for the next volume.

---

[1] See Deussen, Vedânta, Einleitung, p. 38. *S*aṅkara occasionally refers also to the Paiṅgi, Agnirahasya, *G*âbâla, and Nârâya*n*îya Upanishads.

[2] Deussen, loc. cit. p. 82.

[3] I state this on the authority of Professor Cowell. See also Fitzedward Hall, Index to the Bibliography of the Indian Philosophical Systems, pp. 116 and 236.

It is more difficult to determine which of the Upanishads
were chosen by *Sa*ṅkara or deserving the honour of a special
commentary. We possess his commentaries on the eleven
Upanishads mentioned before[1], with the exception of the
Kaushîtaki[2]-upanishad. We likewise possess his commentary on the Mâ*nd*ûkya-upanishad, but we do not know for
certain whether he left commentaries on any of the other
Upanishads. Some more or less authoritative statements
have been made that he wrote commentaries on some of the
minor Upanishads, such as the Atharva*s*iras, Atharva-*s*ikhâ,
and the N*r*isi*m*hatâpanî[3]. But as, besides *Sa*ṅkarâ*k*ârya, the
disciple of Govinda, there is *Sa*ṅkarânanda, the disciple of
Ânandâtman, another writer of commentaries on the Upanishads, it is possible that the two names may have been
confounded by less careful copyists[4].

With regard to the N*r*isi*m*hatâpanî all uncertainty might
seem to be removed, after Professor Râmamaya Tarkaratna has actually published its text with the commentary
of *Sa*ṅkarâ*k*ârya in the Bibliotheca Indica, Calcutta, 1871.
But some uncertainty still remains. While at the end of
each Kha*nd*a of the N*r*isi*m*ha-pûrvatâpanî we read that
the Bhâshya was the work of the Paramaha*m*sa-parivrâ-
*g*akâ*k*ârya *Sr*î-*Sa*ṅkara, the pupil of Govinda, we have no
such information for the N*r*isi*m*ha-uttaratâpanî, but are
told on the contrary that the words *Sr*î-Govindabhagavat
&c. have been added at the end by the editor, because he
thought fit to do so. This is, to say the least, very suspicious,
and we must wait for further confirmation. There is another
commentary on this Upanishad by Nârâya*n*abha*tt*a, the son
of Bha*tt*a Ratnâkara[5], who is well known as the author of
Dîpikâs on several Upanishads.

---

[1] They have been published by Dr. Roer in the Bibliotheca Indica.

[2] Dr. Weber's statement that *Sa*ṅkara wrote a commentary on the Kaushîtaki-
upanishad has been corrected by Deussen, loc. cit. p. 39.

[3] See Deussen, loc. cit. p. 39.

[4] A long list of works ascribed to *Sa*ṅkara may be seen in Regnaud, Philosophie de l'Inde, p. 34, chiefly taken from Fitzedward Hall's Index of Indian
Philosophical Systems.

[5] See Tarkaratna's Vig*ñ*âpana, p. 3, l. 5.

I subjoin a list of thirty of the smaller Upanishads, published by Professor Râmamaya Tarkaratna in the Bibliotheca Indica, with the commentaries of Nârâya*n*abha*tt*a.

We owe to the same editor in the earlier numbers of the Bibliotheca the following editions:

Nrisimhapûrvatâpanî-upanishad, with commentary.
Nrisimhottaratâpanî-upanishad, with commentary.
Shatkakra-upanishad, with commentary by Nârâyana.

Lastly, Harakandra Vidyâbhûshana and Visvanâtha Sâstrî have published in the Bibliotheca Indica an edition of the Gopâlatâpanî-upanishad, with commentary by Visvesvara.

These editions of the text and commentaries of the Upanishads are no doubt very useful, yet there are many passages where the text is doubtful, still more where the commentaries leave us without any help.

Whatever other scholars may think of the difficulty of translating the Upanishads, I can only repeat what I have said before, that I know of few Sanskrit texts presenting more formidable problems to the translator than these philosophical treatises. It may be said that most of them had been translated before. No doubt they have been, and a careful comparison of my own translation with those of my predecessors will show, I believe, that a small advance, at all events, has now been made towards a truer understanding of these ancient texts. But I know full well how much still remains to be done, both in restoring a correct text, and in discovering the original meaning of the Upanishads; and I have again and again had to translate certain passages tentatively only, or following the commentators, though conscious all the time that the meaning which they extract from the text cannot be the right one.

As to the text, I explained in my preface to the first volume that I attempted no more than to restore the text, such as it must have existed at the time when Sankara wrote his commentaries. As Sankara lived during the ninth century A.D.[1], and as we possess no MSS. of so early a date, all reasonable demands of textual criticism would thereby seem to be satisfied. Yet, this is not quite so. We may draw such a line, and for the present keep within it, but scholars who hereafter take up the study of the

---

[1] India, What can it teach us? p. 360.

Upanishads will probably have to go beyond. Where I had an opportunity of comparing other commentaries, besides those of Sankara, it became quite clear that they often followed a different text, and when, as in the case of the Maitrâya*n*a-brâhma*n*a-upanishad, I was enabled to collate copies which came from the South of India, the opinion which I have often expressed of the great value of Southern MSS. received fresh confirmation. The study of Grantha and other Southern MSS. will inaugurate, I believe, a new period in the critical treatment of Sanskrit texts, and the text of the Upanishads will, I hope, benefit quite as much as later texts by the treasures still concealed in the libraries of the Dekhan.

The rule which I have followed myself, and which I have asked my fellow translators to follow, has been adhered to in this new volume also, viz. whenever a choice has to be made between what is not quite faithful and what is not quite English, to surrender without hesitation the idiom rather than the accuracy of the translation. I know that all true scholars have approved of this, and if some of our critics have been offended by certain unidiomatic expressions occurring in our translations, all I can say is, that we shall always be most grateful if they would suggest translations which are not only faithful, but also idiomatic. For the purpose we have in view, a rugged but faithful translation seems to us more useful than a smooth but misleading one.

However, we have laid ourselves open to another kind of censure also, namely, of having occasionally not been literal enough. It is impossible to argue these questions in general, but every translator knows that in many cases a literal translation may convey an entirely wrong meaning. I shall give at least one instance.

My old friend, Mr. Nehemiah Goreh—at least I hope he will still allow me to call him so—in the 'Occasional Papers on Missionary Subjects,' First Series, No. 6, quotes, on p. 39, a passage from the *Kh*ândogya-upanishad, translates it into English, and then remarks that I had not translated it accurately. But the fault seems to me to lie entirely with him, in attempting to translate a passage without considering the whole chapter of which it forms a part. Mr. Nehemiah Goreh states the beginning of the story rightly when he says that a youth by name *S*veta-ketu went, by the advice of his father, to a teacher to study under him. After spending twelve years, as was customary, with the teacher, when he returned home he appeared rather elated. Then the father asked him:

Uta tam âde*s*am aprâksho[1] yenâ*s*ruta*m s*rutam bhavaty amatam matam avi*gñ*âta*m* vi*gñ*âtam iti?

I translated this: 'Have you ever asked for that instruction by which we hear what cannot be heard, by which we perceive what cannot be perceived, by which we know what cannot be known?'

Mr. Nehemiah Goreh translates: 'Hast thou asked (of thy teacher) for that instruction by which what is not heard becomes heard, what is not comprehended becomes comprehended, what is not known becomes known?'

I shall not quarrel with my friend for translating m a n by to comprehend rather than by to perceive. I prefer my own translation, because manas is one side of the common sensory (anta*h*kara*n*a), buddhi, the other; the original differ-ence between the two being, so far as I can see, that the manas originally dealt with percepts, the buddhi with con-cepts[2]. But the chief difference on which my critic lays stress is that I translated a*s*rutam, amatam, and avi*gñ*âtam not by 'not heard, not comprehended, not known,' but by 'what cannot be heard, what cannot be perceived, what cannot be known.'

Now, before finding fault, why did he not ask himself what possible reason I could have had for deviating from the original, and for translating avi*gñ*âta by unknowable or

---

[1] Mr. Nehemiah Goreh writes aprâkshyo, and this is no doubt the reading adopted by Roer in his edition of the *Kh*ândogya-upanishad in the Bibliotheca Indica, p. 384. In *S*ankara's commentary also the same form is given. Still grammar requires aprâksho.

[2] The Pa*ñk*adasî (I, 20) distinguishes between manas and buddhi, by saying, mano vimar*s*arûpa*m* syâd buddhi*h* syân ni*s*/ayâtmikâ, which places the difference between the two rather in the degree of certainty, ascribing deliberation to manas, decision to buddhi.

what cannot be known, rather than by unknown, as every one would be inclined to translate these words at first sight? If he had done so, he would have seen in a moment, that without the change which I introduced in the idiom, the translation would not have conveyed the sense of the original, nay, would have conveyed no sense at all. What could Svetaketu have answered, if his father had asked him, whether he had not asked for that instruction by which what is not heard becomes heard, what is not comprehended becomes comprehended, what is not known becomes known? He would have answered, 'Yes, I have asked for it; and from the first day on which I learnt the Siksha, the A B C, I have every day heard something which I had not heard before, I have comprehended something which I had not comprehended before, I have known something which I had not known before.' Then why does he say in reply, 'What is that instruction?' Surely Mr. Nehemiah Goreh knew that the instruction which the father refers to, is the instruction regarding Brahman, and that in all which follows the father tries to lead his son by slow degrees to a knowledge of Brahman[1]. Now that Brahman is called again and again 'that which cannot be seen, cannot be heard, cannot be perceived, cannot be conceived,' in the ordinary sense of these words; can be learnt, in fact, from the Veda only[2]. It was in order to bring out this meaning that I translated asrutam not by 'not heard,' but by 'not hearable,' or, in better English, by 'what cannot be heard[3].'

---

[1] In the Vedânta-Sâra, Sadânanda lays great stress on the fact that in this very chapter of the Khândogya-upanishad, the principal subject of the whole chapter is mentioned both in the beginning and in the end. Tatra prakaranaprati-pâdyasyârthasya tadâdyantayor upâdânam upakramasamhâram. Yathâ Khân-dogyashashthaprapâthake prakaranapratipâdyasyâdvitîyavastuna ekam evâ-dvitîyam (VI, 2, 1) ityâdâv aitadâtmyam idam sarvam (VI, 16, 3) ity ante ka pratipâdanam. 'The beginning with and ending with' imply that the matter to be declared in any given section is declared both at the beginning and at the end thereof:—as, for instance, in the sixth section of the Khândogya-upanishad, 'the Real, besides which there is nought else'—which is to be explained in that section—is declared at the outset in the terms, 'One only, without a second,' and at the end in the terms 'All this consists of That.'

[2] Vedânta-Sâra, No. 118, tatraivâdvitîyavastuno mânântarâvishayîkaranam.

[3] See Mund. Up. I, 1, 6, adresyam agrâhyam.

Any classical scholar knows how often we must translate invictus by invincible, and how Latin tolerates even invictissimus, which we could never render in English by 'the most unconquered,' but 'the unconquerable.' English idiom, therefore, and common sense required that avig*ñ*âta should be translated, not by inconceived, but by inconceivable, if the translation was to be faithful, and was to give to the reader a correct idea of the original.

Let us now examine some other translations, to see whether the translators were satisfied with translating literally, or whether they attempted to translate thoughtfully.

Anquetil Duperron's translation, being in Latin, cannot help us much. He translates: 'Non auditum, auditum fiat; et non scitum, scitum; et non cognitum, cognitum.'

Rajendralal Mitra translates: 'Have you enquired of your tutor about that subject which makes the unheard-of heard, the unconsidered considered, and the unsettled settled?'

He evidently knew that Brahman was intended, but his rendering of the three verbs is not exact.

Mr. Gough (p. 43) translates: 'Hast thou asked for that instruction by which the unheard becomes heard, the unthought thought, the unknown known?'

But now let us consult a scholar who, in a very marked degree, always was a thoughtful translator, who felt a real interest in the subject, and therefore was never satisfied with mere words, however plausible. The late Dr. Ballantyne, in his translation of the Vedânta-Sâra[1], had occasion to translate this passage from the *Kh*ândogya-upanishad, and how did he translate it? 'The eulogizing of the subject is the glorifying of what is set forth in this or that section (of the Veda); as, for example, in that same section, the sixth chapter of the *Kh*ândogya-upanishad, the glorifying of the Real, besides whom there is nought else, in the following terms: "Thou, O disciple, hast asked for that instruction whereby the unheard-of becomes heard, the inconceiv-

---

[1] Lecture on the Vedânta, embracing the text of the Vedânta-Sâra, Allahabad, 1851, p. 69. Vedântasâra, with N*ri*simha-Sarasvatî's Subodhinî, and Râmatîrtha's Vidvanmanora*ñ*ginî, Calcutta, 1860, p. 89. Here we find the right reading, aprâksha*h*.

able becomes conceived, and the unknowable becomes thoroughly known."'

Dr. Ballantyne therefore felt exactly what I felt, that in our passage a strictly literal translation would be wrong, would convey no meaning, or a wrong meaning ; and Mr. Nehemiah Goreh will see that he ought not to express blame, without trying to find out whether those whom he blames for want of exactness, were not in reality more scrupulously exact in their translation than he has proved himself to be.

Mr. Nehemiah Goreh has, no doubt, great advantages in interpreting the Upanishads, and when he writes without any theological bias, his remarks are often very useful. Thus he objects rightly, I think, to my translation of a sentence in the same chapter of the *Kh*ândogya-upanishad, where the father, in answer to his son's question, replies : 'Sad eva, Somya, idam agra âsîd ekam evâdvitîyam.' I had tried several translations of these words, and yet I see now that the one I proposed in the end is liable to be mis-understood. I had translated : 'In the beginning, my dear, there was that only which is, one only, without a second.' The more faithful translation would have been : 'The being alone was this in the beginning.' But 'the being' does not mean in English that which is, τὸ ὄν, and therefore, to avoid any misunderstanding, I translated 'that which is.' I might have said, however, 'The existent, the real, the true (satyam) was this in the beginning,' just as in the Aitareya-upani-shad we read : 'The Self was all this, one alone, in the beginning[1].' But in that case I should have sacrificed the gender, and this in our passage is of great importance, being neuter, and not masculine.

What, however, is far more important, and where Mr. Nehemiah Goreh seems to me to have quite misapprehended the original Sanskrit, is this, that sat, τὸ ὄν, and âtmâ, the Self, are the subjects in these sentences, and not predicates. Now Mr. Nehemiah Goreh translates : 'This was the ex-istent one. itself before, one only without a second ;' and he

---

[1] Âtmâ vâ idam eka evâgra âsît.

explains: 'This universe, before it was developed in the
present form, was the existent one, Brahma, itself.' This
cannot be. If 'idam,' this, i. e. the visible world, were the
subject, how could the Upanishad go on and say, tad
aikshata bahu syâm pra*g*âyeyeti tat te*g*o 'sri*g*ata, 'that
thought, may I be many, may I grow forth. It sent forth
fire.' This can be said of the Sat only, that is, the
Brahman[1]. Sat, therefore, is the subject, not idam, for
a Vedântist may well say that Brahman is the world, or
sent forth the world, but not that the world, which is a
mere illusion, was, in the beginning, Brahman.

This becomes clearer still in another passage, Maitr. Up.
VI, 17, where we read: Brahma ha vâ idam agra âsîd eko
'nanta*h*, 'In the beginning Brahman was all this. He was
one, and infinite.' Here the transition from the neuter to
the masculine gender shows that Brahman only can be the
subject, both in the first and in the second sentence.

In English it may seem to make little difference whether
we say, 'Brahman was this,' or 'this was Brahman.' In
Sanskrit too we find, Brahma khalv idam vâva sarvam,
'Brahman indeed is all this' (Maitr. Up. IV, 6), and Sarva*m*
khalv idam Brahma, 'all this is Brahman indeed' (*Kh*ând.
Up. III, 14, 1). But the logical meaning is always that
Brahman was all this, i. e. all that we see now, Brahman
being the subject, idam the predicate. Brahman becomes
idam, not idam Brahman.

Thus the Pañ*k*adasî, I, 18, says:

Ekada*s*endriyair yuktyâ *s*âstre*n*âpy avagamyate
    Yâvat ki*m*k*id bhaved etad ida*m*sabdodita*m* *g*agat,
which Mr. A. Venis (Pandit, V, p. 667) translates: 'Whatever may be apprehended through the eleven organs, by
argument and revelation, i. e. the world of phenomena, is
expressed by the word idam, this.' The Pañ*k*adasî then
goes on:

Ida*m* sarvam purâ sri*sh*te*r* ekam evâdvitîyakam
    Sad evâsîn nâmarûpe nâstâm ity Âru*n*e va*k*a*h*.
This Mr. Venis translates: 'Previous to creation, all this

<hr>

[1] *S*ankara says (p. 398, l. 5): ekam evâdvitîyam paramârthata idam buddhi-
kâle 'pi tat sad aikshata.

was the existent (sat), one only without a second : name and form were not :—this is the declaration of the son of Aru*n*a.'

This is no doubt a translation grammatically correct, but from the philosophical standpoint of the Vedânta, what is really meant is that, before the s*ri*sh*ti* (which is not creation, but the sending forth of the world, and the sending forth of it, not as something real, but as a mere illusion), the Real alone, i. e. the Brahman, was, instead of this, i. e. instead of this illusory world. The illusion was not, but the Real, i.e. Brahman, was. What became, or what seemed to change, was Brahman, and therefore the only possible subject, logically, is Brahman, everything else being a predicate, and a phenomenal predicate only.

If I were arguing with a European, not with an Indian scholar, I should venture to go even a step further, and try to prove that the idam, in this and similar sentences, does not mean this, i. e. this world, but that originally it was intended as an adverb, meaning now, or here. This use of idam, unsuspected by native scholars, is very frequent in Vedic literature, and instances may be seen in Boehtlingk's Dictionary. In that case the translation would be : ' The real (τὸ ὄν), O friend, was here in the beginning.' This meaning of idam, however, would apply only to the earliest utterances of ancient Brahmavâdins, while in later times idam was used and understood in the sense of all that is seen, the visible universe, just as iyam by itself is used in the sense of the earth.

However, difficulties of this kind may be overcome, if once we have arrived at a clear conception of the general drift of the Upanishads. The real difficulties are of a very different character. They consist in the extraordinary number of passages which seem to us utterly meaningless and irrational, or, at all events, so far-fetched that we can hardly believe that the same authors who can express the deepest thoughts on religion and philosophy with clearness, nay, with a kind of poetical eloquence, could have uttered in the same breath such utter rubbish. Some of the sacrificial technicalities, and their philosophical interpretations with which the Upanishads abound, may perhaps in time assume a clearer meaning, when we shall have more fully mastered the intricacies of the Vedic ceremonial. But there will always remain in the Upanishads a vast amount of what we can only call meaningless jargon, and for the presence of which in these ancient mines of thought I, for my own part, feel quite unable to account. 'Yes,' a friend of mine wrote to me, after reading some of the Sacred Books of the East, 'you are right, how tremendously ahead of other sacred books is the Bible. The difference strikes one as almost unfairly great.' So it does, no doubt. But some of the most honest believers and admirers of the Bible have expressed a similar disappointment, because they had formed their ideas of what a Sacred Book ought to be, theoretically, not historically. The Rev. J. M. Wilson, in his excellent Lectures on the Theory of Inspiration, p. 32, writes: 'The Bible is so unlike what you would expect; it does not consist of golden sayings and rules of life; give explanations of the philosophical and social problems of the past, the present, and the future; contain teachings immeasurably unlike those of any other book; but it contains history, ritual, legislation, poetry, dialogue, prophecy, memoirs, and letters; it contains much that is foreign to your idea of what a revelation ought to be. But this is not all. There is not only much that is foreign, but much that is opposed, to your preconceptions. The Jews tolerated slavery, polygamy, and other customs and cruelties of imperfect civilisation. There are the vindictive psalms, too, with their bitter hatred against enemies,—psalms which we chant in our churches. How can we do so? There are stories of immorality, of treachery, of crime. How can we read them?' Still the Bible has been and is a truly sacred, because a truly historical book, for there is nothing more sacred in this world than the history of man, in his search after his highest ideals. All ancient books which have once been called sacred by man, will have their lasting place in the history of mankind, and those who possess the courage, the perseverance, and the self-denial of the true miner, and of the true scholar, will find even in the darkest and dustiest shafts what they are seeking for,—real nuggets of thought, and precious jewels of faith and hope.

I.

THE KA*TH*A-UPANISHAD.

THE Ka*th*a-upanishad is probably more widely known than any other Upanishad. It formed part of the Persian translation, was rendered into English by Râmmohun Roy, and has since been frequently quoted by English, French, and German writers as one of the most perfect specimens of the mystic philosophy and poetry of the ancient Hindus.

It was in the year 1845 that I first copied at Berlin the text of this Upanishad, the commentary of *S*aṅkara (MS. 127 Chambers[1]), and the gloss of Gopâlayogin (MS. 224 Chambers). The text and commentary of *S*aṅkara and the gloss of Ânandagiri have since been edited by Dr. Roer in the Bibliotheca Indica, with translation and notes. There are other translations, more or less perfect, by Râmmohun Roy, Windischmann, Poley, Weber, Muir, Regnaud, Gough, and others. But there still remained many difficult and obscure portions, and I hope that in some at least of the passages where I differ from my predecessors, not excepting *S*aṅkara, I may have succeeded in rendering the original meaning of the author more intelligible than it has hitherto been.

The text of the Ka*th*a-upanishad is in some MSS. ascribed to the Ya*g*ur-veda. In the Chambers MS. of the commentary also it is said to belong to that Veda[2], and in the Muktikopanishad it stands first among the Upanishads of the Black Ya*g*ur-veda. According to Colebrooke (Miscellaneous Essays, I, 96, note) it is referred to the Sâma-veda also. Generally, however, it is counted as one of the Âtharva*n*a Upanishads.

The reason why it is ascribed to the Ya*g*ur-veda, is probably because the legend of Na*k*iketas occurs in the Brâhma*n*a of the Taittirîya Ya*g*ur-veda. Here we read (III, 1, 8):

Vâ*g*a*s*ravasa, wishing for rewards, sacrificed all his

---

[1] MS. 133 is a mere copy of MS. 127.
[2] Ya*g*urvede Ka*th*avallîbhâshyam.

wealth. He had a son, called Na*k*iketas. While he was
still a boy, faith entered into him at the time when the
cows that were to be given (by his father) as presents to
the priests, were brought in. He said: 'Father, to whom
wilt thou give me?' He said so a second and third time.
The father turned round and said to him: 'To Death, I
give thee.'

Then a voice said to the young Gautama, as he stood
up: 'He (thy father) said, Go away to the house of Death,
I give thee to Death.' Go therefore to Death when he is
not at home, and dwell in his house for three nights without eating. If he should ask thee, 'Boy, how many nights
hast thou been here?' say, 'Three.' When he asks thee,
'What didst thou eat the first night?' say, 'Thy offspring.' 'What didst thou eat the second night?' say,
'Thy cattle.' 'What didst thou eat the third night?'
say, 'Thy good works.'

He went to Death, while he was away from home, and
he dwelt in his house for three nights without eating. When
Death returned, he asked: 'Boy, how many nights hast
thou been here?' He answered: 'Three.' 'What didst
thou eat the first night?' 'Thy offspring.' 'What didst thou
eat the second night?' 'Thy cattle.' 'What didst thou eat
the third night?' 'Thy good works.'

Then he said: 'My respect to thee, O venerable sir!
Choose a boon.'

'May I return living to my father,' he said.

'Choose a second boon.'

'Tell me how my good works may never perish.'

Then he explained to him this Nâ*k*iketa fire (sacrifice),
and hence his good works do not perish.

'Choose a third boon.'

'Tell me the conquest of death again.'

Then he explained to him this (chief) Nâ*k*iketa fire
(sacrifice), and hence he conquered death again [1].

This story, which in the Brâhma*n*a is told in order to
explain the name of a certain sacrificial ceremony called

---

[1] The commentator explains punar-m*ri*tyu as the death that follows after
the present inevitable death.

Nâ*k*iketa, was used as a peg on which to hang the doctrines of the Upanishad. In its original form it may have constituted one Adhyâya only, and the very fact of its division into two Adhyâyas may show that the compilers of the Upanishad were still aware of its gradual origin. We have no means, however, of determining its original form, nor should we even be justified in maintaining that the first Adhyâya ever existed by itself, and that the second was added at a much later time. Whatever its component elements may have been before it was an Upanishad, when it was an Upanishad it consisted of six Vallîs, neither more nor less.

The name of vallî, lit. creeper, as a subdivision of a Vedic work, is important. It occurs again in the Taittirîya Upanishads. Professor Weber thinks that vallî, creeper, in the sense of chapter, is based on a modern metaphor, and was primarily intended for a creeper, attached to the *s*âkhâs or branches of the Veda[1]. More likely, however, it was used in the same sense as parvan, a joint, a shoot, a branch, i. e. a division.

Various attempts have been made to distinguish the more modern from the more ancient portions of our Upanishad[2]. No doubt there are peculiarities of metre, grammar, language, and thought which indicate the more primitive or the more modern character of certain verses. There are repetitions which offend us, and there are several passages which are clearly taken over from other Upanishads, where they seem to have had their original place. Thirty-five years ago, when I first worked at this Upanishad, I saw no difficulty in re-establishing what I thought the original text of the Upanishad must have been. I now feel that we know so little of the time and the circumstances when these half-prose and half-metrical Upanishads were first put together, that I should hesitate

---

[1] History of Indian Literature, p. 93, note ; p. 157.

[2] Though it would be unfair to hold Professor Weber responsible for his remarks on this and other questions connected with the Upanishads published many years ago (Indische Studien, 1853, p. 197), and though I have hardly ever thought it necessary to criticise them, some of his remarks are not without their value even now.

before expunging even the most modern-sounding lines from the original context of these Vedântic essays[1].

The mention of Dhâtri, creator, for instance (Ka*th*. Up. II, 20), is certainly startling, and seems to have given rise to a very early conjectural emendation. But dhâtri and vidhâtri occur in the hymns of the Rig-veda (X, 82, 2), and in the Upanishads (Maitr. Up. VI, 8); and Dhâtri, as almost a personal deity, is invoked with Pra*g*âpati in Rig-veda X, 184, 1. Deva, in the sense of God (Ka*th*. Up. II, 12), is equally strange, but occurs in other Upanishads also (Maitr. Up. VI, 23; *S*vetâ*s*v. Up. I, 3). Much might be said about setu, bridge (Ka*th*. Up. III, 2; Mu*nd*. Up. II, 2, 5), âdar*s*a, mirror (Ka*th*. Up. VI, 5), as being characteristic of a later age. But setu is not a bridge, in our sense of the word, but rather a wall, a bank, a barrier, and occurs frequently in other Upanishads (Maitr. Up. VII,. 7; *K*hând. Up. VIII, 4; B*ri*h. Up. IV, 4, 22, &c.), while âdar*s*as, or mirrors, are mentioned in the B*ri*hadâra*n*yaka and the *S*rauta-sûtras. Till we know something more about the date of the first and the last composition or compilation of the Upanishads, how are we to tell what subjects and what ideas the first author or the last collector was familiar with? To attempt the impossible may seem courageous, but it is hardly scholarlike.

With regard to faulty or irregular readings, we can never know whether they are due to the original composers, the compilers, the repeaters, or lastly the writers of the Upanishads. It is easy to say that adre*s*ya (Mu*nd*. Up. I, 1, 6) ought to be ad*ri*sya; but who would venture to correct that form? Whenever that verse is quoted, it is quoted with adre*s*ya, not ad*ri*sya. The commentators themselves tell us sometimes that certain forms are either Vedic or due to carelessness (pramâdapâ*th*a); but that very fact shows that such a form, for instance, as samîyâta (*K*hând. Up. I, 12, 3) rests on an old authority.

No doubt, if we have the original text of an author, and can prove that his text was corrupted by later compilers

---

[1] See Regnaud, Le Pessimisme Brahmanique, Annales du Musée Guimet, 1880; tom. i, p. 101.

or copyists or printers, we have a right to remove those later alterations, whether they be improvements or corruptions. But where, as in our case, we can never hope to gain access to original documents, and where we can only hope, by pointing out what is clearly more modern than the rest or, it may be, faulty, to gain an approximate conception of what the original composer may have had in his mind, before handing his composition over to the safe keeping of oral tradition, it is almost a duty to discourage, as much as lies in our power, the work of reconstructing an old text by so-called conjectural emendations or critical omissions.

I have little doubt, for instance, that the three verses 16–18 in the first Vallî of the Ka*th*a-upanishad are later additions, but I should not therefore venture to remove them. Death had granted three boons to Na*k*iketas, and no more. In a later portion, however, of the Upanishad (II, 3), the expression s*ri*ṅkâ vittamayî occurs, which I have translated by 'the road which leads to wealth.' As it is said that Na*k*iketas did not choose that s*ri*ṅkâ, some reader must have supposed that a s*ri*ṅkâ was offered him by Death. S*ri*ṅkâ, however, meant commonly a string or necklace, and hence arose the idea that Death must have offered a necklace as an additional gift to Na*k*iketas. Besides this, there was another honour done to Na*k*iketas by M*ri*tyu, namely, his allowing the sacrifice which he had taught him, to be called by his name. This also, it was supposed, ought to have been distinctly mentioned before, and hence the insertion of the three verses 16–18. They are clumsily put in, for after punar evâha, 'he said again,' verse 16 ought not to have commenced by tam abravît, 'he said to him.' They contain nothing new, for the fact that the sacrifice is to be called after Na*k*iketas was sufficiently indicated by verse 19, 'This, O Na*k*iketas, is thy fire which leads to heaven, which thou hast chosen as thy second boon.' But so anxious was the interpolator to impress upon his hearers the fact that the sacrifice should in future go by that name, that, in spite of the metre, he inserted tavaiva, 'of thee alone,' in verse 19.

II.

THE MU*N*DAKA-UPANISHAD.

THIS is an Upanishad of the Atharva-veda. It is a Mantra-upanishad, i. e. it has the form of a Mantra. But, as the commentators observe, though it is written in verse, it is not, like other Mantras, to be used for sacrificial purposes. Its only object is to teach the highest knowledge, the knowledge of Brahman, which cannot be obtained either by sacrifices or by worship (upâsana), but by such teaching only as is imparted in the Upanishad. A man may a hundred times restrain his breath, &c., but without the Upanishad his ignorance does not cease. Nor is it right to continue for ever in the performance of sacrificial and other good works, if one wishes to obtain the highest knowledge of Brahman. The Sannyâsin alone, who has given up everything, is qualified to know and to become Brahman. And though it might seem from Vedic legends that Gr*i*hasthas also who continued to live with their families, performing all the duties required of them by law, had been in possession of the highest knowledge, this, we are told, is a mistake. Works and knowledge can be as little together as darkness and light.

This Upanishad too has been often translated since it first appeared in the Persian translation of Dârâ Shukoh. My own copy of the text and *S*ankara's commentary from the MS. in the Chambers Collection was made in October 1844. Both are now best accessible in the Bibliotheca Indica, where Dr. Roer has published the text, the comcommentary by *S*ankara, a gloss by Ânanda*g*ñâna, and an English translation with notes.

The title of the Upanishad, Mu*n*daka, has not yet been explained. The Upanishad is called Mu*n*daka-upanishad, and its three chapters are each called Mu*n*dakam. Native commentators explain it as the shaving Upanishad, that is, as the Upanishad which cuts off the errors of the mind, like a razor. Another Upanishad also is called Kshurikâ, the razor, a name which is explained in the text itself as meaning an instrument for removing illusion and error. The title is all the more strange because Mu*nd*aka, in its commonest acceptation, is used as a term of reproach for Buddhist mendicants, who are called ' Shavelings,' in opposition to the Brâhmans, who dress their hair carefully, and often display by its peculiar arrangement either their family or their rank. Many doctrines of the Upanishads are, no doubt, pure Buddhism, or rather Buddhism is on many points the consistent carrying out of the principles laid down in the Upanishads. Yet, for that very reason, it seems impossible that this should be the origin of the name, unless we suppose that it was the work of a man who was, in one sense, a Mu*nd*aka, and yet faithful to the Brahmanic law.

III.

THE TAITTIRÎYAKA-UPANISHAD.

THE Taittirîyaka-upanishad seems to have had its original place in the Taittirîya-Âra*ny*aka. This Âra*ny*aka consists, as Rajendralal Mitra has shown in the Introduction to his edition of the work in the Bibliotheca Indica, of three portions. Out of its ten Prapâ*th*akas, the first six form the Âra*ny*aka proper, or the Karma-kâ*nd*a, as Sâya*n*a writes. Then follow Prapâ*th*akas VII, VIII, and IX, forming the Taittirîyaka-upanishad; and lastly, the tenth Prapâ*th*aka, the Yâg*ñ*ikî or Mahânârâya*n*a-upanishad, which is called a Khila, and was therefore considered by the Brâhmans themselves as a later and supplementary work.

*S*ankara, in his commentary on the Taittirîyaka-upanishad, divides his work into three Adhyâyas, and calls the first *S*ikshâ-vallî, the second the Brahmânanda-vallî, while he gives no special name to the Upanishad explained in the third Adhyâya. This, however, may be due to a mere accident, for whenever the division of the Taittirîyaka-upanishad into Vallîs is mentioned, we always-have three[1], the

---

[1] *S*ankara (ed. Roer, p. 141) himself speaks of two Vallîs, teaching the paramâtmag*ñ*âna (the *S*ikshâ-vallî has nothing to do with this), and Anquetil has Anandbli = Ânanda-vallî, and Bharkbli = Bh*ri*gu-vallî.

*S*iksha-vallî, the Brahmânanda-vallî, and the Bh*r*igu-vallî[1]. Properly, however, it is only the second Anuvâka of the seventh Prapâ*th*aka which deserves and receives in the text itself the name of *S*ikshâdhyâya, while the rest of the first Vallî ought to go by the name of Sa*m*hitâ-upanishad[2], or Sâ*m*hitî-upanishad.

Sâya*n*a[3], in his commentary on the Taittirîya-âra*n*yaka, explains the seventh chapter, the *S*ikshâdhyâya (twelve anuvâkas), as Sâ*m*hitî-upanishad. His commentary, however, is called *S*ikshâ-bhâshya. The same Sâya*n*a treats the eighth and ninth Prapâ*th*akas as the Vâru*n*y-upanishad[4].

The Ânanda-vallî and Bh*r*igu-vallî are quoted among the Upanishads of the Âtharva*n*a[5].

At the end of each Vallî there is an index of the Ânuvâkas which it contains. That at the end of the first Vallî is intelligible. It gives the Pratîkas, i. e the initial words, of each Anuvâka, and states their number as twelve. At the end of the first Anuvâka, we have the final words 'satyam vadishyâmi,' and pa*ñk*a *k*a, i. e. five short paragraphs at the end. At the end of the second Anuvâka, where we expect the final words, we have the initial, i. e. *s*ikshâm, and then pa*ñk*a, i. e. five sections in the Anuvâka. At the end of the third Anuvâka, we have the final words, but no number of sections. At the end of the fourth Anuvâka, we have the final words of the three sections, followed by one paragraph ; at the end of the fifth Anuvâka, three final words, and two paragraphs, though the first paragraph belongs clearly to the third section. In the sixth Anuvâka, we have the final words of the two Anuvâkas, and one paragraph. In the seventh Anuvâka, there is the final word

---

[1] The third Vallî ends with Bh*r*igur ity upanishat.

[2] See Taittirîyaka-upanishad, ed. Roer, p. 12.

[3] See M. M., Alphabetisches Verzeichniss der Upanishads, p. 144.

[4] The Anukrama*n*î of the Âtreyî school (see Weber, Indische Studien, II, p. 208) of the Taittirîyaka gives likewise the name of Vâru*n*î to the eighth and ninth Prapâ*th*aka, while it calls the seventh Prapâ*th*aka the Sâmhitî, and the tenth Prapâ*th*aka the Yâg*ñ*ikî-upanishad. That Anukrama*n*î presupposes, however, a different text, as may be seen both from the number of Anuvâkas, and from the position assigned to the Yâg*ñ*ikî as between the Sâmhitî and Vâru*n*î Upanishads.

[5] See M. M., Alphabetisches Verzeichniss der Upanishads.

sarvam, and one paragraph added. In the eighth Anuvâka,
we have the initial word, and the number of sections, viz.
ten. In the ninth Anuvâka, there are the final words of one
section, and six paragraphs. In the tenth Anuvâka, there
is the initial word, and the number of paragraphs, viz. six.
In the eleventh Anuvâka, we have the final words of four
sections, and seven paragraphs, the first again forming an
integral portion of the last section. The twelfth Anuvâka
has one section, and five paragraphs. If five, then the *s*ânti
would here have to be included, while, from what is said
afterwards, it is clear that as the first word of the Vallî is
*s*am na*h*, so the last is vaktâram.

In the second Vallî the index to each Anuvâka is given
at the end of the Vallî.

1st Anuvâka: pratîka: brahmavid, and some other catchwords, idam, ayam, idam. Number of sections, 21.
2nd Anuvâka: pratîka: annâd, and other catchwords;
last word, pu*kkh*a. Sections, 26.
3rd Anuvâka: pratîka: prâ*n*am, and other catchwords;
last word, pu*kkh*a. Sections, 22.
4th Anuvâka: pratîka: yata*h*, and other catchwords;
last word, pu*kkh*a. Sections, 18.
5th Anuvâka: pratîka: vig*ñ*ânam, and other catchwords;
last word, pu*kkh*a. Sections, 22.
6th Anuvâka: pratîka: asanneva, then atha (deest in
Taitt. Âr. 7). Sections, 28.
7th Anuvâka: pratîka: asat. Sections, 16.
8th Anuvâka: pratîka: bhîshâsmât, and other catchwords; last word, upasankrâmati. Sections, 51.
9th Anuvâka: pratîka: yata*h*—kuta*s*kana; then tam
(deest in Taitt. Âr.). Sections, 11.
In the third Vallî the Anukrama*n*î stands at the end.
1. The first word, bh*r*igu*h*, and some other catchwords.
Sections, 13.
2. The first word, annam. Sections, 12.
3. The first word, prâ*n*am. Sections, 12.
4. The first word, mana*h*. Sections, 12.
5. The first word, vig*ñ*ânam, and some other words. Sections, 12.

6. The first word, ânanda, and some other words. Sections, 10.

7. The first words, anna*m* na nindyât, prâ*nah*, *s*arîram. Sections, 11.

8. The first words, anna*m* na pari*k*akshîta, âpo *g*yoti*h*. Sections, 11.

9. The first words, annam bahu kurvîta p*r*ithivîm âkâ*s*a. Sections, 11.

10. The first words, na ka*ñk*ana. Sections 61. The last words of each section are given for the tenth Anuvâka.

IV.

THE B*R*IHADÂRA*N*YAKA-UPANISHAD.

THIS Upanishad has been so often edited and discussed that it calls for no special remarks. It forms part of the *S*atapatha-brâhma*n*a. In the Mâdhyandina-*s*âkhâ of that Brâhma*n*a, which has been edited by Professor Weber, the Upanishad, consisting of six adhyâyas, begins with the fourth adhyâya (or third prapâ*th*aka) of the fourteenth book.

There is a commentary on the B*r*ihadâra*n*yaka-upanishad by Dvideda*s*rînârâya*n*asûnu Dvivedaga*n*ga, which has been carefully edited by Weber in his great edition of the *S*atapatha-brâhma*n*a from a MS. in the Bodleian Library, formerly belonging to Dr. Mill, in which the Upanishad is called Mâdhyandinîya-brâhma*n*a-upanishad.

In the Kâ*n*va-*s*âkhâ the B*r*ihadâra*n*yaka-upanishad forms the seventeenth book of the *S*atapatha-brâhma*n*a, consisting of six adhyâyas.

As *S*ankara's commentary and the gloss of Ânandatîrtha, edited by Dr. Roer in the Bibliotheca Indica, follow the Kâ*n*va-*s*âkhâ, I have followed the same text in my translation.

Besides Dr. Roer's edition of the text, commentary, and gloss of this Upanishad, there is Poley's edition of the text. There is also a translation of it by Dr. Roer, with large extracts from *S*ankara's commentary.

V.

THE SVETÂSVATARA-UPANISHAD.

THE Svetâsvatara-upanishad has been handed down as one of the thirty-three Upanishads of the Taittirîyas, and though this has been doubted, no real argument has ever been brought forward to invalidate the tradition which represents it as belonging to the Taittirîya or Black Yagur-veda.

It is sometimes called Svetâsvatarânâm Mantropanishad (p. 274), and is frequently spoken of in the plural, as Svetâsvataropanishadah. At the end of the last Adhyâya we read that Svetâsvatara told it to the best among the hermits, and that it should be kept secret, and not be taught to any one except to a son or a regular pupil. It is also called Svetâsva[1], though, it would seem, for the sake of the metre only. The Svetâsvataras are mentioned as a Sâkhâ[2], subordinate to the Karakas; but of the literature belonging to them in particular, nothing is ever mentioned beyond this Upanishad.

Svetâsvatara means a white mule, and as mules were known and prized in India from the earliest times, Svetâsvatara, as the name of a person, is no more startling than Svetâsva, white horse, an epithet of Arguna. Now as no one would be likely to conclude from the name of one of the celebrated Vedic Rishis, Syâvâsva, i. e. black horse, that negro influences might be discovered in his hymns, it is hardly necessary to say that all speculations as to Christian influences, or the teaching of white Syro-Christian missionaries, being indicated by the name of Svetâsvatara, are groundless[3].

The Svetâsvatara-upanishad holds a very high rank among the Upanishads. Though we cannot say that it is quoted by name by Bâdarâyana in the Vedânta-sûtras,

---

[1] Vâkaspatyam, p. 1222.

[2] Catal. Bodl. p. 271 a ; p. 222 a.

[3] See Weber, Ind. Stud. I, pp. 400, 421.

it is distinctly referred to as *s*ruta or revealed[1]. It is one of the twelve Upanishads chosen by Vidyâra*n*ya in his Sarvopanishad-arthânabhûtiprakâ*s*a, and it was singled out by *S*aṅkara as worthy of a special commentary.

The *S*vetâ*s*vatara-upanishad seems to me one of the most difficult, and at the same time one of the most interesting works of its kind. Whether on that and on other grounds it should be assigned to a more ancient or to a more modern period is what, in the present state of our knowledge, or, to be honest, of our ignorance of minute chronology during the Vedic period, no true scholar would venture to assert. We must be satisfied to know that, as a class, the Upanishads are presupposed by the Kalpa-sûtras, that some of them, called Mantra-upanishads, form part of the more modern Sa*m*hitâs, and that there are portions even in the Rig-veda-sa*m*hitâ[2] for which the name of Upanishad is claimed by the Anukrama*n*îs. We find them most frequent, however, during the Brâhma*n*a-period, in the Brâhma*n*as themselves, and, more especially, in those portions which are called Âra*n*yakas, while a large number of them is referred to the Atharva-veda. That, in imitation of older Upanishads, similar treatises were composed to a comparatively recent time, has, of course, long been known[3].

But when we approach the question whether among the ancient and genuine Upanishads one may be older than the other, we find that, though we may guess much, we can prove nothing. The Upanishads belonged to Parishads or settlements spread all over India. There is a stock of ideas, even of expressions, common to most of them. Yet, the ideas collected in the Upanishads cannot all have grown up in one and the same place, still less in regular succession. They must have had an independent growth, deter-mined by individual and local influences, and opinions which in one village might seem far advanced, would in another be looked upon as behind the world. We may

---

[1] See Deussen, Vedânta, p. 24; Ved. Sûtra I, 1, 11; I, 4, 8; II, 3, 22.
[2] See Sacred Books of the East, vol. i, p. lxvi.
[3] Loc. cit. p. lxvii.

admire the ingeniousness of those who sometimes in this, sometimes in that peculiarity see a clear indication of the modern date of an Upanishad, but to a conscientious scholar such arguments are really distasteful for the very sake of their ingeniousness. He knows that they will convince many who do not know the real difficulties; he knows they will have to be got out of the way with no small trouble, and he knows that, even if they should prove true in the end, they will require very different support from what they have hitherto received, before they can be admitted to the narrow circle of scientific facts.

While fully admitting therefore that the Svetâsvatara-upanishad has its peculiar features and its peculiar difficulties, I must most strongly maintain that no argument that has as yet been brought forward, seems to me to prove, in any sense of the word, its modern character.

It has been said, for instance, that the Svetâsvatara-upanishad is a sectarian Upanishad, because, when speaking of the Highest Self or the Highest Brahman, it applies such names to him as Hara (I, 10), Rudra (II, 17; III, 2; 4; IV, 12; 21; 22), Siva (III, 14; IV, 10), Bhagavat (III, 14), Agni, Âditya, Vâyu, &c. (IV, 2). But here it is simply taken for granted that the idea of the Highest Self was developed first, and, after it had reached its highest purity, was lowered again by an identification with mythological and personal deities. The questions whether the conception of the Highest Self was formed once and once only, whether it was formed after all the personal and mythological deities had first been merged into one Lord (Pragâpati), or whether it was discovered behind the veil of any other name in the mythological pantheon of the past, have never been mooted. Why should not an ancient Rishi have said: What we have hitherto called Rudra, and what we worship as Agni, or Siva, is in reality the Highest Self, thus leaving much of the ancient mythological phraseology to be used with a new meaning? Why should we at once conclude that late sectarian worshippers of mythological gods replaced again the Highest Self, after their fathers had discovered it, by their own sectarian names? If we adopt the former

view, the Upanishads, which still show these rudera of
the ancient temples, would have to be considered as more
primitive even than those in which the idea of the Brahman or the Highest Self has reached its utmost purity.

It has been considered a very strong argument in support of the modern and sectarian character of the Svetâsvatara-upanishad, that 'it inculcates what is called Bhakti[1],
or implicit reliance on the favour of the deity worshipped.'
Now it is quite true that this Upanishad possesses a very
distinct character of its own, by the stress which it lays on
the personal, and sometimes almost mythical character of
the Supreme Spirit; but, so far from inculcating bhakti,
in the modern sense of the word, it never mentions that
word, except in the very last verse, a verse which, if necessary, certain critics would soon dispose of as a palpable
addition.   But that verse says no more than this : ' If these
truths (of the Upanishad) have been told to a high-minded
man, who feels the highest devotion for God, and for his
Guru as for God, then they will shine forth indeed.' Does
that prove the existence of Bhakti as we find it in the
Sândilya-sûtras[2]?

Again, it has been said that the Svetâsvatara-upanishad
is sectarian in a philosophical sense, that it is in fact an
Upanishad of the Sânkhya system of philosophy, and not
of the Vedânta.   Now I am quite willing to admit that, in
its origin, the Vedânta philosophy is nearer to the Vedic
literature than any other of the six systems of philosophy,
and that if we really found doctrines, peculiar to the Sânkhya, and opposed to the Vedânta, in the Svetâsvatara-
upanishad, we might feel inclined to assign to our Upanishad a later date.   But where is the proof of this?

No doubt there are expressions in this Upanishad which
remind us of technical terms used at a later time in the
Sânkhya system of philosophy, but of Sânkhya doctrines,
which I had myself formerly suspected in this Upanishad,

---

[1] Weber, Ind. Stud. I, 422; and History of Indian Literature, p. 238.
[2] The Aphorisms of Sândilya, or the Hindu Doctrine of Faith, translated by
E. B. Cowell, Calcutta, 1878.

I can on closer study find very little. I think it was Mr. Gough who, in his Philosophy of the Upanishads, for the first time made it quite clear that the teaching of our Upanishad is, in the main, the same as that of the other Upanishads. 'The Svetâsvatara-upanishad teaches,' as he says, 'the unity of souls in the one and only Self; the unreality of the world as a series of figments of the self-feigning world-fiction ; and as the first of the fictitious emanations, the existence of the Demiurgos or universal soul present in every individual soul, the deity that projects the world out of himself, that the migrating souls may find the recompense of their works in former lives.'

I do not quite agree with this view of the Îsvara, whom Mr. Gough calls the Demiurgos, but he seems to me per-fectly right when he says that the Svetâsvatara-upanishad propounds in Sânkhya terms the very principles that the Sânkhya philosophers make it their business to subvert. One might doubt as to the propriety of calling certain terms ' Sânkhya terms' in a work written at a time when a Sânkhya philosophy, such as we know it as a system, had as yet no existence, and when the very name sânkhya meant something quite different from the Sânkhya system of Kapila. Sânkhya is derived from sankhyâ, and that meant counting, number, name, corresponding very nearly to the Greek λόγος. Sânkhya, as derived from it, meant originally no more than theoretic philosophy, as opposed to yoga, which meant originally practical religious exer-cises and penances, to restrain the passions and the senses in general. All other interpretations of these words, when they had become technical names, are of later date.

But even in their later forms, whatever we may think of the coincidences and differences between the Sânkhya and Vedânta systems of philosophy, there is one point on which
· they are diametrically opposed. Whatever else the Sân-khya may be, it is dualistic; whatever else the Vedânta may be, it is monistic. In the Sânkhya, nature, or whatever else we may call it, is independent of the purusha ; in the Vedânta it is not. Now the Svetâsvatara-upanishad states distinctly that nature, or what in the Sânkhya philosophy

is intended by Pradhâna, is not an independent power, but
a power (sakti) forming the very self of the Deva. 'Sages,'
we read, 'devoted to meditation and concentration, have
seen the power belonging to God himself, hidden in its own
qualities.'

What is really peculiar in the Svetâsvatara-upanishad is
the strong stress which it lays on the personality of the
Lord, the Îsvara. Deva, in the passage quoted, is perhaps
the nearest approach to our own idea of a personal God,
though without the background which the Vedânta always
retains for it. It is God as creator and ruler of the world,
as îsvara, lord, but not as Paramâtman, or the Highest Self.
The Paramâtman constitutes, no doubt, his real essence,
but creation and creator have a phenomenal character
only[1]. The creation is mâyâ, in its original sense of work,
then of phenomenal work, then of illusion. The creator
is mâyin, in its original sense of worker or maker, but
again, in that character, phenomenal only[2]. The Gunas
or qualities arise, according to the Vedânta, from prakriti
or mâyâ, within, not beside, the Highest Self, and this
is the very idea which is here expressed by 'the Self-power
of God, hidden in the gunas or determining qualities.' How
easily that sakti or power may become an independent
being, as Mâyâ, we see in such verses as:

Sarvabhûteshu sarvâtman yâ saktir aparâbhavâ
Gunâsrayâ namas tasyai sasvatâyai paresvara[3].

But the important point is this, that in the Svetâsvatara-
upanishad this change has not taken place. Throughout
the whole of it we have one Being only, as the cause of
everything, never two. Whatever Sânkhya philosophers
of a later date may have imagined that they could discover
in that Upanishad in support of their theories[4], there is not
one passage in it which, if rightly interpreted, not by itself,
but in connection with the whole text, could be quoted in

[1] Prathamam îsvarâtmanâ mâyirûpenâvatishthate brahma; see p. 280, l. 5.
[2] Mâyî srigate sarvam etat.
[3] See p. 279, l. 5. Sarvâtman seems a vocative, like paresvara.
[4] See Sarvadarsanasangraha, p. 152.

support of a dualistic philosophy such as the Sâṅkhya, as a system, decidedly is.

If we want to understand, what seems at first sight contradictory, the existence of a God, a Lord, a Creator, a Ruler, and at the same time the existence of the super-personal Brahman, we must remember that the orthodox view of the Vedânta[1] is not what we should call Evolution, but Illusion. Evolution of the Brahman, or Pariṇâma, is heterodox, illusion or Vivarta is orthodox Vedânta. Brahman is a concept involving such complete perfection that with it evolution, or a tendency towards higher perfection, is impossible. If therefore there is change, that change can only be illusion, and can never claim the same reality as Brahman. To put it metaphorically, the world, according to the orthodox Vedântin, does not proceed from Brahman as a tree from a germ, but as a mirage from the rays of the sun. The world is, as we express it, phenomenal only, but whatever objective reality there is in it, is Brahman, 'das Ding an sich,' as Kant might call it.

Then what is Îsvara or Deva, the Lord or God? The answers given to this question are not very explicit. Historically, no doubt, the idea of the Îsvara, the personal God, the creator and ruler, the omniscient and omnipotent, existed before the idea of the absolute Brahman, and after the idea of the Brahman had been elaborated, the difficulty of effecting a compromise between the two ideas, had to be overcome. Îsvara, the Lord, is Brahman, for what else could he be? But he is Brahman under a semblance, the semblance, namely, of a personal creating and governing God. He is not created, but is the creator, an office too low, it was supposed, for Brahman. The power which enabled Îsvara to create, was a power within him, not independent of him, whether we call it Devâtmasakti, Mâyâ, or Prakṛiti. That power is really inconceivable, and it has assumed such different forms in the mind of different Vedântists, that in the end Mâyâ herself is represented as the creating power, nay, as having created Îsvara himself.

---

[1] Vedântaparibhâshâ, in the Pandit, vol. iv, p. 496.

In our Upanishad, however, Îsvara is the creator, and though, philosophically speaking, we should say that he was conceived as phenomenal, yet we must never forget that the phenomenal is the form of the real, and Îsvara there- fore an aspect of Brahman[1]. 'This God,' says Pramâda Dâsa Mitra[2], 'is the spirit conscious of the universe. Whilst an extremely limited portion, and that only of the material universe, enters into my consciousness, the whole of the conscious universe, together, of course, with the material one that hangs upon it, enters into the conscious- ness of God.' And again, 'Whilst we (the *g*îvâtmans) are subject to Mâyâ, Mâyâ is subject to Îsvara. If we truly know Îsvara, we know him as Brahman; if we truly know ourselves, we know ourselves as Brahman. This being so, we must not be surprised if sometimes we find Îsvara sharply distinguished from Brahman, whilst at other times Îsvara and Brahman are interchanged.'

Another argument in support of the sectarian character of the *S*vetâ*s*vatara-upanishad is brought forward, not by European students only, but by native scholars, namely, that the very name of Kapila, the reputed founder of the Sâṅkhya philosophy, occurs in it. Now it is quite true that if we read the second verse of the fifth Adhyâya by itself, the occurrence of the word Kapila may seem startling. But if we read it in connection with what precedes and fol- lows, we shall see hardly anything unusual in it. It says:

'It is he who, being one only, rules over every germ (cause), over all forms, and over all germs; it is he who, in the beginning, bears in his thoughts the wise son, the fiery, whom he wished to look on while he was born.'

Now it is quite clear to me that the subject in this verse is the same as in IV, 11, where the same words are used, and where yo yoni*m* yonim adhitish*th*aty eka*h* refers clearly to Brahman. It is equally clear that the prasûta, the son, the offspring of Brahman, in the Vedânta sense, can only be the same person who is elsewhere called Hira*n*yagarbha,

---

[1] Savisesham Brahma, or sabalam Brahma.
[2] Journal of the Royal Asiatic Society, 1878, p. 40.

the personified Brahman. Thus we read before, III, 4, 'He the creator and supporter of the gods, Rudra, the great seer (maharshi), the lord of all, formerly gave birth to Hira*n*yagarbha;' and in IV, 11, we have the very expression which is used here, namely, 'that he saw Hira*n*yagarbha being born.' Unfortunately, a new adjective is applied in our verse to Hira*n*yagarbha, namely, kapila, and this has called forth interpretations totally at variance with the general tenor of the Upanishad. If, instead of kapilam, reddish, fiery[1], any other epithet had been used of Hira*n*yagarbha, no one, I believe, would have hesitated for a moment to recognise the fact that our text simply repeats the description of Hira*n*yagarbha in his relation to Brahman, for the other epithet *ri*shim, like maharshim, is too often applied to Brahman himself and to Hira*n*yagarbha to require any explanation.

But it is a well known fact that the Hindus, even as early as the Brâhma*n*a-period, were fond of tracing their various branches of knowledge back to Brahman or to Brahman Svayambhû and then through· Pra*g*âpati, who even in the Rig-veda (X, 121, 10) replaces Hira*n*yagarbha, and sometimes through the Devas, such as M*ri*tyu, Vâyu, Indra, Agni[2], &c., to the various ancestors of their ancient families.

In the beginning of the Mu*nd*akopanishad we are told that Brahman told it to Atharvan, Atharvan to A*n*gir, A*n*gir to Satyavâha Bhâradvâ*g*a, Bhâradvâ*g*a to A*n*giras, A*n*giras to *S*aunaka. Manu, the ancient lawgiver, is called both Haira*n*yagarbha and Svâyambhuva, as descended from Svayambhu or from Hira*n*yagarbha[3]. Nothing therefore was more natural than that the same tendency should have led some one to assign the authorship of a great philosophical system like the Sânkhya to Hira*n*yagarbha, if not to Brahman Svayambhû. And if the name of Hira*n*yagarbha had been used already for the ancestors of other sages, and the inspirers of other systems, what could be more natural than that another name of the same Hira*n*ya-

---

[1] Other colours, instead of kapila, are nîla, harita, lohitâksha; see IV, 1; 4.
[2] See Va*m*sa-brâhma*n*a, ed. Burnell, p. 10; Br*i*hadâra*n*yaka-up. pp. 185, 224.
[3] See M. M., India, p. 372.

garbha should be chosen, such as Kapila. If we are told that Kapila handed his knowledge to Âsuri, Âsuri to Pañkaṣikha, this again is in perfect keeping with the character of literary tradition in India. Âsuri occurs in the Vaṃsas of the Ṣatapatha-brâhmaṇa (see above, pp. 187, 226); Pañkaṣikha[1], having five tufts, might be either a general name or a proper name of an ascetic, Buddhist or otherwise. He is quoted in the Sâṅkhya-sûtras, V, 32; VI, 68.

But after all this was settled, after Kapila had been accepted, like Hiraṇyagarbha, as the founder of a great system of philosophy, there came a reaction. People had now learnt to believe in a real Kapila, and when looking out for credentials for him, they found them wherever the word Kapila occurred in old writings. The question whether there ever was a real historical person who took the name of Kapila and taught the Sâṅkhya-sûtras, does not concern us here. I see no evidence for it. What is instructive is this, that our very passage, which may have suggested at first the name of Kapila, as distinct from Hiraṇyagarbha Kapila, was later on appealed to to prove the primordial existence of a Kapila, the founder of the Sâṅkhya philosophy. However, it requires but a very slight acquaintance with Sanskrit literature and very little reflection in order to see that the author of our verse could never have dreamt of elevating a certain Kapila, known to him as a great philosopher, if there ever was such a man, to a divine rank[2]. Hiraṇyagarbha kapila may have given birth to Kapila, the hero of the Sâṅkhya philosophers, but Kapila, a real human person, was never changed into Hiraṇyagarbha kapila.

Let us see now what the commentators say. Saṅkara first explains kapilam by kanakaṃ[3] kapilavarṇam .... Hiraṇyagarbham. Kapilo 'graga iti purâṇavakanât. Kapilo Hiraṇyagarbho vâ nirdiṣyate. But he afterwards quotes some verses in support of the theory that Kapila was a

---

[1] For fuller information on Pañkaṣikha, Kapila, &c., see F. Hall's Preface to Sâṅkhya-pravakana-bhâshya, p. 9 seq.; Weber, Ind. Stud. I, p. 433.

[2] Weber, Hist. of Indian Literature, p. 236.

[3] This ought to be Kanakavarṇam, and I hope will not be identified with the name of Buddha in a former existence.

Paramarshi, a portion of Vish*n*u, intended to destroy error in the K*ri*ta Yuga, a teacher of the Sânkhya philosophy.

Vig*ñâ*nâtman explains the verse rightly, and without any reference to Kapila, the Sânkhya teacher.

*S*ankarânanda goes a step further, and being evidently fully aware of the misuse that had been made of this passage, even in certain passages of the Mahâbhârata (XII, 13254, 13703), and elsewhere, declares distinctly that kapila cannot be meant for the teacher of the Sânkhya (na tu sânkhyapra*n*etâ kapila*h*, nâmamâtrasâmyena tadgraha*n*e syâd atiprasanga*h*). He is fully aware of the true interpretation, viz. avyâk*ri*tasya prathamakâryabhûta*m* kapila*m* vi*k*itravar*n*am *g*ñânakriyâ*s*aktyâtmaka*m* Hira*n*yagarbham ityartha*h*, but he yields to another temptation, and seems to prefer another view which makes Kapila Vâsudevasyâvatârabhûta*m* Sagaraputrâ*n*â*m* dagdhâram, an Avatâra of Vâsudeva, the burner of the sons of Sagara. What vast conclusions may be drawn from no facts, may be seen in Weber's Indische Studien, vol. i, p. 430, and even in his History of Indian Literature, published in 1878.

Far more difficult to explain than these supposed allusions to the authors and to the teaching of the Sânkhya philosophy are the frequent references in the *S*vetâ*s*vatara-upanishad to definite numbers, which are supposed to point to certain classes of subjects as arranged in the Sânkhya and other systems of philosophy. The Sânkhya philosophy is fond of counting and arranging, and its very name is sometimes supposed to have been chosen because it numbers (sankhyâ) the subjects of which it treats. It is certainly true that if we meet, as we do in the *S*vetâ*s*vatara-upanishad, with classes of things[1], numbered as one, two, three, five, eight, sixteen, twenty, forty-eight, fifty and more, and if some of these numbers agree with those recognised in the later Sânkhya and Yoga systems, we feel doubtful as to whether these coincidences are accidental, or whether, if not accidental, they are due to borrowing on the part of those later systems, or on the part of the Upanishads. I feel

---

[1] See I, 4; 5; VI, 3.

it impossible to come to a decision on this point. Even so early as the hymns of the Rig-veda we meet with these numbers assigned to days and months and seasons, rivers and countries, sacrifices and deities. They clearly prove the existence of a considerable amount of intellectual labour which had become fixed and traditional before the composition of certain hymns, and they prove the same in the case of certain Upanishads. But beyond this, for the present, I should not like to go; and I must say that the attempts of most of the Indian commentators at explaining such numbers by a reference to later systems of philosophy or cosmology, are generally very forced and unsatisfactory.

One more point I ought to mention as indicating the age of the Svetâsvatara-upanishad, and that is the obscurity of many of its verses, which may be due to a corruption of the text, and the number of various readings, recognised as such, by the commentators. Some of them have been mentioned in the notes to my translation.

The text of this Upanishad was printed by Dr. Roer in the Bibliotheca Indica, with Sankara's commentary. I have consulted besides, the commentary of Vignânâtman, the pupil of Paramahamsa-parivrâgakâkârya-srîmag-Gñânottamâkârya, MS. I. O. 1133; and a third commentary, by Sankarânanda, the pupil of Paramahamsa-parivrâgakâkâryânandâtman, MS. I. O. 1878. These were kindly lent me by Dr. Rost, the learned and liberal librarian of the India Office.

VI.

PRASÑA-UPANISHAD.

THIS Upanishad is called the Prasña or Shat-prasña-upanishad, and at the end of a chapter we find occasionally iti prasñaprativakanam, i. e. thus ends the answer to the question. It is ascribed to the Atharva-veda, and occasionally to the Pippalâda-sâkhâ, one of the most important sâkhâs of that Veda. Pippalâda is mentioned in the Upanishad as the name of the principal teacher.

Sankara, in the beginning of his commentary, says:

Mantroktasyârthasya vistarânuvâdîdam Brâhma*n*am ârabhyate, which would mean 'this Brâhma*n*a is commenced as more fully repeating what has been declared in the Mantra.' This, however, does not, I believe, refer to a Mantra or hymn in the Atharva-veda-sa*m*hitâ, but to the Mu*nd*aka-upanishad, which, as written in verse, is sometimes spoken of as a Mantra, or Mantropanishad. This is also the opinion of Ânandagiri, who says, 'one might think that it was mere repetition (punarukti), if the essence of the Self, which has been explained by the Mantras, were to be taught here again by the Brâhma*n*a.' For he adds, 'by the Mantras "Brahma devânâm," &c.,' and this is evidently meant for the beginning of the Mu*nd*aka-upanishad, 'Brahmâ devânâm.' Ânandagiri refers again to the Mu*nd*aka in order to show that the Pra*sn*a is not a mere repetition, and if *S*ankara calls the beginning of it a Brâhma*n*a, this must be taken in the more general sense of 'what is not Mantra[1].' Mantropanishad is a name used of several Upanishads which are written in verse, and some of which, like the Îsâ, have kept their place in the Sa*m*hitâs.

VII.

MAITRÂYA*N*A-BRÂHMA*N*A-UPANISHAD.

In the case of this Upanishad we must first of all attempt to settle its right title. Professor Cowell, in his edition and translation of it, calls it Maitri or Maitrâya*n*îya-upanishad, and states that it belongs to the Maitrâya*n*îya-*s*âkhâ of the Black Yagur-veda, and that it formed the concluding portion of a lost Brâhma*n*a of that *S*âkhâ, being preceded by the sacrificial (karma) portion, which consisted of four books.

In his MSS. the title varied between Maitry-upanishad and Maitrî-*s*âkhâ-upanishad. A Poona MS. calls it Maitrâya*n*îya-*s*âkhâ-upanishad, and a MS. copied for Baron von Eckstein, Maitrâya*n*îyopanishad. I myself in the Alphabetical List of the Upanishads, published in the Journal of

---

[1] Mantravyatiriktabhâge tu brâhma*n*asabda*h*, Rig-veda, Sâyana's Introduction, vol. i, p. 23.

the German Oriental Society, called it, No. 104, Maitrâya*n*a
or Maitri-upanishad, i. e. either the Upanishad of the Maitrâya*n*as, or the Upanishad of Maitri, the principal teacher.

In a MS. which I received from Dr. Burnell, the title of
our Upanishad is Maitrâya*n*i-brâhma*n*a-upanishad, varying
with Maitrâya*n*î-brâhma*n*a-upanishad, and *S*rîya*g*u*ss*âkhâyâm Maitrâya*n*îya-brâhma*n*a-upanishad.

The next question is by what name this Upanishad is
quoted by native authorities. Vidyâra*n*ya, in his Sarvo-
panishad-arthânubhûtiprakâ*s*a[1], v. 1, speaks of the Maitrâya*n*îyanâmnî yâ*g*ushî *s*âkhâ, and he mentions Maitra (not
Maitri) as the author of that *S*âkhâ (vv. 55, 150).

In the Muktikâ-upanishad[2] we meet with the name of
Maitrâya*n*î as the twenty-fourth Upanishad, with the
name of Maitreyî as the twenty-ninth; and again, in the
list of the sixteen Upanishads of the Sâma-veda, we find
Maitrâya*n*î and Maitreyî as the fourth and fifth.

Looking at all this evidence, I think we should come to
the conclusion that our Upanishad derives its name from
the *S*âkhâ of the Maitrâya*n*as, and may therefore be called
Maitrâya*n*a-upanishad or Maitrâya*n*î Upanishad. Maitrâya*n*a-brâhma*n*a-upanishad seems likewise correct, and
Maitrâya*n*i-brâhma*n*a-upanishad, like Kaushîtaki-brâh-
ma*n*a-upanishad and Vâ*g*asaneyi-sa*m*hitopanishad, might
be defended, if Maitrâyanin were known as a further deri-
vative of Maitrâya*n*a. If the name is formed from the
teacher Maitri or Maitra, the title of Maitri-upanishad
would also be correct, but I doubt whether Maitrî-upani-
shad would admit of any grammatical justification[3].

Besides this Maitrâya*n*a-brâhma*n*a-upanishad, however,
I possess a MS. of what is called the Maitreyopanishad,
sent to me likewise by the late Dr. Burnell. It is very
short, and contains no more than the substance of the first
Prapâ*th*aka of the Maitrâya*n*a-brâhma*n*a-upanishad. I give

---

[1] See Cowell, Maitr. Up. pref. p. iv.

[2] Calcutta, 1791 (1869), p. 4; also as quoted in the Mahâvâkya-ratnâvalî, p. 2[b].

[3] Dr. Burnell, in his Tanjore Catalogue, mentions, p. 35[a], a Maitrâya*n*î-
brâhma*n*opanishad, which can hardly be a right title, and p. 36[b] a Maitrâya*n*îya and Maitreyîbrâhma*n*a.

the text of it, as far as it can be restored from the one MS. in my possession:

Hari*h* Om. B*ri*hadratho vai nâma râ*g*â vairâ*g*ye putra*m* nidhâpayitvedam asâ*s*vatam manyamâna*h* *s*arîra*m* vairâ-gyam upeto 'ra*n*ya*m* nir*g*agâma. Sa tatra paramam tapa[1] âdityam udîkshamâ*n*a ûrdhvas tish*th*aty. Ante sahasrasya muner antikam â*g*agâma[2]. Atha B*ri*hadratho brahmavit-pravaram munîndra*m* sampû*g*ya stutvâ bahu*s*a*h* pra*n*âmam akarot. So 'bravîd agnir ivâdhûmakas te*g*asâ nirdahann ivâtmavid Bhagavâñ *kh*âkâyanya, uttish*th*ottish*th*a vara*m* v*ri*nîshveti râ*g*ânam abravît[3]. Sa tasmai punar namask*ri*-tyovâ*k*a, Bhagavan nâ(ha)mâtmavit tva*m* tattvavi*k* *kh*u-*s*rumo vayam; sa tva*m* no brûhîty etad vratam purastâd a*s*akyam mâ p*rikkh*a pra*s*ñam Aikshvâkânyân kâmân v*ri*nîshveti *S*âkâyanya*h*. *S*arîrasya *s*arîre (sic) *k*ara*n*âv abhim*ri*syamâno râ*g*emâ*m* gâthâ*m* *g*agâda. 1

Bhagavann, asthi*k*armasnâyuma*gg*âmâ*m*sa*s*ukla*s*o*n*ita-*s*reshmâ*s*rudashikâvi*n*mûtrapittakaphasa*m*ghâte durgandhe ni*h*sâre 'smiñ *kh*arîre ki*m* kâmabhogai*h*. 2

Kâmakrodhalobhamohabhayavishâdershesh*t*aviyogânish-*t*asamprayogakshutpipâsâ*g*arâm*ri*tyuroga*s*okâdyair abhiha-te 'smiñ *kh*arîre ki*m* kâmabhogai*h*. 3

Sarva*m* *k*eda*m* kshayish*n*u pa*s*yâmo yatheme da*m*sama-*s*akâdayas t*ri*navan[4] na*s*yata yodbhûtapradhva*m*sina*h*. 4

Atha kim etair vâ pare 'nye dhamarthar夜a*s* (sic) *k*akra-vartina*h* Sudyumnabhûridyumnakuvalayâ*s*vayauvanâ*s*va-vaddh*ri*yâ*s*vâsvapati*h* *s*a*s*abindur hari*s*andro 'm*b*arîsho nanukastvayâtir yayâtir a*n*ara*n*yokshasenâdayo maruta-bharataprabh*ri*tayo râ*g*âno mishato bandhuvargasya ma-hatî*m* *s*riya*m* tyaktvâsmâl lokâd amu*m* lokam prayânti. 5.

Atha kim etair vâ pare 'nye gandharvâsurayaksharâksha-sabhûtaga*n*api*s*â*k*oragrahâdînâ*m* nirodhanam pa*s*yâma*h*. 6

Atha kim etair vânyânâ*m* *s*osha*n*am mahâr*n*avânâ*m*

---

[1] One expects âsthâya.
[2] This seems better than the Maitrâya*n*a text. He went near a Muni, viz. *S*âkâyanya.
[3] This seems unnecessary.
[4] There may be an older reading hidden in this, from which arose the reading of the Maitrâya*n*a B. U. t*ri*navanaspatayodbhûtapradhva*m*sina*h*, or yo bhûtapradhva*m*sina*h*.

*s*ikhari*n*âm prapatana*m* dhruvasya pra*k*alana*m* vâtarû*n*â*m* nima*gg*anam p*ri*thivyâ*h* sthânâpasara*n*am surâ*n*âm. So 'ham ity etadvidhe 'smin sa*m*sâre ki*m* kâmopabhogair yair evâ*s*ritasya sak*ri*d âvartanam d*ri*s*y*ata ity uddhartum arhasi tyandodapânabheka ivâham asmin sa*m* Bhagavas tva*m* gatis tva*m* no gatir iti. 7

Ayam[1] agnir vai*s*vânaro yo 'yam anta*h* purushe yenedam annam pa*k*yate yad idam adyate tasyaisha ghosho bhavati yam etat karn*â*v apidhâya *s*ri*n*oti, sa yadotkramishyan[2] bhavati naina*m* ghosha*m* *s*ri*n*oti. 8

Yathâ[3] nirindhano vahni*h* svayonâv upa*s*âmyati. 9[4]

Sa *s*iva*h* so 'nte vai*s*vânaro bhûtvâ sa dagdhvâ sarvâ*n*i bhûtâni p*ri*thivyapsu pralîyate[5], âpas te*g*asi lîyante[6], te*g*o vâyau pralîyate[7], vâyur âkâ*s*e vilîyate[8], âkâ*s*am indriyeshv, indriyâ*n*i tanmâtreshu, tanmâtrâ*n*i bhûtâdau vilîyante[9], bhûtâdi mahati vilîyate[10], mahân avyakte vilîyate[11], avyaktam akshare vilîyate[12], aksharam tamasi vilîyate[13], tama ekîbhavati parasmin, parastân na[14] san nâsan na sad ityetan nirvâ*n*am anu*s*âsanam iti vedânu*s*âsanam.

We should distinguish therefore between the large Maitrâ-ya*n*a-brâhma*n*a-upanishad and the smaller Maitreyopani-shad. The title of Maitreyî-brâhma*n*a has, of course, a totally different origin, and simply means the Brâhma*n*a which tells the story of Maitreyî[15].

As Professor Cowell, in the Preface to his edition and translation of the Maitrâya*n*a-brâhma*n*a-upanishad, has discussed its peculiar character, I have little to add on that subject. I agree with him in thinking that this Upanishad has grown, and contains several accretions. The Sanskrit commentator himself declares the sixth and seventh chapters to be Khilas or supplementary. Possibly the Maitreya-upanishad, as printed above, contains the earliest framework. Then we have traces of various recensions. Professor Cowell (Preface, p. vi) mentions a MS., copied

---

[1] Maitr. Up. II, 6; p. 32.   [2] kramishyân, m.   [3] Yadhâ, m.
[4] Maitr. Up. VI, 34; p. 178.   [5] lipyate. ·   [6] lipyante.   [7] lîyyate.
[8] lîyyate.   [9] liyante.   [10] liyyate.   [11] lipyate.   [12] liyyate.
[13] liyyate.   [14] tânasannâ.   [15] See *Kh*ând. Up. p. 623.

for Baron Eckstein, apparently from a Telugu original, which contains the first five chapters only, numbered as four. The verses given in VI, 34 (p. 177), beginning with atreme *sloka* bhavanti, are placed after IV, 3. In my own MS. these verses are inserted at the beginning of the fifth chapter[1]. Then follows in Baron Eckstein's MS. as IV, 5, what is given in the printed text as V, 1, 2 (pp. 69-76). In my own MS., which likewise comes from the South, the Upanishad does not go beyond VI, 8, which is called the sixth chapter and the end of the Upanishad.

We have in fact in our Upanishad the first specimen of that peculiar Indian style, so common in the later fables and stories, which delights in enclosing one story within another. The kernel of our Upanishad is really the dialogue between the Vâlakhilyas and Pra*g*âpati Kratu. This is called by the commentator (see p. 331, note) a Vyâkhyâna, i. e. a fuller explanation of the Sûtra which comes before, and which expresses in the few words, 'He is the Self, this is the immortal, the fearless, this is Brahman,' the gist of the whole Upanishad.

This dialogue, or at all events the doctrine which it was meant to illustrate, was communicated by Maitri (or Maitra) to *S*âkâyanya, and by *S*âkâyanya to King B*ri*hadratha Aikshvâka, also called Marut (II, 1; VI, 30). This dialogue might seem to come to an end in VI, 29, and likewise the dialogue between *S*âkâyanya and B*ri*hadratha; but it is carried on again to the end of VI, 30, and followed afterwards by a number of paragraphs which may probably be considered as later additions.

But though admitting all this, I cannot bring myself to follow Professor Cowell in considering, as he does, even the earlier portion of the Upanishad as dating from a late period, while the latter portions are called by him comparatively modern, on account of frequent Vaish*n*ava quotations. What imparts to this Upanishad, according to my opinion, an exceptionally genuine and ancient character, is the preservation in it of that peculiar Sandhi which,

---

[1] See p. 303, note 1; p. 305. note 1; p. 312, note 1.

thanks to the labours of Dr. von Schroeder, we now know
to be characteristic of the Maitrâya*n*a-*s*âkhâ. In that *S*âkhâ
final unaccented as and e are changed into â, if the next word
begins with an accented vowel, except a. Before initial a,
however, e remains unchanged, and as becomes o, and the
initial a is sometimes elided, sometimes not. Some of these
rules, it must be remembered, run counter to Pâ*n*ini, and
we may safely conclude therefore that texts in which they
are observed, date from the time before Pâ*n*ini. In some
MSS., as, for instance, in my own MS. of the Maitrâya*n*a-
brâhma*n*a-upanishad, these rules are not observed, but this
makes their strict observation in other MSS. all the more
important. Besides, though to Dr. von Schroeder belongs,
no doubt, the credit of having, in his edition of the
Maitrâya*n*î Sa*m*hitâ, first pointed out these phonetic peculiarities, they were known as such to the commentators,
who expressly point out these irregular Sandhis as dis-
tinctive of the Maitrâya*n*î *s*âkhâ. Thus we read Maitr. Up.
II, 3 (p. 18), that tigmate*g*asâ ûrdhvaretaso, instead of
tigmate*g*asa, is eva*m*vidha eta*kkh*âkhâsaṅketapâ*th*as *kh*ândasa*h* sarvatra, i.e. is throughout the Vedic reading indica-
tory of that particular *S*âkhâ, namely the Maitrâya*n*î.

A still stranger peculiarity of our *S*âkhâ is the change of
a final t before initial *s* into *ñ*. This also occurs in our
Upanishad. In VI, 8, we read svâ*ñ* sarîrâd; in VI, 27, ya*ñ*
*s*arîrasya. Such a change seems phonetically so unnatural,
that the tradition must have been very strong to perpetuate
it among the Maitrâya*n*as.

Now what is important for our purposes is this, that these
phonetic peculiarities run through all the seven chapters of
our Upanishad. This will be seen from the following list:

I. Final as changed into â before initial vowel[1]:

    II, 3, tigmate*g*asâ ûrdhvaretaso (Comm. eta*kkh*âkhâ-
    saṅketapâ*th*as *kh*ândasa*h* sarvatra).

    II, 5, vibodhâ evam.   II, 7, avasthitâ iti.

---

[1] I have left out the restriction as to the accent of the vowels, because
they are disregarded in the Upanishad. It should be observed that this peculiar
Sandhi occurs in the Upanishad chiefly before iti.

III, 5, etair abhibhûtâ iti.   IV, 1, vidyatâ iti.

VI, 4, pra*n*avâ iti ; bhûmyâdayâ eko.

VI, 6, âdityâ iti ; âhavanîyâ iti ; sûryâ iti ; ahaṅkârâ
iti ; vyânâ iti.   VI, 7, bhargâ iti.

VI, 7, sannivish*t*â iti.   VI, 23, devâ oṅkâro.

VI, 30, prâyâtâ iti.   VI, 30, vinirgatâ iti.

II. Final e before initial vowels becomes â. For
instance :

I, 4, d*ri*syatâ iti.   II, 2, nishpadyatâ iti.

III, 2, âpadyatâ iti.   III, 2, pushkarâ iti.

IV, 1, vidyatâ iti.   VI, 10, bhuṅktâ iti.

VI, 20, a*s*nutâ iti.   VI, 30, ekâ âhur.

Even prag*ri*hya e is changed to â in—

VI, 23, etâ upâsîta, i. e. ete uktalaksha*n*e brahma*n*î.

In VI, 31, instead of te etasya, the commentator seems to
have read te vâ etasya.

III. Final as before â, u, and au becomes a, and is then
contracted.   For instance :

I, 4, vanaspatayodbhûta, instead of vanaspataya
udbhûta. (Comm. Sandhi*s* *kh*ândaso vâ, ukâro
vâtra lupto drash*t*avya*h*.)

II, 6, devaush*n*yam, instead of deva aush*n*yam.
(Comm. Sandhi*s* *kh*ândasa*h*.)

VI, 24, atamâvish*t*am, instead of atama-âvish*t*am
(Comm. Sandhi*s* *kh*ândasa*h*); cf. *Kh*ând. Up.

VI, 8, 3, a*s*anâyeti (Comm. visarga*n*îyalopa*h*).

IV. Final e before i becomes a, and is then contracted.
For instance :

VI, 7, âtmâ *g*anîteti for *g*anîta iti. (Comm. *g*ânîte,
*g*ânâti.)

VI, 28, ava*t*aiva for avata iva. (Comm. Sandhi-
v*ri*ddhî *kh*ândase.)

V. Final au before initial vowels becomes â. For instance :

II, 6, yena vâ etâ anug*ri*hîtâ iti.

VI, 22, asâ abhidhyâtâ.

On abhibhûyamânay iva, see p. 295, note 2.

V, 2, asâ âtmâ (var. lect. asâv âtmâ).

VI. Final o of atho produces elision of initial ă. For instance:

> III, 2, atho 'bhibhûtatvât. (Comm. Sandhi*s* *kh*ân-dasa*h*.) Various reading, ato 'bhibhûtatvât.
>
> VI, 1, so antar is explained as sa u.

VII. Other irregularities:

> VI, 7, âpo pyâyanât, explained by pyâyanât and âpyâyanât. Might it be, âpo 'py ayanât?
>
> VI, 7, âtmano tmâ netâ.
>
> II, 6, so tmânam abhidhyâtvâ.
>
> VI, 35, dvidharmondham for dvidharmândham. (Comm. *kh*ândasa.)
>
> VI, 35, te*g*asendham, i.e. te*g*asâ-iddhan. (In explaining other irregular compounds, too, as in I, 4, the commentator has recourse to a *kh*ândasa or prâmâdika licence.)
>
> VI, 1, hira*n*yavasthât for hira*n*yâvasthât. Here the dropping of a in avasthât is explained by a reference to Bhâguri (vash*t*i Bhâgurir allopam avâpyor upasargayo*h*). See Vopadeva III, 171.

VIII. Vi*s*lish*t*apâtha:

> VII, 2, brahmadhîyâlambana. (Comm. vi*s*lish*t*a-pâtha*s* *kh*ândasa*h*.)
>
> VI, 35, apyay ankurâ for apy ankurâ. (Comm. yakâra*h* pramâdapa*th*ita*h*.)

On the contrary VI, 35, vlîyânte for vilîyante.

If on the grounds which we have hitherto examined there seems good reason to ascribe the Maitrâya*n*a-brâhma*n*a-upanishad to an early rather than to a late period, possibly to an ante-Pâ*n*inean period, we shall hardly be persuaded to change this opinion on account of supposed references to Vaish*n*ava or to Bauddha doctrines which some scholars have tried to discover in it.

As to the worship of Vish*n*u, as one of the many manifestations of the Highest Spirit, we have seen it alluded to in other Upanishads, and we know from the Brâhma*n*as that the name of Vish*n*u was connected with many of the earliest Vedic sacrifices.

As to Bauddha doctrines, including the very name of Nirvâ*na* (p. xlvi, l. 19), we must remember, as I have often remarked, that there were Bauddhas before Buddha. B*ri*haspati, who is frequently quoted in later philosophical writings as the author of an heretical philosophy, denying the authority of the Vedas, is mentioned by name in our Upanishad (VII, 9), but we are told that this B*ri*haspati, having become *S*ukra, promulgated his erroneous doctrines in order to mislead the Asuras, and thus to insure the safety of Indra, i.e. of the old faith.

The fact that the teacher of King B*ri*hadratha in our Upanishad is called *S*âkâyanya, can never be used in support of the idea that, being a descendant of *S*âka[1], he must have been, like *S*âkyamuni, a teacher of Buddhist doctrines. He is the very opposite in our Upanishad, and warns his hearers against such doctrines as we should identify with the doctrines of Buddha. As I have pointed out on several occasions, the breaking through the law of the Âsramas is the chief complaint which orthodox Brâhmans make against Buddhists and their predecessors, and this is what *S*âkâyanya condemns. A Brâhman may become a Sannyâsin, which is much the same as a Buddhist Bhikshu, if he has first passed through the three stages of a student, a householder, and a Vânaprastha. But to become a Bhikshu without that previous discipline, was heresy in the eyes of the Brâhmans, and it was exactly that heresy which the Bauddhas preached and practised. That this social laxity was gaining ground at the time when our Upanishad was written is clear (see VII, 8). We hear of people who wear red dresses (like the Buddhists) without having a right to them ; we even hear of books, different from the Vedas, against which the true Brâhmans are warned. All this points to times when what we call Buddhism was in the air, say the sixth century B.C., the very time to which I have always assigned the origin of the genuine and classical Upanishads.

The Upanishads are to my mind the germs of Buddhism,

---

[1] *S*âkâyanya means a grandson or further descendant of *S*âka; see Ga*n*aratnâvalî (Baroda, 1874), p. 57[n].

while Buddhism is in many respects the doctrine of the Upanishads carried out to its last consequences, and, what is important, employed as the foundation of a new social system. In doctrine the highest goal of the Vedânta, the knowledge of the true Self, is no more than the Buddhist Samyaksambodhi; in practice the Sannyâsin is the Bhikshu, the friar, only emancipated alike from the tedious discipline of the Brâhmanic student, the duties of the Brâhmanic householder, and the yoke of useless penances imposed on the Brâhmanic dweller in the forest. The spiritual freedom of the Sannyâsin becomes in Buddhism the common property of the Sangha, the Fraternity, and that Fraternity is open alike to the young and the old, to the Brâhman and the *S*ûdra, to the rich and the poor, to the wise and the foolish. In fact there is no break between the India of the Veda and the India of the Tripi*t*aka, but there is an historical continuity between the two, and the connecting link between extremes that seem widely separated must be sought in the Upanishads[1].

F. MAX MÜLLER.

Oxford, February, 1884.

---

[1] As there is room left on this page, I subjoin a passage from the Abhidharma-kosha-vyâkhyâ, ascribed to the Bhagavat, but which, as far as style and thought are concerned, might be taken from an Upanishad: Ukta*m* hi Bhagavatâ: P*ri*thivî bho Gautama kutra pratish*th*itâ? P*ri*thivî Brâhma*n*a abma*n*dale pratish*th*itâ. Abma*n*dalam bho Gautama kva pratish*th*itam? Vâyau pratish-*th*itam. Vâyur bho Gautama kva pratish*th*ita*h*? Âkâ*s*e pratish*th*ita*h*. Âkâsam bho Gautama kutra pratish*th*itam? Atisarasi Mahâbrâhma*n*a, atisarasi Mahâbrâhma*n*a. Âkâsam Brâhma*n*âpratish*th*itam, anâlambanam iti vistara*h*. Tasmâd asty âkâ*s*am iti Vaibhâshikâ*h*. (See B*ri*had-Âr. Up. III, 6, 1. Burnouf, Introduction à l'histoire du Buddhisme, p. 449.)

'For it is said by the Bhagavat: "O Gautama, on what does the earth rest?" "The earth, O Brâhma*n*a, rests on the sphere of water." "O Gautama, on what does the sphere of water rest?" "It rests on the air." "O Gautama, on what does the air rest?" "It rests on the ether (âkâ*s*a)." "O Gautama, on what does the ether rest?" "Thou goest too far, great Brâhma*n*a; thou goest too far, great Brâhma*n*a. The ether, O Brâhma*n*a, does not rest. It has no support." Therefore the Vaibhâshikas hold that there is an ether,' &c.

KATHA-UPANISHAD.

KA*TH*A-UPANISHAD.

FIRST ADHYÂYA.

FIRST VALLÎ.

1. VÂGA*S*RAVASA[1], desirous (of heavenly rewards), surrendered (at a sacrifice) all that he possessed. He had a son of the name of Na*k*iketas.

2. When the (promised) presents were being given (to the priests), faith entered into the heart of Na*k*iketas, who was still a boy, and he thought:

3. 'Unblessed[2], surely, are the worlds to which a man goes by giving (as his promised present at a sacrifice) cows which have drunk water, eaten hay, given their milk[3], and are barren.'

4. He (knowing that his father had promised to give up all that he possessed, and therefore his son also) said to his father: 'Dear father, to whom wilt thou give me?'

---

[1] Vâga*s*ravasa is called Âru*n*i Auddâlaki Gautama, the father of Na*k*iketas. The father of *S*vetaketu, another enlightened pupil (see *Kh*ând. Up. VI, 1, 1), is also called Âru*n*i (Uddâlaka, comm. Kaush. Up. I, 1) Gautama. *S*vetaketu himself is called Âru*n*eya, i. e. the son of Âru*n*i, the grandson of Aru*n*a, and likewise Auddâlaki. Auddâlaki is a son of Uddâlaka, but *S*ankara (Kâ*th*.Up. I, 11) takes Auddâlaki as possibly the same as Uddâlaka. See B*ri*h. Âr. Up. III, 6, 1.

[2] As to ânanda, unblessed, see B*ri*h. Âr. Up. IV, 4, 11; Vâga*s*. Sa*m*h. Up. 3 (Sacred Books of the East, vol. i, p. 311).

[3] Ânandagiri explains that the cows meant here are cows no longer able to drink, to eat, to give milk, and to calve.

He said it a second and a third time.   Then the father replied (angrily):

   'I shall give thee[1] unto Death.'

(The father, having once said so, though in haste, had to be true to his word and to sacrifice his son.)

   5. The son said: 'I go as the first, at the head of many (who have still to die); I go in the midst of many (who are now dying).   What will be the work of Yama (the ruler of the departed) which to-day he has to do unto me[2]?

---

   [1] Dadâmi, I give, with the meaning of the future.   Some MSS. write dâsyâmi.

   [2] I translate these verses freely, i. e. independently of the commentator, not that I ever despise the traditional interpretation which the commentators have preserved to us, but because I think that, after having examined it, we have a right to judge for ourselves.   *S*ankara says that the son, having been addressed by his father full of anger, was sad, and said to himself: 'Among many pupils I am the first, among many middling pupils I am the middlemost, but nowhere am I the last.   Yet though I am such a good pupil, my father has said that he will consign me unto death.   What duty has he to fulfil toward Yama which he means to fulfil to-day by giving me to him?   There may be no duty, he may only have spoken in haste.   Yet a father's word must not be broken.'   Having considered this, the son comforted his father, and exhorted him to behave like his forefathers, and to keep his word.   I do not think this view of *S*ankara's could have been the view of the old poet.   He might have made the son say that he was the best or one of the best of his father's pupils, but hardly that he was also one of his middling pupils, thus implying that he never was among the worst.   That would be out of keeping with the character of Na*k*iketas, as drawn by the poet himself.   Na*k*iketas is full of faith and wishes to die, he would be the last to think of excuses why he should not die.   The second half of the verse may be more doubtful.   It may mean what *S*ankara thinks it means, only that we should get thus again an implied complaint of Na*k*iketas against his father, and this is not in keeping with his character.   The mind of Na*k*iketas is bent on what is to come, on what he will see after death, and on what Yama will do unto him.   'What has Yama to do,' he asks, 'what can he do, what is it that he will to-day do unto

6. ' Look back how it was with those who came
before, look forward how it will be with those who
come hereafter.   A mortal ripens like corn, like
corn he springs up again [1].'

(Na*k*iketas enters into the abode of Yama Vaivasvata, and there is no one to receive him.
Thereupon one of the attendants of Yama is supposed to say :)

7. ' Fire enters into the houses, when a Brâhma*n*a
enters as a guest[2].   That fire is quenched by this
peace-offering ;—bring water, O Vaivasvata [3]!

8. ' A Brâhma*n*a that dwells in the house of a
foolish man without receiving food to eat, destroys
his hopes and expectations, his possessions, his
righteousness, his sacred and his good deeds, and
all his sons and cattle [4].'

(Yama, returning to his house after an absence
of three nights, during which time Na*k*iketas had
received no hospitality from him, says :)

9. ' O Brâhma*n*a, as thou, a venerable guest, hast
dwelt in my house three nights without eating,

---

me ?' This seems to me consistent with the tenor of the ancient story,
while *S*ankara's interpretations and interpolations savour too much
of the middle ages of India.

[1] Sasya, corn rather than grass; *eîa, ἥἱον*, Benfey ; Welsh haidd,
according to Rhys; different from *s*ash-pa, ces-pes, Benfey.

[2] Cf. Vasish*th*a XI, 13 ; Sacred Books of the East, vol. xiv, p. 51.

[3] Vaivasvata, a name of Yama, the ruler of the departed.   Water
is the first gift to be offered to a stranger who claims hospitality.

[4] Here again some words are translated differently from *S*ankara.
He explains âsâ as asking for a wished-for object, pratîkshâ as looking forward with a view to obtaining an unknown object.   Sangata
he takes as reward for intercourse with good people ; sûn*r*itâ, as
usual, as good and kind speech ; ish*t*a as rewards for sacrifices ;
pûrta as rewards for public benefits.

therefore choose now three boons. Hail to thee! and welfare to me!'

10. Na*k*iketas said: 'O Death, as the first of the three boons I choose that Gautama, my father, be pacified, kind, and free from anger towards me; and that he may know me and greet me, when I shall have been dismissed by thee.'

11. Yama said: 'Through my favour Auddâlaki Âru*n*i, thy father, will know thee, and be again towards thee as he was before. He shall sleep peacefully through the night, and free from anger, after having seen thee freed from the mouth of death.'

12. Na*k*iketas said: 'In the heaven-world there is no fear; thou art not there, O Death, and no one is afraid on account of old age. Leaving behind both hunger and thirst, and out of the reach of sorrow, all rejoice in the world of heaven.'

13. 'Thou knowest, O Death, the fire-sacrifice which leads us to heaven; tell it to me, for I am full of faith. Those who live in the heaven-world reach immortality,—this I ask as my second boon.'

14. Yama said: 'I tell it thee, learn it from me, and when thou understandest that fire-sacrifice which leads to heaven, know, O Na*k*iketas, that it is the attainment of the endless worlds, and their firm support, hidden in darkness[1].'

15. Yama then told him that fire-sacrifice, the beginning of all the worlds[2], and what bricks are

---

[1] The commentator translates: 'I tell it thee, attend to me who knows the heavenly fire.' Here the nom. sing. of the participle would be very irregular, as we can hardly refer it to bravîmi. Then, 'Know this fire as a means of obtaining the heavenly world, know that fire as the rest or support of the world, when it assumes the form of Virâ*g*, and as hidden in the heart of men.'

[2] *S*ankara: the first embodied, in the shape of Virâ*g*.

required for the altar, and how many, and how they
are to be placed. And Na*k*iketas repeated all as it
had been told to him. Then M*ri*tyu, being pleased
with him, said again :

16. The generous [1], being satisfied, said to him :
'I give thee now another boon; that fire-sacrifice
shall be named after thee, take also this many-
coloured chain [2].'

17. 'He who has three times performed this Nâ*k*i-
keta rite, and has been united with the three (father,
mother, and teacher), and has performed the three
duties (study, sacrifice, almsgiving) overcomes birth
and death. When he has learnt and understood
this fire, which knows (or makes us know) all that is
born of Brahman [3], which is venerable and divine,
then he obtains everlasting peace.'

18. 'He who knows the three Nâ*k*iketa fires, and
knowing the three, piles up the Nâ*k*iketa sacrifice, he,
having first thrown off the chains of death, rejoices
in the world of heaven, beyond the reach of grief.'

19. 'This, O Na*k*iketas, is thy fire which leads
to heaven, and which thou hast chosen as thy second
boon. That fire all men will proclaim [4]. Choose now,
O Na*k*iketas, thy third boon.'

20. Na*k*iketas said : 'There is that doubt, when a
man is dead,—some saying, he is ; others, he is not.
This I should like to know, taught by thee ; this is
the third of my boons.'

21. Death said : 'On this point even the gods

---

[1] Verses 16–18 seem a later addition.

[2] This arises probably from a misunderstanding of verse II, 3.

[3] *G*âtavedas.

[4] Tavaiva is a later addition, caused by the interpolation of
verses 15–18.

have doubted formerly; it is not easy to understand. That subject is subtle. Choose another boon, O Nakiketas, do not press me, and let me off that boon.'

22. Nakiketas said: 'On this point even the gods have doubted indeed, and thou, Death, hast declared it to be not easy to understand, and another teacher like thee is not to be found:—surely no other boon is like unto this.'

23. Death said : 'Choose sons and grandsons who shall live a hundred years, herds of cattle, elephants, gold, and horses. Choose the wide abode of the earth, and live thyself as many harvests as thou desirest.'

24. 'If you can think of any boon equal to that, choose wealth, and long life. Be (king), Nakiketas, on the wide earth [1]. I make thee the enjoyer of all desires.'

25. 'Whatever desires are difficult to attain among mortals, ask for them according to thy wish;—these fair maidens with their chariots and musical instruments,—such are indeed not to be obtained by men,—be waited on by them whom I give to thee, but do not ask me about dying.'

26. Nakiketas said : 'These things last till to-morrow, O Death, for they wear out this vigour of all the senses. Even the whole of life is short. Keep thou thy horses, keep dance and song for thyself.'

27. 'No man can be made happy by wealth. Shall we possess wealth, when we see thee ? Shall we live,

---

[1] Mahâbhûmau, on the great earth, has been explained also by mahâ bhûmau, be great on the earth. It is doubtful, however, whether mahâ for mahân could be admitted in the Upanishads, and whether it would not be easier to write mahân bhûmau.

as long as thou rulest? Only that boon (which I
have chosen) is to be chosen by me.'

28. 'What mortal, slowly decaying here below, and
knowing, after having approached them, the freedom
from decay enjoyed by the immortals, would delight
in a long life, after he has pondered on the pleasures
which arise from beauty and love [1]?'

29. 'No, that on which there is this doubt, O Death,
tell us what there is in that great Hereafter. Nakiketas does not choose another boon but that which
enters into the hidden world.'

---

[1] A very obscure verse. Sankara gives a various reading kva
tadâsthah for kvadhahsthah, in the sense of 'given to these pleasures,'
which looks like an emendation. I have changed agîryatâm into
agâryatâm, and take it for an acc. sing., instead of a gen. plur.,
which could hardly be governed by upetya.

SECOND VALLÎ.

1. Death said: 'The good is one thing, the pleasant another; these two, having different objects, chain a man. It is well with him who clings to the good; he who chooses the pleasant, misses his end.'

2. 'The good and the pleasant approach man: the wise goes round about them and distinguishes them. Yea, the wise prefers the good to the pleasant, but the fool chooses the pleasant through greed and avarice.'

3. 'Thou, O Nakiketas, after pondering all pleasures that are or seem delightful, hast dismissed them all. Thou hast not gone into the road[1] that leadeth to wealth, in which many men perish.'

4. 'Wide apart and leading to different points are these two, ignorance, and what is known as wisdom. I believe Nakiketas to be one who desires knowledge, for even many pleasures did not tear thee away[2].'

5. 'Fools dwelling in darkness, wise in their own conceit, and puffed up with vain knowledge, go round and round, staggering to and fro, like blind men led by the blind[3].'

6. 'The Hereafter never rises before the eyes of the careless child, deluded by the delusion of wealth. "This is the world," he thinks, "there is no other;"— thus he falls again and again under my sway.'

7. 'He (the Self) of whom many are not even able

---

[1] Cf. I, 16.

[2] The commentator explains lolupantah by vikkhedam kritavantah. Some MSS. read lolupante and lolupanti, but one expects either lolupyante or lolupati.

[3] Cf. Mund. Up. II, 8.

to hear, whom many, even when they hear of him, do not comprehend; wonderful is a man, when found, who is able to teach him (the Self); wonderful is he who comprehends him, when taught by an able teacher[1].'

8. 'That (Self), when taught by an inferior man, is not easy to be known, even though often thought upon[2]; unless it be taught by another, there is no way to it, for it is inconceivably smaller than what is small[3].'

9. 'That doctrine is not to be obtained[4] by argument, but when it is declared by another, then, O dearest, it is easy to understand. Thou hast obtained it now[5]; thou art truly a man of true resolve. May we have always an inquirer like thee[6]!'

10. Nakiketas said: 'I know that what is called a treasure is transient, for that eternal is not obtained by things which are not eternal. Hence the Nâki-keta fire(-sacrifice) has been laid by me (first); then, by means of transient things, I have obtained what is not transient (the teaching of Yama)[7].'

11. Yama said: 'Though thou hadst seen the fulfilment of all desires, the foundation of the world, the endless rewards of good deeds, the shore where

[1] Cf. Bhag. Gîtâ II, 29.   [2] Cf. Mund. Up II, 4.
[3] I read anupramânât. Other interpretations: If it is taught by one who is identified with the Self, then there is no uncertainty. If it has been taught as identical with ourselves, then there is no perception of anything else. If it has been taught by one who is identified with it, then there is no failure in understanding it (agati).
[4] Âpaneyâ; should it be âpanâya, as afterwards sugñânâya?
[5] Because you insist on my teaching it to thee.
[6] Unless no is negative, for Yama, at first, does not like to communicate his knowledge.
[7] The words in parentheses have been added in order to remove the otherwise contradictory character of the two lines.

there is no fear, that which is magnified by praise, the wide abode, the rest [1], yet being wise thou hast with firm resolve dismissed it all.'

12. 'The wise who, by means of meditation on his Self, recognises the Ancient, who is difficult to be seen, who has entered into the dark, who is hidden in the cave, who dwells in the abyss, as God, he indeed leaves joy and sorrow far behind [2].'

13. 'A mortal who has heard this and embraced it, who has separated from it all qualities, and has thus reached the subtle Being, rejoices, because he has obtained what is a cause for rejoicing. The house (of Brahman) is open, I believe, O Na*k*iketas.'

14. Na*k*iketas said: 'That which thou seest as neither this nor that, as neither effect nor cause, as neither past nor future, tell me that.'

15. Yama said: 'That word (or place) which all the Vedas record, which all penances proclaim, which men desire when they live as religious students, that word I tell thee briefly, it is Om [3].'

16. 'That (imperishable) syllable means Brahman, that syllable means the highest (Brahman); he who knows that syllable, whatever he desires, is his.'

17. 'This is the best support, this is the highest support; he who knows that support is magnified in the world of Brahmâ.'

18. 'The knowing (Self) is not born, it dies not; it sprang from nothing, nothing sprang from it. The

---

[1] Cf. *Kh*ând. Up. VII, 12, 2.

[2] Yama seems here to propound the lower Brahman only, not yet the highest. Deva, God, can only be that as what the Old, i. e. the Self in the heart, is to be recognised. It would therefore mean, he who finds God or the Self in his heart. See afterwards, verse 21.

[3] Cf. *S*vet. Up. IV, 9; Bhag. Gîtâ VIII, 11.

Ancient is unborn, eternal, everlasting; he is not killed, though the body is killed [1].'

19. 'If the killer thinks that he kills, if the killed thinks that he is killed, they do not understand; for this one does not kill, nor is that one killed.'

20. 'The Self [2], smaller than small, greater than great, is hidden in the heart of that creature. A man who is free from desires and free from grief, sees the majesty of the Self by the grace of the Creator [3].'

21. 'Though sitting still, he walks far; though lying down, he goes everywhere [4]. Who, save myself, is able to know that God who rejoices and rejoices not?'

22. 'The wise who knows the Self as bodiless within the bodies, as unchanging among changing things, as great and omnipresent, does never grieve.'

23. 'That Self [5] cannot be gained by the Veda, nor by understanding, nor by much learning. He whom the Self chooses, by him the Self can be gained. The Self chooses him (his body) as his own.'

24. 'But he who has not first turned away from his wickedness, who is not tranquil, and subdued, or whose mind is not at rest, he can never obtain the Self (even) by knowledge.'

25. 'Who then knows where He is, He to whom the Brahmans and Kshatriyas are (as it were) but food [6], and death itself a condiment?'

---

[1] As to verses 18 and 19, see Bhag. Gîtâ II, 19, 20.

[2] Cf. Svet. Up. III, 20; Taitt. Âr. X, 12, 1.

[3] The commentator translates 'through the tranquillity of the senses,' i. e. dhâtuprasâdât, taking prasâda in the technical sense of samprasâda. As to kratu, desire, or rather, will, see Brih. Âr. IV, 4, 5.

[4] Cf. Tal. Up. 5.

[5] Cf. I, 7–9; Mund. Up. III, 2, 3; Bhag. Gîtâ I, 53.

[6] In whom all disappears, and in whom even death is swallowed up.

THIRD VALLÎ.

1. 'There are the two[1], drinking their reward in the world of their own works, entered into the cave (of the heart), dwelling on the highest summit (the ether in the heart). Those who know Brahman call them shade and light; likewise, those householders who perform the Trinâkiketa sacrifice.'

2. 'May we be able to master that Nâkiketa rite which is a bridge for sacrificers; also that which is the highest, imperishable Brahman for those who wish to cross over to the fearless shore[2].'

3. 'Know the Self to be sitting in the chariot, the body to be the chariot, the intellect (buddhi) the charioteer, and the mind the reins[3].'

4. 'The senses they call the horses, the objects of the senses their roads. When he (the Highest Self) is in union with the body, the senses, and the mind, then wise people call him the Enjoyer.'

5. 'He who has no understanding and whose mind

---

[1] The two are explained as the higher and lower Brahman, the former being the light, the latter the shadow. *Rita* is explained as reward, and connected with suk*ri*ta, lit. good deeds, but frequently used in the sense of svakr*i*ta, one's own good and evil deeds. The difficulty is, how the highest Brahman can be said to drink the reward (r*i*tapa) of former deeds, as it is above all works and above all rewards. The commentator explains it away as a metaphorical expression, as we often speak of many, when we mean one. (Cf. Mu*nd.* Up. III, 1, 1.) I have joined sukr*i*tasya with loke, loka meaning the world, i. e. the state, the environment, which we made to ourselves by our former deeds.

[2] These two verses may be later additions.

[3] The simile of the chariot has some points of similarity with the well-known passage in Plato's Phædros, but Plato did not borrow this simile from the Brahmans, as little as Xenophon need have consulted our Upanishad (II, 2) in writing his prologue of Prodikos.

(the reins) is never firmly held, his senses (horses) are
unmanageable, like vicious horses of a charioteer.'

6. ' But he who has understanding and whose mind
is always firmly held, his senses are under control,
like good horses of a charioteer.'

7. ' He who has no understanding, who is unmind-
ful and always impure, never reaches that place, but
enters into the round of births.'

8. ' But he who has understanding, who is mindful
and always pure, reaches indeed that place, from
whence he is not born again.'

9. ' But he who has understanding for his charioteer, and who holds the reins of the mind, he
reaches the end of his journey, and that is the
highest place of Vishnu.'

10. ' Beyond the senses there are the objects, beyond
the objects there is the mind, beyond the mind there
is the intellect, the Great Self is beyond the intellect.'

11. ' Beyond the Great there is the Undeveloped,
beyond the Undeveloped there is the Person
(purusha). Beyond the Person there is nothing—
this is the goal, the highest road.'

12. ' That Self is hidden in all beings and does not
shine forth, but it is seen by subtle seers through
their sharp and subtle intellect.'

13. ' A wise man should keep down speech and
mind [1]; he should keep them within the Self which
is knowledge; he should keep knowledge within the
Self which is the Great; and he should keep that
(the Great) within the Self which is the Quiet.'

14. ' Rise, awake! having obtained your boons [2],

---

[1] Sankara interprets, he should keep down speech in the mind.
[2] Comm., excellent teachers.

understand them! The sharp edge of a razor is
difficult to pass over; thus the wise say the path (to
the Self) is hard.'

15. 'He who has perceived that which is without
sound, without touch, without form, without decay,
without taste, eternal, without smell, without beginning, without end, beyond the Great, and unchangeable, is freed from the jaws of death.'

16. 'A wise man who has repeated or heard the
ancient story of Na*k*iketas told by Death, is magnified in the world of Brahman.'

17. 'And he who repeats this greatest mystery in
an assembly of Brâhmans, or full of devotion at the
time of the *S*râddha sacrifice, obtains thereby infinite
rewards.'

SECOND ADHYÂYA.

FOURTH VALLÎ.

1. Death said: 'The Self-existent pierced the openings (of the senses) so that they turn forward: therefore man looks forward, not backward into himself. Some wise man, however, with his eyes closed and wishing for immortality, saw the Self behind.'

2. 'Children follow after outward pleasures, and fall into the snare of wide-spread death. Wise men only, knowing the nature of what is immortal, do not look for anything stable here among things unstable.'

3. 'That by which we know form, taste, smell, sounds, and loving touches, by that also we know what exists besides. This is that (which thou hast asked for).'

4. 'The wise, when he knows that that by which he perceives all objects in sleep or in waking is the great omnipresent Self, grieves no more.'

5. 'He who knows this living soul which eats honey (perceives objects) as being the Self, always near, the Lord of the past and the future, henceforward fears no more. This is that.'

6. 'He who (knows) him[1] who was born first from

---

[1] The first manifestation of Brahman, commonly called Hira*n*ya-garbha, which springs from the tapas of Brahman. Afterwards only water and the rest of the elements become manifested. The text of these verses is abrupt, possibly corrupt. The two accusatives, tish*thh*antam and tish*thh*antîm, seem to me to require veda to be supplied from verse 4.

the brooding heat[1] (for he was born before the water),
who, entering into the heart, abides therein, and was
perceived from the elements.   This is that.'

7. '(He who knows) Aditi also, who is one with
all deities, who arises with Prâna (breath or Hiranyagarbha), who, entering into the heart, abides therein,
and was born from the elements.   This is that.'

8. 'There is Agni (fire), the all-seeing, hidden in
the two fire-sticks, well-guarded like a child (in the
womb) by the mother, day after day to be adored by
men when they awake and bring oblations.   This
is that.'

9. 'And that whence the sun rises, and whither
it goes to set, there all the Devas are contained, and
no one goes beyond.   This is that[2].'

10. 'What is here (visible in the world), the same
is there (invisible in Brahman); and what is there,
the same is here.   He who sees any difference here
(between Brahman and the world), goes from death
to death.'

11. 'Even by the mind this (Brahman) is to be
obtained, and then there is no difference whatsoever.
He goes from death to death who sees any difference
here.'

12. 'The person (purusha), of the size of a thumb[3],
stands in the middle of the Self (body?), as lord of
the past and the future, and henceforward fears
no more.   This is that.'

13. 'That person, of the size of a thumb, is like
a light without smoke, lord of the past and the
future, he is the same to-day and to-morrow.   This
is that.'

---

[1] Cf. srishtikrama.　　　　　　　[2] Cf. V, 8.
[3] Svet. Up. III, 13.

14. 'As rain-water that has fallen on a mountain-ridge runs down the rocks on all sides, thus does he, who sees a difference between qualities, run after them on all sides.'

15. 'As pure water poured into pure water remains the same, thus, O Gautama, is the Self of a thinker who knows.'

FIFTH VALLÎ.

1. 'There is a town with eleven [1] gates belonging to the Unborn (Brahman), whose thoughts are never crooked. He who approaches it, grieves no more, and liberated (from all bonds of ignorance) becomes free. This is that.'

2. 'He (Brahman) [2] is the swan (sun), dwelling in the bright heaven; he is the Vasu (air), dwelling in the sky; he is the sacrificer (fire), dwelling on the hearth; he is the guest (Soma), dwelling in the sacrificial jar; he dwells in men, in gods (vara), in the sacrifice (*ri*ta), in heaven; he is born in the water, on earth, in the sacrifice (*ri*ta), on the mountains; he is the True and the Great.'

3. 'He (Brahman) it is who sends up the breath (prâ*n*a), and who throws back the breath (apâna). All the Devas (senses) worship him, the adorable (or the dwarf), who sits in the centre.'

4. 'When that incorporated (Brahman), who dwells in the body, is torn away and freed from the body, what remains then? This is that.'

5. 'No mortal lives by the breath that goes up and by the breath that goes down. We live by another, in whom these two repose.'

6. 'Well then, O Gautama, I shall tell thee this mystery, the old Brahman, and what happens to the Self, after reaching death.'

---

[1] Seven apertures in the head, the navel, two below, and the one at the top of the head through which the Self escapes. Cf. *S*vet. Up. III, 18; Bhag. Gîtâ V, 13.

[2] Cf. Rig-veda IV, 40, 5.

7. 'Some enter the womb in order to have a body, as organic beings, others go into inorganic matter, according to their work and according to their knowledge [1].'

8. 'He, the highest Person, who is awake in us while we are asleep, shaping one lovely sight after another, that indeed is the Bright, that is Brahman, that alone is called the Immortal. All worlds are contained in it, and no one goes beyond. This is that [2].'

9. 'As the one fire, after it has entered the world, though one, becomes different according to whatever it burns, thus the one Self within all things becomes different, according to whatever it enters, and exists also without [3].'

10. 'As the one air, after it has entered the world, though one, becomes different according to whatever it enters, thus the one Self within all things becomes different, according to whatever it enters, and exists also without.'

11. 'As the sun, the eye of the whole world, is not contaminated by the external impurities seen by the eyes, thus the one Self within all things is never contaminated by the misery of the world, being himself without [4].'

12. 'There is one ruler, the Self within all things, who makes the one form manifold. The wise who perceive him within their Self, to them belongs eternal happiness, not to others [5].'

13. 'There is one eternal thinker, thinking non-

---

[1] Cf. Br*i*h. Âr. II, 2, 13.   [2] Cf. IV, 9; VI, 1.
[3] Cf. Br*i*h. Âr. II, 5, 19.   [4] Cf. Bhag. Gîtâ XIII, 52.
[5] Cf. *S*vet. Up. VI, 12.

eternal thoughts, who, though one, fulfils the desires of many. The wise who perceive him within their Self, to them belongs eternal peace, not to others [1].'

14. 'They perceive that highest indescribable pleasure, saying, This is that. How then can I understand it? Has it its own light, or does it reflect light?'

15. 'The sun does not shine there, nor the moon and the stars, nor these lightnings, and much less this fire. When he shines, everything shines after him; by his light all this is lighted [2].'

---

[1] Cf. Svet. Up. VI, 13.

[2] Cf. Svet. Up. VI, 14; Mund. Up. II, 2, 10; Bhag. Gîtâ XV, 6.

SIXTH VALLÎ.

1. 'There is that ancient tree[1], whose roots grow upward and whose branches grow downward;—that[2] indeed is called the Bright[3], that is called Brahman, that alone is called the Immortal[4]. All worlds are contained in it, and no one goes beyond. This is that.'

2. 'Whatever there is, the whole world, when gone forth (from the Brahman), trembles in its breath[5]. That Brahman is a great terror, like a drawn sword. Those who know it become immortal.'

3. 'From terror of Brahman fire burns, from terror the sun burns, from terror Indra and Vâyu, and Death, as the fifth, run away[6].'

4. 'If a man could not understand it before the falling asunder of his body, then he has to take body again in the worlds of creation[7].'

---

[1] The fig-tree which sends down its branches so that they strike root and form new stems, one tree growing into a complete forest.

[2] Cf. Bhag. Gîtâ XV, 1–3.   [3] Cf. V, 8.

[4] The commentator says that the tree is the world, and its root is Brahman, but there is nothing to support this view in the original, where tree, roots, and branches are taken together as representing the Brahman in its various manifestations.

[5] According to the commentator, in the highest Brahman.

[6] Cf. Taitt. Up. II, 8, 1.

[7] The commentator translates: 'If a man is able to understand (Brahman), then even before the decay of his body, he is liberated. If he is not able to understand it, then he has to take body again in the created worlds.' I doubt whether it is possible to supply so much, and should prefer to read iha ken nâsakad, though I find it difficult to explain how so simple a text should have been misunderstood and corrupted.

5. 'As in a mirror, so (Brahman may be seen clearly) here in this body; as in a dream, in the world of the Fathers; as in the water, he is seen about in the world of the Gandharvas; as in light and shade [1], in the world of Brahmâ.'

6. 'Having understood that the senses are distinct [2] (from the Âtman), and that their rising and setting (their waking and sleeping) belongs to them in their distinct existence (and not to the Âtman), a wise man grieves no more.'

7. 'Beyond the senses is the mind, beyond the mind is the highest (created) Being [3], higher than that Being is the Great Self, higher than the Great, the highest Undeveloped.'

8. 'Beyond the Undeveloped is the Person, the all-pervading and entirely imperceptible. Every creature that knows him is liberated, and obtains immortality.'

9. 'His form is not to be seen, no one beholds him with the eye. He is imagined by the heart, by wisdom, by the mind. Those who know this, are immortal [4].'

10. 'When the five instruments of knowledge stand still together with the mind, and when the intellect does not move, that is called the highest state.'

11. 'This, the firm holding back of the senses, is what is called Yoga. He must be free from thoughtlessness then, for Yoga comes and goes [5].'

---

[1] Roer: 'As in a picture and in the sunshine.'

[2] They arise from the elements, ether, &c.

[3] Buddhi or intellect, cf. III, 10.

[4] Much better in Svet. Up. IV, 20: 'Those who know him by the heart as being in the heart, and by the mind, are immortal.'

[5] Sankara explains apyaya by apâya.

12. ' He (the Self) cannot be reached by speech, by mind, or by the eye. How can it be apprehended except by him who says : " He is ? " '

13. ' By the words " He is," is he to be apprehended, and by (admitting) the reality of both (the invisible Brahman and the visible world, as coming from Brahman). When he has been apprehended by the words " He is," then his reality reveals itself.'

14. ' When all desires that dwell in his heart cease, then the mortal becomes immortal, and obtains Brahman.'

15. ' When all the ties [1] of the heart are severed here on earth, then the mortal becomes immortal— here ends the teaching [2].'

16. ' There are a hundred and one arteries of the heart [3], one of them penetrates the crown of the head [4]. Moving upwards by it, a man (at his death) reaches the Immortal [5]; the other arteries serve for departing in different directions.'

17. ' The Person not larger than a thumb, the inner Self, is always settled in the heart of men [6]. Let a man draw that Self forth from his body with steadi-

---

[1] Ignorance, passion, &c.   Cf. Mu*nd*. Up. II, 1, 10; II, 2, 9.

[2] The teaching of the Vedânta extends so far and no farther. (Cf. Pra*s*na Up. VI, 7.)   What follows has reference, according to the commentator, not to him who knows the highest Brahman, for he becomes Brahman at once and migrates no more; but to him who does not know the highest Brahman fully, and therefore migrates to the Brahmaloka, receiving there the reward for his partial knowledge and for his good works.

[3] Cf. *Kh*ând. Up. VIII, 6, 6.

[4] It passes out by the head.

[5] The commentator says: He rises through the sun (Mu*nd*. Up. I, 2, 11) to a world in which he enjoys some kind of immortality.

[6] *S*vet. Up. III, 13.

ness, as one draws the pith from a reed¹. Let him know that Self as the Bright, as the Immortal; yes, as the Bright, as the Immortal².'

18. Having received this knowledge taught by Death and the whole rule of Yoga (meditation), Na*k*iketa became free from passion³ and death, and obtained Brahman. Thus it will be with another also who knows thus what relates to the Self.

19. May He protect us both! May He enjoy us both! May we acquire strength together! May our knowledge become bright! May we never quarrel⁴! Om! Peace! peace! peace! Hari*h*, Om!

---

¹ Roer: 'As from a painter's brush a fibre.'

² This repetition marks, as usual, the end of a chapter.

³ Vira*g*a, free from vice and virtue. It may have been vi*g*ara, free from old age. See, however, Mu*nd*. Up. I, 2, 11.

⁴ Cf. Taitt. Up. III, 1; III, 10, note.

MU*N*DAKA-UPANISHAD.

MU*N*DAKA-UPANISHAD.

FIRST MU*N*DAKA.

FIRST KHA*N*DA.

1. BRAHMÂ was the first of the Devas, the maker of the universe, the preserver of the world. He told the knowledge of Brahman, the foundation of all knowledge, to his eldest son Atharva[1].

2. Whatever Brahmâ told Atharvan, that knowledge of Brahman Atharvan formerly told to Angir; he told it to Satyavâha Bhâradvâ*g*a, and Bhâradvâ*g*a told it in succession to Angiras.

3. *S*aunaka, the great householder, approached Angiras respectfully and asked: 'Sir, what is that through which, if it is known, everything else becomes known?'

4. He said to him: 'Two kinds of knowledge must be known, this is what all who know Brahman tell us, the higher and the lower knowledge.'

5. 'The lower knowledge is the *R*ig-veda, Ya*g*ur-veda, Sâma-veda, Atharva-veda, *S*ikshâ (phonetics), Kalpa (ceremonial), Vyâkara*n*a (grammar), Niruk*t*a (etymology), *Kh*andas (metre), *G*yotisha (astronomy)[2];

---

[1] The change between Atharva and Atharvan, like that between Na*k*iketas and Nâ*k*iketa, shows the freedom of the phraseology of the Upanishad, and cannot be used for fixing the date of the constituent elements of the Upanishad.

[2] Other MSS. add here itihâsa-purâ*n*a-nyâya-mîmâm*s*â-dharma-*s*âstrâ*n*i.

but the higher knowledge is that by which the Indestructible (Brahman) is apprehended.'

6. 'That which cannot be seen, nor seized, which has no family and no caste [1], no eyes nor ears, no hands nor feet, the eternal, the omnipresent (all-pervading), infinitesimal, that which is imperishable, that it is which the wise regard as the source of all beings.'

7. 'As the spider sends forth and draws in its thread, as plants grow on the earth, as from every man hairs spring forth on the head and the body, thus does everything arise here from the Indestructible.'

8. 'The Brahman swells by means of brooding (penance) [2]; hence is produced matter (food); from matter breath [3], mind, the true [4], the worlds (seven), and from the works (performed by men in the worlds), the immortal (the eternal effects, rewards, and punishments of works).'

---

[1] I translate var*n*a by caste on account of its conjunction with gotra. The commentator translates, 'without origin and without qualities.' We should say that which belongs to no genus or species.

[2] I have translated tapas by brooding, because this is the only word in English which combines the two meanings of warmth and thought. Native authorities actually admit two roots, one tap, to burn, the other tap, to meditate; see commentary on Parâ-*s*ara-smr*i*ti, p. 39[b] (MS. Bodl.), Tapa*h* k*rikkh*ra*k*andrâya*n*âdirû-pe*n*âhâravarga*n*am. Nanu Vyâsena tapo 'nyathâ smaryate, tapa*h* svadharma-vartitva*m* sau*k*am sa*n*ganibarha*n*am iti; nâya*m* dosha*h*, k*rikkh*râder api svadharmavi*s*eshât. Tapa sa*m*tâpa ity asmad dhâtor utpannasya tapa*h*-*s*abdasya deha*s*osha*n*e v*ri*ttir mukhyâ.... Yat tu tatraivokta*m*, ko 'yam moksha*h* katha*m* tena sa*m*sâram prati-pannavân ity âlo*k*anam artha*gñ*âs tapa*h* sa*m*santi pa*nd*îtâ iti so 'nya eva tapa*h*sabda*h*, tapa âlo*k*ana ity asmâd dhâtor utpanna*h*.

[3] Hira*n*yagarbha, the living world as a whole. Comm.

[4] Satya, if we compare Ka*th*. VI, 7 and III, 10, seems to mean buddhi. Here it is explained by the five elements.

9. 'From him who perceives all and who knows all, whose brooding (penance) consists of knowledge, from him (the highest Brahman) is born that Brahman[1], name, form[2], and matter (food).'

---

[1] Hira*n*yagarbha. Comm.

[2] Nâmarûpam, a very frequent concept in Buddhistic literature.

SECOND KHA*N*DA.

1. This is the truth[1]: the sacrificial works which they (the poets) saw in the hymns (of the Veda) have been performed in many ways in the Tretâ age[2]. Practise[3] them diligently, ye lovers of truth, this is your path that leads to the world of good works[4]!

2. When the fire is lighted and the flame flickers, let a man offer his oblations between the two portions of melted butter, as an offering with faith.

3. If a man's Agnihotra sacrifice[5] is not followed

---

[1] In the beginning of the second Kha*n*da the lower knowledge is first described, referring to the performance of sacrifices and other good deeds. The reward of them is perishable, and therefore a desire is awakened after the higher knowledge.

[2] The Tretâ age is frequently mentioned as the age of sacrifices. I should prefer, however, to take tretâ in the sense of trayî vidyâ, and santata as developed, because the idea that the Tretâ age was distinguished by its sacrifices, seems to me of later origin. Even the theory of the four ages or yugas, though known in the Ait. Brâhma*n*a, is not frequently alluded to in the older Upanishads. See Weber, Ind. Stud. I, p. 283.

[3] The termination tha for ta looks suspiciously Buddhistic; see 'Sanskrit Texts discovered in Japan,' J. R. A. S. 1880, p. 180.

[4] Svak*ri*ta and suk*ri*ta are constantly interchanged. They mean the same, good deeds, or deeds performed by oneself and believed to be good.

[5] At the Agnihotra, the first of all sacrifices, and the type of many others, two portions of âg*y*a are sacrificed on the right and left side of the Âhavanîya altar. The place between the two is called the Âvâpasthâna, and here the oblations to the gods are to be offered. There are two oblations in the morning to Sûrya and Prag*â*pati, two in the evening to Agni and Prag*â*pati. Other sacrifices, such as the Dar*s*a and Pûr*n*amâsa, and those mentioned in verse 3, are connected with the Agnihotra.

by the new-moon and full-moon sacrifices, by the
four-months' sacrifices, and by the harvest sacrifice,
if it is unattended by guests, not offered at all, or
without the Vai*s*vadeva ceremony, or not offered
according to rule, then it destroys his seven worlds [1].

4. Kâlî (black), Karâlî (terrific), Mano*g*avâ (swift
as thought), Sulohitâ (very red), Sudhûmravar*n*â
(purple), Sphuli*n*ginî (sparkling), and the brilliant
Vi*s*varûpî [2] (having all forms), all these playing about
are called the seven tongues (of fire).

5. If a man performs his sacred works when these
flames are shining, and the oblations follow at the
right time, then they lead him as sun-rays to where
the one Lord of the Devas dwells.

6. Come hither, come hither! the brilliant oblations say to him, and carry the sacrificer on the rays
of the sun, while they utter pleasant speech and
praise him, saying: ' This is thy holy Brahma-world
(Svarga), gained by thy good works.'

7. But frail, in truth, are those boats, the sacrifices, the eighteen, in which this lower ceremonial
has been told [3]. Fools who praise this as the highest
good, are subject again and again to old age and
death.

---

[1] The seven worlds form the rewards of a pious sacrificer, the
first is Bhu*h*, the last Satya. The seven worlds may also be explained as the worlds of the father, grandfather, and great-grand-
father, of the son, the grandson, and great-grandson, and of the
sacrificer himself.

[2] Or Vi*s*varu*k*î, if there is any authority for this reading in Mahîdhara's commentary to the Vâ*g*as. Sa*m*hitâ XVII, 79. The Râjah
of Besmah's edition has vi*s*varukî, which is also the reading adopted
by Rammohun Roy, see Complete Works, vol. i, p. 579.

[3] The commentator takes the eighteen for the sixteen priests,
the sacrificer, and his wife. But such an explanation hardly yields
a satisfactory meaning, nor does plava mean perishable.

8. Fools dwelling in darkness, wise in their own conceit, and puffed up with vain knowledge, go round and round staggering to and fro, like blind men led by the blind [1].

9. Children, when they have long lived in ignorance, consider themselves happy. Because those who depend on their good works are, owing to their passions, improvident, they fall and become miserable when their life (in the world which they had gained by their good works) is finished.

10. Considering sacrifice and good works as the best, these fools know no higher good, and having enjoyed (their reward) on the height of heaven, gained by good works, they enter again this world or a lower one.

11. But those [2] who practise penance and faith in the forest, tranquil, wise, and living on alms, depart free from passion through the sun to where that immortal Person dwells whose nature is imperishable [3].

12. Let a Brâhma*n*a, after he has examined all these worlds which are gained by works, acquire freedom from all desires. Nothing that is eternal (not made) can be gained by what is not eternal (made). Let him, in order to understand this, take

---

[1] Cf. Ka*th*. Up. II, 5.

[2] According to the commentator, this verse refers to those who know the uselessness of sacrifices and have attained to a knowledge of the qualified Brahman. They live in the forest as Vânaprasthas and Sa*m*nyâsins, practising tapas, i.e. whatever is proper for their state, and *s*raddhâ, i.e. a knowledge of Hira*n*yagarbha. The wise are the learned Gr*i*hasthas, while those who live on alms are those who have forsaken their family.

[3] That person is Hira*n*yagarbha. His immortality is relative only, it lasts no longer than the world (sa*m*sâra).

fuel in his hand and approach a Guru who is learned and dwells entirely in Brahman.

13. To that pupil who has approached him respectfully, whose thoughts are not troubled by any desires, and who has obtained perfect peace, the wise teacher truly told that knowledge of Brahman through which he knows the eternal and true Person.

SECOND MUN̈DAKA.

FIRST KHAN̈DA.

1. This is the truth. As from a blazing fire sparks, being like unto fire[1], fly forth a thousandfold, thus are various beings brought forth from the Imperishable, my friend, and return thither also.

2. That heavenly Person is without body, he is both without and within, not produced, without breath and without mind, pure, higher than the high Imperishable[2].

3. From him (when entering on creation) is born breath, mind, and all organs of sense, ether, air, light, water, and the earth, the support of all.

4. Fire (the sky) is his head, his eyes the sun and the moon, the quarters his ears, his speech the Vedas disclosed, the wind his breath, his heart the universe; from his feet came the earth; he is indeed the inner Self of all things[3].

5. From him comes Agni (fire)[4], the sun being the fuel; from the moon (Soma) comes rain (Parganya); from the earth herbs; and man gives seed unto the woman. Thus many beings are begotten from the Person (purusha).

6. From him come the *Rik*, the Sâman, the

---

[1] Cf. Br̈h. Âr. II, 1, 20.

[2] The high Imperishable is here the creative, the higher the non-creative Brahman.

[3] Called Vishn̈u and Virâg̈ by the commentators.

[4] There are five fires, those of heaven, rain, earth, man, and woman. Comm.

Ya*g*ush, the Dîkshâ (initiatory rites), all sacrifices and offerings of animals, and the fees bestowed on priests, the year too, the sacrificer, and the worlds, in which the moon shines brightly and the sun.

7. From him the many Devas too are begotten, the Sâdhyas (genii), men, cattle, birds, the up and down breathings, rice and corn (for sacrifices), penance, faith, truth, abstinence, and law.

8. The seven senses (prâ*n*a) also spring from him, the seven lights (acts of sensation), the seven kinds of fuel (objects by which the senses are lighted), the seven sacrifices (results of sensation), these seven worlds (the places of the senses, the worlds determined by the senses) in which the senses move, which rest in the cave (of the heart), and are placed there seven and seven.

9. Hence come the seas and all the mountains, from him flow the rivers of every kind ; hence come all herbs and the juice through which the inner Self subsists with the elements.

10. The Person is all this, sacrifice, penance, Brahman, the highest immortal; he who knows this hidden in the cave (of the heart), he, O friend, scatters the knot of ignorance here on earth.

SECOND KHA*N*DA.

1. Manifest, near, moving in the cave (of the heart) is the great Being. In it everything is centred which ye know as moving, breathing, and blinking, as being and not-being, as adorable, as the best, that is beyond the understanding of creatures.

2. That which is brilliant, smaller than small, that on which the worlds are founded and their inhabitants, that is the indestructible Brahman, that is the breath, speech, mind; that is the true, that is the immortal. That is to be hit. Hit it, O friend!

3. Having taken the Upanishad as the bow, as the great weapon, let him place on it the arrow, sharpened by devotion! Then having drawn it with a thought directed to that which is, hit the mark, O friend, viz. that which is the Indestructible!

4. Om is the bow, the Self is the arrow, Brahman is called its aim. It is to be hit by a man who is not thoughtless; and then, as the arrow (becomes one with the target), he will become one with Brahman.

5. In him the heaven, the earth, and the sky are woven, the mind also with all the senses. Know him alone as the Self, and leave off other words! He is the bridge of the Immortal.

6. He moves about becoming manifold within the heart where the arteries meet, like spokes fastened to the nave. Meditate on the Self as Om! Hail to you, that you may cross beyond (the sea of) darkness!

7. He who understands all and who knows all, he to whom all this glory in the world belongs, the

Self, is placed in the ether, in the heavenly city of Brahman (the heart). He assumes the nature of mind, and becomes the guide of the body of the senses. He subsists in food, in close proximity to the heart. The wise who understand this, behold the Immortal which shines forth full of bliss.

8. The fetter of the heart is broken, all doubts are solved, all his works (and their effects) perish when He has been beheld who is high and low (cause and effect)[1].

9. In the highest golden sheath there is the Brahman without passions and without parts. That is pure, that is the light of lights, that is it which they know who know the Self.

10. The[2] sun does not shine there, nor the moon and the stars, nor these lightnings, and much less this fire. When he shines, everything shines after him; by his light all this is lighted[3].

11. That immortal Brahman is before, that Brahman is behind, that Brahman is right and left. It has gone forth below and above; Brahman alone is all this, it is the best.

---

[1] Cf. Ka*th*. Up. VI, 15.   [2] Ka*th*. Up. V, 15.
[3] *S*vet. Up. VI, 14; Bhag. Gîtâ IX, 15, 6.

THIRD MU*N*DAKA.

First Kha*n*da.

1. Two birds, inseparable friends, cling to the same tree. One of them eats the sweet fruit, the other looks on without eating [1].

2. On the same tree man sits grieving, immersed, bewildered by his own impotence (an-*îsâ*). But when he sees the other lord (*îsa*) contented and knows his glory, then his grief passes away [2].

3. When the seer sees the brilliant maker and lord (of the world) as the Person who has his source in Brahman, then he is wise, and shaking off good and evil, he reaches the highest oneness, free from passions;

4. For he is the Breath shining forth in all beings, and he who understands this becomes truly wise, not a talker only. He revels in the Self, he delights in the Self, and having performed his works (truthfulness, penance, meditation, &c.) he rests, firmly established in Brahman, the best of those who know Brahman [3].

---

[1] Cf. Rv. I, 164, 20; Nir. XIV, 30; *S*vet. Up. IV, 6; Ka*th*. Up. III, 1.

[2] Cf. *S*vet. Up. IV, 7.

[3] The commentator states that, besides âtmarati*h* kriyâvân, there was another reading, viz. âtmaratikriyâvân. This probably owed its origin to a difficulty felt in reconciling kriyâvân, performing acts, with the brahmavidâ*m* varish*th*a*h*, the best of those who know Brahman, works being utterly incompatible with a true knowledge of Brahman. Kriyâvân, however, as *S*ankara points out, may mean here simply, having performed meditation and other acts conducive to a knowledge of Brahman. Probably truthfulness,

5. By truthfulness, indeed, by penance, right knowledge, and abstinence must that Self be gained; the
Self whom spotless anchorites gain is pure, and like
a light within the body.

6. The true prevails, not the untrue; by the true
the path is laid out, the way of the gods (devayâna*h*),
on which the old sages, satisfied in their desires,
proceed to where there is that highest place of the
True One.

7. That (true Brahman) shines forth grand, divine,
inconceivable, smaller than small; it is far beyond
what is far and yet near here, it is hidden in the
cave (of the heart) among those who see it even
here.

8. He is not apprehended by the eye, nor by
speech, nor by the other senses, not by penance or
good works[1]. When a man's nature has become
purified by the serene light of knowledge, then he
sees him, meditating on him as without parts.

9. That subtle Self is to be known by thought
(*k*etas) there where breath has entered fivefold;
for every thought of men is interwoven with the
senses, and when thought is purified, then the Self
arises.

10. Whatever state a man whose nature is purified imagines, and whatever desires he desires (for
himself or for others)[2], that state he conquers and

---

penance, &c., mentioned in the next following verse, are the kriyâs
or works intended. For grammatical reasons also this reading is
preferable. But the last foot esha brahmavidâ*m* varish*th*a*h* is
clearly defective. If we examine the commentary, we see that
*S*ankara read brahmanish*th*a*h*, and that he did not read esha, which
would give us the correct metre, brahmanish*th*o brahmavidâ*m*
varish*th*a*h*.

[1] Cf. Ka*th*. Up. VI, 12.   [2] Cf. Br*i*h. Âr. I, 4, 15.

those desires he obtains. Therefore let every man who desires happiness worship the man who knows the Self[1].

SECOND KHA*N*DA.

1. He (the knower of the Self) knows that highest home of Brahman[2], in which all is contained and shines brightly. The wise who, without desiring happiness, worship that Person[3], transcend this seed, (they are not born again.)

2. He who forms desires in his mind, is born again through his desires here and there. But to him whose desires are fulfilled and who is conscious of the true Self (within himself) all desires vanish, even here on earth.

3. That Self[4] cannot be gained by the Veda, nor by understanding, nor by much learning. He whom the Self chooses, by him the Self can be gained. The Self chooses him (his body) as his own.

4. Nor is that Self to be gained by one who is destitute of strength, or without earnestness, or without right meditation. But if a wise man strives after it by those means (by strength, earnestness, and right meditation), then his Self enters the home of Brahman.

5. When they have reached him (the Self), the sages become satisfied through knowledge, they are conscious of their Self, their passions have passed

---

[1] All this is said by the commentator to refer to a knowledge of the conditioned Brahman only.

[2] See verse 4.

[3] The commentator refers purusha to the knower of the Self.

[4] Ka*th*. Up. II, 23.

away, and they are tranquil. The wise, having reached Him who is omnipresent everywhere, devoted to the Self, enter into him wholly.

6. Having well ascertained the object of the knowledge of the Vedânta[1], and having purified their nature by the Yoga[2] of renunciation, all anchorites, enjoying the highest immortality, become free at the time of the great end (death) in the worlds of Brahmâ.

7. Their fifteen parts[3] enter into their elements, their Devas (the senses) into their (corresponding) Devas[4]. Their deeds and their Self with all his knowledge become all one in the highest Imperishable.

8. As the flowing rivers disappear in the sea[5], losing their name and their form, thus a wise man, freed from name and form, goes to the divine Person, who is greater than the great[6].

9. He who knows that highest Brahman, becomes even Brahman. In his race no one is born ignorant of Brahman. He overcomes grief, he overcomes evil; free from the fetters of the heart, he becomes immortal.

10. And this is declared by the following *Rik*-verse: 'Let a man tell this science of Brahman to those only who have performed all (necessary) acts, who are versed in the Vedas, and firmly established in (the lower) Brahman, who themselves offer as

---

[1] Cf. Taitt. Âr. X, 12, 3; *S*vet. Up. VI, 22; Kaiv. Up. 3; see Weber, Ind. Stud. I, p. 288.

[2] By the Yoga system, which, through restraint (yoga), leads a man to true knowledge.

[3] Cf. Pra*s*na Up. VI, 4.   [4] The eye into the sun, &c.

[5] Cf. Pra*s*na Up. VI, 5.

[6] Greater than the conditioned Brahman. Comm.

an oblation the one *Ri*shi (Agni), full of faith, and by whom the rite of (carrying fire on) the head has been performed, according to the rule (of the Âtharva*n*as).'

11. The *Ri*shi Aṅgiras formerly told this true (science[1]); a man who has not performed the (proper) rites, does not read it. Adoration to the highest *Ri*shis! Adoration to the highest *Ri*shis!

---

[1] To *S*aunaka, cf. I, 1, 3.

TAITTIRÎYAKA-
UPANISHAD.

TAITTIRÎYAKA-UPANISHAD.

FIRST VALLÎ,

Or, the Chapter on *Sî*kshâ (pronunciation).

First Anuvâka [1].

1. HARI*h*, Om! May Mitra be propitious to us, and Varu*n*a, Aryaman also, Indra, B*ri*haspati, and the wide-striding Vish*n*u [2].

Adoration to Brahman! Adoration to thee, O Vâyu (air)! Thou indeed art the visible Brahman. I shall proclaim thee alone as the visible Brahman. I shall proclaim the right. I shall proclaim the true (scil. Brahman).

(1–5) [3] May it protect me! May it protect the teacher! yes, may it protect me, and may it protect the teacher! Om! Peace! peace! peace!

---

[1] This invocation is here counted as an Anuvâka; see Taitt. Âr., ed. Rajendralal Mitra, p. 725.

[2] This verse is taken from Rig-veda-sa*m*hitâ I, 90, 9. The deities are variously explained by the commentators: Mitra as god of the Prâ*n*a (forth-breathing) and of the day; Varu*n*a as god of the Apâna (off-breathing) and of the night. Aryaman is supposed to represent the eye or the sun; Indra, strength; B*ri*haspati, speech or intellect; Vish*n*u, the feet. Their favour is invoked, because it is only if they grant health that the study of the highest wisdom can proceed without fail.

[3] Five short sentences, in addition to the one paragraph. Such sentences occur at the end of other Anuvâkas also, and are counted separately.

Second Anuvâka.

1. Om[1]! Let us explain *Sîkshâ*, the doctrine of pronunciation, viz. letter, accent, quantity, effort (in the formation of letters), modulation, and union of letters (sandhi). This is the lecture on *Sîkshâ*.

Third Anuvâka.

1. May glory come to both of us (teacher and pupil) together! May Vedic light belong to both of us!

Now let us explain the Upanishad (the secret meaning) of the union (sa*m*hitâ)[2], under five heads, with regard to the worlds, the heavenly lights, knowledge, offspring, and self (body). People call these the great Sa*m*hitâs.

First, with regard to the worlds. The earth is the former element, heaven the latter, ether their union;

2. That union takes place through Vâyu (air). So much with regard to the worlds.

Next, with regard to the heavenly lights. Agni (fire) is the former element, Âditya (the sun) the latter, water their union. That union takes place through lightning. So much with regard to the heavenly lights.

Next, with regard to knowledge. The teacher is the former element,

3. The pupil the latter, knowledge their union. That union takes place through the recitation of the Veda. So much with regard to knowledge.

Next, with regard to offspring. The mother is

---

[1] Cf. Rig-veda-prâti*s*âkhya, ed. M. M., p. iv seq.

[2] Cf. Aitareya-âra*n*yaka III, 1, 1 (Sacred Books, vol. i, p. 247).

the former element, the father the latter, offspring
their union. That union takes place through procreation. So much with regard to offspring.

4. Next, with regard to the self (body). The
lower jaw is the former element, the upper jaw the
latter, speech their union. That union takes place
through speech. So much with regard to the Self.
These are the great Samhitâs. He who knows
these Samhitâs (unions), as here explained, becomes
united with offspring, cattle, Vedic light, food, and
with the heavenly world.

FOURTH ANUVÂKA.

1. May he[1] who is the strong bull of the Vedas,
assuming all forms, who has risen from the Vedas,
from the Immortal, may that Indra (lord) strengthen
me with wisdom! May I, O God, become an upholder
of the Immortal!

May my body be able, my tongue sweet, may
I hear much with my ears! Thou (Om) art the
shrine (of Brahman), covered by wisdom. Guard
what I have learnt[2].

She (Srî, happiness) brings near and spreads,

2. And makes, without delay, garments for herself,
cows, food, and drink at all times; therefore bring
that Srî (happiness) hither to me, the woolly, with

---

[1] The next verses form the prayer and oblation of those who
wish for wisdom and happiness. In the first verse it is supposed
that the Om is invoked, the most powerful syllable of the Vedas,
the essence extracted from all the Vedas, and in the end a name
of Brahman. See Khând. Up. p. 1 seq.

[2] Here end the prayers for the attainment of wisdom, to be followed by oblations for the attainment of happiness.

her cattle [1]! Svâhâ [2]! May the Brahman-students
come to me, Svâhâ! May they come from all
sides, Svâhâ! May they come forth to me, Svâhâ!
May they practise restraint, Svâhâ! May they enjoy
peace, Svâhâ!

3. May I be a glory among men, Svâhâ! May
I be better than the richest, Svâhâ! May I enter
into thee, O treasure (Om), Svâhâ! Thou, O
treasure [3], enter into me, Svâhâ! In thee, consisting of a thousand branches, in thee, O treasure,
I am cleansed, Svâhâ! As water runs downward, as
the months go to the year, so, O preserver of the
world, may Brahman-students always come to me
from all sides, Svâhâ!

(1) Thou art a refuge! Enlighten me! Take possession of me!

FIFTH ANUVÂKA.

1. Bhû, Bhuvas, Suvas [4], these are the three sacred
interjections (vyâhriti). Mâhâkamasya taught a
fourth, viz. Mahas, which is Brahman, which is the
Self. The others (devatâs) are its members.

Bhû is this world, Bhuvas is the sky, Suvas is
the other world.

2. Mahas is the sun. All the worlds are increased
by the sun. Bhû is Agni (fire), Bhuvas is Vâyu
(air), Suvas is Âditya (sun). Mahas is the moon. All
the heavenly lights are increased by the moon.

---

[1] The construction is not right. Woolly, lomasâ, is explained
as ' possessed of woolly sheep.'

[2] With the interjection Svâhâ each oblation is offered.

[3] Bhaga, here explained as bhagavat.

[4] The text varies between Bhû, Bhuvas, Suvas, Mahas, and Bhû,
Bhuvar, Suvar, Mahar.

Bhû is the *Rik*-verses, Bhuvas is the Sâman-verses, Suvas is the Ya*g*us-verses.

3. Mahas is Brahman. All the Vedas are increased by the Brahman.

(1–2) Bhû is Prâ*n*a (up-breathing), Bhuvas is Apâna (down-breathing), Suvas is Vyâna (back-breathing). Mahas is food. All breathings are increased by food.

Thus there are these four times four, the four and four sacred interjections. He who knows these,

(1–2) Knows the Brahman. All Devas bring offerings to him.

SIXTH ANUVÂKA.

1. There is the ether within the heart, and in it there is the Person (purusha) consisting of mind, immortal, golden.

Between the two palates there hangs the uvula, like a nipple—that is the starting-point of Indra (the lord)[1]. Where the root of the hair divides, there he opens the two sides of the head, and saying Bhû, he enters Agni (the fire); saying Bhuvas, he enters Vâyu (air);

2. Saying Suvas, he enters Âditya (sun); saying Mahas, he enters Brahman. He there obtains lordship, he reaches the lord of the mind. He becomes lord of speech, lord of sight, lord of hearing, lord of knowledge. Nay, more than this. There is the Brahman whose body is ether, whose nature is true, rejoicing in the senses (prâ*n*a), delighted in the mind, perfect in peace, and immortal.

(1) Worship thus, O Prâ*k*înayogya!

---

[1] Cf. I, 4, 1.

SEVENTH ANUVÂKA.

1. 'The earth, the sky, heaven, the four quarters, and the intermediate quarters,'—'Agni (fire), Vâyu (air), Âditya (sun), *K*andramas (moon), and the stars,'—'Water, herbs, trees, ether, the universal Self (virâ*g*),'—so much with reference to material objects (bhûta).

Now with reference to the self (the body): 'Prâ*n*a (up-breathing), Apâna (down-breathing), Vyâna (back-breathing), Udâna (out-breathing), and .Samâ*n*a (on-breathing),'—'The eye, the ear, mind, speech, and touch,'—'The skin, flesh, muscle, bone, and marrow.' Having dwelt on this (fivefold arrangement of the worlds, the gods, beings, breathings, senses, and elements of the body), a Rishi said: 'Whatever exists is fivefold (pâṅkta)[1].'

(1) By means of the one fivefold set (that referring to the body) he completes the other fivefold set.

EIGHTH ANUVÂKA.

1. Om means Brahman.   2. Om means all this. 3. Om means obedience.   When they have been told, 'Om, speak,' they speak.   4. After Om they sing Sâmans.   5. After Om they recite hymns. 6. After Om the Adhvaryu gives the response. 7. After Om the Brahman-priest gives orders. 8. After Om he (the sacrificer) allows the performance of the Agnihotra.   9. When a Brâhma*n*a is going to begin his lecture, he says, 10. 'Om, may I acquire Brahman (the Veda).'   He thus acquires the Veda.

---

[1] Cf. Br*i*h. Âr. Up. I, 4, 17.

NINTH ANUVÂKA [1].

1. (What is necessary?) The right, and learning and practising the Veda. The true, and learning and practising the Veda. Penance, and learning and practising the Veda. Restraint, and learning and practising the Veda. Tranquillity, and learning and practising the Veda. The fires (to be consecrated), and learning and practising the Veda. The Agnihotra sacrifice, and learning and practising the Veda. Guests (to be entertained), and learning and practising the Veda. Man's duty, and learning and practising the Veda. Children, and learning and practising the Veda.

(1–6) Marriage, and learning and practising the Veda. Children's children, and learning and practising the Veda.

Satyava*k*as Râthîtara thinks that the true only is necessary. Taponitya Paura*s*ish*t*i thinks that penance only is necessary. Nâka Maudgalya thinks that learning and practising the Veda only are necessary,—for that is penance, that is penance.

TENTH ANUVÂKA.

1. 'I am he who shakes the tree (i.e. the tree of the world, which has to be cut down by knowledge). 2. My glory is like the top of a mountain. 3. I, whose pure light (of knowledge) has risen high, am that which is truly immortal, as it resides in the sun.

---

[1] This chapter is meant to show that knowledge alone, though it secures the highest object, is not sufficient by itself, but must be preceded by works. The learning of the Veda by heart and the practising of it so as not to forget it again, these two must always have been previously performed.

4. I am the brightest treasure. 5. I am wise, immortal, imperishable [1].' 6. This is the teaching of the Veda, by the poet Trisanku.

ELEVENTH ANUVÂKA.

1. After having taught the Veda, the teacher instructs the pupil: 'Say what is true! Do thy duty! Do not neglect the study of the Veda! After having brought to thy teacher his proper reward, do not cut off the line of children! Do not swerve from the truth! Do not swerve from duty! Do not neglect what is useful! Do not neglect greatness! Do not neglect the learning and teaching of the Veda!

2. 'Do not neglect the (sacrificial) works due to the Gods and Fathers! Let thy mother be to thee like unto a god! Let thy father be to thee like unto a god! Let thy teacher be to thee like unto a god! Let thy guest be to thee like unto a god! Whatever actions are blameless, those should be regarded, not others. Whatever good works have been performed by us, those should be observed by thee,—

3. 'Not others. And there are some Brâhmanas better than we. They should be comforted by thee by giving them a seat. Whatever is given should be given with faith, not without faith,—with joy, with modesty, with fear, with kindness. If there should

---

[1] This verse has been translated as the commentator wishes it to be understood, in praise of that knowledge of Self which is only to be obtained after all other duties, and, more particularly, the study of the Veda, have been performed. The text is probably corrupt, and the interpretation fanciful.

be any doubt in thy mind with regard to any sacred act or with regard to conduct,—

4. 'In that case conduct thyself as Brâhma*n*as who possess good judgment conduct themselves therein, whether they be appointed or not[1], as long as they are not too severe, but devoted to duty. And with regard to things that have been spoken against, as Brâhma*n*as who possess good judgment conduct themselves therein, whether they be appointed or not, as long as they are not too severe, but devoted to duty,

(1–7) Thus conduct thyself. 'This is the rule. This is the teaching. This is the true purport (Upanishad) of the Veda. This is the command. Thus should you observe. Thus should this be observed.'

TWELFTH ANUVÂKA.

1. May Mitra be propitious to us, and Varu*n*a, Aryaman also, Indra, Br*i*haspati, and the wide-striding Vish*n*u! Adoration to Brahman! Adoration to thee, O Vâyu! Thou indeed art the visible Brahman. I proclaimed thee alone as the visible Brahman.

(1–5) I proclaimed the right. I proclaimed the true. It protected me. It protected the teacher. Yes, it protected me, it protected the teacher. Om! Peace! peace! peace!

---

[1] Aparaprayuktâ iti svatantrâ*h*. For other renderings, see Weber, Ind. Stud. II, p. 216.

SECOND VALLÎ,

Or, the Chapter on Ânanda (bliss).

Hari*h*, Om! May it (the Brahman) protect us both (teacher and pupil)! May it enjoy us both! May we acquire strength together! May our knowledge become bright! May we never quarrel! Peace! peace! peace [1]!

First Anuvâka.

He who knows the Brahman attains the highest (Brahman). On this the following verse is recorded:

'He who knows Brahman, which is (i.e. cause, not effect), which is conscious, which is without end, as hidden in the depth (of the heart), in the highest ether, he enjoys all blessings, at one with the omniscient Brahman.'

From that Self [2] (Brahman) sprang ether (âkâ*s*a, that through which we hear); from ether air (that through which we hear and feel); from air fire (that through which we hear, feel, and see); from fire water (that through which we hear, feel, see, and taste); from water earth (that through which we hear, feel, see, taste, and smell). From earth herbs, from herbs food, from food seed, from seed man. Man thus consists of the essence of food. This is his head,

---

[1] Not counted here as an Anuvâka. The other Anuvâkas are divided into a number of small sentences.

[2] Compare with this sr*i*sh*t*ikrama, *Kh*ând. Up. VI, 2; Ait. Âr. II, 4, 1.

this his right arm, this his left arm, this his trunk (âtman), this the seat (the support)[1].

On this there is also the following *S*loka :

SECOND ANUVÂKA.

'From food[2] are produced all creatures which dwell on earth. Then they live by food, and in the end they return to food. For food is the oldest of all beings, and therefore it is called panacea (sarvaushadha, i. e. consisting of all herbs, or quieting the heat of the body of all beings).'

They who worship food as Brahman[3], obtain all food. For food is the oldest of all beings, and therefore it is called panacea. From food all creatures are produced; by food, when born, they grow. Because it is fed on, or because it feeds on beings, therefore it is called food (anna).

Different from this, which consists of the essence of food, is the other, the inner Self, which consists of breath. The former is filled by this. It also has the shape of man. Like the human shape of the former is the human shape of the latter. Prâ*n*a (up-breathing) is its head. Vyâna (back-breathing) is its right arm. Apâna (down-breathing) is its left arm. Ether is its trunk. The earth the seat (the support).

On this there is also the following *S*loka :

---

[1] The text has 'the tail, which is his support.' But pratish*thâ* seems to have been added, the Anuvâka ending originally with pu*kkh*a, which is explained by nâbher adhastâd yad a*n*gam. In the Persian translation the different members are taken for members of a bird, which is not unlikely.

[2] Anna is sometimes used in the more general sense of matter.

[3] Worship consisting in the knowledge that they are born of food, live by food, and end in food, which food is Brahman.

THIRD ANUVÂKA.

'The Devas breathe after breath (prâ*n*a), so do men and cattle. Breath is the life of beings, therefore it is called sarvâyusha (all-enlivening).'

They who worship breath as Brahman, obtain the full life. For breath is the life of all beings, and therefore it is called sarvâyusha. The embodied Self of this (consisting of breath) is the same as that of the former (consisting of food).

Different from this, which consists of breath, is the other, the inner Self, which consists of mind. The former is filled by this. It also has the shape of man. Like the human shape of the former is the human shape of the latter. Ya*g*us is its head. *Rik* is its right arm. Sâman is its left arm. The doctrine (âde*s*a, i.e. the Brâhma*n*a) is its trunk. The Atharvâṅgiras (Atharva-hymns) the seat (the support).

On this there is also the following *S*loka:

FOURTH ANUVÂKA[1].

'He who knows the bliss of that Brahman, from whence all speech, with the mind, turns away unable to reach it, he never fears.' The embodied Self of this (consisting of mind) is the same as that of the former (consisting of breath).

Different from this, which consists of mind, is the other, the inner Self, which consists of understanding. The former is filled by this. It also has the shape of man. Like the human shape of the former is the human shape of the latter. Faith is its head. What is right is its right arm. What is true is its left arm.

---

[1] Cf. II, 9.

Absorption (yoga) is its trunk. The great (intellect?) is the seat (the support).

On this there is also the following *Sloka* :

Fifth Anuvâka.

' Understanding performs the sacrifice, it performs all sacred acts. All Devas worship understanding as Brahman, as the oldest. If a man knows understanding as Brahman, and if he does not swerve from it, he leaves all evils behind in the body, and attains all his wishes.' The embodied Self of this (consisting of understanding) is the same as that of the former (consisting of mind).

Different from this, which consists of understanding, is the other inner Self, which consists of bliss. The former is filled by this. It also has the shape of man. Like the human shape of the former is the human shape of the latter. Joy is its head. Satisfaction its right arm. Great satisfaction is its left arm. Bliss is its trunk. Brahman is the seat (the support).

On this there is also the following *Sloka* :

Sixth Anuvâka.

' He who knows the Brahman as non-existing, becomes himself non-existing. He who knows the Brahman as existing, him we know himself as existing.' The embodied Self of this (bliss) is the same as that of the former (understanding).

Thereupon follow the questions of the pupil :

' Does any one who knows not, after he has departed this life, ever go to that world ? Or does he who knows, after he has departed, go to that world[1]?'

---

[1] As he who knows and he who knows not, are both sprung from Brahman, the question is supposed to be asked by the pupil, whether both will equally attain Brahman.

The answer is: He wished, may I be many[1],
may I grow forth. He brooded over himself (like
a man performing penance). After he had thus
brooded, he sent forth (created) all, whatever there
is. Having sent forth, he entered into it. Having
entered it, he became sat (what is manifest) and
tyat (what is not manifest), defined and undefined,
supported and not supported, (endowed with) knowledge and without knowledge (as stones), real and
unreal[2]. The Sattya (true) became all this whatsoever, and therefore the wise call it (the Brahman)
Sat-tya (the true).

On this there is also this *Sloka*:

SEVENTH ANUVÂKA.

'In the beginning this was non-existent (not yet
defined by form and name). From it was born what
exists. That made itself its Self, therefore it is
called the Self-made[3].' That which is Self-made is
a flavour[4] (can be tasted), for only after perceiving a
flavour can any one perceive pleasure. Who could
breathe, who could breathe forth, if that bliss (Brah-

---

[1] In the *Kh*ândogya-upanishad VI, 2, 1, where a similar account
of the creation is given, the subject is spoken of as tad, neuter. It
is said there: 'In the beginning there was that only which is, one
only, without a second. It willed, may I be many,' &c. (Cf. Br*i*h.
Âr. Up. vol. ii, p. 52.)

[2] What appears as real and unreal to the senses, not the really
real and unreal.

[3] Cf. Ait. Up. I, 2, 3.

[4] As flavour is the cause of pleasure, so Brahman is the cause
of all things. The wise taste the flavour of existence, and know
that it proceeds from Brahman, the Self-made. See Kaushîtaki-
upanishad I, 5; Sacred Books, vol. i, p. 277.

man) existed not in the ether (in the heart)? For
he alone causes blessedness.

When he finds freedom from fear and rest in that
which is invisible, incorporeal, undefined, unsup-
ported, then he has obtained the fearless. For if
he makes but the smallest distinction in it, there
is fear for him[1]. But that fear exists only for
one who thinks himself wise[2], (not for the true
sage.)

On this there is also this *S*loka:

EIGHTH ANUVÂKA.

(1) 'From terror of it (Brahman) the wind blows,
from terror the sun rises; from terror of it Agni
and Indra, yea Death runs as the fifth[3].'

Now this is an examination of (what is meant by)
Bliss (ânanda):

Let there be a noble young man, who is well
read (in the Veda), very swift, firm, and strong, and
let the whole world be full of wealth for him, that is
one measure of human bliss.

One hundred times that human bliss (2) is one
measure of the bliss of human Gandharvas (genii),

---

[1] Fear arises only from what is not ourselves. Therefore, as
soon as there is even the smallest distinction made between our Self
and the real Self, there is a possibility of fear. The explanation
ud=api, aram=alpam is very doubtful, but recognised in the
schools. It could hardly be a proverbial expression, 'if he makes
another stomach' meaning as much as, 'if he admits another person.'
According to the commentator, we should translate, 'for one who
knows (a difference), and does not know the oneness.'

[2] I read manvânasya, the commentator amanvânasya.

[3] Ka*th*. Up. VI, 3.

and likewise of a great sage (learned in the Vedas) who is free from desires.

One hundred times that bliss of human Gandharvas is one measure of the bliss of divine Gandharvas (genii), and likewise of a great sage who is free from desires.

One hundred times that bliss of divine Gandharvas is one measure of the bliss of the Fathers, enjoying their long estate, and likewise of a great sage who is free from desires.

One hundred times that bliss of the Fathers is one measure of the bliss of the Devas, born in the Âgâna heaven (through the merit of their lawful works), (3) and likewise of a great sage who is free from desires.

One hundred times that bliss of the Devas born in the Âgâna heaven is one measure of the bliss of the sacrificial Devas, who go to the Devas by means of their Vaidik sacrifices, and likewise of a great sage who is free from desires.

One hundred times that bliss of the sacrificial Devas is one measure of the bliss of the (thirty-three) Devas, and likewise of a great sage who is free from desires.

One hundred times that bliss of the (thirty-three) Devas is one measure of the bliss of Indra, (4) and likewise of a great sage who is free from desires.

One hundred times that bliss of Indra is one measure of the bliss of Brihaspati, and likewise of a great sage who is free from desires.

One hundred times that bliss of Brihaspati is one measure of the bliss of Pragâpati, and likewise of a great sage who is free from desires.

One hundred times that bliss of Pragâpati is one

measure of the bliss of Brahman, and likewise of a great sage who is free from desires.

(5) He[1] who is this (Brahman) in man, and he who is that (Brahman) in the sun, both are one[2].

---

[1] Cf. III, 10, 4.

[2] In giving the various degrees of happiness, the author of the Upanishad gives us at the same time the various classes of human and divine beings which we must suppose were recognised in his time. We have Men, human Gandharvas, divine Gandharvas, Fathers (pitaras *k*iralokalokâ*h*), born Gods (â*g*âna*g*â devâ*h*), Gods by merit (karmadevâ*h*), Gods, Indra, Br*i*haspati, Pra*g*âpati, Brahman. Such a list would seem to be the invention of an individual rather than the result of an old tradition, if it did not occur in a very similar form in the *S*atapatha-brâhma*n*a, Mâdhyandina-*s*âkhâ XIV, 7, 1, 31, Kâ*n*va-*s*âkhâ (Br*i*h. Âr. Up. IV, 3, 32). Here, too, the highest measure of happiness is ascribed to the Brahmaloka, and other beings are supposed to share a certain measure only of its supreme happiness. The scale begins in the Mâdhyandina-*s*âkhâ with men, who are followed by the Fathers (pitaro *g*italokâ*h*), the Gods by merit (karmadevâ*h*), the Gods by birth (â*g*ânadevâ*h*, with whom the *S*rotriya is joined), the world of Gods, the world of Gandharvas, the world of Pra*g*âpati, the world of Brahman. In the Br*i*had-âra*n*yaka-upanishad we have Men, Fathers, Gandharvas, Gods by merit, Gods by birth, Pra*g*âpati, and Brahman. If we place the three lists side by side, we find—

TAITTIRÎYA-UPAN.	*S*ATAPATHA-BRÂH.	BR*I*HADÂRA*N*.-UPAN.
Men	Men	Men
Human Gandharvas (and *S*rotriya)	—	—
Divine Gandharvas	—	—
Fathers (*k*iraloka)	Fathers (*g*italoka)	Fathers (*g*italoka)
	—	Gandharvas
Gods by birth	Gods by merit	Gods by merit
Gods by merit	Gods by birth (and *S*rotriya)	Gods by birth (and *S*rotriya)
Gods	Gods	—
Indra	Gandharvas	—
Br*i*haspati	—	—
Pra*g*âpati	Pra*g*âpati	Pra*g*âpati
Brahman	Brahman	Brahman.

The commentators do not help us much. *S*ankara on the Taitti-

He who knows this, when he has departed this
world, reaches and comprehends the Self which consists of food, the Self which consists of breath, the
Self which consists of mind, the Self which consists
of understanding, the Self which consists of bliss.
    On this there is also this *S*loka :

---

rîyaka-upanishad explains the human Gandharvas as men who
have become Gandharvas, a kind of fairies; divine Gandharvas, as
Gandharvas by birth. The Fathers or Manes are called *K*iraloka,
because they remain long, though not for ever, in their world. The
âgâna*g*a Gods are explained as born in the world of the Devas
through their good works (smârta), while the Karmadevas are explained as born there through their sacred works (vaidika). The
Gods are the thirty-three, whose lord is Indra, and whose teacher
Br*i*haspati. Pra*g*âpati is Virâ*g*, Brahman Hira*n*yagarbha. Dvivedaga*n*ga, in his commentary on the *S*atapatha-brâhma*n*a, explains
the Fathers as those who, proceeding on the Southern path, have
conquered their world, more particularly by having themselves
offered in their life sacrifices to their Fathers. The Karmadevas,
according to him, are those who have become Devas by sacred
works (*s*rauta), the Â*g*ânadevas those who were gods before there
were men. The Gods are Indra and the rest, while the Gandharvas
are not explained. Pra*g*âpati is Virâ*g*, Brahman is Hira*n*yagarbha.
Lastly, *S*ankara, in his commentary on the Br*i*hadâra*n*yaka-
upanishad, gives nearly the same explanation as before; only that
he makes â*g*ânadevâ*h* still clearer, by explaining them as gods
â*g*ânata*h*, i. e. utpattita*h*, from their birth.
    The arrangement of these beings and their worlds, one rising
above the other, reminds us of the cosmography of the Buddhists,
but the elements, though in a less systematic form, existed evidently
before. Thus we find in the so-called Gargî-brâhma*n*a (*S*atapatha-
brâhma*n*a XIV, 6, 6, 1) the following succession: Water, air, ether[a],
the worlds of the sky[b], heaven, sun, moon, stars, gods, Gandharvas[c],
Pra*g*âpati, Brahman. In the Kaushîtaki-upanishad I, 3 (Sacred
Books of the East, vol. i, p. 275) there is another series, the worlds
of Agni, Vâyu, Varu*n*a, Indra, Pra*g*âpati, and Brahman. See Weber,
Ind. Stud. II, p. 224.

    [a] Deest in Kâ*n*va-*s*âkhâ.
    [b] Between sky and sun, the Kâ*n*va-*s*âkhâ places the Gandharvaloka (Br*i*h. Âr.
Up. III, 6, 1, p. 609).
    [c] Instead of Gandharvas, the Br*i*h. Âr. Up. places Indra.

Ninth Anuvâka[1].

'He who knows the bliss of that Brahman, from whence all speech, with the mind, turns away unable to reach it, he fears nothing[2].'

He does not distress himself with the thought, Why did I not do what is good? Why did I do what is bad? He who thus knows these two (good and bad), frees himself. He who knows both, frees himself[3]. This is the Upanishad[4].

---

[1] Cf. II, 4.

[2] Even if there is no fear from anything else, after the knowledge of Self and Brahman has been obtained, it might be thought that fear might still arise from the commission of evil deeds, and the omission of good works. Therefore the next paragraphs have been added.

[3] The construction of these two sentences is not clear to me.

[4] Here follows the Anukramanî, and in some MSS. the same invocation with which the next Vallî begins.

THIRD VALLÎ,

Or, the Chapter of Bhr*i*gu.

Har*ih*, Om! May it (the Brahman) protect us both! May it enjoy us both! May we acquire strength together! May our knowledge become bright! May we never quarrel! Peace! peace! peace [1]!

First Anuvâka.

Bh*ri*gu Vâru*n*i went to his father Varu*n*a, saying: 'Sir, teach me Brahman.' He told him this, viz. Food, breath, the eye, the ear, mind, speech.

Then he said again to him: 'That from whence these beings are born, that by which, when born, they live, that into which they enter at their death, try to know that. That is Brahman.'

He performed penance. Having performed penance—

Second Anuvâka.

He perceived that food is Brahman, for from food these beings are produced; by food, when born, they live; and into food they enter at their death.

Having perceived this, he went again to his father Varu*n*a, saying: 'Sir, teach me Brahman.' He said to him: 'Try to know Brahman by penance, for penance is (the means of knowing) Brahman.'

He performed penance. Having performed penance—

---

[1] The same paragraph, as before (II, 1), occurs at the end of the Ka*th*a-upanishad, and elsewhere.

THIRD ANUVÂKA.

He perceived that breath [1] is Brahman, for from breath these beings are born; by breath, when born, they live; into breath they enter at their death.

Having perceived this, he went again to his father Varuna, saying: 'Sir, teach me Brahman.' He said to him: 'Try to know Brahman by penance, for penance is (the means of knowing) Brahman.'

He performed penance. Having performed penance—

FOURTH ANUVÂKA.

He perceived that mind (manas) is Brahman, for from mind these beings are born; by mind, when born, they live; into mind they enter at their death.

Having perceived this, he went again to his father Varuna, saying: 'Sir, teach me Brahman.' He said to him: 'Try to know Brahman by penance, for penance is (the means of knowing) Brahman.'

He performed penance. Having performed penance—

FIFTH ANUVÂKA.

He perceived that understanding (vigñâna) was Brahman, for from understanding these beings are born; by understanding, when born, they live; into understanding they enter at their death.

Having perceived this, he went again to his father Varuna, saying: 'Sir, teach me Brahman.' He said to him: 'Try to know Brahman by penance, for penance is (the means of knowing) Brahman.'

---

[1] Or life; see Brih. Âr. Up. IV, 1, 3.

He performed penance. Having performed penance—

SIXTH ANUVÂKA.

He perceived that bliss is Brahman, for from bliss these beings are born ; by bliss, when born, they live; into bliss they enter at their death.

This is the knowledge of Bh*r*igu and Varu*n*a[1], exalted in the highest heaven (in the heart). He who knows this becomes exalted, becomes rich in food, and able to eat food (healthy), becomes great by offspring, cattle, and the splendour of his knowledge (of Brahman), great by fame.

SEVENTH ANUVÂKA.

Let him never abuse food, that is the rule.

Breath is food[2], the body eats the food. The body rests on breath, breath rests on the body. This is the food resting on food. He who knows this food resting on food[3], rests exalted, becomes rich in food, and able to eat food (healthy), becomes great by offspring, cattle, and the splendour of his knowledge (of Brahman), great by fame.

EIGHTH ANUVÂKA.

Let him never shun food, that is the rule. Water is food, the light eats the food. The light rests on water, water rests on light. This is the food resting

---

[1] Taught by Varu*n*a, learnt by Bh*r*igu Vâru*n*i.

[2] Because, like food, it is inside the body.

[3] The interdependence of food and breath. The object of this discussion is to show (see *S*ankara's commentary, p. 135) that the world owes its origin to there being an enjoyer (subject) and what is enjoyed (object), but that this distinction does not exist in the Self.

on food [1]. He who knows this food resting on food, rests exalted, becomes rich in food, and able to eat food (healthy), becomes great by offspring, cattle, and the splendour of his knowledge (of Brahman), great by fame.

Ninth Anuvâka.

Let him acquire much food, that is the rule. Earth is food, the ether eats the food. The ether rests on the earth, the earth rests on the ether. This is the food resting on food. He who knows this food resting on food, rests exalted, becomes rich in food, and able to eat food (healthy), becomes great by offspring, cattle, and the splendour of his knowledge (of Brahman), great by fame.

Tenth Anuvâka.

1. Let him never turn away (a stranger) from his house, that is the rule. Therefore a man should by all means acquire much food, for (good) people say (to the stranger): 'There is food ready for him.' If he gives food amply, food is given to him amply. If he gives food fairly, food is given to him fairly. If he gives food meanly, food is given to him meanly.

2. He who knows this, (recognises and worships Brahman [2]) as possession in speech, as acquisition and possession in up-breathing (prâna) and down-breathing (apâna); as action in the hands; as walking in the feet; as voiding in the anus. These are the human recognitions (of Brahman as manifested in human actions). Next follow the recognitions (of

---

[1] The interdependence of water and light.

[2] Brahmana upâsanaprakârah.

Brahman) with reference to the Devas, viz. as satisfaction in rain; as power in lightning;

3. As glory in cattle; as light in the stars; as
procreation, immortality, and bliss in the member;
as everything in the ether. Let him worship that
(Brahman) as support, and he becomes supported.
Let him worship that (Brahman) as greatness (maha*h*),
and he becomes great. Let him worship that (Brahman) as mind, and he becomes endowed with mind.

4. Let him worship that (Brahman) as adoration,
and all desires fall down before him in adoration.
Let him worship that (Brahman) as Brahman, and
he will become possessed of Brahman. Let him
worship this as the absorption of the gods [1] in Brahman, and the enemies who hate him will die all
around him, all around him will die the foes whom
he does not love.

He [2] who is this (Brahman) in man, and he who is
that (Brahman) in the sun, both are one.

5. He who knows this, when he has departed this
world, after reaching and comprehending the Self
which consists of food, the Self which consists of
breath, the Self which consists of mind, the Self
which consists of understanding, the Self which consists of bliss, enters and takes possession of these
worlds, and having as much food as he likes, and
assuming as many forms as he likes, he sits down
singing this Sâman (of Brahman): 'Hâvu, hâvu,
hâvu!

---

[1] Cf. Kaush. Up. II, 12. Here the absorption of the gods of fire,
sun, moon, and lightning in the god of the air (vâyu) is described.
Sankara adds the god of rain, and shows that air is identical with
ether.

[2] Cf. II, 8.

6. 'I am food (object), I am food, I am food! I am the eater of food (subject), I am the eater of food, I am the eater of food! I am the poet (who joins the two together), I am the poet, I am the poet! I am the first-born of the Right (*ri*ta). Before the Devas I was in the centre of all that is immortal. He who gives me away, he alone preserves me: him who eats food, I eat as food.

'I overcome the whole world, I, endowed with golden light[1]. He who knows this, (attains all this).' This is the Upanishad[2].

---

[1] If we read suvar*n*agyoti*h*. The commentator reads suvar *n*a *g*yoti*h*. i. e. the light is like the sun.

[2] After the Anukrama*n*î follows the same invocation as in the beginning of the third Vallî, 'May it protect us both,' &c.

BR*I*HADÂRA*N*YAKA-
UPANISHAD.

B*RI*HADÂRA*N*YAKA-
UPANISHAD.

FIRST ADHYÂYA[1].

FIRST BRÂHMA*N*A.

1. Verily[2] the dawn is the head of the horse which is fit for sacrifice, the sun its eye, the wind its breath, the mouth the Vai*s*vânara[3] fire, the year the body of the sacrificial horse. Heaven is the back, the sky the belly, the earth the chest[4], the quarters the two sides, the intermediate quarters the ribs, the members the seasons, the joints the months and half-months, the feet days and nights, the bones the stars, the

---

[1] It is the third Adhyâya of the Âra*n*yaka, but the first of the Upanishad.

[2] This Brâhma*n*a is found in the Mâdhyandina text of the *S*atapatha, ed. Weber, X, 6, 4. Its object is there explained by the commentary to be the meditative worship of Virâ*g*, as represented metaphorically in the members of the horse. Sâya*n*a dispenses with its explanation, because, as part of the B*ri*hadâra*n*yaka-upanishad, according to the Kâ*n*va-*s*âkhâ, it had been enlarged on by the Vârttikakâra and explained.

[3] Agni or fire, as pervading everything, as universally present in nature.

[4] Pâ*g*asya is doubtful. The commentator suggests pâd-asya, the place of the feet, i. e. the hoof. The Greek Pēgasos, or ἵπποι πηγοί, throws no light on the word. The meaning of hoof would hardly be appropriate here, and I prefer chest on account of ur as in I, 2, 3. Deussen (Vedânta, p. 8) translates, die Erde seiner Füsse Schemel; but we want some part of the horse.

flesh the clouds. The half-digested food is the sand, the rivers the bowels[1], the liver and the lungs[2] the mountains, the hairs the herbs and trees. As the sun rises, it is the forepart, as it sets, the hindpart of the horse. When the horse shakes itself[3], then it lightens; when it kicks, it thunders; when it makes water, it rains; voice[4] is its voice.

2. Verily Day arose after the horse as the (golden) vessel[5], called Mahiman (greatness), which (at the sacrifice) is placed before the horse. Its place is in the Eastern sea. The Night arose after the horse as the (silver) vessel, called Mahiman, which (at the sacrifice) is placed behind the horse. Its place is in the Western sea. Verily, these two vessels (or greatnesses) arose to be on each side of the horse.

As a racer he carried the Devas, as a stallion the Gandharvas, as a runner the Asuras, as a horse men. The sea is its kin, the sea is its birthplace.

SECOND BRÂHMA*N*A[6].

1. In the beginning there was nothing (to be per-

---

[1] Guda, being in the plural, is explained by nâ*d*î, channel, and sirâ*h*; for we ought to read sirâ or hirâgraha*n*e for *s*irâ, p. 22, l. 16.

[2] Klomâna*h* is explained as a plurale tantum (nityam bahuva-*k*anam ekasmin), and being described as a lump below the heart, on the opposite side of the liver, it is supposed to be the lungs.

[3] 'When it yawns.' Ânandagiri.

[4] Voice is sometimes used as a personified power of thunder and other aerial sounds, and this is identified with the voice of the horse.

[5] Two vessels, to hold the sacrificial libations, are placed at the A*s*vamedha before and behind the horse, the former made of gold, the latter made of silver. They are called Mahiman in the technical language of the ceremonial. The place in which these vessels are set, is called their yoni. Cf. Vâ*g*as. Sa*m*hitâ XXIII, 2.

[6] Called the Agni-brâhma*n*a, and intended to teach the origin of

ceived) here whatsoever. By Death indeed all this
was concealed,—by hunger; for death is hunger.
Death (the first being) thought, 'Let me have a
body.' Then he moved about, worshipping. From
him thus worshipping water was produced. And he
said: 'Verily, there appeared to me, while I worshipped (ar*k*ate), water (ka).' This is why water is
called ar-ka[1]. Surely there is water (or pleasure)
for him who thus knows the reason why water is
called arka.

2. Verily water is arka. And what was there as
the froth of the water, that was hardened, and became
the earth. On that earth he (Death) rested, and from
him, thus resting and heated, Agni (Virâ*g*) proceeded,
full of light.

3. That being divided itself threefold, Âditya (the
sun) as the third, and Vâyu (the air) as the third[2].
That spirit (prâ*n*a)[3] became threefold. The head was
the Eastern quarter, and the arms this and that quarter

Agni, the fire, which is here used for the Horse-sacrifice. It is
found in the *S*atapatha-brâhma*n*a, Mâdhyandina-*s*âkhâ X, 6, 5, and
there explained as a description of Hira*n*yagarbha.

[1] We ought to read arkasyârkatvam, as in Poley's edition, or
ark-kasyârkkatvam, to make the etymology still clearer. The commentator takes arka in the sense of fire, more especially the sacrificial fire employed at the Horse-sacrifice. It may be so, but the
more natural interpretation seems to me to take arka here as water,
from which indirectly fire is produced. From water springs the
earth; on that earth he (M*ri*tyu or Pra*g*âpati) rested, and from
him, while resting there, fire (Virâ*g*) was produced. That fire
assumed three forms, fire, sun, and air, and in that threefold form
it is called prâ*n*a, spirit.

[2] As Agni, Vâyu, and Âditya.

[3] Here Agni (Virâ*g*) is taken as representing the fire of the altar
at the Horse-sacrifice, which is called Arka. The object of the
whole Brâhma*n*a was to show the origin and true character of that
fire (arka).

(i. e. the N. E. and S. E., on the left and right sides). Then the tail was the Western quarter, and the two legs this and that quarter (i.e. the N. W. and S. W.) The sides were the Southern and Northern quarters, the back heaven, the belly the sky, the dust the earth. Thus he (M*ri*tyu, as arka) stands firm in the water, and he who knows this stands firm wherever he goes.

4. He desired[1], 'Let a second body be born of me,' and he (Death or Hunger) embraced Speech in his mind. Then the seed became the year. Before that time there was no year. Speech[2] bore him so long as a year, and after that time sent him forth. Then when he was born, he (Death) opened his mouth, as if to swallow him. He cried Bhâ*n*! and that became speech[3].

5. He thought, 'If I kill him, I shall have but little food.' He therefore brought forth by that speech and by that body (the year) all whatsoever exists, the *Rik*, the Ya*g*us, the Sâman, the metres, the sacrifices, men, and animals.

And whatever he (Death) brought forth, that he resolved to eat (ad). Verily because he eats everything, therefore is Aditi (Death) called Aditi. He who thus knows why Aditi is called Aditi, becomes an eater of everything, and everything becomes his food[4].

---

[1] He is the same as what was before called m*ri*tyu, death, who, after becoming self-conscious, produced water, earth, fire, &c. He now wishes for a second body, which is the year, or the annual sacrifice, the year being dependent on the sun (Âditya).

[2] The commentator understands the father, instead of Speech, the mother.

[3] The interjectional theory.

[4] All these are merely fanciful etymologies of a*s*vamedha and arka.

6. He desired to sacrifice again with a greater sacrifice. He toiled and performed penance. And while he toiled and performed penance, glorious power[1] went out of him. Verily glorious power means the senses (prâna). Then when the senses had gone out, the body took to swelling (sva-yitum), and mind was in the body.

7. He desired that this body should be fit for sacrifice (medhya), and that he should be embodied by it. Then he became a horse (asva), because it swelled (asvat), and was fit for sacrifice (medhya); and this is why the horse-sacrifice is called Asva-medha.

Verily he who knows him thus, knows the Asvamedha. Then, letting the horse free, he thought[2], and at the end of a year he offered it up for himself, while he gave up the (other) animals to the deities. Therefore the sacrificers offered up the purified horse belonging to Pragâpati, (as dedicated) to all the deities.

Verily the shining sun is the Asvamedha-sacrifice, and his body is the year; Agni is the sacrificial fire (arka), and these worlds are his bodies. These two are the sacrificial fire and the Asvamedha-sacrifice, and they are again one deity, viz. Death. He (who knows this) overcomes another death, death does not reach him, death is his Self, he becomes one of those deities.

---

[1] Or glory (senses) and power. Comm.
[2] He considered himself as the horse. Roer.

THIRD BRÂHMA*N*A [1].

1. There were two kinds of descendants of Pra*g*â-pati, the Devas and the Asuras [2]. Now the Devas were indeed the younger, the Asuras the elder ones [3]. The Devas, who were struggling in these worlds, said: 'Well, let us overcome the Asuras at the sacrifices (the *G*yotish*t*oma) by means of the udgîtha.'

2. They said to speech (Vâ*k*): 'Do thou sing out for us (the udgîtha).' 'Yes,' said speech, and sang (the udgîtha). Whatever delight there is in speech, that she obtained for the Devas by singing (the three pavamânas); but that she pronounced well (in the other nine pavamânas), that was for herself. The Asuras knew: 'Verily, through this singer they will overcome us.' They therefore rushed at the singer and pierced her with evil. That evil which consists in saying what is bad, that is that evil.

3. Then they (the Devas) said to breath (scent): 'Do thou sing out for us.' 'Yes,' said breath, and sang. Whatever delight there is in breath (smell), that he obtained for the Devas by singing; but that he smelled well, that was for himself. The Asuras knew: 'Verily, through this singer they will overcome us.' They therefore rushed at the singer, and

---

[1] Called the Udgîtha-brâhma*n*a. In the Mâdhyandina-*s*âkhâ, the Upanishad, which consists of six adhyâyas, begins with this Brâhma*n*a (cf. Weber's edition, p. 1047; Commentary, p. 1109).

[2] The Devas and Asuras are explained by the commentator as the senses, inclining either to sacred or to worldly objects, to good or to evil.

[3] According to the commentator, the Devas were the less numerous and less strong, the Asuras the more numerous and more powerful.

pierced him with evil. That evil which consists in smelling what is bad, that is that evil.

4. Then they said to the eye : 'Do thou sing out for us.' 'Yes,' said the eye, and sang. Whatever delight there is in the eye, that he obtained for the Devas by singing; but that he saw well, that was for himself. The Asuras knew : 'Verily, through this singer they will overcome us.' They therefore rushed at the singer, and pierced him with evil. That evil which consists in seeing what is bad, that is that evil.

5. Then they said to the ear : 'Do thou sing out for us.' 'Yes,' said the ear, and sang. Whatever delight there is in the ear, that he obtained for the Devas by singing; but that he heard well, that was for himself. The Asuras knew : 'Verily, through this singer they will overcome us.' They therefore rushed at the singer, and pierced him with evil. That evil which consists in hearing what is bad, that is that evil.

6. Then they said to the mind : 'Do thou sing out for us.' 'Yes,' said the mind, and sang. Whatever delight there is in the mind, that he obtained for the Devas by singing; but that he thought well, that was for himself. The Asuras knew: 'Verily, through this singer they will overcome us.' They therefore rushed at the singer, and pierced him with evil. That evil which consists in thinking what is bad, that is that evil.

Thus they overwhelmed these deities with evils, thus they pierced them with evil.

7. Then they said to the breath in the mouth[1]: 'Do thou sing for us.' 'Yes,' said the breath, and sang. The Asuras knew: 'Verily, through this singer

---

[1] This is the chief or vital breath, sometimes called mukhya.

they will overcome us.' They therefore rushed at
him and pierced him with evil. Now as a ball of
earth will be scattered when hitting a stone, thus
they perished, scattered in all directions. Hence
the Devas rose, the Asuras fell. He who knows
this, rises by his self, and the enemy who hates
him falls.

8. Then they (the Devas) said: ' Where was he
then who thus stuck to us[1]?' It was (the breath)
within the mouth (âsye 'ntar[2]), and therefore called
Ayâsya; he was the sap (rasa) of the limbs (a*n*ga),
and therefore called Â*n*girasa.

9. That deity was called Dûr, because Death was
far (dûran) from it. From him who knows this,
Death is far off.

10. That deity, after having taken away the evil
of those deities, viz. death, sent it to where the
end of the quarters of the earth is. There he
deposited their sins. Therefore let no one go to
a man, let no one go to the end (of the quarters
of the earth[3]), that he may not meet there with
evil, with death.

11. That deity, after having taken away the evil of
those deities, viz. death, carried them beyond death.

12. He carried speech across first. When speech
had become freed from death, it became (what it
had been before) Agni (fire). That Agni, after
having stepped beyond death, shines.

13. Then he carried breath (scent) across. When
breath had become freed from death, it became

---

[1] Asakta from sa*n*g, to embrace; cf. Rig-veda I, 33, 3. Here
it corresponds to the German anhänglich.

[2] See Deussen, Vedânta, p. 359.

[3] To distant people.

Vâyu (air). That Vâyu, after having stepped beyond death, blows.

14. Then he carried the eye across. When the eye had become freed from death, it became Âditya (the sun). That Âditya, after having stepped beyond death, burns.

15. Then he carried the ear across. When the ear had become freed from death, it became the quarters (space). These are our quarters (space), which have stepped beyond death.

16. Then he carried the mind across. When the mind had become freed from death, it became the moon (*K*andramas). That moon, after having stepped beyond death, shines. Thus does that deity carry him, who knows this, across death.

17. Then breath (vital), by singing, obtained for himself eatable food. For whatever food is eaten, is eaten by breath alone, and in it breath rests[1].

The Devas said: 'Verily, thus far, whatever food there is, thou hast by singing acquired it for thyself. Now therefore give us a share in that food.' He said: 'You there, enter into me.' They said Yes, and entered all into him. Therefore whatever food is eaten by breath, by it the other senses are satisfied.

18. If a man knows this, then his own relations come to him in the same manner; he becomes their supporter, their chief leader, their strong ruler[2]. And if ever any one tries to oppose[3] one who is possessed of such knowledge among his own relatives, then he

---

[1] This is done by the last nine Pavamânas, while the first three were used for obtaining the reward common to all the prâ*n*as.

[2] Here annâda is well explained by anâmayâvin, and vyâdhirahita, free from sickness, strong.

[3] Read pratiprati*h*; see Poley, and Weber, p. 1180.

will not be able to support his own belongings. But
he who follows the man who is possessed of such
knowledge, and who with his permission wishes to
support those whom he has to support, he indeed
will be able to support his own belongings.

19. He was called Ayâsya Ângirasa, for he is the
sap (rasa) of the limbs (anga). Verily, breath is
the sap of the limbs. Yes, breath is the sap of the
limbs. Therefore from whatever limb breath goes
away, that limb withers, for breath verily is the sap
of the limbs.

20. He (breath) is also Brihaspati, for speech is
Brihatî (Rig-veda), and he is her lord; therefore he
is Brihaspati.

21. He (breath) is also Brahmanaspati, for speech
is Brahman (Yagur-veda), and he is her lord; therefore he is Brahmanaspati.

He (breath) is also Sâman (the Udgîtha), for
speech is Sâman (Sâma-veda), and that is both
speech (sâ) and breath (ama)[1]. This is why Sâman
is called Sâman.

22. Or because he is equal (sama) to a grub, equal
to a gnat, equal to an elephant, equal to these three
worlds, nay, equal to this universe, therefore he is
Sâman. He who thus knows this Sâman, obtains
union and oneness with Sâman.

23. He (breath) is Udgîtha[2]. Breath verily is Ut,
for by breath this universe is upheld (uttabdha); and
speech is Gîthâ, song. And because he is ut and
gîthâ, therefore he (breath) is Udgîtha.

---

[1] Cf. Khând. Up. V, 2, 6.
[2] Not used here in the sense of song or hymn, but as an act of
worship connected with the Sâman. Comm.

24. And thus Brahmadatta *K*aikitâneya (the grandson of *K*ikitâna), while taking Soma (râ*g*an), said: 'May this Soma strike my head off, if Ayâsya Ângirasa sang another Udgîtha than this. He sang it indeed as speech and breath.'

25. He who knows what is the property of this Sâman, obtains property. Now verily its property is tone only. Therefore let a priest, who is going to perform the sacrificial work of a Sâma-singer, desire that his voice may have a good tone, and let him perform the sacrifice with a voice that is in good tone. Therefore people (who want a priest) for a sacrifice, look out for one who possesses a good voice, as for one who possesses property. He who thus knows what is the property of that Sâman, obtains property.

26. He who knows what is the gold of that Sâman, obtains gold. Now verily its gold is tone only. He who thus knows what is the gold of that Sâman, obtains gold.

27. He who knows what is the support of that Sâman, he is supported. Now verily its support is speech only. For, as supported in speech, that breath is sung as that Sâman. Some say the support is in food.

Next follows the Abhyâroha[1] (the ascension) of the Pavamâna verses. Verily the Prastot*ri* begins to sing the Sâman, and when he begins, then let him (the sacrificer) recite these (three Ya*g*us-verses):

'Lead me from the unreal to the real! Lead me

---

[1] The ascension is a ceremony by which the performer reaches the gods, or becomes a god. It consists in the recitation of three Ya*g*us, and is here enjoined to take place when the Prastot*ri* priest begins to sing his hymn.

from darkness to light! Lead me from death to immortality!'

Now when he says, 'Lead me from the unreal to the real,' the unreal is verily death, the real immortality. He therefore says, 'Lead me from death to immortality, make me immortal.'

When he says, 'Lead me from darkness to light,' darkness is verily death, light immortality. He therefore says, 'Lead me from death to immortality, make me immortal.'

When he says, 'Lead me from death to immortality,' there is nothing there, as it were, hidden (obscure, requiring explanation)[1].

28. Next come the other Stotras with which the priest may obtain food for himself by singing them. Therefore let the sacrificer, while these Stotras are being sung, ask for a boon, whatever desire he may desire. An Udgât*ri* priest who knows this obtains by his singing whatever desire he may desire either for himself or for the sacrificer. This (knowledge) indeed is called the conqueror of the worlds. He who thus knows this Sâman[2], for him there is no fear of his not being admitted to the worlds[3].

---

[1] See Deussen, Vedânta, p. 86.

[2] He knows that he is the Prâ*n*a, which Prâ*n*a is the Sâman. That Prâ*n*a cannot be defeated by the Asuras, i. e. by the senses which are addicted to evil; it is pure, and the five senses finding refuge in him, recover there their original nature, fire, &c. The Prâ*n*a is the Self of all things, also of speech (*R*ig-yagu*h*-sâmodgîtha), and of the Sâman that has to be sung and well sung. The Prâ*n*a pervades all creatures, and he who identifies himself with that Prâ*n*a, obtains the rewards mentioned in the Brâhma*n*a. Comm.

[3] In connection with loka*g*it, lokyatâ is here explained, and may probably have been intended, as worthiness to be admitted to the highest world. Originally lokyatâ and alokyatâ meant right and wrong. See also I, 5, 17.

FOURTH BRÂHMANA [1].

1. In the beginning this was Self alone, in the shape of a person (purusha). He looking round saw nothing but his Self. He first said, 'This is I;' therefore he became I by name. Therefore even now, if a man is asked, he first says, 'This is I,' and then pronounces the other name which he may have. And because before (pûrva) all this, he (the Self) burnt down (ush) all evils, therefore he was a person (pur-usha). Verily he who knows this, burns down every one who tries to be before him.

2. He feared, and therefore any one who is lonely fears. He thought, 'As there is nothing but myself, why should I fear?' Thence his fear passed away. For what should he have feared? Verily fear arises from a second only.

3. But he felt no delight. Therefore a man who is lonely feels no delight. He wished for a second. He was so large as man and wife together. He then made this his Self to fall in two (pat), and thence arose husband (pati) and wife (patnî). Therefore Yâgñavalkya said : 'We two [2] are thus (each of us) like half a shell [3].' Therefore the void which was

---

[1] Called Purushavidhabrâhmana (Mâdhyandina-sâkhâ, p. 1050). See Muir, Original Sanskrit Texts, vol. i, p. 24.

[2] The Comm. explains svah by âtmanah, of himself. But see Boehtlingk, Sanskrit Chrestomathie, p. 357.

[3] Roer translates : 'Therefore was this only one half of himself, as a split pea is of a whole.' Brigala is a half of anything. Muir (Orig. Sansk. Texts, vol. i, p. 25) translates : 'Yâgñavalkya has said that this one's self is like the half of a split pea.' I have translated the sentence according to Professor Boehtlingk's conjecture (Chrestomathie, 2nd ed. p. 357), though the singular after the dual (svah) is irregular.

there, is filled by the wife. He embraced her, and men were born.

4. She thought, 'How can he embrace me, after having produced me from himself? I shall hide myself.'

She then became a cow, the other became a bull and embraced her, and hence cows were born. The one became a mare, the other a stallion; the one a male ass, the other a female ass. He embraced her, and hence one-hoofed animals were born. The one became a she-goat, the other a he-goat; the one became a ewe[1], the other a ram. He embraced her, and hence goats and sheep were born. And thus he created everything that exists in pairs, down to the ants.

5. He knew, 'I indeed am this creation, for I created all this.' Hence he became the creation, and he who knows this lives in this his creation.

6. Next he thus produced fire by rubbing. From the mouth, as from the fire-hole, and from the hands he created fire[2]. Therefore both the mouth and the hands are inside without hair, for the fire-hole is inside without hair.

And when they say, 'Sacrifice to this or sacrifice to that god,' each god is but his manifestation, for he is all gods.

Now, whatever there is moist, that he created from seed; this is Soma. So far verily is this universe either food or eater. Soma indeed is food, Agni eater. This is the highest creation of Brah-

---

[1] The reading avir itaro, i. e. itarâ u, is not found in the Kâ*n*va text. See Boehtlingk, Chrestomathie, p. 357.

[2] He blew with the mouth while he rubbed with the hands.

man, when he created the gods from his better part[1], and when he, who was (then) mortal[2], created the immortals. Therefore it was the highest creation. And he who knows this, lives in this his highest creation.

7. Now all this was then undeveloped. It became developed by form and name, so that one could say, 'He, called so and so, is such a one[3].' Therefore at present also all this is developed by name and form, so that one can say, 'He, called so and so, is such a one.'

He (Brahman or the Self) entered thither, to the very tips of the finger-nails, as a razor might be fitted in a razor-case, or as fire in a fire-place[4].

He cannot be seen, for, in part only, when breathing, he is breath by name; when speaking, speech by name; when seeing, eye by name; when hearing, ear by name; when thinking, mind by name. All these are but the names of his acts. And he who worships (regards) him as the one or the other, does not know him, for he is apart from this (when qualified) by the one or the other (predicate). Let men worship him as Self, for in the Self all these are one. This Self is the footstep of everything, for through it one knows everything[5]. And as one can find again by footsteps what was lost, thus he who knows this finds glory and praise.

---

[1] Or, when he created the best gods.

[2] As man and sacrificer. Comm.

[3] The Comm. takes asau-nâmâ as a compound, instead of idam-nâmâ. I read asau nâma, he is this by name, viz. Devadatta, &c. Dr. Boehtlingk, who in his Chrestomathie (2nd ed. p. 31) had accepted the views of the Commentator, informs me that he has changed his view, and thinks that we should read asaú nãma.

[4] Cf. Kaush. Br. Up. VI, 19.

[5] 'As one finds lost cattle again by following their footsteps, thus one finds everything, if one has found out the Self.' Comm.

8. This, which is nearer to us than anything, this Self, is dearer than a son, dearer than wealth, dearer than all else.

And if one were to say to one who declares another than the Self dear, that he will lose what is dear to him, very likely it would be so. Let him worship the Self alone as dear. He who worships the Self alone as dear, the object of his love will never perish[1].

9. Here they say: 'If men think that by knowledge of Brahman they will become everything, what then did that Brahman know, from whence all this sprang?'

10. Verily in the beginning this was Brahman, that Brahman knew (its) Self only, saying, 'I am Brahman.' From it all this sprang. Thus, whatever Deva was awakened (so as to know Brahman), he indeed became that (Brahman); and the same with Rishis and men. The Rishi Vâmadeva saw and understood it, singing, 'I was Manu (moon), I was the sun.' Therefore now also he who thus knows that he is Brahman, becomes all this, and even the Devas cannot prevent it, for he himself is their Self.

Now if a man worships another deity, thinking the deity is one and he another, he does not know. He is like a beast for the Devas. For verily, as many beasts nourish a man, thus does every man nourish the Devas. If only one beast is taken away, it is not pleasant; how much more when many are taken! Therefore it is not pleasant to the Devas that men should know this.

11. Verily in the beginning this was Brahman, one

---

[1] On rudh, to lose, see Taitt. Samh. II, 6, 8, 5, pp. 765, 771, as pointed out by Dr. Boehtlingk. On îsvaro (yat) tathaiva syât, see Boehtlingk, s. v.

only. That being one, was not strong enough. It created still further the most excellent Kshatra (power), viz. those Kshatras (powers) among the Devas,—Indra, Varuna, Soma, Rudra, Parganya, Yama, Mrityu, Îsâna. Therefore there is nothing beyond the Kshatra, and therefore at the Râgasûya sacrifice the Brâhmana sits down below the Kshatriya. He confers that glory on the Kshatra alone. But Brahman is (nevertheless) the birth-place of the Kshatra. Therefore though a king is exalted, he sits down at the end (of the sacrifice) below the Brahman, as his birth-place. He who injures him, injures his own birth-place. He becomes worse, because he has injured one better than himself.

12. He[1] was not strong enough. He created the Vis (people), the classes of Devas which in their different orders are called Vasus, Rudras, Âdityas, Visve Devas, Maruts.

13. He was not strong enough. He created the Sûdra colour (caste), as Pûshan (as nourisher). This earth verily is Pûshan (the nourisher); for the earth nourishes all this whatsoever.

14. He was not strong enough. He created still further the most excellent Law (dharma). Law is the Kshatra (power) of the Kshatra[2], therefore there is nothing higher than the Law. Thenceforth even a weak man rules a stronger with the help of the Law, as with the help of a king. Thus the Law is what is called the true. And if a man declares what is true, they say he declares the Law; and if he declares the Law, they say he declares what is true. Thus both are the same.

---

[1] Observe the change from tad, it, to sa, he.
[2] More powerful than the Kshatra or warrior caste. Comm.

15. There are then this Brahman, Kshatra, Vis, and Sûdra. Among the Devas that Brahman existed as Agni (fire) only, among men as Brâhmana, as Kshatriya through the (divine) Kshatriya, as Vaisya through the (divine) Vaisya, as Sûdra through the (divine) Sûdra. Therefore people wish for their future state among the Devas through Agni (the sacrificial fire) only; and among men through the Brâhmana, for in these two forms did Brahman exist.

Now if a man departs this life without having seen his true future life (in the Self), then that Self, not being known, does not receive and bless him, as if the Veda had not been read, or as if a good work had not been done. Nay, even if one who does not know that (Self), should perform here on earth some great holy work, it will perish for him in the end. Let a man worship the Self only as his true state. If a man worships the Self only as his true state, his work does not perish, for whatever he desires that he gets from that Self.

16. Now verily this Self (of the ignorant man) is the world [1] of all creatures. In so far as man sacrifices and pours out libations, he is the world of the Devas; in so far as he repeats the hymns, &c., he is the world of the Rishis; in so far as he offers cakes to the Fathers and tries to obtain offspring, he is the world of the Fathers; in so far as he gives shelter and food to men, he is the world of men; in so far as he finds fodder and water for the animals, he is the world of the animals; in so far as quadrupeds, birds, and even ants live in his houses, he is their world. And as every one wishes his own world not to be injured,

---

[1] Is enjoyed by them all. Comm.

thus all beings wish that he who knows this should not be injured. Verily this is known and has been well reasoned.

17. In the beginning this was Self alone, one only. He desired, 'Let there be a wife for me that I may have offspring, and let there be wealth for me that I may offer sacrifices.' Verily this is the whole desire, and, even if wishing for more, he would not find it. Therefore now also a lonely person desires, 'Let there be a wife for me that I may have offspring, and let there be wealth for me that I may offer sacrifices.' And so long as he does not obtain either of these things, he thinks he is incomplete. Now his completeness (is made up as follows): mind is his self (husband); speech the wife; breath the child; the eye all worldly wealth, for he finds it with the eye; the ear his divine wealth, for he hears it with the ear. The body (âtman) is his work, for with the body he works. This is the fivefold[1] sacrifice, for fivefold is the animal, fivefold man, fivefold all this whatsoever. He who knows this, obtains all this.

FIFTH BRÂHMA*N*A[2].

1. 'When the father (of creation) had produced by knowledge and penance (work) the seven kinds of food, one of his (foods) was common to all beings, two he assigned to the Devas, (1)

'Three he made for himself, one he gave to the animals. In it all rests, whatsoever breathes and breathes not. (2)

---

[1] Fivefold, as consisting of mind, speech, breath, eye, and ear. See Taitt. Up. I, 7, 1.

[2] Mâdhyandina text, p. 1054.

'Why then do these not perish, though they are always eaten? He who knows this imperishable one, he eats food with his face. (3)

'He goes even to the Devas, he lives on strength.' (4)

2. When it is said, that 'the father produced by knowledge and penance the seven kinds of food,' it is clear that (it was he who) did so. When it is said, that 'one of his (foods) was common,' then that is that common food of his which is eaten. He who worships (eats) that (common food), is not removed from evil, for verily that food is mixed (property)[1]. When it is said, that 'two he assigned to the Devas,' that is the huta, which is sacrificed in fire, and the prahuta, which is given away at a sacrifice. But they also say, the new-moon and full-moon sacrifices are here intended, and therefore one should not offer them as an ishti or with a wish.

When it is said, that 'one he gave to animals,' that is milk. For in the beginning (in their infancy) both men and animals live on milk. And therefore they either make a new-born child lick ghrita (butter), or they make it take the breast. And they call a new-born creature 'atrinâda,' i. e. not eating herbs. When it is said, that 'in it all rests, whatsoever breathes and breathes not,' we see that all this, whatsoever breathes and breathes not, rests and depends on milk.

And when it is said (in another Brâhmana), that a man who sacrifices with milk a whole year[2], overcomes death again, let him not think so. No, on

---

[1] It belongs to all beings.

[2] This would imply 360 sacrificial days, each with two oblations, i. e. 720 oblations.

the very day on which he sacrifices, on that day he overcomes death again; for he who knows this, offers to the gods the entire food (viz. milk).

When it is said, 'Why do these not perish, though they are always eaten,' we answer, Verily, the Person is the imperishable, and he produces that food again and again[1].

When it is said, 'He who knows this imperishable one,' then, verily, the Person is the imperishable one, for he produces this food by repeated thought, and whatever he does not work by his works, that perishes.

When it is said, that 'he eats food with his face,' then face means the mouth, he eats it with his mouth.

When it is said, that 'he goes even to the Devas, he lives on strength,' that is meant as praise.

3. When it is said, that 'he made three for himself,' that means that he made mind, speech, and breath for himself. As people say, 'My mind was elsewhere, I did not see; my mind was elsewhere, I did not hear,' it is clear that a man sees with his mind and hears with his mind[2]. Desire, representation, doubt, faith, want of faith, memory[3], forgetfulness, shame, reflexion, fear, all this is mind. Therefore even if a man is touched on the back, he knows it through the mind.

Whatever sound there is, that is speech. Speech indeed is intended for an end or object, it is nothing by itself.

---

[1] Those who enjoy the food, become themselves creators. Comm.
[2] See Deussen, Vedânta, p. 358.
[3] Firmness, strength. Comm.

The up-breathing, the down-breathing, the back-breathing, the out-breathing, the on-breathing, all that is breathing is breath (prâ*n*a) only. Verily that Self consists of it; that Self consists of speech, mind, and breath.

4. These are the three worlds: earth is speech, sky mind, heaven breath.

5. These are the three Vedas: the Rig-veda is speech, the Ya*g*ur-veda mind, the Sâma-veda breath.

6. These are the Devas, Fathers, and men: the Devas are speech, the Fathers mind, men breath.

7. These are father, mother, and child: the father is mind, the mother speech, the child breath.

8. These are what is known, what is to be known, and what is unknown.

What is known, has the form of speech, for speech is known. Speech, having become this, protects man [1].

9. What is to be known, has the form of mind, for mind is what is to be known. Mind, having become this, protects man.

10. What is unknown, has the form of breath, for breath is unknown. Breath, having become this, protects man [2].

11. Of that speech (which is the food of Pra*g*â-pati) earth is the body, light the form, viz. this fire. And so far as speech extends, so far extends the earth, so far extends fire.

12. Next, of this mind heaven is the body, light the form, viz. this sun. And so far as this mind

---

[1] 'The food (speech), having become known, can be consumed.' Comm.

[2] This was adhibhautika, with reference to bhûtas, beings. Next follows the adhidaivika, with reference to the devas, gods. Comm.

extends, so far extends heaven, so far extends the sun. If they (fire and sun) embrace each other, then wind is born, and that is Indra, and he is without a rival. Verily a second is a rival, and he who knows this, has no rival.

13. Next, of this breath water is the body, light the form, viz. this moon. And so far as this breath extends, so far extends water, so far extends the moon.

These are all alike, all endless. And he who worships them as finite, obtains a finite world, but he who worships them as infinite, obtains an infinite world.

14. That Pra*g*âpati is the year, and he consists of sixteen digits. The nights[1] indeed are his fifteen digits, the fixed point[2] his sixteenth digit. He is increased and decreased by the nights. Having on the new-moon night entered with the sixteenth part into everything that has life, he is thence born again in the morning. Therefore let no one cut off the life of any living thing on that night, not even of a lizard, in honour (pû*g*ârtham) of that deity.

15. Now verily that Pra*g*âpati, consisting of sixteen digits, who is the year, is the same as a man who knows this. His wealth constitutes the fifteen digits, his Self the sixteenth digit. He is increased and decreased by that wealth. His Self is the nave, his wealth the felly. Therefore even if he loses everything, if he lives but with his Self, people say, he lost the felly (which can be restored again).

16. Next there are verily three worlds, the world of men, the world of the Fathers, the world of the Devas. The world of men can be gained by a son

---

[1] Meant for nychthemera.
[2] When he is just invisible at the new moon.

only, not by any other work. By sacrifice the world of the Fathers, by knowledge the world of the Devas is gained. The world of the Devas is the best of worlds, therefore they praise knowledge.

17. Next follows the handing over. When a man thinks he is going to depart, he says to his son: 'Thou art Brahman (the Veda, so far as acquired by the father); thou art the sacrifice (so far as performed by the father); thou art the world.' The son answers: 'I am Brahman, I am the sacrifice, I am the world.' Whatever has been learnt (by the father) that, taken as one, is Brahman. Whatever sacrifices there are, they, taken as one, are the sacrifice. Whatever worlds there are, they, taken as one, are the world. Verily here ends this (what has to be done by a father, viz. study, sacrifice, &c.) 'He (the son), being all this, preserved me from this world[1],' thus he thinks. Therefore they call a son who is instructed (to do all this), a world-son (lokya), and therefore they instruct him.

When a father who knows this, departs this world, then he enters into his son together with his own spirits (with speech, mind, and breath). If there is anything done amiss by the father, of all that the son delivers him, and therefore he is called Putra, son[2]. By help of his son the father stands firm in this world[3]. Then these divine immortal spirits (speech, mind, and breath) enter into him.

---

[1] Roer seems to have read samnaya, 'all this multitude.' I read, etan mâ sarvam sann ayam ito 'bhunagad iti.

[2] The Comm. derives putra from pu (pûr), to fill, and tra (trâ), to deliver, a deliverer who fills the holes left by the father, a stop-gap. Others derive it from put, a hell, and trâ, to protect; cf. Manu IX, 138.

[3] 'The manushya-loka, not the pitri-loka and deva-loka.' Comm.

18. From the earth and from fire, divine speech enters into him. And verily that is divine speech whereby, whatever he says, comes to be.

19. From heaven and the sun, divine mind enters into him. And verily that is divine mind whereby he becomes joyful, and grieves no more.

20. From water and the moon, divine breath (spirit) enters into him. And verily that is divine breath which, whether moving or not moving, does not tire, and therefore does not perish. He who knows this, becomes the Self of all beings. As that deity (Hiranyagarbha) is, so does he become. And as all beings honour that deity (with sacrifice, &c.), so do all beings honour him who knows this.

Whatever grief these creatures suffer, that is all one[1] (and therefore disappears). Only what is good approaches him; verily, evil does not approach the Devas.

21. Next follows the consideration of the observances[2] (acts). Pragâpati created the actions (active senses). When they had been created, they strove among themselves. Voice held, I shall speak; the eye held, I shall see; the ear held, I shall hear; and thus the other actions too, each according to its own act. Death, having become weariness, took them and seized them. Having seized them, death held them back (from their work). Therefore speech grows weary, the eye grows weary, the ear grows weary. But death did not seize the central breath. Then the others tried to know him, and

---

[1] 'Individuals suffer, because one causes grief to another. But in the universal soul, where all individuals are one, their sufferings are neutralised.' Comm.

[2] The upâsana or meditative worship.

said: 'Verily, he is the best of us, he who, whether moving or not, does not tire and does not perish. Well, let all of us assume his form.' Thereupon they all assumed his form, and therefore they are called after him 'breaths' (spirits).

In whatever family there is a man who knows this, they call that family after his name. And he who strives with one who knows this, withers away and finally dies. So far with regard to the body.

22. Now with regard to the deities.

Agni (fire) held, I shall burn; Âditya (the sun) held, I shall warm; *K*andramas (the moon) held, I shall shine; and thus also the other deities, each according to the deity. And as it was with the central breath among the breaths, so it was with Vâyu, the wind among those deities. The other deities fade, not Vâyu. Vâyu is the deity that never sets.

23. And here there is this *S*loka:

'He from whom the sun rises, and into whom it sets' (he verily rises from the breath, and sets in the breath)

'Him the Devas made the law, he only is to-day, and he to-morrow also' (whatever these Devas determined then, that they perform to-day also[1]).

Therefore let a man perform one observance only, let him breathe up and let him breathe down, that the evil death may not reach him. And when he performs it, let him try to finish it. Then he obtains through it union and oneness with that deity (with prâ*n*a).

---

[1] The prâ*n*a-vrata and vâyu-vrata. Comm.

Sixth Brâhmawa[1].

1. Verily this is a triad, name, form, and work. Of these names, that which is called Speech is the Uktha (hymn, supposed to mean also origin), for from it all names arise. It is their Sâman (song, supposed to mean also sameness), for it is the same as all names. It is their Brahman (prayer, supposed to mean also support), for it supports all names.

2. Next, of the forms, that which is called Eye is the Uktha (hymn), for from it all forms arise. It is their Sâman (song), for it is the same as all forms. It is their Brahman (prayer), for it supports all forms.

3. Next, of the works, that which is called Body is the Uktha (hymn), for from it all works arise. It is their Sâman (song), for it is the same as all works. It is their Brahman (prayer), for it supports all works.

That being a triad is one, viz. this Self; and the Self, being one, is that triad. This is the immortal, covered by the true. Verily breath is the immortal, name and form are the true, and by them the immortal is covered.

---

[1] Mâdhyandina text, p. 1058.

SECOND ADHYÂYA[1].

FIRST BRÂHMA*N*A[2].

1. There[3] was formerly the proud Gârgya Bâlâki[4], a man of great reading. He said to A*g*âta*s*atru of Kâ*s*i, 'Shall I tell you Brahman?' A*g*âta*s*atru said: 'We give a thousand (cows) for that speech (of yours), for verily all people run away, saying, *G*anaka (the king of Mithilâ) is our father (patron)[5].'

2. Gârgya said: 'The person that is in the sun[6], that I adore as Brahman.' A*g*âta*s*atru said to him: 'No, no! Do not speak to me on this. I adore him

---

[1] Mâdhyandina text, p. 1058.

[2] Whatever has been taught to the end of the third (according to the counting of the Upanishad, the first) Adhyâya, refers to avidyâ, ignorance. Now, however, vidyâ, the highest knowledge, is to be taught, and this is done, first of all, by a dialogue between Gârgya Dr*i*ptabâlâki and king A*g*âta*s*atru, the former, though a Brâhma*n*a, representing the imperfect, the latter, though a Kshatriya, the perfect knowledge of Brahman. While Gârgya worships the Brahman as the sun, the moon, &c., as limited, as active and passive, A*g*âta*s*atru knows the Brahman as the Self.

[3] Compare with this the fourth Adhyâya of the Kaushîtaki-upanishad, Sacred Books of the East, vol. i, p. 300; Gough, Philosophy of the Upanishads, p. 144.

[4] Son of Balâkâ, of the race of the Gârgyas.

[5] *G*anaka, known as a wise and liberal king. There is a play on his name, which means father, and is understood in the sense of patron, or of teacher of wisdom. The meaning is obscure; and in the Kaush. Up. IV. 1, the construction is still more difficult. What is intended seems to be that A*g*âta*s*atru is willing to offer any reward to a really wise man, because all the wise men are running after *G*anaka and settling at his court.

[6] The commentator expatiates on all these answers and brings them more into harmony with Vedânta doctrines. Thus he adds that the person in the sun is at the same time the person in the eye, who is both active and passive in the heart, &c.

verily as the supreme, the head of all beings, the king. Whoso adores him thus, becomes supreme, the head of all beings, a king.'

3. Gârgya said: 'The person that is in the moon (and in the mind), that I adore as Brahman.' Agâtasatru said to him: 'No, no! Do not speak to me on this. I adore him verily as the great, clad in white raiment, as Soma, the king.' Whoso adores him thus, Soma is poured out and poured forth for him day by day, and his food does not fail [1].

4. Gârgya said: 'The person that is in the lightning (and in the heart), that I adore as Brahman.' Agâtasatru said to him: 'No, no! Do not speak to me on this. I adore him verily as the luminous.' Whoso adores him thus, becomes luminous, and his offspring becomes luminous.

5. Gârgya said: 'The person that is in the ether (and in the ether of the heart), that I adore as Brahman.' Agâtasatru said to him: 'No, no! Do not speak to me on this. I adore him as what is full, and quiescent.' Whoso adores him thus, becomes filled with offspring and cattle, and his offspring does not cease from this world.

6. Gârgya said: 'The person that is in the wind (and in the breath), that I adore as Brahman.' Agâtasatru said to him: 'No, no! Do not speak to me on this. I adore him as Indra Vaikuntha, as the unconquerable army (of the Maruts).' Whoso adores him thus, becomes victorious, unconquerable, conquering his enemies.

---

[1] We miss the annasyâtmâ, the Self of food, mentioned in the Kaush. Up., and evidently referred to in the last sentence of our paragraph. Suta and prasuta, poured out and poured forth, are explained as referring to the principal and the secondary sacrifices.

7. Gârgya said : 'The person that is in the fire (and in the heart), that I adore as Brahman.' A*g*âta*s*atru said to him: 'No, no! Do not speak to me on this. I adore him as powerful.' Whoso adores him thus, becomes powerful, and his offspring becomes powerful.

8. Gârgya said: ' The person that is in the water (in seed, and in the heart), that I adore as Brahman.' A*g*âta*s*atru said to him : 'No, no! Do not speak to me on this. I adore him as likeness.' Whoso adores him thus, to him comes what is likely (or proper), not what is improper; what is born from him, is like unto him[1].

9. Gârgya said : ' The person that is in the mirror, that I adore as Brahman.' A*g*âta*s*atru said to him : ' No, no! Do not speak to me on this. I adore him verily as the brilliant.' Whoso adores him thus, he becomes brilliant, his offspring becomes brilliant, and with whomsoever he comes together, he outshines them.

10. Gârgya said : ' The sound that follows a man while he moves, that I adore as Brahman.' A*g*âta*s*atru said to him : ' No, no! Do not speak to me on this. I adore him verily as life.' Whoso adores him thus, he reaches his full age in this world, breath does not leave him before the time.

11. Gârgya said : 'The person that is in space, that I adore as Brahman.' A*g*âta*s*atru said to him : ' No, no! Do not speak to me on this. I adore him verily as the second who never leaves us.'

---

[1] Here the Kaush. Up. has the Self of the name, instead of pratirûpa, likeness. The commentator thinks that they both mean the same thing, because a name is the likeness of a thing. Another text of the Kaush. Up. gives here the Self of light. Pratirûpa in the sense of likeness comes in later in the Kaush. Up., § 11.

Whoso adores him thus, becomes possessed of a
second, his party is not cut off from him.

12. Gârgya said : 'The person that consists of the
shadow, that I adore as Brahman.' Agâtaśatru said
to him : 'No, no! Do not speak to me on this.
I adore him verily as death.' Whoso adores him
thus, he reaches his whole age in this world, death
does not approach him before the time.

13. Gârgya said : 'The person that is in the body[1],
that I adore as Brahman.' Agâtaśatru said to him :
'No, no! Do not speak to me on this. I adore him
verily as embodied.' Whoso adores him thus, becomes
embodied, and his offspring becomes embodied [2].

Then Gârgya became silent.

14. Agâtaśatru said : 'Thus far only?' 'Thus far
only,' he replied. Agâtaśatru said : 'This does not
suffice to know it (the true Brahman).' Gârgya
replied : 'Then let me come to you, as a pupil.'

15. Agâtaśatru said : 'Verily, it is unnatural that
a Brâhmaña should come to a Kshatriya, hoping
that he should tell him the Brahman. However, I
shall make you know him clearly,' thus saying he
took him by the hand and rose.

And the two together came to a person who was
asleep. He called him by these names, 'Thou,
great one, clad in white raiment, Soma, King [3].' He

---

[1] 'In the Âtman, in Pragâpati, in the Buddhi, and in the heart.'
Comm.

[2] It is difficult to know what is meant here by âtman and âtmanvin. In the Kaush. Up. Agâtaśatru refers to Pragâpati, and the
commentator here does the same, adding, however, buddhi and
hrid. Gough translates âtmanvin by 'having peace of mind.'
Deussen, p. 195, passes it over.

[3] These names are given here as they occur in the Kaushîtaki-
upanishad, not as in the Brihadârañyaka-upanishad, where the

did not rise.   Then rubbing him with his hand, he woke him, and he arose.

16. Agâtasatru said : ' When this man was thus asleep, where was then the person (purusha), the intelligent ? and from whence did he thus come back?' Gârgya did not know this ?

17. Agâtasatru said : ' When this man was thus asleep, then the intelligent person (purusha), having through the intelligence of the senses (prânas) absorbed within himself all intelligence, lies in the ether, which is in the heart [1].   When he takes in these different kinds of intelligence, then it is said that the man sleeps (svapiti) [2].   Then the breath is kept in, speech is kept in, the ear is kept in, the eye is kept in, the mind is kept in.

18. But when he moves about in sleep (and dream), then these are his worlds.   He is, as it were, a great king; he is, as it were, a great Brâhmana ; he rises, as it were, and he falls.   And as a great king might keep in his own subjects, and move about, according to his pleasure, within his own domain, thus does that person (who is endowed with intelligence) keep in the various senses (prânas) and move about, according to his pleasure, within his own body (while dreaming).

19. Next, when he is in profound sleep, and knows

---

first name was atishthâh sarveshâm bhûtânâm mûrdhâ râgâ.   This throws an important light on the composition of the Upanishads.

[1] The ether in the heart is meant for the real Self.   He has come to himself, to his Self, i.e. to the true Brahman.

[2] Svapiti, he sleeps, is explained as sva, his own Self, and apiti for apyeti, he goes towards, so that 'he sleeps' must be interpreted as meaning ' he comes to his Self.'   In another passage it is explained by svam apîto bhavati.   See Sankara's Commentary on the Brih. Âr. Up. vol. i, p. 372.

nothing, there are the seventy-two thousand arteries called Hita, which from the heart spread through the body[1]. Through them he moves forth and rests in the surrounding body. And as a young man, or a great king, or a great Brâhmana, having reached the summit of happiness, might rest, so does he then rest.

20. As the spider comes out with its thread, or as small sparks come forth from fire, thus do all senses, all worlds, all Devas, all beings come forth from that Self. The Upanishad (the true name and doctrine) of that Self is 'the True of the True.' Verily the senses are the true, and he is the true of the true.

SECOND BRÂHMANA [2].

1. Verily he who knows the babe[3] with his place[4], his chamber[5], his post[6], and his rope[7], he keeps off the seven relatives[8] who hate him. Verily by the young is meant the inner life, by his place this (body)[9], by his chamber this (head), by his post the vital breath, by his rope the food.

2. Then the seven imperishable ones[10] approach him. There are the red lines in the eye, and by them Rudra clings to him. There is the water

---

[1] 'Not the pericardium only, but the whole body.' Comm.

[2] Mâdhyandina text, p. 1061.

[3] The lingâtman, or subtle body which has entered this body in five ways. Comm.

[4] The body.   [5] The head.   [6] The vital breath.

[7] Food, which binds the subtle to the coarse body.

[8] The seven organs of the head through which man perceives and becomes attached to the world.

[9] The commentator remarks that while saying this, the body and the head are pointed out by touching them with the hand (pânipeshapratibodhanena).

[10] See before, I, 5, 1, 2. They are called imperishable, because they produce imperishableness by supplying food for the prâna, here called the babe.

in the eye, and by it Par*g*anya clings to him. There is the pupil, and by it Âditya (sun) clings to him. There is the dark iris, and by it Agni clings to him. There is the white eye-ball, and by it Indra clings to him. With the lower eye-lash the earth, with the upper eye-lash the heaven clings to him. He who knows this, his food does never perish.

3. On this there is this *S*loka :

' There [1] is a cup having its mouth below and its bottom above. Manifold glory has been placed into it. On its lip sit the seven *R*ishis, the tongue as the eighth communicates with Brahman.' What is called the cup having its mouth below and its bottom above is this head, for its mouth (the mouth) is below, its bottom (the skull) is above. When it is said that manifold glory has been placed into it, the senses verily are manifold glory, and he therefore means the senses. When he says that the seven *R*ishis sit on its lip, the *R*ishis are verily the (active) senses, and he means the senses. And when he says that the tongue as the eighth communicates with Brahman, it is because the tongue, as the eighth, does communicate with Brahman.

4. These two (the two ears) are the *R*ishis Gautama and Bharadvâ*g*a; the right Gautama, the left Bharadvâ*g*a. These two (the eyes) are the *R*ishis Vi*s*vâmitra and *G*amadagni; the right Vi*s*vâmitra, the left *G*amadagni. These two (the nostrils) are the *R*ishis Vasish*th*a and Ka*s*yapa ; the right Vasish*th*a, the left Ka*s*yapa. The tongue is Atri, for with the tongue food is eaten, and Atri is meant for Atti, eating. He who knows this, becomes an eater of everything, and everything becomes his food.

---

[1] Cf. Atharva-veda-sa*m*h. X, 8, 9.

THIRD BRÂHMANA[1].

1. There are two forms of Brahman, the material and the immaterial, the mortal and the immortal, the solid and the fluid, sat (being) and tya (that), (i.e. sat-tya, true)[2].

2. Everything except air and sky is material, is mortal, is solid, is definite. The essence of that which is material, which is mortal, which is solid, which is definite is the sun that shines, for he is the essence of sat (the definite).

3. But air and sky are immaterial, are immortal, are fluid, are indefinite. The essence of that which is immaterial, which is immortal, which is fluid, which is indefinite is the person in the disk of the sun, for he is the essence of tyad (the indefinite). So far with regard to the Devas.

4. Now with regard to the body. Everything except the breath and the ether within the body is material, is mortal, is solid, is definite. The essence of that which is material, which is mortal, which is solid, which is definite is the Eye, for it is the essence of sat (the definite).

5. But breath and the ether within the body are immaterial, are immortal, are fluid, are indefinite. The essence of that which is immaterial, which is immortal, which is fluid, which is indefinite is the person in the right eye, for he is the essence of tyad (the indefinite).

6. And what is the appearance of that person? Like a saffron-coloured raiment, like white wool,

---

[1] Mâdhyandina text, p. 1062.
[2] Sat is explained by definite, tya or tyad by indefinite.

like cochineal, like the flame of fire, like the white lotus, like sudden lightning. He who knows this, his glory is like unto sudden lightning.

Next follows the teaching (of Brahman) by No, no[1]! for there is nothing else higher than this (if one says): 'It is not so.' Then comes the name 'the True of the True,' the senses being the True, and he (the Brahman) the True of them.

FOURTH BRÂHMA*N*A[2].

1. Now when Yâg*ñ*avalkya was going to enter upon another state, he said : ' Maitreyî[3], verily I am going away from this my house (into the forest[4]). Forsooth, let me make a settlement between thee and that Kâtyâyanî (my other wife).'

2. Maitreyî said : ' My Lord, if this whole earth, full of wealth, belonged to me, tell me, should I be immortal by it[5]?'

---

[1] See III, 9, 26; IV, 2, 4; IV, 4, 22; IV, 5, 15.

[2] Mâdhyandina text, p. 1062. To the end of the third Brâhma*n*a of the second Adhyâya, all that has been taught does not yet impart the highest knowledge, the identity of the personal and the true Self, the Brahman. In the fourth Brâhma*n*a, in which the knowledge of the true Brahman is to be set forth, the Sa*m*nyâsa, the retiring from the world, is enjoined, when all desires cease, and no duties are to be performed (Sa*m*nyâsa, pârivrâg*y*a). The story is told again with slight variations in the Br*i*hadâra*n*yaka-upanishad IV, 5. The more important variations, occurring in IV, 5, are added here, marked with B. There are besides the various readings of the Mâdhyandina-*s*âkhâ of the *S*atapatha-brâhma*n*a. See also Deussen, Vedânta, p. 185.

[3] In Br*i*h. Up. IV, 5, the story begins: Yâg*ñ*avalkya had two wives, Maitreyî and Kâtyâyanî. Of these Maitreyî was conversant with Brahman, but Kâtyâyanî possessed such knowledge only as women possess.

[4] Instead of udyâsyan, B. gives pravrag*i*shyan, the more technical term.

[5] Should I be immortal by it, or no? B.

'No,' replied Yâg*n*avalkya; 'like the life of rich people will be thy life. But there is no hope of immortality by wealth.'

3. And Maitreyî said: 'What should I do with that by which I do not become immortal? What my Lord knoweth (of immortality), tell that to me[1].'

4. Yâg*n*avalkya replied: 'Thou who art truly dear to me, thou speakest dear words[2]. Come, sit down, I will explain it to thee, and mark well what I say.'

5. And he said: 'Verily, a husband is not dear, that you may love the husband; but that you may love the Self, therefore a husband is dear.

'Verily, a wife is not dear, that you may love the wife; but that you may love the Self, therefore a wife is dear.

'Verily, sons are not dear, that you may love the sons; but that you may love the Self, therefore sons are dear.

'Verily, wealth is not dear, that you may love wealth; but that you may love the Self, therefore wealth is dear[3].

'Verily, the Brahman-class is not dear, that you may love the Brahman-class; but that you may love the Self, therefore the Brahman-class is dear.

'Verily, the Kshatra-class is not dear, that you may love the Kshatra-class; but that you may love the Self, therefore the Kshatra-class is dear.

'Verily, the worlds are not dear, that you may love the worlds; but that you may love the Self, therefore the worlds are dear.

---

[1] Tell that clearly to me. B.

[2] Thou who art dear to me, thou hast increased what is dear (to me in this). B.

[3] B. adds, Verily, cattle are not dear, &c.

'Verily, the Devas are not dear, that you may love the Devas; but that you may love the Self, therefore the Devas are dear [1].

'Verily, creatures are not dear, that you may love the creatures; but that you may love the Self, therefore are creatures dear.

'Verily, everything is not dear that you may love everything; but that you may love the Self, therefore everything is dear.

'Verily, the Self is to be seen, to be heard, to be perceived, to be marked, O Maitreyî! When we see, hear, perceive, and know the Self [2], then all this is known.

6. 'Whosoever looks for the Brahman-class elsewhere than in the Self, was [3] abandoned by the Brahman-class. Whosoever looks for the Kshatra-class elsewhere than in the Self, was abandoned by the Kshatra-class. Whosoever looks for the worlds elsewhere than in the Self, was abandoned by the worlds. Whosoever looks for the Devas elsewhere than in the Self, was abandoned by the Devas [4]. Whosoever looks for creatures elsewhere than in the Self, was abandoned by the creatures. Whosoever looks for anything elsewhere than in the Self, was abandoned by everything. This Brahman-class, this Kshatra-class, these worlds, these Devas [5], these [6] creatures, this everything, all is that Self.

7. 'Now as [7] the sounds of a drum, when beaten,

---

[1] B. inserts, Verily, the Vedas are not dear, &c.
[2] When the Self has been seen, heard, perceived, and known. B.
[3] The commentator translates, 'should be abandoned.'
[4] B. inserts, Whosoever looks for the Vedas, &c.
[5] B. adds, these Vedas.   [6] B. has, all these creatures.
[7] I construe sa yathâ with evam vai in § 12, looking upon

cannot be seized externally (by themselves), but the sound is seized, when the drum is seized or the beater of the drum;

8. 'And as the sounds of a conch-shell, when blown, cannot be seized externally (by themselves), but the sound is seized, when the shell is seized or the blower of the shell;

9. 'And as the sounds of a lute, when played, cannot be seized externally (by themselves), but the sound is seized, when the lute is seized or the player of the lute;

10. 'As clouds of smoke proceed by themselves out of a lighted fire kindled with damp fuel, thus, verily, O Maitreyî, has been breathed forth from this great Being what we have as *Ri*g-veda, Ya*g*ur-veda, Sâma-veda, Atharvâṅgirasas, Itihâsa (legends), Purâ*n*a (cosmogonies), Vidyâ (knowledge), the Upanishads, *S*lokas (verses), Sûtras (prose rules), Anuvyâkhyânas (glosses), Vyâkhyânas (commentaries)[1]. From him alone all these were breathed forth.

11. 'As all waters find their centre in the sea, all touches in the skin, all tastes in the tongue, all smells in the nose, all colours in the eye, all sounds in the ear, all percepts in the mind, all knowledge in the heart, all actions in the hands, all movements in the feet, and all the Vedas in speech,—

12. 'As a lump of salt[2], when thrown into water, becomes dissolved into water, and could not be taken

§ 11 as probably a later insertion.   The sa is not the pronoun, but a particle, as in sa yadi, sa *k*et, &c.

[1] B. adds, what is sacrificed, what is poured out, food, drink, this world and the other world, and all creatures.

[2] See *Kh*ând. Up. VI, 13.

out again, but wherever we taste (the water) it is
salt,—thus verily, O Maitreyî, does this great Being,
endless, unlimited, consisting of nothing but knowledge[1], rise from out these elements, and vanish again
in them. When he has departed, there is no more
knowledge (name), I say, O Maitreyî.' Thus spoke
Yâ*g*ñavalkya.

13. Then Maitreyî said: 'Here thou hast bewildered me, Sir, when thou sayest that having
departed, there is no more knowledge[2].'

But Yâ*g*ñavalkya replied: 'O Maitreyî, I say nothing
that is bewildering. This is enough, O beloved, for
wisdom[3].

'For when there is as it were duality, then one
sees the other, one smells the other, one hears the
other[4], one salutes the other[5], one perceives the
other[6], one knows the other; but when the Self only
is all this, how should he smell another[7], how should
he see[8] another[9], how should he hear[10] another, how
should he salute[11] another, how should he perceive
another[12], how should he know another? How
should he know Him by whom he knows all this?

---

[1] As a mass of salt has neither inside nor outside, but is altogether
a mass of taste, thus indeed has that Self neither inside nor outside,
but is altogether a mass of knowledge. B.

[2] 'Here, Sir, thou hast landed me in utter bewilderment. Indeed,
I do not understand him.' B.

[3] Verily, beloved, that Self is imperishable, and of an indestructible nature. B.

[4] B. inserts, one tastes the other.

[5] B. inserts, one hears the other.

[6] B. inserts, one touches the other.   [7] See, B.

[8] Smell, B.   [9] B. inserts taste.

[10] Salute, B.   [11] Hear, B.

[12] B. inserts, how should he touch another?

How, O beloved, should he know (himself), the Knower[1]?'

FIFTH BRÂHMAZA [2].

1. This earth is the honey [3] (madhu, the effect) of all beings, and all beings are the honey (madhu, the effect) of this earth.   Likewise this bright, immortal person in this earth, and that bright immortal person incorporated in the body (both are madhu).   He indeed is the same as that Self, that Immortal, that Brahman, that All.

2. This water is the honey of all beings, and all beings are the honey of this water.   Likewise this bright, immortal person in this water, and that bright, immortal person, existing as seed in the body (both are madhu).   He indeed is the same as that Self, that Immortal, that Brahman, that All.

---

[1] Instead of the last line, B. adds (IV, 5, 15): 'That Self is to be described by No, no!   He is incomprehensible, for he cannot be comprehended; he is imperishable, for he cannot perish; he is unattached, for he does not attach himself; unfettered, he does not suffer, he does not fail.   How, O beloved, should he know the Knower?   Thus, O Maitreyî, thou hast been instructed.   Thus far goes immortality.'   Having said so, Yâgñavalkya went away (into the forest). 15.   See also *Kh*ând. Up. VII, 24, 1.

[2] Mâdhyandina text, p. 1064.

[3] Madhu, honey, seems to be taken here as an instance of something which is both cause and effect, or rather of things which are mutually dependent on each other, or cannot exist without one other.   As the bees make the honey, and the honey makes or supports the bees, bees and honey are both cause and effect, or at all events are mutually dependent on one other.   In the same way the earth and all living beings are looked upon as mutually dependent, living beings presupposing the earth, and the earth presupposing living beings.   This at all events seems to be the general idea of what is called the Madhuvidyâ, the science of honey, which Dadhya*k* communicated to the A*s*vins.

3. This fire is the honey of all beings, and all beings are the honey of this fire. Likewise this bright, immortal person in this fire, and that bright, immortal person, existing as speech in the body (both are madhu). He indeed is the same as that Self, that Immortal, that Brahman, that All.

4. This air is the honey of all beings, and all beings are the honey of this air. Likewise this bright, immortal person in this air, and that bright, immortal person existing as breath in the body (both are madhu). He indeed is the same as that Self, that Immortal, that Brahman, that All.

5. This sun is the honey of all beings, and all beings are the honey of this sun. Likewise this bright, immortal person in this sun, and that bright, immortal person existing as the eye in the body (both are madhu). He indeed is the same as that Self, that Immortal, that Brahman, that All.

6. This space (di*sah*, the quarters) is the honey of all beings, and all beings are the honey of this space. Likewise this bright, immortal person in this space, and that bright, immortal person existing as the ear in the body (both are madhu). He indeed is the same as that Self, that Immortal, that Brahman, that All.

7. This moon is the honey of all beings, and all beings are the honey of this moon. Likewise this bright, immortal person in this moon, and that bright, immortal person existing as mind in the body (both are madhu). He indeed is the same as that Self, that Immortal, that Brahman, that All.

8. This lightning is the honey of all beings, and all beings are the honey of this lightning. Likewise this bright, immortal person in this lightning, and

that bright, immortal person existing as light in the body (both are madhu). He indeed is the same as that Self, that Immortal, that Brahman, that All.

9. This thunder[1] is the honey of all beings, and all beings are the honey of this thunder. Likewise this bright, immortal person in this thunder, and that bright, immortal person existing as sound and voice in the body (both are madhu). He indeed is the same as that Self, that Immortal, that Brahman, that All.

10. This ether is the honey of all beings, and all beings are the honey of this ether. Likewise this bright, immortal person in this ether, and that bright, immortal person existing as heart-ether in the body (both are madhu). He indeed is the same as that Self, that Immortal, that Brahman, that All.

11. This law (dharmaḥ) is the honey of all beings, and all beings are the honey of this law. Likewise this bright, immortal person in this law, and that bright, immortal person existing as law in the body (both are madhu). He indeed is the same as that Self, that Immortal, that Brahman, that All.

12. This true[2] (satyam) is the honey of all beings, and all beings are the honey of this true. Likewise this bright, immortal person in what is true, and that bright, immortal person existing as the true in the body (both are madhu). He indeed is the same as that Self, that Immortal, that Brahman, that All.

13. This mankind is the honey of all beings, and all beings are the honey of this mankind. Likewise

---

[1] Stanayitnu, thunder, is explained by the commentator as Parganya.

[2] Satyam, the true, the real, not, as it is generally translated, the truth.

this bright, immortal person in mankind, and that bright, immortal person existing as man in the body (both are madhu). He indeed is the same as that Self, that Immortal, that Brahman, that All.

14. This Self is the honey of all beings, and all beings are the honey of this Self. Likewise this bright, immortal person in this Self, and that bright, immortal person, the Self (both are madhu). He indeed is the same as that Self, that Immortal, that Brahman, that All.

15. And verily this Self is the lord of all beings, the king of all beings. And as all spokes are contained in the axle and in the felly of a wheel, all beings, and all those selfs (of the earth, water, &c.) are contained in that Self.

16. Verily Dadhya*k* Âtharva*n*a proclaimed this honey (the madhu-vidyâ) to the two A*s*vins, and a *Ri*shi, seeing this, said (Rv. I, 116, 12):

'O ye two heroes (A*s*vins), I make manifest that fearful deed of yours (which you performed) for the sake of gain [1], like as thunder [2] makes manifest the rain. The honey (madhu-vidyâ) which Dadhya*k* Âtharva*n*a proclaimed to you through the head of a horse,' . . .

17. Verily Dadhya*k* Âtharva*n*a [3] proclaimed this honey to the two A*s*vins, and a *Ri*shi, seeing this, said (Rv. I, 117, 22):

'O A*s*vins, you fixed a horse's head on Âtharva*n*a Dadhya*k*, and he, wishing to be true (to his promise),

---

[1] The translation here follows the commentary.

[2] Tanyatu, here explained as Par*g*anya.

[3] *S*a*n*kara distinguishes here between Atharva*n*a and Âtharva*n*a, if the text is correct.

proclaimed to you the honey, both that of Tvash*tri*[1]
and that which is to be your secret, O ye strong
ones.'

18. Verily Dadhya*k* Âtharva*n*a proclaimed this
honey to the two A*s*vins, and a *Ri*shi, seeing this,
said:

'He (the Lord) made bodies with two feet, he
made bodies with four feet. Having first become
a bird, he entered the bodies as purusha (as the
person).' This very purusha is in all bodies the puri-
*s*aya, i.e. he who lies in the body (and is therefore
called purusha). There is nothing that is not
covered by him, nothing that is not filled by him.

19. Verily Dadhya*k* Âtharva*n*a proclaimed this
honey to the two A*s*vins, and a *Ri*shi, seeing this,
said (Rv. VI, 47, 18):

'He (the Lord) became like unto every form[2], and
this is meant to reveal the (true) form of him (the
Âtman). Indra (the Lord) appears multiform through
the Mâyâs (appearances), for his horses (senses) are
yoked, hundreds and ten.'

This (Âtman) is the horses, this (Âtman) is the
ten, and the thousands, many and endless. This is
the Brahman, without cause and without effect, without anything inside or outside; this Self is Brahman,
omnipresent and omniscient. This is the teaching
(of the Upanishads).

---

[1] *S*ankara explains Tvash*tri* as the sun, and the sun as the head
of the sacrifice which, having been cut off, was to be replaced by
the pravargya rite. The knowledge of this rite forms the honey
of Tvash*tri*. The other honey which is to be kept secret is the
knowledge of the Self, as taught before in the Madhu-brâhma*n*a.

[2] He assumed all forms, and such forms, as two-footed or four-
footed animals, remained permanent. Comm.

SIXTH BRÂHMANA.

1. Now follows the stem [1]:

  1. Pautimâshya from Gaupavana,

  2. Gaupavana from Pautimâshya,

  3. Pautimâshya from Gaupavana,

  4. Gaupavana from Kausika,

  5. Kausika from Kaundinya,

  6. Kaundinya from Sândilya,

  7. Sândilya from Kausika and Gautama,

  8. Gautama

2. from Âgnivesya,

  9. Âgnivesya from Sândilya and Ânabhimlâta,

  10. Sândilya and Ânabhimlâta from Ânabhimlâta,

  11. Ânabhimlâta from Ânabhimlâta,

  12. Ânabhimlâta from Gautama,

  13. Gautama from Saitava and Prâkînayogya,

  14. Saitava and Prâkînayogya from Pârasarya,

  15. Pârasarya from Bhâradvâga,

  16. Bhâradvâga from Bhâradvâga and Gautama,

  17. Gautama from Bhâradvâga,

---

[1] The line of teachers and pupils by whom the Madhukânda (the fourth Brâhmana) was handed down. The Mâdhyandina-sâkhâ begins with ourselves, then 1. Saurpanâyya, 2. Gautama, 3. Vâtsya, 4. Vâtsya and Pârâsarya, 5. Sânkritya and Bhâradvâga, 6. Audavâhi and Sândilya, 7. Vaigavâpa and Gautama, 8. Vaigavâpâyana and Vaishtapureya, 9. Sândilya and Rauhinâyana, 10. Saunaka, Âtreya, and Raibhya, 11. Pautimâshyâyana and Kaundinyâyana, 12. Kaundinya, 13. Kaundinya, 14. Kaundinya and Âgnivesya, 15. Saitava, 16. Pârâsarya, 17. Gâtukarnya, 18. Bhâradvâga, 19. Bhâradvâga, Âsurâyana, and Gautama, 20. Bhâradvâga, 21. Vaigavâpâyana. Then the same as the Kânvas to Gâtukarnya, who learns from Bhâradvâga, who learns from Bhâradvâga, Âsurâyana, and Yâska. Then Traivani &c. as in the Kânva-vamsa.

18. Bhâradvâga from Pârasarya,

19. Pârasarya from Vaigavâpâyana,

20. Vaigavâpâyana from Kausikâyani,

21[1]. Kausikâyani

3. from Ghritakausika,

22. Ghritakausika from Pârasaryâyana,

23. Pârasaryâyana from Pârasarya,

24. Pârasarya from Gâtûkarnya[2],

25. Gâtûkarnya from Âsurâyana and Yâska[3],

26. Âsurâyana and Yâska from Traivani,

27. Traivani from Aupagandhani,

28. Aupagandhani from Âsuri,

29. Âsuri from Bhâradvâga,

30. Bhâradvâga from Âtreya,

31. Âtreya from Mânti,

32. Mânti from Gautama,

33. Gautama from Gautama,

34. Gautama from Vâtsya,

35. Vâtsya from Sândilya,

36. Sândilya from Kaisorya Kâpya,

37. Kaisorya Kâpya from Kumârahârita,

38. Kumârahârita from Gâlava,

39. Gâlava from Vidarbhî-kaundinya,

40. Vidarbhî - kaundinya from Vatsanapât Bâbhrava,

41. Vatsanapât Bâbhrava from Pathi Saubhara,

42. Pathi Saubhara from Ayâsya Ângirasa,

43. Ayâsya Ângirasa from Âbhûti Tvâshtra,

44. Âbhûti Tvâshtra from Visvarûpa Tvâshtra,

45. Visvarûpa Tvâshtra from Asvinau,

---

[1] From here the Vamsa agrees with the Vamsa at the end of IV, 6.

[2] Bhâradvâga, in Mâdhyandina text.

[3] Bhâradvâga, Âsurâyana, and Yâska, in Mâdhyandina text.

46. Asvinau from Dadhyak Âtharvaṇa,
47. Dadhyak Âtharvaṇa from Atharvan Daiva,
48. Atharvan Daiva from Mrityu Prâdhvaṃsana,
49. Mrityu Prâdhvaṃsana from Pradhvaṃsana,
50. Pradhvaṃsana from Ekarshi,
51. Ekarshi from Viprakitti [1],
52. Viprakitti from Vyashti,
53. Vyashti from Sanâru,
54. Sanâru from Sanâtana,
55. Sanâtana from Sanaga,
56. Sanaga from Parameshthin,
57. Parameshthin from Brahman,
58. Brahman is Svayambhu, self-existent.
Adoration to Brahman [2].

---

[1] Vipragitti, in Mâdhyandina text.
[2] Similar genealogies are found Brĭh. Âr. Up. IV, 6, and VI, 5.

THIRD ADHYÂYA.

Adoration to the Highest Self (Paramâtman)!

1. *G*anaka Vaideha (the king of the Videhas) sacrificed with a sacrifice at which many presents were offered to the priests of (the A*s*vamedha). Brâhma*n*as of the Kurus and the Pâ*ñk*âlas had come thither, and *G*anaka Vaideha wished to know, which of those Brâhma*n*as was the best read. So he enclosed a thousand cows, and ten pâdas (of gold)[2] were fastened to each pair of horns.

2. And *G*anaka spoke to them : ' Ye venerable Brâhma*n*as, he who among you is the wisest, let him drive away these cows.'

Then those Brâhma*n*as durst not, but Yâ*gñ*avalkya said to his pupil : ' Drive them away, my dear.'

He replied : ' O glory of the Sâman [3],' and drove them away.

The Brâhma*n*as became angry and said : ' How could he call himself the wisest among us ?'

Now there was A*s*vala, the Hot*ri* priest of *G*anaka Vaideha. He asked him : ' Are you indeed the

---

[1] Mâdhyandina text, p. 1067.

[2] Pala*k*aturbhâga*h* pâda*h* suvar*n*asya.   Comm.

[3] One expects iti after uda*g*a, but Sâma*s*ravas is applied to Yâ*gñ*avalkya, and not to the pupil.   Yâ*gñ*avalkya, as the commentator observes, was properly a teacher of the Ya*g*ur-veda, but as the pupil calls him Sâma*s*ravas, he shows that Yâ*gñ*avalkya knew all the four Vedas, because the Sâmans are taken from the Rig-veda, and the Atharva-veda is contained in the other three Vedas.   Regnaud, however, refers it to the pupil, and translates, ' Ô toi qui apprends le Sâma-veda.'

wisest among us, O Yâg*ñ*avalkya?' He replied: 'I
bow before the wisest (the best knower of Brahman),
but I wish indeed to have these cows.'

Then A*s*vala, the Hot*ri* priest, undertook to
question him.

3. 'Yâg*ñ*avalkya,' he said, 'everything here (connected with the sacrifice) is reached by death, everything is overcome by death. By what means then
is the sacrificer freed beyond the reach of death?'

Yâg*ñ*avalkya said: 'By the Hot*ri* priest, who is
Agni (fire), who is speech. For speech is the Hot*ri*
of the sacrifice (or the sacrificer), and speech is
Agni, and he is the Hot*ri*. This constitutes freedom, and perfect freedom (from death).'

4. 'Yâg*ñ*avalkya,' he said, 'everything here is
reached by day and night, everything is overcome by
day and night. By what means then is the sacrificer
freed beyond the reach of day and night?'

Yâg*ñ*avalkya said: 'By the Adhvaryu priest, who
is the eye, who is Âditya (the sun)[1]. For the eye is
the Adhvaryu of the sacrifice, and the eye is the sun,
and he is the Adhvaryu. This constitutes freedom,
and perfect freedom.'

5. 'Yâg*ñ*avalkya,' he said, 'everything here is
reached by the waxing and waning of the moon,
everything is overcome by the waxing and waning
of the moon. By what means then is the sacrificer
freed beyond the reach of the waxing and waning
of the moon?'

Yâg*ñ*avalkya said: 'By the Udgât*ri* priest, who
is Vâyu (the wind), who is the breath. For the

---

[1] One expects âdityena *k*akshushâ, instead of *k*akshushâdityena,
but see § 6.

breath is the Udgât*ri* of the sacrifice, and the breath is the wind, and he is the Udgât*ri*. This constitutes freedom, and perfect freedom.'

6. 'Yâ*gñ*avalkya,' he said, 'this sky is, as it were, without an ascent (staircase.) By what approach does the sacrificer approach the Svarga world?'

Yâ*gñ*avalkya said : 'By the Brahman priest, who is the mind (manas), who is the moon. For the mind is the Brahman of the sacrifice, and the mind is the moon, and he is the Brahman. This constitutes freedom, and perfect freedom. These are the complete deliverances (from death).'

Next follow the achievements.

7. 'Yâ*gñ*avalkya,' he said, 'how many *Rik* verses will the Hot*ri* priest employ to-day at this sacrifice?'

'Three,' replied Yâ*gñ*avalkya.

'And what are these three?'

'Those which are called Puronuvâkyâ, Yâ*g*yâ, and, thirdly, *S*asyâ [1].'

'What does he gain by them?'

'All whatsoever has breath.'

8. 'Yâ*gñ*avalkya,' he said, 'how many oblations (âhuti) will the Adhvaryu priest employ to-day at this sacrifice?'

'Three,' replied Yâ*gñ*avalkya.

'And what are these three?'

'Those which, when offered, flame up; those which, when offered, make an excessive noise; and those which, when offered, sink down [2].'

---

[1] The Puronuvâkyâs are hymns employed before the actual sacrifice, the Yâ*g*yâs accompany the sacrifice, the *S*asyâs are used for the *S*astra. All three are called Stotriyâs.

[2] These oblations are explained as consisting of wood and oil, of flesh, and of milk and Soma. The first, when thrown on the

'What does he gain by them?'

'By those which, when offered, flame up, he gains the Deva (god) world, for the Deva world flames up, as it were. By those which, when offered, make an excessive noise, he gains the Pit*ri* (father) world, for the Pit*ri* world is excessively (noisy)[1]. By those which, when offered, sink down, he gains the Manushya (man) world, for the Manushya world is, as it were, down below.'

9. 'Yâg*ñ*avalkya,' he said, 'with how many deities does the Brahman priest on the right protect to-day this sacrifice?'

'By one,' replied Yâg*ñ*avalkya.

'And which is it?'

'The mind alone; for the mind is endless, and the Vi*s*vedevas are endless, and he thereby gains the endless world.'

10. 'Yâg*ñ*avalkya,' he said, 'how many Stotriyâ hymns will the Udgât*ri* priest employ to-day at this sacrifice?'

'Three,' replied Yâg*ñ*avalkya.

'And what are these three?'

'Those which are called Puronuvâkyâ, Yâg*yâ*, and, thirdly, *S*asyâ.'

'And what are these with regard to the body (adhyâtmam)?'

'The Puronuvâkyâ is Prâ*n*a (up-breathing), the Yâg*yâ* the Apâna (down-breathing), the *S*asyâ the Vyâna (back-breathing).'

---

fire, flame up. The second, when thrown on the fire, make a loud hissing noise. The third, consisting of milk, Soma, &c., sink down into the earth.

[1] On account of the cries of those who wish to be delivered out of it. Comm.

'What does he gain by them?'
'He gains the earth by the Puronuvâkyâ, the sky by the Yâgyâ, heaven by the Sasyâ.'
After that Asvala held his peace.

SECOND BRÂHMAÑA [1].

1. Then Gâratkârava Ârtabhâga [2] asked. 'Yâgña-valkya,' he said, 'how many Grahas are there, and how many Atigrahas [3]?'
'Eight Grahas,' he replied, 'and eight Atigrahas.'
'And what are these eight Grahas and eight Atigrahas?'

2. 'Prâña (breath) is one Graha, and that is seized by Apâna (down-breathing) as the Atigrâha [4], for one smells with the Apâna.'

3. 'Speech (vâk) is one Graha, and that is seized by name (nâman) as the Atigrâha, for with speech one pronounces names.'

4. 'The tongue is one Graha, and that is seized by taste as the Atigrâha, for with the tongue one perceives tastes.'

5. 'The eye is one Graha, and that is seized by form as the Atigrâha, for with the eye one sees forms.'

6. 'The ear is one Graha, and that is seized by sound as the Atigrâha, for with the ear one hears sounds.'

7. 'The mind is one Graha, and that is seized by

---

[1] Mâdhyandina text, p. 1069.
[2] A descendant of Ritabhâga of the family of Garatkâru.
[3] Graha is probably meant originally in its usual sacrificial sense, as a vessel for offering oblations. But its secondary meaning, in which it is here taken, is a taker, a grasper, i. e. an organ of sense, while atigraha is intended for that which is grasped, i. e. an object of sense.
[4] Here the â is long, khândasatvât.

desire as the Atigrâha, for with the mind one desires desires.'

8. 'The arms are one Graha, and these are seized by work as the Atigrâha, for with the arms one works work.'

9. 'The skin is one Graha, and that is seized by touch as the Atigrâha, for with the skin one perceives touch. These are the eight Grahas and the eight Atigrahas.'

10. 'Yâg*ñ*avalkya,' he said, 'everything is the food of death. What then is the deity to whom death is food?'

'Fire (agni) is death, and that is the food of water. Death is conquered again.'

11. 'Yâg*ñ*avalkya,' he said, 'when such a person (a sage) dies, do the vital breaths (prâ*n*as) move out of him or no?'

'No,' replied Yâg*ñ*avalkya; 'they are gathered up in him, he swells, he is inflated, and thus inflated the dead lies at rest.'

12. 'Yâg*ñ*avalkya,' he said, 'when such a man dies, what does not leave him?'

'The name,' he replied; 'for the name is endless, the Vi*s*vedevas are endless, and by it he gains the endless world.'

13. 'Yâg*ñ*avalkya,' he said, 'when the speech of this dead person enters into the fire[1], breath into the air, the eye into the sun, the mind into the moon, the hearing into space, into the earth the body, into the ether the self, into the shrubs the hairs of the body, into the trees the hairs of the head, when the

---

[1] The commentator explains purusha here by asamyagdar*s*in, one who does not know the whole truth. See also Deussen, Vedânta, p. 405, and p. 399, note.

blood and the seed are deposited in the water, where is then that person?'

Yâgñavalkya said: 'Take my hand, my friend. We two alone shall know of this; let this question of ours not be (discussed) in public.' Then these two went out and argued, and what they said was karman (work), what they praised was karman[1], viz. that a man becomes good by good work, and bad by bad work. After that Gâratkârava Ârtabhâga held his peace.

THIRD BRÂHMANA[2].

1. Then Bhugyu Lâhyâyani asked. 'Yâgñavalkya,' he said, 'we wandered about as students[3], and came to the house of Patañkala Kâpya. He had a daughter who was possessed by a Gandharva. We asked him, 'Who art thou?' and he (the Gandharva) replied: 'I am Sudhanvan, the Âṅgirasa.' And when we asked him about the ends of the world, we said to him, 'Where were the Pârikshitas[4]? Where then were the Pârikshitas, I ask thee, Yâgñavalkya, where were the Pârikshitas?'

2. Yâgñavalkya said: 'He said to thee, I suppose, that they went where those go who have performed a horse-sacrifice.'

He said: 'And where do they go who have performed a horse-sacrifice?'

---

[1] What is intended is that the samsâra continues by means of karman, while karman by itself never leads to moksha.

[2] Mâdhyandina text, p. 1070.

[3] The commentator explains karakâh as adhyayanârtham vratakaranâk karakâh, adhvaryavo vâ. See Professor R. G. Bhandarkar, in Indian Antiquary, 1883, p. 145.

[4] An old royal race, supposed to have vanished from the earth.

Yâgñavalkya replied : 'Thirty-two journeys of the car of the sun is this world. The earth surrounds it on every side, twice as large, and the ocean surrounds this earth on every side, twice as large. Now there is between[1] them a space as large as the edge of a razor or the wing of a mosquito. Indra, having become a bird, handed them (through the space) to Vâyu (the air), and Vâyu (the air), holding them within himself, conveyed them to where they dwell who have performed a horse-sacrifice. Somewhat in this way did he praise Vâyu indeed. Therefore Vâyu (air) is everything by itself, and Vâyu is all things together. He who knows this, conquers death.' After that Bhugyu Lâhyâyani held his peace.

FOURTH BRÂHMANA[2].

1. Then Ushasta Kâkrâyana asked. 'Yâgñavalkya,' he said, 'tell me the Brahman which is visible, not invisible[3], the Self (âtman), who is within all.'

Yâgñavalkya replied: 'This, thy Self, who is within all.'

'Which Self, O Yâgñavalkya, is within all?'

Yâgñavalkya replied: 'He who breathes in the up-breathing, he is thy Self, and within all. He who breathes in the down-breathing, he is thy Self, and within all. He who breathes in the on-breathing, he is thy Self, and within all. He who breathes in

---

[1] The commentator explains that this small space or hole is between the two halves of the mundane egg.

[2] Mâdhyandina text, p. 1071. It follows after what is here the fifth Brâhmana, treating of Kahoda Kaushîtakeya.

[3] Deussen, Vedânta, p. 163, translates, 'das immanente, nicht transcendente Brahman,' which is right, but too modern.

the out-breathing, he is thy Self, and within all. This is thy Self, who is within all.'

2. Ushasta Kâkrâyana said: 'As one might say, this is a cow, this is a horse, thus has this been explained by thee. Tell me the Brahman which is visible, not invisible, the Self, who is within all.'

Yâgñavalkya replied: 'This, thy Self, who is within all.'

'Which Self, O Yâgñavalkya, is within all?'

Yâgñavalkya replied: 'Thou couldst not see the (true) seer of sight, thou couldst not hear the (true) hearer of hearing, nor perceive the perceiver of perception, nor know the knower of knowledge. This is thy Self, who is within all. Everything also is of evil.' After that Ushasta Kâkrâyana held his peace.

FIFTH BRÂHMANA [1].

1. Then Kahola Kaushîtakeya asked. 'Yâgña-valkya,' he said, 'tell me the Brahman which is visible, not invisible, the Self (âtman), who is within all.'

Yâgñavalkya replied: 'This, thy Self, who is within all.'

'Which Self, O Yâgñavalkya, is within all?'

Yâgñavalkya replied: 'He who overcomes hunger and thirst, sorrow, passion, old age, and death. When Brâhmanas know that Self, and have risen above the desire for sons [2], wealth, and (new) worlds [3], they wander about as mendicants. For a desire for sons is desire for wealth, a desire for wealth is desire for worlds. Both these are indeed desires. There-fore let a Brâhmana, after he has done with learning,

---

[1] Mâdhyandina text, p. 1071, standing before the fourth Brâhmana.
[2] See Brih. Âr. Up. IV, 4, 22.
[3] Life in the world of the Fathers, or in the world of the Gods.

wish to stand by real strength[1]; after he has done
with that strength and learning, he becomes a Muni
(a Yogin); and after he has done with what is not
the knowledge of a Muni, and with what is the
knowledge of a Muni, he is a Brâhma*n*a. By whatever means he has become a Brâhma*n*a, he is such
indeed[2]. Everything else is of evil.' After that
Kahola Kaushîtakeya held his peace.

Sixth Brâhma*n*a[3].

1. Then Gârgî Vâ*k*aknavî asked. ' Yâ*gñ*avalkya,'
she said, ' everything here is woven, like warp and
woof, in water. What then is that in which water is
woven, like warp and woof ?'

' In air, O Gârgî,' he replied.

' In what then is air woven, like warp and woof ?'

' In the worlds of the sky, O Gârgî,' he replied.

' In what then are the worlds of the sky woven,
like warp and woof ?'

' In the worlds of the Gandharvas, O Gârgî,' he
replied.

---

[1] Knowledge of the Self, which enables us to dispense with all
other knowledge.

[2] Mr. Gough proposes as an alternative rendering: ' Let a
Brâhma*n*a renounce learning and become as a child; and after
renouncing learning and a childlike mind, let him become a
quietist; and when he has made an end of quietism and non-
quietism, he shall become a Brâhma*n*a, a Brâhma*n*a indeed.'
Deussen takes a similar view, but I doubt whether 'the knowledge
of babes' is not a Christian rather than an Indian idea, in spite of
*S*ankara's remarks on Ved. Sûtra, III, 4, 50, which are strangely at
variance with his commentary here. Possibly the text may be corrupt, for tish*th*âset too is a very peculiar form. We might conjecture
balyena, as we have abalyam, in IV, 4, 1. In Kaush. Up. III, 3,
âbâlyam stands for âbǎlyam, possibly for ǎbǎlyam. The construction of kena syâd yena syât tened*ri*sa eva, however, is well known.

[3] Mâdhyandina text, p. 1072.

'In what then are the worlds of the Gandharvas woven, like warp and woof?'

'In the worlds of Âditya (sun), O Gârgî,' he replied.

'In what then are the worlds of Âditya (sun) woven, like warp and woof?'

'In the worlds of Kandra (moon), O Gârgî,' he replied.

'In what then are the worlds of Kandra (moon) woven, like warp and woof?'

'In the worlds of the Nakshatras (stars), O Gârgî,' he replied.

'In what then are the worlds of the Nakshatras (stars) woven, like warp and woof?'

'In the worlds of the Devas (gods), O Gârgî,' he replied.

'In what then are the worlds of the Devas (gods) woven, like warp and woof?'

'In the worlds of Indra, O Gârgî,' he replied.

'In what then are the worlds of Indra woven, like warp and woof?'

'In the worlds of Pragâpati, O Gârgî,' he replied.

'In what then are the worlds of Pragâpati woven, like warp and woof?'

'In the worlds of Brahman, O Gârgî,' he replied.

'In what then are the worlds of Brahman woven, like warp and woof?'

Yâgñavalkya said: 'O Gârgî, Do not ask too much, lest thy head should fall off. Thou askest too much about a deity about which we are not to ask too much [1]. Do not ask too much, O Gârgî.' After that Gârgî Vâkaknavî held her peace.

---

[1] According to the commentator questions about Brahman are to be answered from the Scriptures only, and not to be settled by argument.

SEVENTH BRÂHMANA [1].

1. Then Uddâlaka Âruni [2] asked. 'Yâgñavalkya,' he said, 'we dwelt among the Madras in the houses of Patañkala Kâpya, studying the sacrifice. His wife was possessed of a Gandharva, and we asked him: "Who art thou?" He answered: "I am Kabandha Âtharvana." And he said to Patañkala Kâpya and to (us) students: "Dost thou know, Kâpya, that thread by which this world and the other world, and all beings are strung together?" And Patañkala Kâpya replied: "I do not know it, Sir." He said again to Patañkala Kâpya and to (us) students: "Dost thou know, Kâpya, that puller (ruler) within (antaryâmin), who within pulls (rules) this world and the other world and all beings?" And Patañkala Kâpya replied: "I do not know it, Sir." He said again to Patañkala Kâpya and to (us) students: "He, O Kâpya, who knows that thread and him who pulls (it) within, he knows Brahman, he knows the worlds, he knows the Devas, he knows the Vedas, he knows the Bhûtas (creatures), he knows the Self, he knows everything." Thus did he (the Gandharva) say to them, and I know it. If thou, O Yâgñavalkya, without knowing that string and the puller within, drivest away those Brahma-cows (the cows offered as a prize to him who best knows Brahman), thy head will fall off.'

Yâgñavalkya said: 'O Gautama, I believe I know that thread and the puller within.'

---

[1] Mâdhyandina text, p. 1072.
[2] Afterwards addressed as Gautama ; see before, p. 1, note.

The other said : 'Anybody may say, I know, I know. Tell what thou knowest.'

2. Yâgñavalkya said : 'Vâyu (air) is that thread, O Gautama. By air, as by a thread, O Gautama, this world and the other world, and all creatures are strung together. Therefore, O Gautama, people say of a dead person that his limbs have become unstrung; for by air, as by a thread, O Gautama, they were strung together.'

The other said : 'So it is, O Yâgñavalkya. Tell now (who is) the puller within.'

3. Yâgñavalkya said : 'He who dwells in the earth, and within the earth[1], whom the earth does not know, whose body the earth is, and who pulls (rules) the earth within, he is thy Self, the puller (ruler) within, the immortal.'

4. 'He who dwells in the water, and within the water, whom the water does not know, whose body the water is, and who pulls (rules) the water within, he is thy Self, the puller (ruler) within, the immortal.'

5. 'He who dwells in the fire, and within the fire, whom the fire does not know, whose body the fire is, and who pulls (rules) the fire within, he is thy Self, the puller (ruler) within, the immortal.'

6. 'He who dwells in the sky, and within the sky, whom the sky does not know, whose body the sky is, and who pulls (rules) the sky within, he is thy Self, the puller (ruler) within, the immortal.'

7. 'He who dwells in the air (vâyu), and within the air, whom the air does not know, whose body the

---

[1] I translate antara by 'within,' according to the commentator, who explains it by abhyantara, but I must confess that I should prefer to translate it by 'different from,' as Deussen does, l. c. p. 160, particularly as it governs an ablative.

air is, and who pulls (rules) the air within, he is thy
Self, the puller (ruler) within, the immortal.'

8. 'He who dwells in the heaven (dyu), and within
the heaven, whom the heaven does not know, whose
body the heaven is, and who pulls (rules) the heaven
within, he is thy Self, the puller (ruler) within, the
immortal.'

9. 'He who dwells in the sun (âditya), and within
the sun, whom the sun does not know, whose body
the sun is, and who pulls (rules) the sun within, he
is thy Self, the puller (ruler) within, the immortal.'

10. 'He who dwells in the space (disa*h*), and
within the space, whom the space does not know,
whose body the space is, and who pulls (rules) the
space within, he is thy Self, the puller (ruler) within,
the immortal.'

11. 'He who dwells in the moon and stars (*k*an-
dra-târakam), and within the moon and stars, whom
the moon and stars do not know, whose body the
moon and stars are, and who pulls (rules) the moon
and stars within, he is thy Self, the puller (ruler)
within, the immortal.'

12. 'He who dwells in the ether (âkâ*s*a), and
within the ether, whom the ether does not know,
whose body the ether is, and who pulls (rules) the
ether within, he is thy Self, the puller (ruler) within,
the immortal.'

13. 'He who dwells in the darkness (tamas), and
within the darkness, whom the darkness does not
know, whose body the darkness is, and who pulls
(rules) the darkness within, he is thy Self, the puller
(ruler) within, the immortal.'

14. 'He who dwells in the light (te*g*as), and within
the light, whom the light does not know, whose

body the light is, and who pulls (rules) the light within, he is thy Self, the puller (ruler) within, the immortal.'

So far with respect to the gods (adhidaivatam); now with respect to beings (adhibhûtam).

15. Yâgñavalkya said: 'He who dwells in all beings, and within all beings, whom all beings do not know, whose body all beings are, and who pulls (rules) all beings within, he is thy Self, the puller (ruler) within, the immortal.'

16. 'He who dwells in the breath (prâna), and within the breath, whom the breath does not know, whose body the breath is, and who pulls (rules) the breath within, he is thy Self, the puller (ruler) within, the immortal.'

17. 'He who dwells in the tongue (vâk), and within the tongue, whom the tongue does not know, whose body the tongue is, and who pulls (rules) the tongue within, he is thy Self, the puller (ruler) within, the immortal.'

18. 'He who dwells in the eye, and within the eye, whom the eye does not know, whose body the eye is, and who pulls (rules) the eye within, he is thy Self, the puller (ruler) within, the immortal.'

19. 'He who dwells in the ear, and within the ear, whom the ear does not know, whose body the ear is, and who pulls (rules) the ear within, he is thy Self, the puller (ruler) within, the immortal.'

20. 'He who dwells in the mind, and within the mind, whom the mind does not know, whose body the mind is, and who pulls (rules) the mind within, he is thy Self, the puller (ruler) within, the immortal.'

21. 'He who dwells in the skin, and within the skin, whom the skin does not know, whose body the

skin is, and who pulls (rules) the skin within, he is thy Self, the puller (ruler) within, the immortal.'

22. 'He who dwells in knowledge[1], and within knowledge, whom knowledge does not know, whose body knowledge is, and who pulls (rules) knowledge within, he is thy Self, the puller (ruler) within, the immortal.'

23. 'He who dwells in the seed, and within the seed, whom the seed does not know, whose body the seed is, and who pulls (rules) the seed within, he is thy Self, the puller (ruler) within, the immortal; unseen, but seeing; unheard, but hearing; unperceived, but perceiving; unknown, but knowing. There is no other seer but he, there is no other hearer but he, there is no other perceiver but he, there is no other knower but he. This is thy Self, the ruler within, the immortal. Everything else is of evil.' After that Uddâlaka Âruni held his peace.

EIGHTH BRÂHMANA[2].

1. Then Vâkaknavî[3] said: 'Venerable Brâhmanas, I shall ask him two questions. If he will answer them, none of you, I think, will defeat him in any argument concerning Brahman.'

Yâgñavalkya said: 'Ask, O Gârgî.'

2. She said: 'O Yâgñavalkya, as the son of a warrior from the Kâsîs or Videhas might string his loosened bow, take two pointed foe-piercing arrows in his hand and rise to do battle, I have risen to

---

[1] Self, i.e. the individual Self, according to the Mâdhyandina school; see Deussen, p. 161.

[2] Mâdhyandina text, p. 1075.

[3] Gârgî, not the wife of Yâgñavalkya.

fight thee with two questions. Answer me these questions.'

Yâg͂navalkya said : 'Ask, O Gârgî.'

3. She said : 'O Yâg͂navalkya, that of which they say that it is above the heavens, beneath the earth, embracing heaven and earth[1], past, present, and future, tell me in what is it woven, like warp and woof?'

4. Yâg͂navalkya said : 'That of which they say that it is above the heavens, beneath the earth, embracing heaven and earth, past, present, and future, that is woven, like warp and woof, in the ether (âkâsa).'

5. She said : 'I bow to thee, O Yâg͂navalkya, who hast solved me that question. Get thee ready for the second.'

Yâg͂navalkya said[2] : 'Ask, O Gârgî.'

6. She said : 'O Yâg͂navalkya, that of which they say that it is above the heavens, beneath the earth, embracing heaven and earth, past, present, and future, tell me in what is it woven, like warp and woof?'

7. Yâg͂navalkya said : 'That of which they say that it is above the heavens, beneath the earth, embracing heaven and earth, past, present, and future, that is woven, like warp and woof, in the ether.'

Gârgî said : 'In what then is the ether woven, like warp and woof?'

8. He said : 'O Gârgî, the Brâhman̄as call this the Akshara (the imperishable). It is neither coarse nor fine, neither short nor long, neither red (like fire) nor fluid (like water); it is without shadow, without darkness, without air, without ether, without

---

[1] Deussen, p. 143, translates, 'between heaven and earth,' but that would be the antariksha.

[2] This repetition does not occur in the Mâdhyandina text.

attachment [1], without taste, without smell, without
eyes, without ears, without speech, without mind,
without light (vigour), without breath, without a
mouth (or door), without measure, having no within
and no without, it devours nothing, and no one
devours it.'

9. 'By the command of that Akshara (the imperishable), O Gârgî, sun and moon stand apart [2].
By the command of that Akshara, O Gârgî,
heaven and earth stand apart. By the command of
that Akshara, O Gârgî, what are called moments
(nimesha), hours (muhûrta), days and nights, half-
months, months, seasons, years, all stand apart.
By the command of that Akshara, O Gârgî, some
rivers flow to the East from the white mountains,
others to the West, or to any other quarter. By
the command of that Akshara, O Gârgî, men praise
those who give, the gods follow the sacrificer, the
fathers the Darvî-offering.'

10. 'Whosoever, O Gârgî, without knowing that
Akshara (the imperishable), offers oblations in this
world, sacrifices, and performs penance for a thousand years, his work will have an end. Whosoever,
O Gârgî, without knowing this Akshara, departs this
world, he is miserable (like a slave) [3]. But he, O
Gârgî, who departs this world, knowing this Akshara,
he is a Brâhma*n*a.'

11. 'That Brahman,' O Gârgî, 'is unseen, but
seeing; unheard, but hearing; unperceived, but perceiving; unknown, but knowing. There is nothing

---

[1] Not adhering to anything, like lac or gum.

[2] Each follows its own course.

[3] 'He stores up the effects from work, like a miser his riches,'
Roer. 'He is helpless,' Gough.

that sees but it, nothing that hears but it, nothing that perceives but it, nothing that knows but it. In that Akshara then, O Gârgî, the ether is woven, like warp and woof.'

12. Then said Gârgî : 'Venerable Brâhmans, you may consider it a great thing, if you get off by bowing before him. No one, I believe, will defeat him in any argument concerning Brahman.' After that Vâkaknavî held her peace.

NINTH BRÂHMANA [1].

1. Then Vidagdha Sâkalya asked him[2]: 'How many gods are there, O Yâgñavalkya?' He replied with this very Nivid[3]: 'As many as are mentioned in the Nivid of the hymn of praise addressed to the Visvedevas, viz. three and three hundred, three and three thousand[4].'

'Yes,' he said, and asked again : ' How many gods are there really, O Yâgñavalkya ?'

'Thirty-three,' he said.

---

[1] Mâdhyandina text, p. 1076.

[2] This disputation between Yâgñavalkya and Vidagdha Sâkalya occurs in a simpler form in the Satapatha-brâhmana, XI, p. 873. He is here represented as the first who defies Yâgñavalkya, and whom Yâgñavalkya asks at once, whether the other Brâhmans had made him the ulmukâvakshayana, the cat's paw, literally one who has to take a burning piece of wood out of the fire (ardha-dagdhakâshtham ulmukam; tasya vahirnirasanam avakshayanam vinâsah). The end, however, is different, for on asking the nature of the one god, the Prâna, he is told by Yâgñavalkya that he has asked for what he ought not to ask, and that therefore he will die and thieves will carry away his bones.

[3] Nivid, old and short invocations of the gods ; devatâsankhyâ-vâkakâni mantrapadâni kânikid vaisvadeve sastre sasyante. Sankara and Dvivedaganga.

[4] This would make 3306 devatâs.

'Yes,' he said, and asked again : ' How many gods
are there really, O Yâgñavalkya?'
'Six,' he said.
'Yes,' he said, and asked again : ' How many gods
are there really, O Yâgñavalkya?'
'Three,' he said.
'Yes,' he said, and asked again : ' How many gods
are there really, O Yâgñavalkya?'
'Two,' he said.
'Yes,' he said, and asked again : ' How many gods
are there really, O Yâgñavalkya?'
'One and a half (adhyardha),' he said.
'Yes,' he said, and asked again : 'How many gods
are there really, O Yâgñavalkya?'
'One,' he said.
'Yes,' he said, and asked : 'Who are these three
and three hundred, three and three thousand?'
2. Yâgñavalkya replied : 'They are only the
various powers of them, in reality there are only
thirty-three gods [1].'
He asked : 'Who are those thirty-three?'
Yâgñavalkya replied : 'The eight Vasus, the eleven
Rudras, the twelve Âdityas. They make thirty-one,
and Indra and Pragâpati make the thirty-three [2].'
3. He asked : 'Who are the Vasus.'
Yâgñavalkya replied : 'Agni (fire), Prithivî
(earth), Vâyu (air), Antariksha (sky), Âditya (sun),
Dyu (heaven), Kandramas (moon), the Nakshatras
(stars), these are the Vasus, for in them all that
dwells (this world) [3] rests ; and therefore they are
called Vasus.'

---

[1] 'The glories of these are three and thirty.' Gough, p. 172.

[2] Trayastrimsau, i. e. trayastrimsatah pûranau.

[3] The etymological explanation of Vasu is not quite clear, and

4. He asked: 'Who are the Rudras?'

Yâgñavalkya replied: 'These ten vital breaths (prânas, the senses, i. e. the five gñânendriyas, and the five karmendriyas), and Âtman[1], as the eleventh. When they depart from this mortal body, they make us cry (rodayanti), and because they make us cry, they are called Rudras.'

5. He asked: 'Who are the Âdityas?'

Yâgñavalkya replied: 'The twelve months of the year, and they are Âdityas, because they move along (yanti), taking up everything[2] (âdadânâh). Because they move along, taking up everything, therefore they are called Âdityas.'

6. He asked: 'And who is Indra, and who is Pragâpati?'

Yâgñavalkya replied: 'Indra is thunder, Pragâpati is the sacrifice.'

He asked: 'And what is the thunder?'

Yâgñavalkya replied: 'The thunderbolt.'

He asked: 'And what is the sacrifice?'

Yâgñavalkya replied: 'The (sacrificial) animals.'

7. He asked: 'Who are the six?'

Yâgñavalkya replied: 'Agni (fire), Prithivî (earth), Vâyu (air), Antariksha (sky), Âditya (sun), Dyu (heaven), they are the six, for they are all[3] this, the six.'

8. He asked: 'Who are the three gods?'

the commentator hardly explains our text. Perhaps vasu is meant for the world or the dwellers therein. The more usual explanation occurs in the Satap. Brâh. p. 1077, ete hîdam sarvam vâsayante tadyad idam sarvam vâsayante tasmâd vasava iti; or on p. 874, where we read te yad idam sarvam &c.

[1] Âtman is here explained as manas, the common sensory.

[2] The life of men, and the fruits of their work.

[3] They are the thirty-three gods.

Yâg*ñ*avalkya replied : 'These three worlds, for in them all these gods exist.'

He asked : 'Who are the two gods?'

Yâg*ñ*avalkya replied : 'Food and breath.'

He asked : 'Who is the one god and a half?'

Yâg*ñ*avalkya replied : ' He that blows.'

9. Here they say : 'How is it that he who blows like one only, should be called one and a half (adhyardha)?' And the answer is : 'Because, when the wind was blowing, everything grew (adhyardhnot).'

He asked : 'Who is the one god?'

Yâg*ñ*avalkya replied : 'Breath (prâ*n*a), and he is Brahman (the Sûtrâtman), and they call him That (tyad).'

10. *S*âkalya said[1]: 'Whosoever knows that person (or god) whose dwelling (body) is the earth, whose sight (world) is fire[2], whose mind is light,—the prin-

---

[1] I prefer to attribute this to *S*âkalya, who is still the questioner, and not Yâg*ñ*avalkya ; but I am not quite satisfied that I am right in this, or in the subsequent distribution of the parts, assigned to each speaker. If *S*âkalya is the questioner, then the sentence, veda vâ aha*m* tam purusha*m* sarvasyâtmana*h* parâya*n*a*m* yam âttha, must belong to Yâg*ñ*avalkya, because he refers to the words of another speaker. Lastly, the sentence vadaiva has to be taken as addressed to *S*âkalya. The commentator remarks that, he being the questioner, one expects p*r*i*kkh*a instead of vada. But Yâg*ñ*avalkya may also be supposed to turn round on *S*âkalya and ask him a question in turn, more difficult than the question addressed by *S*âkalya to Yâg*ñ*avalkya, and in that case the last sentence must be taken as an answer, though an imperfect one, of *S*âkalya's. The commentator seems to think that after Yâg*ñ*avalkya told *S*âkalya to ask this question, *S*âkalya was frightened and asked it, and that then Yâg*ñ*avalkya answered in turn.

[2] The Mâdhyandina text varies considerably. It has the first time, *k*ashur loka*h* for agnir loka*h*. I keep to the same construction throughout, taking mano *g*yoti*h*, not as a compound, but like agnir loko yasya, as a sentence, i. e. mano *g*yotir yasya.

ciple of every (living) self, he indeed is a teacher, O Yâgñavalkya.'

Yâgñavalkya said : ' I know that person, the principle of every self, of whom thou speakest. This corporeal (material, earthy) person, "he is he." But tell me [1], Sâkalya, who is his devatâ [2] (deity)?'

Sâkalya replied : 'The Immortal [3].'

11. Sâkalya said : 'Whosoever knows that person whose dwelling is love (a body capable of sensual love), whose sight is the heart, whose mind is light,—the principle of every self, he indeed is a teacher, O Yâgñavalkya.'

Yâgñavalkya replied : ' I know that person, the principle of every self, of whom thou speakest. This love-made (loving) person, "he is he." But tell me, Sâkalya, who is his devatâ ?'

Sâkalya replied : ' The women [4].'

12. Sâkalya said : ' Whosoever knows that person whose dwelling are the colours, whose sight is the eye, whose mind is light,—the principle of every self, he indeed is a teacher, O Yâgñavalkya.'

Yâgñavalkya replied : ' I know that person, the principle of every self, of whom thou speakest. That person in the sun, "he is he." But tell me, Sâkalya, who is his devatâ ?'

Sâkalya replied : ' The True [5].'

13. Sâkalya said : ' Whosoever knows that person

---

[1] Ask me. Comm.

[2] That from which he is produced, that is his devatâ. Comm.

[3] According to the commentator, the essence of food, which produces blood, from which the germ receives life and becomes an embryo and a living being.

[4] Because they excite the fire of love. Comm.

[5] The commentator explains satya, the true, by the eye, because the sun owes its origin to the eye.

whose dwelling is ether, whose sight is the ear, whose mind is light,—the principle of every self, he indeed is a teacher, O Yâ*g*ñavalkya.'

Yâ*g*ñavalkya replied: 'I know that person, the principle of every self, of whom thou speakest. The person who hears[1] and answers, "he is he." But tell me, *S*âkalya, who is his devatâ?'

*S*âkalya replied: 'Space.'

14. *S*âkalya said: 'Whosoever knows that person whose dwelling is darkness, whose sight is the heart, whose mind is light,—the principle of every self, he indeed is a teacher, O Yâ*g*ñavalkya.'

Yâ*g*ñavalkya replied: 'I know that person, the principle of every self, of whom thou speakest. The shadowy[2] person, "he is he." But tell me, *S*âkalya, who is his devatâ?'

*S*âkalya replied: 'Death.'

15. *S*âkalya said: 'Whosoever knows that person whose dwelling are (bright) colours, whose sight is the eye, whose mind is light,—the principle of every self, he indeed is a teacher, O Yâ*g*ñavalkya.'

Yâ*g*ñavalkya replied: 'I know that person, the principle of every self, of whom thou speakest. The person in the looking-glass, "he is he." But tell me, *S*âkalya, who is his devatâ?'

*S*âkalya replied: 'Vital breath' (asu).

16. *S*âkalya said: 'Whosoever knows that person whose dwelling is water, whose sight is the heart, whose mind is light,—the principle of every self, he indeed is a teacher, O Yâ*g*ñavalkya.'

---

[1] Read *s*rautra instead of *s*rotra; see Br*i*h. Âr. Up. II, 5, 6.

[2] Shadow, *kh*âyâ, is explained here by a*g*ñâna, ignorance, not by *g*ñâna, knowledge.

Yâgñavalkya replied: 'I know that person, the principle of every self, of whom thou speakest. The person in the water, "he is he." But tell me, Sâkalya, who is his devatâ?'

Sâkalya replied: 'Varuæa.'

17. Sâkalya said: 'Whosoever knows that person whose dwelling is seed, whose sight is the heart, whose mind is light,—the principle of every self, he indeed is a teacher, O Yâgñavalkya.'

Yâgñavalkya replied: 'I know that person, the principle of every self, of whom thou speakest. The filial person, "he is he." But tell me, Sâkalya, who is his devatâ?'

Sâkalya replied: 'Pragâpati.'

18. Yâgñavalkya said: 'Sâkalya, did those Brâh-maæas (who themselves shrank from the contest) make thee the victim[1]?'

Sâkalya said: 'Yâgñavalkya, because thou hast decried the Brâhmaæas of the Kuru-Pañkâlas, what[2] Brahman dost thou know?'

19. Yâgñavalkya said: 'I know the quarters with their deities and their abodes.'

---

[1] Aṅgârâvakshayaæa is explained as a vessel in which coals are extinguished, and Ânandagiri adds that Yâgñavalkya, in saying that Sâkalya was made an aṅgârâvakshayaæa by his fellow Brâhmans, meant that he was given up by them as a victim, in fact that he was being burnt or consumed by Yâgñavalkya. I should prefer to take aṅgârâvakshayaæa in the sense of ulmukâvakshayaæa, an instrument with which one takes burning coals from the fire to extinguish them, a pair of tongs. Read sandaṃsa instead of sandesa. Kshi with ava means to remove, to take away. We should call an aṅgârâvakshayaæa a cat's paw. The Brâhmaæas used Sâkalya as a cat's paw.

[2] It seems better to take kim as the interrogative pronoun than as an interrogative particle.

*S*âkalya said : ' If thou knowest the quarters with their deities and their abodes,

20. 'Which is thy deity in the Eastern quarter?'

Yâg*ñ*avalkya said : ' Âditya (the sun).'

*S*âkalya said : ' In what does that Âditya abide?'

Yâg*ñ*avalkya said : 'In the eye.'

*S*âkalya said : ' In what does the eye abide?'

Yâg*ñ*avalkya said : 'In the colours, for with the eye he sees the colours.'

*S*âkalya said : 'And in what then do the colours abide?'

Yâg*ñ*avalkya said : ' In the heart[1], for we know colours by the heart, for colours abide in the heart[2].'

*S*âkalya said : ' So it is indeed, O Yâg*ñ*avalkya.'

21. *S*âkalya said : 'Which is thy deity in the Southern quarter ?'

Yâg*ñ*avalkya said : ' Yama.'

*S*âkalya said : ' In what does that Yama abide?'

Yâg*ñ*avalkya said : 'In the sacrifice.'

*S*âkalya said : ' In what does the sacrifice abide?'

Yâg*ñ*avalkya said : 'In the Dakshi*n*â (the gifts to be given to the priests).'

*S*âkalya said : ' In what does the Dakshi*n*â abide?'

Yâg*ñ*avalkya said : ' In *S*raddhâ (faith), for if a man believes, then he gives Dakshi*n*â, and Dakshi*n*â truly abides in faith.'

*S*âkalya said : 'And in what then does faith abide?'

Yâg*ñ*avalkya said : 'In the heart, for by the heart faith knows, and therefore faith abides in the heart.'

*S*âkalya said : 'So it is indeed, O Yâg*ñ*avalkya.'

---

[1] Heart stands here for buddhi and manas together.   Comm.

[2] In the text, published by Dr. Roer in the Bibliotheca Indica, a sentence is left out, viz. hr*i*daya ity uvâka, hr*i*dayena hi rûpâ*n*i *g*ânâti, hr*i*daye hy eva rûpâ*n*i pratish*th*itâni bhavantîty.

22. Sâkalya said: 'Which is thy deity in the Western quarter?'

Yâgñavalkya said: 'Varuna.'

Sâkalya said: 'In what does that Varuna abide?'

Yâgñavalkya said: 'In the water.'

Sâkalya said: 'In what does the water abide?'

Yâgñavalkya said: 'In the seed.'

Sâkalya said: 'And in what does the seed abide?'

Yâgñavalkya said: 'In the heart. And therefore also they say of a son who is like his father, that he seems as if slipt from his heart, or made from his heart; for the seed abides in the heart.'

Sâkalya said: 'So it is indeed, O Yâgñavalkya.'

23. Sâkalya said: 'Which is thy deity in the Northern quarter?'

Yâgñavalkya said: 'Soma.'

Sâkalya said: 'In what does that Soma abide?'

Yâgñavalkya said: 'In the Dîkshâ[1].'

Sâkalya said: 'In what does the Dîkshâ abide?'

Yâgñavalkya said: 'In the True; and therefore they say to one who has performed the Dîkshâ, Speak what is true, for in the True indeed the Dîkshâ abides.'

Sâkalya said: 'And in what does the True abide?'

Yâgñavalkya said: 'In the heart, for with the heart do we know what is true, and in the heart indeed the True abides.'

Sâkalya said: 'So it is indeed, O Yâgñavalkya.'

24. Sâkalya said: 'Which is thy deity in the zenith?'

---

[1] Dîkshâ is the initiatory rite for the Soma sacrifice. Having sacrificed with Soma which has to be bought, the sacrificer becomes endowed with wisdom, and wanders to the North, which is the quarter of Soma.

Yâg*n*avalkya said: 'Agni.'

*S*âkalya said : 'In what does that Agni abide.'

Yâg*n*avalkya said : 'In speech.'

*S*âkalya said : 'And in what does speech abide ?'

Yâg*n*avalkya said : 'In the heart.'

*S*âkalya said : 'And in what does the heart abide?'

25. Yâg*n*avalkya said : 'O Ahallika [1], when you think the heart could be anywhere else away from us, if it were away from us, the dogs might eat it, or the birds tear it.'

26. *S*âkalya said : 'And in what dost thou (thy body) and the Self (thy heart) abide?'

Yâg*n*avalkya said : 'In the Prâ*n*a (breath).'

*S*âkalya said : 'In what does the Prâ*n*a abide ?'

Yâg*n*avalkya said : 'In the Apâna (down-breathing) [2].'

*S*âkalya said : 'In what does the Apâna abide?'

Yâg*n*avalkya said : 'In the Vyâna (back-breathing) [3].'

*S*âkalya said : 'In what does the Vyâna abide ?'

Yâg*n*avalkya said : 'In the Udâna (the out-breathing) [4].'

*S*âkalya said : 'In what does the Udâna abide ?'

Yâg*n*avalkya said : 'In the Samâna [5].   That Self

---

[1] A term of reproach, it may be a ghost or preta, because ahani lîyate, it disappears by day.

[2] Because the prâ*n*a would run away, if it were not held back by the apâna.

[3] Because the apâna would run down, and the prâ*n*a up, if they were not held back by the vyâna.

[4] Because all three, the prâ*n*a, apâna, and vyâna, would run away in all directions, if they were not fastened to the udâna.

[5] The Samâna can hardly be meant here for one of the five prâ*n*as, generally mentioned before the udâna, but, as explained by Dvivedaga*n*ga, stands for the Sûtrâtman.   This Sûtrâtman abides in the Antaryâmin, and this in the Brahman (Kû*t*astha), which is

(âtman) is to be described by No, no[1]! He is in-comprehensible, for he cannot be (is not) compre-hended; he is imperishable, for he cannot perish; he is unattached, for he does not attach himself; unfet-tered, he does not suffer, he does not fail.'

'These are the eight abodes (the earth, &c.), the eight worlds (fire, &c.), the eight gods (the immortal food, &c.), the eight persons (the corporeal, &c.) He who after dividing and uniting these persons[2], went beyond (the Samâna), that person, taught in the Upanishads, I now ask thee (to teach me). If thou shalt not explain him to me, thy head will fall.'

Sâkalya did not know him, and his head fell, nay, thieves took away his bones, mistaking them for something else.

27. Then Yâgñavalkya said: 'Reverend Brâh-mañas, whosoever among you desires to do so, may now question me. Or question me, all of you. Or whosoever among you desires it, I shall question him, or I shall question all of you.

But those Brâhmañas durst not (say anything).

28. Then Yâgñavalkya questioned them with these Slokas:

1. 'As a mighty tree in the forest, so in truth is man, his hairs are the leaves, his outer skin is the bark.

2. 'From his skin flows forth blood, sap from the skin (of the tree); and thus from the wounded

---

therefore described next. Could Samâna be here the same as in IV, 3, 7?

[1] See before, II, 3, 6; also IV, 2, 4; IV, 4, 22; IV, 5, 15.

[2] Dividing them according to the different abodes, worlds, and persons, and uniting them at last in the heart.

man[1] comes forth blood, as from a tree that is
struck.

3. 'The lumps of his flesh are (in the tree) the
layers of wood, the fibre is strong like the ten-
dons[2]. The bones are the (hard) wood within, the
marrow is made like the marrow of the tree.

4. 'But, while the tree, when felled, grows up
again more young from the root, from what root,
tell me, does a mortal grow up, after he has been
felled by death?

5. 'Do not say, "from seed," for seed is produced
from the living[3]; but a tree, springing from a grain,
clearly[4] rises again after death[5].

6. 'If a tree is pulled up with the root, it will not
grow again; from what root then, tell me, does a
mortal grow up, after he has been felled by death?

7. 'Once born, he is not born (again); for who
should create him again[6]?'

---

[1] In the Mâdhyandina-*s*âkhâ, p. 1080, tasmât tadâtunnât, instead
of tasmât tadât*rinn*ât.

[2] *S*ankara seems to have read snâvavat, instead of snâva tat
sthiram, as we read in both *S*âkhâs.

[3] Here the Mâdhyandinas (p. 1080) add, *g*âta eva na *g*âyate, ko
nv ena*m g*anayet puna*h*, which the Kâ*n*vas place later.

[4] Instead of a*ñg*asâ, the Mâdhyandinas have anyata*h*.

[5] The Mâdhyandinas have dhânâruha u vai, which is better than
iva vai, the iva being, according to *S*ankara's own confession, useless. The thread of the argument does not seem to have been
clearly perceived by the commentators. What the poet wants to
say is, that a man, struck down by death, does not come to life
again from seed, because human seed comes from the living only,
while trees, springing from grain, are seen to come to life after the
tree (which yielded the grain or the seed) is dead. Pretya-sam-
bhava, like pretya-bhâva, means life after death, and pretyasam-
bhava, as an adjective, means coming to life after death.

[6] This line too is taken in a different sense by the commentator.
According to him, it would mean: 'If you say, He has been born

'Brahman, who is knowledge and bliss, he is the principle, both to him who gives gifts[1], and also to him who stands firm, and knows.'

(and there is an end of all questioning), I say, No; he is born again, and the question is, How?' This is much too artificial. The order of the verses in the Mâdhyandina-*s*âkhâ is better on the whole, leading up more naturally to the question, 'From what root then does a mortal grow up, after he has been felled by death?' When the Brâhmans cannot answer, Yâ*gñ*avalkya answers, or the *S*ruti declares, that the root from whence a mortal springs again, after death, is Brahman.

[1] *S*ankara explains râtir dâtu*h* as râter dâtu*h*, a reading adopted by the Mâdhyandinas. He then arrives at the statement that Brahman is the principle or the last source, also the root of a new life, both for those who practise works and for those who, having relinquished works, stand firm in knowledge. Regnaud (II, p. 138) translates: 'C'est Brahma (qui est) l'intelligence, le bonheur, la richesse, le but suprême de celui qui offre (des sacrifices), et de celui qui réside (en lui), de celui qui connaît.'

FOURTH ADHYÂYA.

FIRST BRÂHMA*N*A.

1. When *G*anaka Vaideha was sitting (to give audience), Yâ*gñ*avalkya approached, and *G*anaka Vaideha said : ' Yâ*gñ*avalkya, for what object did you come, wishing for cattle, or for subtle questions [1] ?'

Yâ*gñ*avalkya replied : ' For both, Your Majesty;

2. 'Let us hear what anybody may have told you.'

*G*anaka Vaideha replied : ' *G*itvan *S*ailini told me that speech (vâ*k*) is Brahman.'

Yâ*gñ*avalkya said : 'As one who had (the benefit of a good) father, mother, and teacher might tell, so did *S*ailini [2] tell you, that speech is Brahman; for what is the use of a dumb person ? But did he tell you the body (âyatana) and the resting-place (pratish*th*â) of that Brahman?'

*G*anaka Vaideha said : ' He did not tell me.'

Yâ*gñ*avalkya said : ' Your Majesty, this (Brahman) stands on one leg only [3].'

*G*anaka Vaideha said: 'Then tell me, Yâ*gñ*avalkya.'

---

[1] A*n*v-anta, formed like Sûtrânta, Siddhânta, and probably Vedânta, means subtle questions.

[2] Roer and Poley give here *S*ailina; Weber also (pp. 1080 and 1081) has twice *S*ailina (*S*ilinasyâpatyam).

[3] This seems to mean that *G*itvan's explanation of Brahman is lame or imperfect, because there are four pâdas of that Brahman, and he taught one only. The other three are its body, its place, and its form of worship (pra*gñ*etîyam upanishad brahma*n*a*s k*aturtha*h* pâda*h*). See also Maitr. Up. VII, p. 221.

Yâgñavalkya said: 'The tongue is its body, ether its place, and one should worship it as knowledge.'

Ganaka Vaideha said: 'What is the nature of that knowledge?'

Yâgñavalkya replied: 'Your Majesty, speech itself (is knowledge). For through speech, Your Majesty, a friend is known (to be a friend), and likewise the Rig-veda, Yagur-veda, Sâma-veda, the Atharvâṅgirasas, the Itihâsa (tradition), Purâña-vidyâ (knowledge of the past), the Upanishads, Slokas (verses), Sûtras (rules), Anuvyâkhyânas and Vyâkhyânas (commentaries [1], &c.); what is sacrificed, what is poured out, what is (to be) eaten and drunk, this world and the other world, and all creatures. By speech alone, Your Majesty, Brahman is known, speech indeed, O King, is the Highest Brahman. Speech does not desert him who worships that (Brahman) with such knowledge, all creatures approach him, and having become a god, he goes to the gods.'

Ganaka Vaideha said: 'I shall give you (for this) a thousand cows with a bull as big as an elephant.'

Yâgñavalkya said: 'My father was of opinion that one should not accept a reward without having fully instructed a pupil.'

3. Yâgñavalkya said: 'Let us hear what anybody may have told you.'

Ganaka Vaideha replied: 'Udaṅka Saulbâyana told me that life (prâña)[2] is Brahman.'

Yâgñavalkya said: 'As one who had (the benefit of a good) father, mother, and teacher might tell, so did

---

[1] See before, II, 4, 10; and afterwards, IV, 5, 11.
[2] See Taitt. Up. III, 3.

Udanka *S*aulbâyana tell you that life is Brahman; for what is the use of a person without life? But did he tell you the body and the resting-place of that Brahman?'

*G*anaka Vaideha said: 'He did not tell me.'

Yâ*gñ*avalkya said: 'Your Majesty, this (Brahman) stands on one leg only.'

*G*anaka Vaideha said: 'Then tell me, Yâ*gñ*avalkya.'

Yâ*gñ*avalkya said: 'Breath is its body, ether its place, and one should worship it as what is dear.'

*G*anaka Vaideha said: 'What is the nature of that which is dear?'

Yâ*gñ*avalkya replied: 'Your Majesty, life itself (is that which is dear);' because for the sake of life, Your Majesty, a man sacrifices even for him who is unworthy of sacrifice, he accepts presents from him who is not worthy to bestow presents, nay, he goes to a country, even when there is fear of being hurt[1], for the sake of life. Life, O King, is the Highest Brahman. Life does not desert him who worships that (Brahman) with such knowledge, all creatures approach him, and having become a god, he goes to the gods.'

*G*anaka Vaideha said: 'I shall give you (for this) a thousand cows with a bull as big as an elephant.'

Yâ*gñ*avalkya said: 'My father was of opinion that one should not accept a reward without having fully instructed a pupil.'

4. Yâ*gñ*avalkya said: 'Let us hear what anybody may have told you.'

---

[1] Or it may mean, he is afraid of being hurt, to whatever country he goes, for the sake of a livelihood.

*G*anaka Vaideha replied: 'Barku Vârsh*n*a told me that sight (*k*akshus) is Brahman.'

Yâ*gñ*avalkya said: 'As one who had (the benefit of a good) father, mother, and teacher might tell, so did Barku Vârsh*n*a tell you that sight is Brahman; for what is the use of a person who cannot see? But did he tell you the body and the resting-place of that Brahman?'

*G*anaka Vaideha said: 'He did not tell me.'

Yâ*gñ*avalkya said: 'Your Majesty, this (Brahman) stands on one leg only.'

*G*anaka Vaideha said: 'Then tell me, Yâ*gñ*a-valkya.'

Yâ*gñ*avalkya said: 'The eye is its body, ether its place, and one should worship it as what is true.'

*G*anaka Vaideha said: 'What is the nature of that which is true?'

Yâ*gñ*avalkya replied: 'Your Majesty, sight itself (is that which is true); for if they say to a man who sees with his eye, "Didst thou see?" and he says, "I saw," then it is true. Sight, O King, is the Highest Brahman. Sight does not desert him who worships that (Brahman) with such knowledge, all creatures approach him, and having become a god, he goes to the gods.'

*G*anaka Vaideha said: 'I shall give you (for this) a thousand cows with a bull as big as an elephant.'

Yâ*gñ*avalkya said: 'My father was of opinion that one should not accept a reward without having fully instructed a pupil.'

5. Yâ*gñ*avalkya said: 'Let us hear what anybody may have told you.'

*G*anaka Vaideha replied: 'Gardabhîvibhîta Bhâ-radvâ*g*a told me that hearing (*s*rotra) is Brahman.'

Yâgñavalkya said : 'As one who had (the benefit of a good) father, mother, and teacher might tell, so did Gardabhîvibhîta Bhâradvâga tell you that hearing is Brahman; for what is the use of a person who cannot hear ? But did he tell you the body and the resting-place of that Brahman ?'

Ganaka Vaideha said : ' He did not tell me.'

Yâgñavalkya said : 'Your Majesty, this (Brahman) stands on one leg only.'

Ganaka Vaideha said: 'Then tell me, Yâgña-valkya.'

Yâgñavalkya said: 'The ear is its body, ether its place, and we should worship it as what is endless.'

Ganaka Vaideha said: 'What is the nature of that which is endless ?'

Yâgñavalkya replied: 'Your Majesty, space (disah) itself (is that which is endless), and therefore to whatever space (quarter) he goes, he never comes to the end of it. For space is endless. Space indeed, O King, is hearing[1], and hearing indeed, O King, is the Highest Brahman. Hearing does not desert him who worships that (Brahman) with such knowledge, all creatures approach him, and having become a god, he goes to the gods.'

Ganaka Vaideha said: 'I shall give you (for this) a thousand cows with a bull as big as an elephant.'

Yâgñavalkya said: 'My father was of opinion that one should not accept a reward without having fully instructed a pupil.'

6. Yâgñavalkya said : 'Let us hear what anybody may have told you.'

---

[1] Dvivedaganga states, digbhâgo hi pârthivâdhishthânâvakkhin-nah srotram ity ukyate, atas tayor ekatvam.

Ganaka Vaideha replied: 'Satyakâma Gâbâla told me that mind [1] (manas) is Brahman.'

Yâgñavalkya said: ' As one who had (the benefit of a good) father, mother, and teacher might tell, so did Satyakâma Gâbâla tell you that mind is Brahman; for what is the use of a person without mind? But did he tell you the body and the resting-place of that Brahman?'

Ganaka Vaideha said: ' He did not tell me.'

Yâgñavalkya said: 'Your Majesty, this (Brahman) stands on one leg only.'

Ganaka Vaideha said: 'Then tell me, Yâgñavalkya.'

Yâgñavalkya said: ' Mind itself is its body, ether its place, and we should worship it as bliss.'

Ganaka Vaideha said: 'What is the nature of bliss?'

Yâgñavalkya replied: ' Your Majesty, mind itself; for with the mind does a man desire a woman, and a like son is born of her, and he is bliss. Mind indeed, O King, is the Highest Brahman. Mind does not desert him who worships that (Brahman) with such knowledge, all creatures approach him, and having become a god, he goes to the gods.'

Ganaka Vaideha said: ' I shall give you (for this) a thousand cows with a bull as big as an elephant.'

Yâgñavalkya said: 'My father was of opinion that one should not accept a reward without having fully instructed a pupil.'

7. Yâgñavalkya said: ' Let us hear what anybody may have told you.'

Ganaka Vaideha replied: 'Vidagdha Sâkalya told me that the heart (hridaya) is Brahman.'

Yâgñavalkya said: ' As one who had (the benefit

---

[1] See also Taitt. Up. III, 4.

of a good) father, mother, and teacher might tell, so did Vidagdha Sâkalya tell you that the heart is Brahman; for what is the use of a person without a heart? But did he tell you the body and the resting-place of that Brahman?'

Ganaka Vaideha said: 'He did not tell me.'

Yâgñavalkya said: 'Your Majesty, this (Brahman) stands on one leg only.'

Ganaka Vaideha said: 'Then tell me, Yâgñavalkya.'

Yâgñavalkya said: 'The heart itself is its body, ether its place, and we should worship it as certainty (sthiti).'

Ganaka Vaideha said: 'What is the nature of certainty?'

Yâgñavalkya replied: 'Your Majesty, the heart itself; for the heart indeed, O King, is the body of all things, the heart is the resting-place of all things, for in the heart, O King, all things rest. The heart indeed, O King, is the Highest Brahman. The heart does not desert him who worships that (Brahman) with such knowledge, all creatures approach him, and having become a god, he goes to the gods.'

Ganaka Vaideha said: 'I shall give you (for this) a thousand cows with a bull as big as an elephant.'

Yâgñavalkya said: 'My father was of opinion that one should not accept a reward without having fully instructed a pupil.'

SECOND BRÂHMANA.

1. Ganaka Vaideha, descending from his throne, said: 'I bow to you, O Yâgñavalkya, teach me.'

Yâgñavalkya said: 'Your Majesty, as a man who wishes to make a long journey, would furnish himself with a chariot or a ship, thus is your mind well furnished by these Upanishads[1]. You are honourable, and wealthy, you have learnt the Vedas and been told the Upanishads. Whither then will you go when departing hence ?'

Ganaka Vaideha said: 'Sir, I do not know whither I shall go.'

Yâgñavalkya said: 'Then I shall tell you this, whither you will go.'

Ganaka Vaideha said: 'Tell it, Sir.'

2. Yâgñavalkya said: 'That person who is in the right eye[2], he is called Indha, and him who is Indha they call indeed[3] Indra mysteriously, for the gods love what is mysterious, and dislike what is evident.

3. 'Now that which in the shape of a person is in the right eye, is his wife, Virâg[4]. Their meeting-place[5] is the ether within the heart, and their food the red lump within the heart. Again, their covering[6] is that which is like net-work within the heart, and the road on which they move (from sleep to waking) is the artery that rises upwards from the heart. Like a hair divided into a thousand parts, so are the veins of it, which are called Hita[7], placed

---

[1] This refers to the preceding doctrines which had been communicated to Ganaka by other teachers, and particularly to the upâsanas of Brahman as knowledge, dear, true, endless, bliss, and certainty.

[2] See also Maitr. Up. VII, p. 216.

[3] The Mâdhyandinas read parokshe*n*eva, but the commentator explains iva by eva. See also Ait. Up. I, 3, 14.

[4] Indra is called by the commentator Vaisvânara, and his wife Virâg. This couple, in a waking state, is Visva; in sleep, Taigasa.

[5] Samstâva, lit. the place where they sing praises together, that is, where they meet.

[6] Prâvara*n*a may also mean hiding-place, retreat.

[7] Hita, a name frequently given to these nâdîs; see IV, 3, 20; Khând. Up. VI, 5, 3, comm.; Kaush. Up. IV, 20. See also Katha Up. VI, 16.

firmly within the heart. Through these indeed that
(food) flows on flowing, and he (the Tai*g*asa) receives
as it were purer food[1] than the corporeal Self (the
Vai*s*vânara).

4. 'His (the Tai*g*asa's) Eastern quarter are the
prâ*n*as (breath) which go to the East;

'His Southern quarter are the prâ*n*as which go
to the South;

'His Western quarter are the prâ*n*as which go to
the West;

'His Northern quarter are the prâ*n*as which go to
the North;

'His Upper (Zenith) quarter are the prâ*n*as which
go upward;

'His Lower (Nadir) quarter are the prâ*n*as which
go downward;

'All the quarters are all the prâ*n*as. And he (the
Âtman in that state) can only be described by No[2],
no! He is incomprehensible, for he cannot be comprehended; he is undecaying, for he cannot decay;
he is not attached, for he does not attach himself;
he is unbound, he does not suffer, he does not perish.
O *G*anaka, you have indeed reached fearlessness,'—
thus said Yâ*gñ*avalkya.

Then *G*anaka said: 'May that fearlessness come
to you also who teachest us fearlessness. I bow to
you. Here are the Videhas, and here am I (thy
slave).'

---

[1] Dvivedaga*n*ga explains that food, when it is eaten, is first of
all changed into the coarse food, which goes away downward, and
into the subtler food. This subtler food is again divided into the
middle juice that feeds the body, and the finest, which is called
the red lump.

[2] See Br*i*h. Up. II, 3, 6; IV, 9, 26.

THIRD BRÂHMANA.

1. Yâgñavalkya came to Ganaka Vaideha, and he did not mean to speak with him[1]. But when formerly

---

[1] The introduction to this Brâhmana has a very peculiar interest, as showing the close coherence of the different portions which together form the historical groundwork of the Upanishads. Ganaka Vaideha and Yâgñavalkya are leading characters in the Brihadâranyaka-upanishad, and whenever they meet they seem to converse quite freely, though each retains his own character, and Yâgñavalkya honours Ganaka as king quite as much as Ganaka honours Yâgñavalkya as a Brâhmana. Now in our chapter we read that Yâgñavalkya did not wish to enter on a discussion, but that Ganaka was the first to address him (pûrvam paprakkha). This was evidently considered not quite correct, and an explanation is given, that Ganaka took this liberty because on a former occasion Yâgñavalkya had granted him permission to address questions to him, whenever he liked. It might be objected that such an explanation looks very much like an after-thought, and we find indeed that in India itself some of the later commentators tried to avoid the difficulty by dividing the words sa mene na vadishya iti, into sam enena vadishya iti, so that we should have to translate, 'Yâgñavalkya came to Ganaka intending to speak with him.' (See Dvivedaganga's Comm. p. 1141.) This is, no doubt, a very ingenious conjecture, which might well rouse the envy of European scholars. But it is no more. The accents decide nothing, because they are changed by different writers, according to their different views of what the Pada text ought to be. What made me prefer the reading which is supported by Sankara and Dvivedaganga, though the latter alludes to the other padakkheda, is that the tmesis, sam enena vadishye, does not occur again, while sa mene is a common phrase. But the most interesting point, as I remarked before, is that this former disputation between Ganaka and Yâgñavalkya and the permission granted to the King to ask any question he liked, is not a mere invention to account for the apparent rudeness by which Yâgñavalkya is forced to enter on a discussion against his will, but actually occurs in a former chapter. In Satap. Br. XI, 6, 2, 10, we read: tasmai ha Yâgñavalkyo varam dadau; sa hovâka, kâma-

*G*anaka Vaideha and Yâg*ñ*avalkya had a disputation on the Agnihotra, Yâg*ñ*avalkya had granted him a boon, and he chose (for a boon) that he might be free to ask him any question he liked. Yâg*ñ*avalkya granted it, and thus the King was the first to ask him a question.

2. 'Yâg*ñ*avalkya,' he said, 'what is the light of man [1]?'

Yâg*ñ*avalkya replied: 'The sun, O King; for, having the sun alone for his light, man sits, moves about, does his work, and returns.'

*G*anaka Vaideha said: 'So indeed it is, O Yâg*ñ*avalkya.'

3. *G*anaka Vaideha said: 'When the sun has set, O Yâg*ñ*avalkya, what is then the light of man?'

Yâg*ñ*avalkya replied: 'The moon indeed is his light; for, having the moon alone for his light, man sits, moves about, does his work, and returns.'

*G*anaka Vaideha said: 'So indeed it is, O Yâg*ñ*avalkya.'

4. *G*anaka Vaideha said: 'When the sun has set, O Yâg*ñ*avalkya, and the moon has set, what is the light of man?'

Yâg*ñ*avalkya replied: 'Fire indeed is his light;

---

pras*n*a eva me tvayi Yâg*ñ*avalkyâsad iti, tato brahmâ *G*anaka âsa. This would show that *G*anaka was considered almost like a Brâh-ma*n*a, or at all events enjoyed certain privileges which were supposed to belong to the first caste only. See, for a different view, Deussen, Vedânta, p. 203; Regnaud (Matériaux pour servir à l'histoire de la philosophie de l'Inde), Errata; and Sacred Books of the East, vol. i, p. lxxiii.

[1] Read ki*m*gyotir as a Bahuvrîhi. Purusha is difficult to translate. It means man, but also the true essence of man, the soul, as we should say, or something more abstract still, the person, as I generally translate it, though a person beyond the Ego.

for, having fire alone for his light, man sits, moves about, does his work, and returns.'

5. *G*anaka Vaideha said: 'When the sun has set, O Yâ*g*ñavalkya, and the moon has set, and the fire is gone out, what is then the light of man?'

Yâ*g*ñavalkya replied: 'Sound indeed is his light; for, having sound alone for his light, man sits, moves about, does his work, and returns. Therefore, O King, when one cannot see even one's own hand, yet when a sound is raised, one goes towards it.'

*G*anaka Vaideha said: 'So indeed it is, O Yâ*g*ña-valkya.'

6. *G*anaka Vaideha said: 'When the sun has set, O Yâ*g*ñavalkya, and the moon has set, and the fire is gone out, and the sound hushed, what is then the light of man?'

Yâ*g*ñavalkya said: 'The Self indeed is his light; for, having the Self alone as his light, man sits, moves about, does his work, and returns.'

7. *G*anaka Vaideha said: 'Who is that Self?'

Yâ*g*ñavalkya replied: 'He who is within the heart, surrounded by the Prâ*n*as[1] (senses), the person of light, consisting of knowledge. He, remaining the same, wanders along the two worlds[2], as if[3] thinking, as if moving. During sleep (in dream) he transcends this world and all the forms of death (all that falls under the sway of death, all that is perishable).

8. 'On being born that person, assuming his body,

---

[1] Sâmîpyalaksha*n*â saptamî, Dvivedaga*n*ga. See B*ri*h. Up. IV, 4, 22.

[2] In this world, while awake or dreaming; in the other world, while in deep sleep.

[3] The world thinks that he thinks, but in reality he does not, he only witnesses the acts of buddhi, or thought.

becomes united with all evils; when he departs and
dies, he leaves all evils behind.

9. 'And there are two states for that person, the
one here in this world, the other in the other world,
and as a third [1] an intermediate state, the state of
sleep. When in that intermediate state, he sees
both those states together, the one here in this
world, and the other in the other world. Now whatever his admission to the other world may be,
having gained that admission, he sees both the evils
and the blessings [2].

'And when he falls asleep, then after having
taken away with him the material from the whole
world, destroying [3] and building it up again, he
sleeps (dreams) by his own light. In that state the
person is self-illuminated.

10. ' There are no (real) chariots in that state, no
horses, no roads, but he himself sends forth (creates)
chariots, horses, and roads. There are no blessings
there, no happiness, no joys, but he himself sends
forth (creates) blessings, happiness, and joys. There

---

[1] There are really two sthânas or states only; the place where
they meet, like the place where two villages meet, belongs to both,
but it may be distinguished as a third. Dvivedaga*n*ga (p. 1141)
uses a curious argument in support of the existence of another
world. In early childhood, he says, our dreams consist of the
impressions of a former world, later on they are filled with the
impressions of our senses, and in old age they contain visions of a
world to come.

[2] By works, by knowledge, and by remembrance of former
things; see Br*i*h. Up. IV, 4, 2.

[3] Dividing and separating the material, i. e. the impressions
received from this world. The commentator explains mâtrâ as a
portion of the impressions which are taken away into sleep.
'Destroying' he refers to the body, which in sleep becomes sense-
less, and 'building up' to the imaginations of dreams.

are no tanks there, no lakes, no rivers, but he himself sends forth (creates) tanks, lakes, and rivers.
He indeed is the maker.

11. 'On this there are these verses :

'After having subdued by sleep all that belongs
to the body, he, not asleep himself, looks down
upon the sleeping (senses). Having assumed light,
he goes again to his place, the golden person[1], the
lonely bird. (1)

12. 'Guarding with the breath (prâna, life) the
lower nest, the immortal moves away from the nest ;
that immortal one goes wherever he likes, the golden
person, the lonely bird. (2)

13. 'Going up and down in his dream, the god
makes manifold shapes for himself, either rejoicing
together with women, or laughing (with his friends),
or seeing terrible sights. (3)

14. 'People may see his playground[2], but himself
no one ever sees. Therefore they say, " Let no one
wake a man suddenly, for it is not easy to remedy,
if he does not get back (rightly to his body)."

'Here some people (object and) say: " No, this
(sleep) is the same as the place of waking, for what
he sees while awake, that only he sees when asleep[3]."

---

[1] The Mâdhyandinas read paurusha, as an adjective to ekahamsa,
but Dvivedaganga explains paurusha as a synonym of purusha,
which is the reading of the Kânvas.

[2] Cf. Susruta III, 7, 1.

[3] I have translated this according to the commentator, who says :
' Therefore the Self is self-illuminated during sleep. But others
say the state of waking is indeed the same for him as sleep ; there
is no other intermediate place, different from this and from the
other world. .... And if sleep is the same as the state of waking,
then is this Self not separate, not cause and effect, but mixed with
them, and the Self therefore not self-illuminated. What he means

No, here (in sleep) the person is self-illuminated (as we explained before).'

*G*anaka Vaideha said: 'I give you, Sir, a thousand. Speak on for the sake of (my) emancipation.'

15. Yâg*ñ*avalkya said: ' That (person) having enjoyed himself in that state of bliss (samprasâda, deep sleep), having moved about and seen both good and evil, hastens back again as he came, to the place from which he started (the place of sleep), to dream [1]. And whatever he may have seen there, he is not followed (affected) by it, for that person is not attached to anything.'

*G*anaka Vaideha said: ' So it is indeed, Yâg*ñ*a-

---

is that others, in order to disprove the self-illumination, say that this sleep is the same as the state of waking, giving as their reason that we see in sleep or in dreams exactly what we see in waking. But this is wrong, because the senses have stopped, and only when the senses have stopped does one see dreams. Therefore there is no necessity for admitting another light in sleep, but only the light inherent in the Self. This has been proved by all that went before.' Dr. Roer takes the same view in his translation, but Deussen (Vedânta, p. 205) takes an independent view, and translates: ' Therefore it is said: It (sleep) is to him a place of waking only, for what he sees waking, the same he sees in sleep. Thus this spirit serves there for his own light.' Though the interpretations of *S*ankara and Dvivedaganga sound artificial, still Dr. Deussen's version does not remove all difficulties. If the purusha saw in sleep no more than what he had seen before in waking, then the whole argument in favour of the independent action, or the independent light of the purusha, would go; anyhow it would be no argument on Yâg*ñ*avalkya's side. See also note to paragraph 9, before.

[1] The Mâdhyandinas speak only of his return from svapnânta to buddhânta, from sleep to waking, instead of his going from samprasâda (deep sleep) to svapnâ (dream), from svapnâ to buddhânta, and from buddhânta again to svapnânta, as the Kâ*n*vas have it. In § 18 the Kâ*n*vas also mention svapnânta and buddhânta only, but the next paragraph refers to sushupti.

valkya. I give you, Sir, a thousand. Speak on for
the sake of emancipation.'

16. Yâg*ñ*avalkya said: 'That (person) having enjoyed himself in that sleep (dream), having moved
about and seen both good and evil, hastens back
again as he came, to the place from which he started,
to be awake. And whatever he may have seen
there, he is not followed (affected) by it, for that
person is not attached to anything.'

*G*anaka Vaideha said: 'So it is indeed, Yâg*ñ*a-
valkya. I give you, Sir, a thousand. Speak on for
the sake of emancipation.'

17. Yâg*ñ*avalkya said: 'That (person) having enjoyed himself in that state of waking, having moved
about and seen both good and evil, hastens back
again as he came, to the place from which he started,
to the state of sleeping (dream).

18. 'In fact, as a large fish moves along the two
banks of a river, the right and the left, so does that
person move along these two states, the state of
sleeping and the state of waking.

19. 'And as a falcon, or any other (swift) bird,
after he has roamed about here in the air, becomes
tired, and folding his wings is carried to his nest, so
does that person hasten to that state where, when
asleep, he desires no more desires, and dreams no
more dreams.

20. 'There are in his body the veins called Hitâ,
which are as small as a hair divided a thousandfold,
full of white, blue, yellow, green, and red[1]. Now

---

[1] Dvivedaga*n*ga explains that if phlegm predominates, qualified
by wind and bile, the juice in the veins is white; if wind predominates, qualified by phlegm and bile, it is blue; if bile predominates,
qualified by wind and phlegm, it is yellow; if wind and phlegm

when, as it were, they kill him, when, as it were,
they overcome him, when, as it were, an elephant
chases him, when, as it were, he falls into a well,
he fancies, through ignorance, that danger which he
(commonly) sees in waking. But when he fancies
that he is, as it were, a god, or that he is, as it
were, a king[1], or " I am this altogether," that is his
highest world[2].

21. 'This indeed is his (true) form, free from
desires, free from evil, free from fear[3]. Now as a
man, when embraced by a beloved wife, knows
nothing that is without, nothing that is within, thus
this person, when embraced by the intelligent (prâ*gñ*a)
Self, knows nothing that is without, nothing that is
within. This indeed is his (true) form, in which
his wishes are fulfilled, in which the Self (only) is

---

predominate, with little bile only, it is green; and if the three elements are equal, it is red. See also Ânandagiri's gloss, where
Su*s*ruta is quoted. Why this should be inserted here, is not quite
clear, except that in sleep the purusha is supposed to move about
in the veins.

[1] Here, again, the commentator seems to be right, but his interpretation does violence to the context. The dangers which a man
sees in his sleep are represented as mere imaginations, so is his
idea of being of god or a king, while the idea that he is all this
(aham eveda*m* sarva*h*, i. e. ida*m* sarvam, see *S*ankara, p. 873, l. 11)
is represented as the highest and real state. But it is impossible to
begin a new sentence with aham eveda*m* sarvam, and though it is
true that all the preceding fancies are qualified by iva, I prefer to
take deva and râ*g*an as steps leading to the sarvâtmatva.

[2] The Mâdhyandinas repeat here the sentence from yatra supto
to pa*s*yati, from the end of § 19.

[3] The Kâ*n*va text reads ati*kkh*andâ apahatapâpmâ. *S*ankara
explains ati*kkh*andâ by ati*kkh*andam, and excuses it as svâdhyâya-
dharma*h* pâ*th*a*h*. The Mâdhyandinas read ati*kkh*ando, but place
the whole sentence where the Kâ*n*vas put âptakâmam &c., at the
end of § 21.

his wish, in which no wish is left,—free from any
sorrow[1].

22. 'Then a father is not a father, a mother not
a mother, the worlds not worlds, the gods not gods,
the Vedas not Vedas. Then a thief is not a thief, a
murderer not a murderer[2], a *Kând*âla[3] not a *Kând*âla,
a Paulkasa[4] not a Paulkasa, a *Sraman*a[5] not a *Sraman*a, a Tâpasa[6] not a Tâpasa. He is not followed
by good, not followed by evil, for he has then overcome all the sorrows of the heart[7].

23. 'And when (it is said that) there (in the
Sushupti) he does not see, yet he is seeing, though
he does not see[8]. For sight is inseparable from the

---

[1] The Kân*v*as read *s*okântaram, the Mâdhyandinas a*s*okântaram,
but the commentators arrive at the same result, namely, that it
means *s*oka*s*ûnyam, free from grief. *S*ankara says: *s*okântara*m*
*s*oka*kkh*idra*m* *s*oka*s*ûnyam ityeta*k*, *kh*okamadhyaman iti vâ; sar-
vathâpy a*s*okam. Dvivedaga*n*ga says: na vidyate *s*oko 'ntare
madhye yasya tad a*s*okântara*m* (ra, Weber) *s*oka*s*ûnyam.

[2] Bhrû*n*ahan, varish*th*abrahmahantâ.

[3] The son of a *S*ûdra father and a Brâhma*n*a mother.

[4] The son of a *S*ûdra father and a Kshatriya mother.

[5] A mendicant.

[6] A Vânaprastha, who performs penances.

[7] I have translated as if the text were ananvâgata*h* pu*n*yena
ananvâgata*h* pâpena. We find anvâgata used in a similar way in
§§ 15, 16, &c. But the Kân*v*as read ananvâgatam pu*n*yena ananvâgatam pâpena, and *S*ankara explains the neuter by referring it
to rûpam (rûpaparatvân napu*m*sakalingam). The Mâdhyandinas, if
we may trust Weber's edition, read ananvâgata*h* pu*n*yenânvâga-
ta*h* pâpena. The second anvâgata*h* may be a mere misprint, but
Dvivedaga*n*ga seems to have read ananvâgatam, like the Kân*v*as,
for he says: ananvâgatam iti rûpavishayo napu*m*sakanirde*s*a*h*.

[8] This is the old Upanishad argument that the true sense is the
Self, and not the eye. Although therefore in the state of profound
sleep, where the eye and the other senses rest, it might be said
that the purusha does not see, yet he is a seer all the time, though
he does not see with the eye. The seer cannot lose his character

seer, because it cannot perish. But there is then no second, nothing else different from him that he could see.

24. 'And when (it is said that) there (in the Sushupti) he does not smell, yet he is smelling, though he does not smell. For smelling is inseparable from the smeller, because it cannot perish. But there is then no second, nothing else different from him that he could smell.

25. 'And when (it is said that) there (in the Sushupti) he does not taste, yet he is tasting, though he does not taste. For tasting is inseparable from the taster, because it cannot perish. But there is then no second, nothing else different from him that he could taste.

26. 'And when (it is said that) there (in the Sushupti) he does not speak, yet he is speaking, though he does not speak. For speaking is inseparable from the speaker, because it cannot perish. But there is then no second, nothing else different from him that he could speak.

27. 'And when (it is said that) there (in the Sushupti) he does not hear, yet he is hearing, though he does not hear. For hearing is inseparable from the hearer, because it cannot perish. But there is then no second, nothing else different from him that he could hear.

28. 'And when (it is said that) there (in the Sushupti) he does not think, yet he is thinking, though he does not think. For thinking is inseparable from the thinker, because it cannot perish.

---

of seeing, as little as the fire can lose its character of burning, so long as it is fire. The Self sees by its own light, like the sun, even where there is no second, no object but the Self, that could be seen.

But there is then no second, nothing else different from him that he could think.

29. 'And when (it is said that) there (in the Sushupti) he does not touch, yet he is touching, though he does not touch. For touching is inseparable from the toucher, because it cannot perish. But there is then no second, nothing else different from him that he could think.

30. 'And when (it is said that) there (in the Sushupti) he does not know, yet he is knowing, though he does not know. For knowing is inseparable from the knower, because it cannot perish. But there is then no second, nothing else different from him that he could know.

31. 'When (in waking and dreaming) there is, as it were, another, then can one see the other, then can one smell the other, then can one speak to the other, then can one hear the other, then can one think the other, then can one touch the other, then can one know the other.

32. 'An ocean[1] is that one seer, without any duality; this is the Brahma-world[2], O King.' Thus did Yâ*gñ*avalkya teach him. This is his highest goal, this is his highest success, this is his highest world, this is his highest bliss. All other creatures live on a small portion of that bliss.

33. 'If a man is healthy, wealthy, and lord of others, surrounded by all human enjoyments, that

---

[1] Salila is explained as salilavat, like the ocean, the seer being one like the ocean, which is one only. Dr. Deussen takes salila as a locative, and translates it 'In dem Gewoge,' referring to *S*vetâ-*s*vatara-upanishad VI, 15.

[2] Or this seer is the Brahma-world, dwells in Brahman, or is Brahman.

is the highest blessing of men. Now a hundred of these human blessings make one blessing of the fathers who have conquered the world (of the fathers). A hundred blessings of the fathers who have conquered this world make one blessing in the Gandharva world. A hundred blessings in the Gandharva world make one blessing of the Devas by merit (work, sacrifice), who obtain their godhead by merit. A hundred blessings of the Devas by merit make one blessing of the Devas by birth, also (of) a *S*rotriya[1] who is without sin, and not overcome by desire. A hundred blessings of the Devas by birth make one blessing in the world of Pra*g*âpati, also (of) a *S*rotriya who is without sin, and not overcome by desire. A hundred blessings in the world of Pra*g*âpati make one blessing in the world of Brahman, also (of) a *S*rotriya who is without sin, and not overcome by desire. And this is the highest blessing[2].

'This is the Brahma-world, O king,' thus spake Yâ*gñ*avalkya.

*G*anaka Vaideha said: 'I give you, Sir, a thousand. Speak on for the sake of (my) emancipation.'

Then Yâ*gñ*avalkya was afraid lest the King, having become full of understanding, should drive him from all his positions[3].

34. And Yâ*gñ*avalkya said: 'That (person), having enjoyed himself in that state of sleeping (dream),

---

[1] An accomplished student of the Veda.

[2] See Taitt. Up. II, 8, p. 59; *Kh*ând. Up. VIII, 2, 1–10; Kaush. Up. I, 3–5; Regnaud, II, p. 33 seq.

[3] *S*ankara explains that Yâ*gñ*avalkya was not afraid that his own knowledge might prove imperfect, but that the king, having the right to ask him any question he liked, might get all his knowledge from him.

having moved about and seen both good and bad, hastens back again as he came, to the place from which he started, to the state of waking[1].

35. ' Now as a heavy-laden carriage moves along groaning, thus does this corporeal Self, mounted by the intelligent Self, move along groaning, when a man is thus going to expire[2].

36. 'And when (the body) grows weak through old age, or becomes weak through illness, at that time that person, after separating himself from his members, as an Amra (mango), or Udumbara (fig), or Pippala-fruit is separated from the stalk, hastens back again as he came, to the place from which he started, to (new) life.

37. 'And as policemen, magistrates, equerries, and governors wait for a king who is coming back, with food and drink, saying, " He comes back, he approaches," thus do all the elements wait on him who knows this, saying, " That Brahman comes, that Brahman approaches."

38. 'And as policemen, magistrates, equerries, and governors gather round a king who is departing, thus do all the senses (prân̄as) gather round the Self at the time of death, when a man is thus going to expire.'

Fourth Brâhman̄a.

1. Yâgñavalkya continued : ' Now when that Self, having sunk into weakness[3], sinks, as it were, into

---

[1] See § 17, before.

[2] Sankara seems to take ukkhvâsî as a noun. He writes: yatraitad bhavati ; etad iti kriyâviseshan̄am ûrdhvôkkhvâsî yatrordhvokkhvâsitvam asya bhavatîtyartha h.

[3] In the Kaush. Up. III, 3, we read yatraitat purusha ârto

unconsciousness, then gather those senses (prâ*n*as) around him, and he, taking with him those elements of light, descends into the heart. When that person in the eye ¹ turns away, then he ceases to know any forms.

2. '" He has become one," they say, " he does not see²." " He has become one," they say, "he does not smell." " He has become one," they say, " he does not taste." " He has become one," they say, "he does not speak." " He has become one," they say, " he does not hear." " He has become one," they say, "he does not think." " He has become one," they say, " he does not touch." " He has become one," they say, " he does not know." The point of his heart³ becomes lighted up, and by that light the Self departs, either through the eye⁴, or through the skull⁵, or through other places of the body. And when he thus departs, life (the chief prâ*n*a) departs after him, and when life thus departs, all the other

---

marishyan âbâlyam etya sammohati. Here âbâlyam should certainly be âbâlyam, as in the commentary; but should it not be äbälyam, as here. See also B*ri*h. Up. III, 5, 1, note.

¹ *K*âkshusha purusha is explained as that portion of the sun which is in the eye, while it is active, but which, at the time of death, returns to the sun.

² Ekîbhavati is probably a familiar expression for dying, but it is here explained by *S*ankara, and probably was so intended, as meaning that the organs of the body have become one with the Self (lingâtman). The same thoughts are found in the Kaush. Up. III, 3, prâ*n*a ekadhâ bhavati.

³ The point where the nâ*d*îs or veins go out from the heart.

⁴ When his knowledge and deeds qualify him to proceed to the sun. *S*ankara.

⁵ When his knowledge and deeds qualify him to proceed to the Brahma-world.

vital spirits (prâ*n*as) depart after it. He is conscious, and being conscious he follows [1] and departs.

'Then both his knowledge and his work take hold of him, and his acquaintance with former things [2].'

3. 'And as a caterpillar, after having reached the end of a blade of grass, and after having made another approach (to another blade) [3], draws itself together towards it, thus does this Self, after having thrown off this body [4] and dispelled all ignorance, and after making another approach (to another body), draw himself together towards it.

4. 'And as a goldsmith, taking a piece of gold, turns it into another, newer and more beautiful shape, so does this Self, after having thrown off this body

---

[1] This is an obscure passage, and the different text of the Mâdhyandinas shows that the obscurity was felt at an early time. The Mâdhyandinas read: Sa*m*g*ñ*ânam anvavakrâmati sa esha g*ñ*a*h* savig*ñ*âno bhavati. This would mean, 'Consciousness departs after. He the knowing (Self) is self-conscious.' The Kâ*n*vas read: Savig*ñ*âno bhavati, savig*ñ*ânam evânvavakrâmati. Roer translates: 'It is endowed with knowledge, endowed with knowledge it departs;' and he explains, with *S*ankara, that the knowledge here intended is such knowledge as one has in a dream, a knowledge of impressions referring to their respective objects, a knowledge which is the effect of actions, and not inherent in the self. Deussen translates: 'Sie (die Seele) ist von Erkenntnissart, und was von Erkenntnissart ist, ziehet ihr nach.' The Persian translator evidently thought that self-consciousness was implied, for he writes: 'Cum quovis corpore addictionem sumat . . . . in illo corpore aham est, id est, ego sum.'

[2] This acquaintance with former things is necessary to explain the peculiar talents or deficiencies which we observe in children. The three words vidyâ, karman, and pûrvapra*g*ñâ often go together (see *S*ankara on Br*i*h. Up. IV, 3, 9). Deussen's conjecture, apûrvapra*g*ñâ, is not called for.

[3] See Br*i*h. Up. IV, 3, 9, a passage which shows how difficult it would be always to translate the same Sanskrit words by the same words in English; see also Brahmopanishad, p. 245.

[4] See Br*i*h. Up. IV, 3, 9, and IV, 3, 13.

and dispelled all ignorance, make unto himself another, newer and more beautiful shape, whether it be like the Fathers, or like the Gandharvas, or like the Devas, or like Praĝâpati, or like Brahman, or like other beings.

5. 'That Self is indeed Brahman, consisting of knowledge, mind, life, sight, hearing, earth, water, wind, ether, light and no light, desire and no desire, anger and no anger, right or wrong, and all things. Now as a man is like this or like that[1], according as he acts and according as he behaves, so will he be :— a man of good acts will become good, a man of bad acts, bad. He becomes pure by pure deeds, bad by bad deeds.

'And here they say that a person consists of desires. And as is his desire, so is his will; and as is his will, so is his deed; and whatever deed he does, that he will reap.

6. 'And here there is this verse: "To whatever object a man's own mind is attached, to that he goes strenuously together with his deed; and having obtained the end (the last results) of whatever deed he does here on earth, he returns again from that world (which is the temporary reward of his deed) to this world of action."

'So much for the man who desires. But as to the man who does not desire, who, not desiring, freed from desires, is satisfied in his desires, or desires the Self only, his vital spirits do not depart elsewhere,—being Brahman, he goes to Brahman.

7. 'On this there is this verse : "When all desires

---

[1] The iti after adomaya is not clear to me, but it is quite clear that a new sentence begins with tadyadetat, which Regnaud, II, p. 101 and p. 139, has not observed.

which once entered his heart are undone, then does the mortal become immortal, then he obtains Brahman."

'And as the slough of a snake lies on an ant-hill, dead and cast away, thus lies this body; but that disembodied immortal spirit (prâna, life) is Brahman only, is only light.'

Ganaka Vaideha said: 'Sir, I give you a thousand.'

8[1]. 'On this there are these verses :

'The small, old path stretching far away[2] has been found by me. On it sages who know Brahman move on to the Svarga-loka (heaven), and thence higher on, as entirely free[3].

9. 'On that path they say that there is white, or blue, or yellow, or green, or red[4]; that path was found by Brahman, and on it goes whoever knows Brahman, and who has done good, and obtained splendour.

10. 'All who worship what is not knowledge (avidyâ) enter into blind darkness: those who delight in knowledge, enter, as it were, into greater darkness[5].

11. 'There are[6] indeed those unblessed worlds,

---

[1] This may be independent matter, or may be placed again into the mouth of Yâgñavalkya.

[2] Instead of vitatah, which perhaps seemed to be in contradiction with anu, there is a Mâdhyandina reading vitara, probably intended originally to mean leading across. The other adjective mâm̐-sprishta I cannot explain. Sankara explains it by mâm sprishtah, mayâ labdhah.

[3] That this is the true meaning, is indicated by the various readings of the Mâdhyandinas, tena dhîrâ apiyanti brahmavida utkramya svargam lokam ito vimuktâh. The road is not to lead to Svarga only, but beyond.

[4] See the colours of the veins as given before, IV, 3, 20.

[5] See Vâg. Up. 9. Sankara in our place explains avidyâ by works, and vidyâ by the Veda, excepting the Upanishads.

[6] See Vâg. Up. 3 ; Katha Up. I, 3.

covered with blind darkness.   Men who are ignorant
and not enlightened go after death to those worlds.

12. 'If a man understands the Self, saying, "I am
He," what could he wish or desire that he should
pine after the body[1].

13. 'Whoever has found and understood the Self
that has entered into this patched-together hiding-
place[2], he indeed is the creator, for he is the maker
of everything, his is the world, and he is the world
itself[3].

14. 'While we are here, we may know this; if not,
I am ignorant[4], and there is great destruction. Those
who know it, become immortal, but others suffer pain
indeed.

15. 'If a man clearly beholds this Self as God,
and as the lord of all that is and will be, then he is
no more afraid.

16. 'He behind whom the year revolves with the
days, him the gods worship as the light of lights, as
immortal time.

17. 'He in whom the five beings[5] and the ether
rest, him alone I believe to be the Self,—I who

---

[1] That he should be willing to suffer once more the pains
inherent in the body.   The Mâdhyandinas read *s*arîram anu
sa*m*karet, instead of sa*ñ*gvaret.

[2] The body is meant, and is called deha from the root dih, to
knead together.   Roer gives sa*m*dehye gahane, which *S*ankara
explains by sa*m*dehe.   Poley has sa*m*deghe, which is the right
Kâ*n*va reading.   The Mâdhyandinas read sa*m*dehe. Gahane might
be taken as an adjective also, referring to sa*m*dehe.

[3] *S*ankara takes loka, world, for âtmâ, self.

[4] I have followed *S*ankara in translating avedi*h* by ignorant, but
the text seems corrupt.

[5] The five *g*anas, i. e. the Gandharvas, Pit*ri*s, Devas, Asuras, and
Rakshas; or the four castes with the Nishâdas; or breath, eye,
ear, food, and mind.

know, believe him to be Brahman; I who am immortal, believe him to be immortal.

18. 'They who know the life of life, the eye of the
eye, the ear of the ear, the mind of the mind, they
have comprehended the ancient, primeval Brahman[1].

19. 'By the mind alone it is to be perceived[2],
there is in it no diversity. He who perceives therein
any diversity, goes from death to death.

20. 'This eternal being that can never be proved,
is to be perceived in one way only; it is spotless,
beyond the ether, the unborn Self, great and eternal.

21. 'Let a wise Brâhmana, after he has discovered
him, practise wisdom[3]. Let him not seek after many
words, for that is mere weariness of the tongue.

22. 'And he is that great unborn Self, who consists
of knowledge, is surrounded by the Prânas, the ether
within the heart[4]. In it there reposes the ruler of all,
the lord of all, the king of all. He does not become
greater by good works, nor smaller by evil works.
He is the lord of all, the king of all things, the protector of all things. He is a bank[5] and a boundary,
so that these worlds may not be confounded. Brâhmanas seek to know him by the study of the Veda, by
sacrifice, by gifts, by penance, by fasting, and he who
knows him, becomes a Muni. Wishing for that
world (for Brahman) only, mendicants leave their
homes.

'Knowing this, the people of old did not wish for
offspring. What shall we do with offspring, they said,

---

[1] See Talavak. Up. I, 2.

[2] See Katha Up. IV, 10–11.

[3] Let him practise abstinence, patience, &c., which are the means
of knowledge.

[4] See Brih. Up. IV, 3, 7.   [5] See Khând. Up. VIII, 4.

we who have this Self and this world (of Brahman)[1]? And they, having risen above the desire for sons, wealth, and new worlds, wander about as mendicants. For desire for sons is desire for wealth, and desire for wealth is desire for worlds. Both these are indeed desires only. He, the Self, is to be described by No, no[2]! He is incomprehensible, for he cannot be comprehended; he is imperishable, for he cannot perish; he is unattached, for he does not attach himself; unfettered, he does not suffer, he does not fail. Him (who knows), these two do not overcome, whether he says that for some reason he has done evil, or for some reason he has done good—he overcomes both, and neither what he has done, nor what he has omitted to do, burns (affects) him.

23. ' This has been told by a verse (*Rik*): " This eternal greatness of the Brâhma*n*a does not grow larger by work, nor does it grow smaller. Let man try to find (know) its trace, for having found (known) it, he is not sullied by any evil deed."

' He therefore that knows it, after having become quiet, subdued, satisfied, patient, and collected[3], sees self in Self, sees all as Self. Evil does not overcome him, he overcomes all evil. Evil does not burn him, he burns all evil. Free from evil, free from spots, free from doubt, he becomes a (true) Brâhma*n*a; this is the Brahma-world, O King,'—thus spoke Yâg*ñ*a-valkya.

*G*anaka Vaideha said : ' Sir, I give you the Videhas, and also myself, to be together your slaves.'

24. This[4] indeed is the great, the unborn Self, the

---

[1] Cf. Br*i*h. Up. III, 5, 1.   [2] See Br*i*h. Up. III, 9, 26 ; IV, 2, 4.
[3] See Deussen, Vedânta, p. 85.
[4] As described in the dialogue between *G*anaka and Yâg*ñ*avalkya.

strong[1], the giver of wealth. He who knows this obtains wealth.

25. This great, unborn Self, undecaying, undying, immortal, fearless, is indeed Brahman. Fearless is Brahman, and he who knows this becomes verily the fearless Brahman.

FIFTH BRÂHMAÑA [2].

1. Yâgñavalkya had two wives, Maitreyî and Kâtyâyanî. Of these Maitreyî was conversant with Brahman, but Kâtyâyanî possessed such knowledge only as women possess. And Yâgñavalkya, when he wished to get ready for another state of life (when he wished to give up the state of a householder, and retire into the forest),

2. Said, 'Maitreyî, verily I am going away from this my house (into the forest). Forsooth, let me make a settlement between thee and that Kâtyâyanî.'

3. Maitreyî said: ' My Lord, if this whole earth, full of wealth, belonged to me, tell me, should I be immortal by it, or no ?'

' No,' replied Yâgñavalkya, ' like the life of rich people will be thy life. But there is no hope of immortality by wealth.'

4. And Maitreyî said: ' What should I do with that by which I do not become immortal? What my Lord knoweth [3] (of immortality), tell that clearly to me.'

5. Yâgñavalkya replied: ' Thou who art truly dear to me, thou hast increased what is dear (to me in

---

[1] Annâda is here explained as ' dwelling in all beings, and eating all food which they eat.'

[2] See before, II, 4.

[3] The Kâñva text has vettha instead of veda.

thee)[1]. Therefore, if you like, Lady, I will explain it to thee, and mark well what I say.'

6. And he said : 'Verily, a husband is not dear, that you may love the husband ; but that you may love the Self, therefore a husband is dear.

'Verily, a wife is not dear, that you may love the wife ; but that you may love the Self, therefore a wife is dear.

'Verily, sons are not dear, that you may love the sons ; but that you may love the Self, therefore sons are dear.

'Verily, wealth is not dear, that you may love wealth ; but that you may love the Self, therefore wealth is dear.

'Verily, cattle [2] are not dear, that you may love cattle ; but that you may love the Self, therefore cattle are dear.

'Verily, the Brahman-class is not dear, that you may love the Brahman-class ; but that you may love the Self, therefore the Brahman-class is dear.

'Verily, the Kshatra-class is not dear, that you may love the Kshatra-class ; but that you may love the Self, therefore the Kshatra-class is dear.

'Verily, the worlds are not dear, that you may love the worlds ; but that you may love the Self, therefore the worlds are dear.

'Verily, the Devas are not dear, that you may love the Devas ; but that you may love the Self, therefore the Devas are dear.

---

[1] The Kânva text has avridhat, which Sankara explains by vardhitavatî nirdhâritavaty asi. The Mâdhyandinas read avritat, which the commentator explains by avartayat, vartitavaty asi.

[2] Though this is added here, it is not included in the summing up in § 6.

'Verily, the Vedas are not dear, that you may love the Vedas; but that you may love the Self, therefore the Vedas are dear.

'Verily, creatures are not dear, that you may love the creatures; but that you may love the Self, therefore are creatures dear.

'Verily, everything is not dear, that you may love everything; but that you may love the Self, therefore everything is dear.

'Verily, the Self is to be seen, to be heard, to be perceived, to be marked, O Maitreyî! When the Self has been seen, heard, perceived, and known, then all this is known.'

7. 'Whosoever looks for the Brahman-class elsewhere than in the Self, was abandoned by the Brahman-class. Whosoever looks for the Kshatra-class elsewhere than in the Self, was abandoned by the Kshatra-class. Whosoever looks for the worlds elsewhere than in the Self, was abandoned by the worlds. Whosoever looks for the Devas elsewhere than in the Self, was abandoned by the Devas. Whosoever looks for the Vedas elsewhere than in the Self, was abandoned by the Vedas. Whosoever looks for the creatures elsewhere than in the Self, was abandoned by the creatures. Whosoever looks for anything elsewhere than in the Self, was abandoned by anything.

'This Brahman-class, this Kshatra-class, these worlds, these Devas, these Vedas, all these beings, this everything, all is that Self.

8. 'Now as the sounds of a drum, when beaten, cannot be seized externally (by themselves), but the sound is seized, when the drum is seized, or the beater of the drum;

9. 'And as the sounds of a conch-shell, when blown, cannot be seized externally (by themselves), but the sound is seized, when the shell is seized, or the blower of the shell;

10. 'And as the sounds of a lute, when played, cannot be seized externally (by themselves), but the sound is seized, when the lute is seized, or the player of the lute;

11. 'As clouds of smoke proceed by themselves out of lighted fire kindled with damp fuel, thus verily, O Maitreyî, has been breathed forth from this great Being what we have as *Ri*g-veda, Ya*g*ur-veda, Sâma-veda, Atharvâṅgirasas, Itihâsa, Purâ*n*a, Vidyâ, the Upanishads, *S*lokas, Sûtras, Anuvyâ-khyânas, Vyâkhyânas, what is sacrificed, what is poured out, food, drink[1], this world and the other world, and all creatures. From him alone all these were breathed forth.

12. 'As all waters find their centre in the sea, all touches in the skin, all tastes in the tongue, all smells in the nose, all colours in the eye, all sounds in the ear, all percepts in the mind, all knowledge in the heart, all actions in the hands, all movements in the feet, and all the Vedas in speech,—

13. 'As a mass of salt has neither inside nor outside, but is altogether a mass of taste, thus indeed has that Self neither inside nor outside, but is altogether a mass of knowledge; and having risen from out these elements, vanishes again in them. When he has departed, there is no more knowledge (name), I say, O Maitreyî,'—thus spoke Yâ*gñ*avalkya.

---

[1] Explained by annadânanimittam and peyadânanimitta*m* dharma*g*âtam. See before, IV, 1, 2.

14. Then Maitreyî said: 'Here, Sir, thou hast landed me in utter bewilderment. Indeed, I do not understand him.'

But he replied: 'O Maitreyî, I say nothing that is bewildering. Verily, beloved, that Self is imperishable, and of an indestructible nature.

15. 'For when there is as it were duality, then one sees the other, one smells the other, one tastes the other, one salutes the other, one hears the other, one perceives the other, one touches the other, one knows the other; but when the Self only is all this, how should he see another, how should he smell another, how should he taste another, how should he salute another, how should he hear another, how should he touch another, how should he know another? How should he know Him by whom he knows all this? That Self is to be described by No, no[1]! He is incomprehensible, for he cannot be comprehended; he is imperishable, for he cannot perish; he is unattached, for he does not attach himself; unfettered, he does not suffer, he does not fail. How, O beloved, should he know the Knower? Thus, O Maitreyî, thou hast been instructed. Thus far goes immortality.' Having said so, Yâgñavalkya went away (into the forest).

SIXTH BRÂHMAÑA.

1. Now follows the stem [2]:
    1. (We) from Pautimâshya,
    2. Pautimâshya from Gaupavana,
    3. Gaupavana from Pautimâshya,

---

[1] See Br*i*h. Up. III, 9, 26; IV, 2, 4; IV, 4, 22.

[2] The line of teachers and pupils by whom the Yâgñavalkya-

4. Pautimâshya from Gaupavana,
5. Gaupavana from Kau*s*ika,
6. Kau*s*ika from Kau*nd*inya,
7. Kau*nd*inya from *S*ân*d*ilya,
8. *S*ân*d*ilya from Kau*s*ika and Gautama,
9. Gautama
2. from Âgnive*s*ya,
10. Âgnive*s*ya from Gârgya,
11. Gârgya from Gârgya,
12. Gârgya from Gautama,
13. Gautama from Saitava,
14. Saitava from Pârâ*s*aryâya*n*a,
15. Pârâ*s*aryâya*n*a from Gârgyâya*n*a,
16. Gârgyâya*n*a from Uddâlakâyana,
17. Uddâlakâyana from *G*âbâlâyana,
18. *G*âbâlâyana from Mâdhyandinâyana,
19. Mâdhyandinâyana from Saukarâya*n*a,
20. Saukarâya*n*a from Kâshâya*n*a,
21. Kâshâya*n*a from Sâyakâyana,
22. Sâyakâyana from Kau*s*ikâyani [1],
23. Kau*s*ikâyani
3. from Gh*ri*takau*s*ika,
24. Gh*ri*takau*s*ika from Pârâ*s*aryâya*n*a,

---

kâ*nd*a was handed down. From 1–10 the Va*m*sa agrees with the Va*m*sa at the end of II, 6.

The Mâdhyandina text begins with vayam, we, and proceeds to 1. *S*aurpanâyya, 2. Gautama, 3. Vâtsya, 4. Pârâ*s*arya, &c., as in the Madhukâ*nd*a, p. 118, except in 10, where it gives *G*aivantâyana for Âtreya. Then after 12. Kau*nd*inyâyana, it gives 13. 14. the two Kau*nd*inyas, 15. the Aur*n*avâbhas, 16. Kau*nd*inya, 17. Kau*nd*inya, 18. Kau*nd*inya and Âgnive*s*ya, 19. Saitava, 20. Pârâ*s*arya, 21. *G*âtukar*n*ya, 22. Bhâradvâ*g*a, 23. Bhâradvâ*g*a, Âsurâya*n*a, and Gautama, 24. Bhâradvâ*g*a, 25. Valâkâkau*s*ika, 26. Kâshâya*n*a, 27. Saukarâya*n*a, 28. Traiva*n*i, 29. Aupa*g*andhani, 30. Sâyakâyana, 31. Kau*s*ikâyani, &c., as in the Kâ*n*va text, from No. 22 to Brahman.

[1] From here the Va*m*sa agrees again with that given at the end of II, 6.

25. Pârâsaryâyana from Pârâsarya,
26. Pârâsarya from Gâtukarnya,
27. Gâtukarnya from Âsurâyana and Yâska[1],
28. Âsurâyana from Travani,
29. Travani from Aupagandhani,
30. Aupagandhani from Âsuri,
31. Âsuri from Bhâradvâga,
32. Bhâradvâga from Âtreya,
33. Âtreya from Mânti,
34. Mânti from Gautama,
35. Gautama from Gautama,
36. Gautama from Vâtsya,
37. Vâtsya from Sândilya,
38. Sândilya from Kaisorya Kâpya,
39. Kaisorya Kâpya from Kumârahârita,
40. Kumârahârita from Gâlava,
41. Gâlava from Vidarbhî-kaundinya,
42. Vidarbhî-kaundinya from Vatsanapât Bâbhrava,
43. Vatsanapât Bâbhrava from Pathi Saubhara,
44. Pathi Saubhara from Ayâsya Ângirasa,
45. Ayâsya Ângirasa from Âbhûti Tvâshtra,
46. Âbhûti Tvâshtra from Visvarûpa Tvâshtra,
47. Visvarûpa Tvâshtra from Asvinau,
48. Asvinau from Dadhyak Âtharvana,
49. Dadhyak Âtharvana from Atharvan Daiva,
50. Atharvan Daiva from Mrityu Prâdhvamsana,
51. Mrityu Prâdhvamsana from Pradhvamsana,
52. Pradhvamsana from Ekarshi,
53. Ekarshi from Viprakitti[2],
54. Viprakitti from Vyashti,

---

[1] The Mâdhyandina text has, 1. Bhâradvâga, 2. Bhâradvâga, Âsurâyana, and Yâska.

[2] Vipragitti, Mâdhyandina text.

55. Vyash*ti* from Sanâru,
56. Sanâru from Sanâtana,
57. Sanâtana from Sanaga,
58. Sanaga from Paramesh*th*in,
59. Paramesh*th*in from Brahman,
60. Brahman is Svayambhu, self-existent.
Adoration to Brahman.

FIFTH ADHYÂYA.

FIRST BRÂHMANA[1].

1. That (the invisible Brahman) is full, this (the visible Brahman) is full[2]. This full (visible Brahman) proceeds from that full (invisible Brahman). On grasping the fulness of this full (visible Brahman) there is left that full (invisible Brahman)[3].

Om (is) ether, (is) Brahman[4]. 'There is the old ether (the invisible), and the (visible) ether of the atmosphere,' thus said Kauravyâyanîputra. This (the Om) is the Veda (the means of knowledge), thus the Brâhmanas know. One knows through it all that has to be known.

SECOND BRÂHMANA.

1. The threefold descendants of Pragâpati, gods, men, and Asuras (evil spirits), dwelt as Brahmakârins (students) with their father Pragâpati. Having finished their studentship the gods said: 'Tell us (something), Sir.' He told them the syllable Da. Then he said: 'Did you understand?' They said: 'We did understand. You told us "Dâmyata," Be subdued.' 'Yes,' he said, 'you have understood.'

2. Then the men said to him : 'Tell us something,

---

[1] This is called a Khila, or supplementary chapter, treating of various auxiliary means of arriving at a knowledge of Brahman.

[2] Full and filling, infinite.

[3] On perceiving the true nature of the visible world, there remains, i.e. there is perceived at once, as underlying it, or as being it, the invisible world or Brahman. This and the following paragraph are called Mantras.

[4] This is explained by Sankara as meaning, Brahman is Kha, the ether, and called Om, i.e. Om and Kha are predicates of Brahman.

Sir.' He told them the same syllable Da. Then he
said : 'Did you understand ?' They said : 'We did
understand. You told us, " Datta," Give.' 'Yes,' he
said, 'you have understood.'

3. Then the Asuras said to him : ' Tell us something, Sir.' He told them the same syllable Da.
Then he said : ' Did you understand ?' They said :
'We did understand. You told us, "Dayadham," Be
merciful.' 'Yes,' he said, 'you have understood.'

The divine voice of thunder repeats the same,
Da Da Da, that is, Be subdued, Give, Be merciful.
Therefore let that triad be taught, Subduing, Giving,
and Mercy.

THIRD BRÂHMA*N*A.

1. Pra*g*âpati is the heart, is this Brahman, is all this.
The heart, h*ri*daya, consists of three syllables. One
syllable is h*ri*, and to him who knows this, his own
people and others bring offerings [1]. One syllable is
da, and to him who knows this, his own people and
others bring gifts. One syllable is yam, and he who
knows this, goes to heaven (svarga) as his world.

FOURTH BRÂHMA*N*A.

1. This (heart) indeed is even that, it was indeed
the true [2] (Brahman). And whosoever knows this
great glorious first-born as the true Brahman, he
conquers these worlds, and conquered likewise may
that (enemy) be [3] ! yes, whosoever knows this great

---

[1] *S*ankara explains that with regard to the heart, i.e. buddhi, the
senses are 'its own people,' and the objects of the senses 'the others.'

[2] The true, not the truth ; the truly existing. The commentator
explains it as it was explained in II, 3, 1, as sat and tya, containing
both sides of the Brahman.

[3] An elliptical expression, as explained by the commentator :
' May that one (his enemy) be conquered, just as that one was

glorious first-born as the true Brahman; for Brahman is the true.

FIFTH BRÂHMANA.

1. In the beginning this (world) was water. Water produced the true[1], and the true is Brahman. Brahman produced Pragâpati[2], Pragâpati the Devas (gods). The Devas adore the true (satyam) alone. This satyam consists of three syllables. One syllable is sa, another t(i), the third[3] yam. The first and last syllables are true, in the middle there is the untrue[4]. This untrue is on both sides enclosed by the true, and thus the true preponderates. The untrue does not hurt him who knows this.

2. Now what is the true, that is the Âditya (the sun), the person that dwells in yonder orb, and the person in the right eye. These two rest on each other, the former resting with his rays in the latter, the latter with his prânas (senses) in the former. When the latter is on the point of departing this life, he sees that orb as white only, and those rays (of the sun) do not return to him.

---

conquered by Brahman. If he conquers the world, how much more his enemy!' It would be better, however, if we could take gita in the sense of vasîkrita or dânta, because we could then go on with ya evam veda.

[1] Here explained by the commentator as Pûtrâtmaka Hiranyagarbha.

[2] Here explained as Virâg.

[3] Satyam is often pronounced satiam, as trisyllabic. Sankara, however, takes the second syllable as t only, and explains the i after it as an anubandha. The Kânva text gives the three syllables as sa, ti, am, which seems preferable; cf. Khând. Up. VIII, 3, 5; Taitt. Up. II, 6.

[4] This is explained by a mere play on the letters, sa and ya having nothing in common with mrityu, death, whereas t occurs in mrityu and anrita. Dvivedaganga takes sa and am as true, because they occur in satya and amrita, and not in mrityu, while ti is untrue, because the t occurs in mrityu and anrita.

3. Now of the person in that (solar) orb Bhû*h* is the head, for the head is one, and that syllable is one; Bhuva*h* the two arms, for the arms are two, and these syllables are two; Svar the foot, for the feet are two, and these syllables are two[1]. Its secret name is Ahar (day), and he who knows this, destroys (hanti) evil and leaves (*g*ahâti) it.

4. Of the person in the right eye Bhû*h* is the head, for the head is one, and that syllable is one; Bhuva*h* the two arms, for the arms are two, and these syllables are two; Svar the foot, for the feet are two, and these syllables are two. Its secret name is Aham (ego), and he who knows this, destroys (hanti) evil and leaves (*g*ahâti) it.

Sixth Brâhma*n*a.

1. That person, under the form of mind (manas), being light indeed[2], is within the heart, small like a grain of rice or barley. He is the ruler of all, the lord of all—he rules all this, whatsoever exists.

Seventh Brâhma*n*a.

1. They say that lightning is Brahman, because lightning (vidyut) is called so from cutting off (vidânât)[3]. Whosoever knows this, that lightning is Brahman, him (that Brahman) cuts off from evil, for lightning indeed is Brahman.

---

[1] Svar has to be pronounced suvar.

[2] Bhâ*h*satya must be taken as one word, as the commentator says, bhâ eva satya*m* sadbhâva*h* svarûpa*m* yasya so 'yam bhâ*h*satyo bhâsvara*h*.

[3] From do, avakha*nd*ane, to cut; the lightning cutting through the darkness of the clouds, as Brahman, when known, cuts through the darkness of ignorance.

EIGHTH BRÂHMANA.

1. Let him meditate on speech as a cow. Her four udders are the words Svâhâ, Vashat, Hanta, and Svadhâ [1]. The gods live on two of her udders, the Svâhâ and the Vashat, men on the Hanta, the fathers on the Svadhâ. The bull of that cow is breath (prâna), the calf the mind.

NINTH BRÂHMANA.

1. Agni Vaisvânara is the fire within man by which the food that is eaten is cooked, i.e. digested. Its noise is that which one hears, if one covers one's ears. When he is on the point of departing this life, he does not hear that noise.

TENTH BRÂHMANA.

1. When the person goes away from this world, he comes to the wind. Then the wind makes room for him, like the hole of a carriage wheel, and through it he mounts higher. He comes to the sun. Then the sun makes room for him, like the hole of a Lambara [2], and through it he mounts higher. He comes to the moon. Then the moon makes room for him, like the hole of a drum, and through it he mounts higher, and arrives at the world where there is no sorrow, no snow [3]. There he dwells eternal years.

---

[1] There are two udders, the Svâhâ and Vashat, on which the gods feed, i. e. words with which oblations are given to the gods. With Hanta they are given to men, with Svadhâ to the fathers.

[2] A musical instrument.

[3] The commentator explains hima by bodily pain, but snow is much more characteristic.

ELEVENTH BRÂHMANA.

1. This is indeed the highest penance, if a man, laid up with sickness, suffers pain[1]. He who knows this, conquers the highest world.

This is indeed the highest penance, if they carry a dead person into the forest[2]. He who knows this, conquers the highest world.

This is indeed the highest penance, if they place a dead person on the fire[3]. He who knows this, conquers the highest world.

TWELFTH BRÂHMANA.

1. Some say that food is Brahman, but this is not so, for food decays without life (prâna). Others say that life (prâna) is Brahman, but this is not so, for life dries up without food. Then these two deities (food and life), when they have become one, reach that highest state (i.e. are Brahman). Thereupon Prâtrida said to his father: 'Shall I be able to do any good to one who knows this, or shall I be able to do him any harm[4]?' The father said to him, beckoning with his hand: 'Not so, O Prâtrida; for who could reach the highest state, if he has only got to the oneness of these two?' He then said to him: 'Vi;

---

[1] The meaning is that, while he is suffering pain from illness, he should think that he was performing penance. If he does that, he obtains the same reward for his sickness which he would have obtained for similar pain inflicted on himself for the sake of performing penance.

[2] This is like the penance of leaving the village and living in the forest.

[3] This is like the penance of entering into the fire.

[4] That is, is he not so perfect in knowledge that nothing can harm him?

verily, food is Vi, for all these beings rest (vish/âni)
on food.' He then said : ' Ram ; verily, life is Ram,
for all these beings delight (ramante) in life. All
beings rest on him, all beings delight in him who
knows this.'

THIRTEENTH BRÂHMAÑA.

1. Next follows the Uktha [1]. Verily, breath (prâña)
is Uktha, for breath raises up (utthâpayati) all this.
From him who knows this, there is raised a wise son,
knowing the Uktha; he obtains union and oneness
with the Uktha.

2. Next follows the Yagus. Verily, breath is
Yagus, for all these beings are joined in breath [2].
For him who knows this, all beings are joined to
procure his excellence; he obtains union and oneness with the Yagus.

3. Next follows the Sâman. Verily, breath is the
Sâman, for all these beings meet in breath. For him
who knows this, all beings meet to procure his excellence; he obtains union and oneness with the Sâman.

4. Next follows the Kshatra. Verily, breath is
the Kshatra, for breath is Kshatra, i.e. breath protects (trâyate) him from being hurt (kshañitoh).
He who knows this, obtains Kshatra (power), which
requires no protection; he obtains union and oneness with Kshatra [3].

---

[1] Meditation on the hymn called uktha. On the uktha, as the
principal part in the Mahâvrata, see Kaush. Up. III, 3; Ait. Âr. II, 1, 2.
The uktha, yagus, sâman, &c. are here represented as forms under
which prâña or life, and indirectly Brahman, is to be meditated on.

[2] Without life or breath nothing can join anything else; therefore life is called yagus, as it were yugus.

[3] Instead of Kshatram atram, another Sâkhâ, i. e. the Mâdhyandina, reads Kshatramâtram, which Dvivedaganga explains as, he

Fourteenth Brâhma*n*a.

1. The words Bhûmi (earth), Antariksha (sky), and Dyu[1] (heaven) form eight syllables. One foot of the Gâyatrî consists of eight syllables. This (one foot) of it is that (i. e. the three worlds). And he who thus knows that foot of it, conquers as far as the three worlds extend.

2. The *Ri*kas, the Ya*g*û*m*shi, and the Sâmâni form eight syllables. One foot (the second) of the Gâyatrî consists of eight syllables. This (one foot) of it is that (i. e. the three Vedas, the *Ri*g-veda, Ya*g*ur-veda, and Sâma-veda). And he who thus knows that foot of it, conquers as far as that threefold knowledge extends.

3. The Prâ*n*a (the up-breathing), the Apâna (the down-breathing), and the Vyâna (the back-breathing) form eight syllables. One foot (the third) of the Gâyatrî consists of eight syllables. This (one foot) of it is that (i. e. the three vital breaths). And he who thus knows that foot of it, conquers as far as there is anything that breathes. And of that (Gâyatrî, or speech) this indeed is the fourth (turîya), the bright (dar*s*ata) foot, shining high above the skies[2]. What is here called turîya (the fourth) is meant for *k*aturtha (the fourth); what is called dar*s*atam padam (the bright foot) is meant for him who is as it were seen (the person in the sun); and what is called paroraga*s* (he who shines high above the

obtains the nature of the Kshatra, or he obtains the Kshatra which protects (Kshatram âtram).

[1] Dyu, nom. Dyaus, must be pronounced Diyaus.

[2] Paroraga*s*, masc., should be taken as one word, like paroksha, viz. he who is beyond all ra*g*as, all visible skies.

skies) is meant for him who shines higher and higher above every sky. And he who thus knows that foot of the Gâyatrî, shines thus himself also with happiness and glory.

4. That Gâyatrî (as described before with its three feet) rests on that fourth foot, the bright one, high above the sky. And that again rests on the True (satyam), and the True is the eye, for the eye is (known to be) true. And therefore even now, if two persons come disputing, the one saying, I saw, the other, I heard, then we should trust the one who says, I saw. And the True again rests on force (balam), and force is life (prâña), and that (the True) rests on life[1]. Therefore they say, force is stronger than the True. Thus does that Gâyatrî rest with respect to the self (as life). That Gâyatrî protects (tatre) the vital breaths (gayas); the gayas are the prâñas (vital breaths), and it protects them. And because it protects (tatre) the vital breaths (gayas), therefore it is called Gâyatrî. And that Sâvitrî verse which the teacher teaches[2], that is it (the life, the prâña, and indirectly the Gâyatrî); and whomsoever he teaches, he protects his vital breaths.

5. Some teach that Sâvitrî as an Anush*t*ubh[3] verse, saying that speech is Anush*t*ubh, and that we teach

---

[1] *S*ankara understood the True (satyam) by tad, not the balam, the force.

[2] The teacher teaches his pupil, who is brought to him when eight years old, the Sâvitrî verse, making him repeat each word, and each half verse, till he knows the whole, and by teaching him that Sâvitrî, he is supposed to teach him really the prâña, the life, as the self of the world.

[3] The verse would be, Rig-veda V, 82, 1:

Tat savitur vri*n*îmahe vaya*m* devasya bho*g*anam
*S*resh*th*am sarvadhâtama*m* turam bhagasya dhîmahi.

that speech. Let no one do this, but let him teach the Gâyatrî as Sâvitrî[1]. And even if one who knows this receives what seems to be much as his reward (as a teacher), yet this is not equal to one foot of the Gâyatrî.

6. If a man (a teacher) were to receive as his fee these three worlds full of all things, he would obtain that first foot of the Gâyatrî. And if a man were to receive as his fee everything as far as this threefold knowledge extends, he would obtain that second foot of the Gâyatrî. And if a man were to receive as his fee everything whatsoever breathes, he would obtain that third foot of the Gâyatrî. But 'that fourth bright foot, shining high above the skies[2]', cannot be obtained by anybody—whence then could one receive such a fee?

7. The adoration[3] of that (Gâyatrî):

'O Gâyatrî, thou hast one foot, two feet, three feet, four feet[4]. Thou art footless, for thou art not known. Worship to thy fourth bright foot above the skies.' If[5] one (who knows this) hates some

---

[1] Because Gâyatrî represents life, and the pupil receives life when he learns the Gâyatrî.

[2] See before, § 2.

[3] Upasthâna is the act of approaching the gods, προσκύνησις, Angehen, with a view of obtaining a request. Here the application is of two kinds, abhi*k*ârika, imprecatory against another, and abhyudayika, auspicious for oneself. The former has two formulas, the latter one. An upasthâna is here represented as effective, if connected with the Gâyatrî.

[4] Consisting of the three worlds, the threefold knowledge, the threefold vital breaths, and the fourth foot, as described before.

[5] I have translated this paragraph very freely, and differently from *S*ankara. The question is, whether dvishyât with iti can be used in the sense of abhi*k*âra, or imprecation. If not, I do not see how the words should be construed. The expression yasmâ upa-

one and says, 'May he not obtain this,' or 'May this wish not be accomplished to him,' then that wish is not accomplished to him against whom he thus prays, or if he says, 'May I obtain this.'

8. And thus Ganaka Vaideha spoke on this point to Budila Âsvatarâsvi[1]: 'How is it that thou who spokest thus as knowing the Gâyatrî, hast become an elephant and carriest me?' He answered: 'Your Majesty, I did not know its mouth. Agni, fire, is indeed its mouth; and if people pile even what seems much (wood) on the fire, it consumes it all. And thus a man who knows this, even if he commits what seems much evil, consumes it all and becomes pure, clean, and free from decay and death.'

FIFTEENTH BRÂHMAṆA.

1. [2]The face of the True (the Brahman) is covered with a golden disk[3]. Open that, O Pûshan[4], that we may see the nature of the True[5].

2. O Pûshan, only seer, Yama (judge), Sûrya (sun), son of Pragâpati[6], spread thy rays and gather them!

---

tishṭhate is rightly explained by Dvivedaganga, yadartham evam upatishṭhate.

[1] Asvatarasyâsvasyâpatyam, Sankara.

[2] These verses, which are omitted here in the Mâdhyandina text, are found at the end of the Vâgasaneyi-upanishad 15–18. They are supposed to be a prayer addressed to Âditya by a dying person.

[3] Mahîdhara on verse 17: 'The face of the true (purusha in the sun) is covered by a golden disk.' Sankara explains here mukha, face, by mukhyam svarûpam, the principal form or nature.

[4] Pûshan is here explained as a name of Savitri, the sun; likewise all the names in the next verse.

[5] Cf. Maitr. Up. VI, 35.

[6] Of Îsvara or Hiraṇyagarbha.

The light which is thy fairest form, I see it.   I am what he is (viz. the person in the sun).

3. Breath to air and to the immortal! Then this my body ends in ashes. Om! Mind, remember! Remember thy deeds! Mind, remember! Remember thy deeds[1]!

4. Agni, lead us on to wealth (beatitude) by a good path[2], thou, O God, who knowest all things! Keep far from us crooked evil, and we shall offer thee the fullest praise! (Rv. I, 189, 1.)

---

[1] The Vâ*g*asaneyi-sa*m*hitâ reads : Om, krato smara, k*l*ibe smara, k*ri*ta*m* smara. Uva*t*a holds that Agni, fire, who has been worshipped in youth and manhood, is here invoked in the form of mind, or that kratu is meant for sacrifice. 'Agni, remember me! Think of the world! Remember my deeds!' K*l*ibe is explained by Mahîdhara as a dative of k*l*ip, k*l*ip meaning loka, world, what is made to be enjoyed (kalpyate bhogâya).

[2] Not by the Southern path, the dark, from which there is a fresh return to life.

SIXTH ADHYÂYA.

First Brâhma*n*a[1].

1. Hari*h*, Om. He who knows the first and the best, becomes himself the first and the best among his people. Breath is indeed the first and the best. He who knows this, becomes the first and the best among his people, and among whomsoever he wishes to be so.

2. He who knows the richest[2], becomes himself the richest among his people. Speech is the richest. He who knows this, becomes the richest among his people, and among whomsoever he wishes to be so.

3. He who knows the firm rest, becomes himself firm on even and uneven ground. The eye indeed is the firm rest, for by means of the eye a man stands firm on even and uneven ground. He who knows this, stands firm on even and uneven ground.

4. He who knows success, whatever desire he desires, it succeeds to him. The ear indeed is success. For in the ear are all these Vedas successful. He who knows this, whatever desire he desires, it succeeds to him.

5. He who knows the home, becomes a home of his own people, a home of all men. The mind

---

[1] This Brâhma*n*a, also called a Khila (p. 1010, l. 8; p. 1029, l. 8), occurs in the Mâdhyandina-*s*âkhâ XIV, 9, 2. It should be compared with the *Kh*ândogya-upanishad V, 1 (Sacred Books of the East, vol. i, p. 72); also with the Ait. Âr. II, 4; Kaush. Up. III, 3; and the Pra*sn*a Up. II, 3.

[2] Here used as a feminine, while in the *Kh*ând. Up. V, 1, it is vasish*th*a.

indeed is the home. He who knows this, becomes a home of his own people and a home of all men.

6. He who knows generation[1], becomes rich in offspring and cattle. Seed indeed is generation. He who knows this, becomes rich in offspring and cattle.

7. These Prânas (senses), when quarrelling together as to who was the best, went to Brahman[2] and said: 'Who is the richest of us?' He replied: 'He by whose departure this body seems worst, he is the richest.'

8. The tongue (speech) departed, and having been absent for a year, it came back and said: 'How have you been able to live without me?' They replied: 'Like unto people, not speaking with the tongue, but breathing with breath, seeing with the eye, hearing with the ear, knowing with the mind, generating with seed. Thus we have lived.' Then speech entered in.

9. The eye (sight) departed, and having been absent for a year, it came back and said: 'How have you been able to live without me?' They replied: 'Like blind people, not seeing with the eye, but breathing with the breath, speaking with the tongue, hearing with the ear, knowing with the mind, generating with seed. Thus we have lived.' Then the eye entered in.

10. The ear (hearing) departed, and having been absent for a year, it came back and said: 'How have you been able to live without me?' They replied: 'Like deaf people, not hearing with the ear,

---

[1] This is wanting in the *Khând.* Up. Roer and Poley read Pragâpati for pragâti. MS. I. O. 375 has pragâti, MS. I. O. 1973 pragâpati.

[2] Here we have Pragâpati, instead of Brahman, in the *Khând.* Up.; also sreshtha instead of vasishtha.

but breathing with the breath, speaking with the tongue, seeing with the eye, knowing with the mind, generating with seed. Thus we have lived.' Then the ear entered in.

11. The mind departed, and having been absent for a year, it came back and said : ' How have you been able to live without me ?' They replied : 'Like fools, not knowing with their mind, but breathing with the breath, seeing with the eye, hearing with the ear, generating with seed. Thus we have lived.' Then the mind entered in.

12. The seed departed, and having been absent for a year, it came back and said : ' How have you been able to live without me ?' They replied : ' Like impotent people, not generating with seed, but breathing with the breath, seeing with the eye, hearing with the ear, knowing with the mind. Thus we have lived.' Then the seed entered in.

13. The (vital) breath, when on the point of departing, tore up these senses, as a great, excellent horse of the Sindhu country might tare up the pegs to which he is tethered. They said to him : ' Sir, do not depart. We shall not be able to live without thee.' He said : ' Then make me an offering.' They said : ' Let it be so.'

14. Then the tongue said : ' If I am the richest, then thou art the richest by it.' The eye said : ' If I am the firm rest, then thou art possessed of firm rest by it.' The ear said : ' If I am success, then thou art possessed of success by it.' The mind said : ' If I am the home, thou art the home by it.' The seed said : ' If I am generation, thou art possessed of generation by it.' He said : ' What shall be food, what shall be dress for me ?'

They replied: 'Whatever there is, even unto dogs, worms, insects, and birds[1], that is thy food, and water thy dress. He who thus knows the food of Ana (the breath)[2], by him nothing is eaten that is not (proper) food, nothing is received that is not (proper) food. *S*rotriyas (Vedic theologians) who know this, rinse the mouth with water when they are going to eat, and rinse the mouth with water after they have eaten, thinking that thereby they make the breath dressed (with water).'

SECOND BRÂHMA*N*A[3].

1. *S*vetaketu Âru*n*eya went to the settlement of the Pa*ñk*âlas. He came near to Pravâha*n*a *G*aivali[4], who was walking about (surrounded by his men). As soon as he (the king) saw him, he said: 'My boy!' *S*vetaketu replied: 'Sir!'

Then the king said: 'Have you been taught by your father!' 'Yes,' he replied.

2. The king said: 'Do you know how men, when they depart from here, separate from each other?' 'No,' he replied.

'Do you know how they come back to this world?' 'No,' he replied[5].

---

[1] It may mean, every kind of food, such as is eaten by dogs, worms, insects, and birds.

[2] We must read, with MS. I.O. 375, anasyânnam, not annasyân-nam, as MS. I.O. 1973, Roer, and Poley read. Weber has the right reading, which is clearly suggested by *Kh*ând. Up. V, 2, 1.

[3] See *Kh*ând. Up. V, 3 ; Muir, Original Sanskrit Texts, I, 433; Deussen, Vedânta, p. 390. The commentator treats this chapter as a supplement, to explain the ways that lead to the pit*ri*loka and the devaloka.

[4] The MSS. I. O. 375 and 1973 give *G*aivali, others *G*aibali. He is a Kshatriya sage, who appears also in *Kh*ând. Up. I, 8, 1, as silencing Brâhma*n*as.

[5] The same question is repeated in Roer's edition, only substi-

'Do you know how that world does never become full with the many who again and again depart thither ?' 'No,' he replied.

'Do you know at the offering of which libation the waters become endowed with a human voice and rise and speak ?' 'No,' he replied.

'Do you know the access to the path leading to the Devas and to the path leading to the Fathers, i.e. by what deeds men gain access to the path leading to the Devas or to that leading to the Fathers ? For we have heard even the saying of a *Ri*shi : " I heard of two paths for men, one leading to the Fathers, the other leading to the Devas. On those paths all that lives moves on, whatever there is between father (sky) and mother (earth)." '

*S*vetaketu said : 'I do not know even one of all these questions.'

3. Then the king invited him to stay and accept his hospitality. But the boy, not caring for hospitality, ran away, went back to his father, and said : 'Thus then you called me formerly well-instructed !' The father said : 'What then, you sage ?' The son replied : 'That fellow of a Râ*g*anya asked me five questions, and I did not know one of them.'

'What were they ?' said the father.

'These were they,' the son replied, mentioning the different heads.

4. The father said : 'You know me, child, that whatever I know, I told you. But come, we shall go thither, and dwell there as students.'

'You may go, Sir,' the son replied.

---

tuting sampadyante for âpadyante. The MSS. I. O. 375 and 1973 do not support this.

Then Gautama went where (the place of) PravâhaƝa Ɠaivali was, and the king offered him a seat,
ordered water for him, and gave him the proper
offerings.   Then he said to him : 'Sir, we offer a
boon to Gautama.'

5. Gautama said : 'That boon is promised to
me ; tell me the same speech which you made in
the presence of my boy.'

6. He said : 'That belongs to divine boons, name
one of the human boons.'

7. He said : 'You know well that I have plenty of
gold, plenty of cows, horses, slaves, attendants, and
apparel ; do not heap on me[1] what I have already in
plenty, in abundance, and superabundance.'

The king said : 'Gautama, do you wish (for instruction from me) in the proper way ?'

Gautama replied : 'I come to you as a pupil.'

In word only have former sages (though Brahmans) come as pupils (to people of lower rank), but
Gautama actually dwelt as a pupil (of PravâhaƝa,
who was a Râƴanya) in order to obtain the fame of
having respectfully served his master[2].

---

[1] Abhyavadânya is explained as niggardly, or unwilling to give,
and derived from vadânya, liberal, a-vadânya, illiberal, and abhi,
towards. This, however, is an impossible form in Sanskrit.
Vadânya means liberal, and stands for avadânya, this being
derived from avadâna, lit. what is cut off, then a morsel, a gift. In
abhyavadânya the original a reappears, so that abhyavadânya
means, not niggardly, but on the contrary, liberal, i. e. giving more
than is required.   Avadânya has never been met with in the sense
of niggardly, and though a rule of PâƝini sanctions the formation of
a-vadânya, it does not say in what sense.   Abhyavadâ in the sense
of cutting off in addition occurs in Ʒatap. Br. II, 5, 2, 40 ; avadânaɱ
karoti, in the sense of making a present, occurs Maitr. Up.VI, 33.

[2] The commentator takes the opposite view. In times of
distress, he says, former sages, belonging to a higher caste, have

8. The king said: 'Do not be offended with us, neither you nor your forefathers, because this knowledge has before now never dwelt with any Brâhmana[1]. But I shall tell it to you, for who could refuse you when you speak thus?

9. 'The altar (fire), O Gautama, is that world (heaven)[2]; the fuel is the sun itself, the smoke his rays, the light the day, the coals the quarters, the sparks the intermediate quarters. On that altar the Devas offer the sraddhâ libation (consisting of water[3]). From that oblation rises Soma, the king (the moon).

10. 'The altar, O Gautama, is Parganya (the god of rain); the fuel is the year itself, the smoke the clouds, the light the lightning, the coals the thunderbolt, the sparks the thunderings. On that altar the Devas offer Soma, the king (the moon). From that oblation rises rain.

11. 'The altar, O Gautama, is this world[4]; the fuel is the earth itself, the smoke the fire, the light the night, the coals the moon, the sparks the stars. On that altar the Devas offer rain. From that oblation rises food.

---

submitted to become pupils to teachers of a lower caste, not, however, in order to learn, but simply in order to live. Therefore Gautama also becomes a pupil in name only, for it would be against all law to act otherwise. See Gautama, Dharma-sûtras VII, 1, ed. Stenzler; translated by Bühler, p. 209.

[1] Here, too, my translation is hypothetical, and differs widely from Sankara.

[2] Cf. Khând. Up. V, 4.

[3] Deussen translates: 'In diesem Feuer opfern die Götter den Glauben.'

[4] Here a distinction is made between ayam loka, this world, and prithivî, earth, while in the Khând. Up. ayam loka is the earth, asau loka the heaven.

12. 'The altar, O Gautama, is man; the fuel the opened mouth, the smoke the breath, the light the tongue, the coals the eye, the sparks the ear. On that altar the Devas offer food. From that oblation rises seed.

13. 'The altar, O Gautama, is woman[1]. On that altar the Devas offer seed. From that oblation rises man. He lives so long as he lives, and then when he dies,

14. 'They take him to the fire (the funeral pile), and then the altar-fire is indeed fire, the fuel fuel, the smoke smoke, the light light, the coals coals, the sparks sparks. In that very altar-fire the Devas offer man, and from that oblation man rises, brilliant in colour.

15. 'Those who thus know this (even G*ri*hasthas), and those who in the forest worship faith and the True [2] (Brahman Hira*n*yagarbha), go to light (ar-*k*is), from light to day, from day to the increasing half, from the increasing half to the six months when the sun goes to the north, from those six months to the world of the Devas (Devaloka), from the world of the Devas to the sun, from the sun to the place of lightning. When they have thus reached the place of lightning a spirit [3] comes near them, and leads them to the worlds of the (conditioned) Brahman. In these worlds of Brahman they dwell exalted for ages. There is no returning for them.

---

[1] Tasyâ upastha eva samil, lomâni dhûmo, yonir ar*k*ir, yad anta*h*karoti te 'ṅgârâ, abhinandâ visphuliṅgâ*h*.

[2] *S*aṅkara translates, 'those who with faith worship the True,' and this seems better.

[3] 'A person living in the Brahma-world, sent forth, i. e. created, by Brahman, by the mind,' *S*aṅkara. 'Der ist nicht wie ein Mensch,' Deussen, p. 392.

16. 'But they who conquer the worlds (future states) by means of sacrifice, charity, and austerity, go to smoke, from smoke to night, from night to the decreasing half of the moon, from the decreasing half of the moon to the six months when the sun goes to the south, from these months to the world of the fathers, from the world of the fathers to the moon. Having reached the moon, they become food, and then the Devas feed on them there, as sacrificers feed on Soma, as it increases and decreases[1]. But when this (the result of their good works on earth) ceases, they return again to that ether, from ether to the air, from the air to rain, from rain to the earth. And when they have reached the earth, they become food, they are offered again in the altar-fire, which is man (see § 11), and thence are born in the fire of woman. Thus they rise up towards the worlds, and go the same round as before.

'Those, however, who know neither of these two paths, become worms, birds, and creeping things.'

Third BrâhmaÆa [2].

1. If a man wishes to reach greatness (wealth for performing sacrifices), he performs the upasad rule during twelve days [3] (i. e. he lives on small quantities of milk), beginning on an auspicious day of the light half of the moon during the northern progress of the sun, collecting at the same time in a cup or a dish

---

[1] See note 4 on *Khând.* Up. V, 10, and Deussen, Vedânta, p. 393. *Sa*ṅkara guards against taking âpyâyasvâpakshîyasva as a Mantra. A similar construction is *g*âyasva m*ri*yasva, see *Khând.* Up. V, 10, 8.

[2] Mâdhyandina text, p. 1103; cf. *Khând.* Up. V, 2, 4–8; Kaush. Up. II, 3.

[3] Yasmin pu*n*ye 'nukûle 'hni karma *k*ikîrshati tata*h* prâk pu*n*yâham evârabhya dvâda*s*âham upasadvratî.

made of Udumbara wood all sorts of herbs, including fruits. He sweeps the floor (near the house-
altar, âvasathya), sprinkles it, lays the fire, spreads
grass round it according to rule [1], prepares the clarified butter (â*g*ya), and on a day, presided over by a
male star (nakshatra), after having properly mixed
the Mantha [2] (the herbs, fruits, milk, honey, &c.),
he sacrifices (he pours â*g*ya into the fire), saying [3]:
' O *G*âtavedas, whatever adverse gods there are in
thee, who defeat the desires of men, to them I offer
this portion ; may they, being pleased, please me
with all desires.'   Svâhâ !

' That cross deity who lies down [4], thinking that
all things are kept asunder by her, I worship thee
as propitious with this stream of ghee.'   Svâhâ !

2. He then says, Svâhâ to the First, Svâhâ to
the Best, pours ghee into the fire, and throws what
remains into the Mantha (mortar).

He then says, Svâhâ to Breath, Svâhâ to her who
is the richest, pours ghee into the fire, and throws
what remains into the Mantha (mortar).

He then says, Svâhâ to Speech, Svâhâ to the
Support, pours ghee into the fire, and throws what
remains into the Mantha (mortar).

He then says, Svâhâ to the Eye, Svâhâ to Success,
pours ghee into the fire, and throws what remains
into the Mantha (mortar).

He then says, Svâhâ to the Ear, Svâhâ to the

---

[1] As the whole act is considered smârta, not *s*rauta, the order to
be observed (âv*ri*t) is that of the sthâlîpâka.

[2] Dravadravye prakshiptâ mathitâ*h* saktava*h* is the explanation
of Mantha, given in *G*aimin. N. M. V. p. 406.

[3] These verses are not explained by *S*ankara, and they are
absent in the *Kh*ând. Up. V, 2, 6, 4.

[4] The Mâdhyandinas read nipadyase.

Home, pours ghee into the fire, and throws what remains into the Mantha (mortar).

He then says, Svâhâ to the Mind, Svâhâ to Off-spring, pours ghee into the fire, and throws what remains into the Mantha (mortar).

He then says, Svâhâ to Seed, pours ghee into the fire, and throws what remains into the Mantha (mortar).

3. He then says, Svâhâ to Agni (fire), pours ghee into the fire, and throws what remains into the Mantha (mortar).

He then says, Svâhâ to Soma, pours ghee into the fire, and throws what remains into the Mantha (mortar).

He then says, Bhû*h* (earth), Svâhâ, pours ghee into the fire, and throws what remains into the Mantha (mortar).

He then says, Bhuva*h* (sky), Svâhâ, pours ghee into the fire, and throws what remains into the Mantha (mortar).

He then says, Sva*h* (heaven), Svâhâ, pours ghee into the fire, and throws what remains into the Mantha (mortar).

He then says, Bhûr, Bhuva*h*, Sva*h*, Svâhâ, pours ghee into the fire, and throws what remains into the Mantha (mortar).

He then says, Svâhâ to Brahman (the priesthood), pours ghee into the fire, and throws what remains into the Mantha (mortar).

He then says, Svâhâ to Kshatra (the knighthood), pours ghee into the fire, and throws what remains into the Mantha (mortar).

He then says, Svâhâ to the Past, pours ghee into the fire, and throws what remains into the Mantha (mortar).

He then says, Svâhâ to the Future, pours ghee into the fire, and throws what remains into the Mantha (mortar).

He then says, Svâhâ to the Universe, pours ghee into the fire, and throws what remains into the Mantha (mortar).

He then says, Svâhâ to all things, pours ghee into the fire, and throws what remains into the Mantha (mortar).

He then says, Svâhâ to Pra*g*âpati, pours ghee into the fire, and throws what remains into the Mantha (mortar).

4. Then he touches it (the Mantha, which is dedicated to Prâ*n*a, breath), saying : ' Thou art fleet (as breath). Thou art burning (as fire). Thou art full (as Brahman). Thou art firm (as the sky). Thou art the abode of all (as the earth). Thou hast been saluted with Hi*n* (at the beginning of the sacrifice by the prastot*ri*). Thou art saluted with Hi*n* (in the middle of the sacrifice by the prastot*ri*). Thou hast been sung (by the udgât*ri* at the beginning of the sacrifice). Thou art sung (by the udgât*ri* in the middle of the sacrifice). Thou hast been celebrated (by the adhvaryu at the beginning of the sacrifice). Thou art celebrated again (by the âgnîdhra in the middle of the sacrifice). Thou art bright in the wet (cloud). Thou art great. Thou art powerful. Thou art food (as Soma). Thou art light (as Agni, fire, the eater). Thou art the end. Thou art the absorption (of all things).'

5. Then he holds it (the Mantha) forth, saying : ' Thou [1] knowest all, we know thy greatness. He is

---

[1] These curious words â ma*m*si â ma*m*hi te mahi are not explained by *S*ankara. Ânandagiri explains them as I have trans-

indeed a king, a ruler, the highest lord. May that king, that ruler make me the highest lord.'

6. Then he eats it, saying: 'Tat savitur vare-*n*yam [1] (We meditate on that adorable light)—The winds drop honey for the righteous, the rivers drop honey, may our plants be sweet as honey! Bhû*h* (earth) Svâhâ!

'Bhargo devasya dhîmahi (of the divine Savit*ri*)—May the night be honey in the morning, may the air above the earth, may heaven, our father, be honey! Bhuva*h* (sky) Svâhâ!

'Dhiyo yo na*h* pro*k*odayât (who should rouse our thoughts)—May the tree be full of honey, may the sun be full of honey, may our cows be sweet like honey! Sva*h* (heaven) Svâhâ!'

He repeats the whole Sâvitrî verse, and all the verses about the honey, thinking, May I be all this! Bhûr, Bhuva*h*, Sva*h*, Svâhâ! Having thus swallowed all, he washes his hands, and sits down behind the altar, turning his head to the East. In the morning he worships Âditya (the sun), with the hymn, 'Thou art the best lotus of the four quarters, may I become the best lotus among men.' Then returning as he came, he sits down behind the altar and recites the genealogical list [2].

7. Uddâlaka Âru*n*i told this (Mantha-doctrine) to his pupil Vâ*g*asaneya Yâ*gñ*avalkya, and said: 'If a man were to pour it on a dry stick, branches would grow, and leaves spring forth.'

---

lated them. They correspond to 'amo nâmâsy amâ hi te sarvam idam' in the *Kh*ând. Up. V, 2, 6, 6. The Mâdhyandinas read: âmo 'sy âma*m* hi te mayi, sa hi râ*g*â, &c. Dvivedaganga translates: 'thou art the knower, thy knowledge extends to me.'

[1] Rv. III, 62, 10.

[2] This probably refers to the list immediately following.

8. Vâgasaneya Yâgñavalkya told the same to his pupil Madhuka Paingya, and said : ' If a man were to pour it on a dry stick, branches would grow, and leaves spring forth.'

9. Madhuka Paingya told the same to his pupil Kûla Bhâgavitti, and said: 'If a man were to pour it on a dry stick, branches would grow, and leaves spring forth.'

10. Kûla Bhâgavitti told the same to his pupil Gânaki Âyasthûna, and said : ' If a man were to pour it on a dry stick, branches would grow, and leaves spring forth.'

11. Gânaki Âyasthûna told the same to his pupil Satyakâma Gâbâla, and said : ' If a man were to pour it on a dry stick, branches would grow, and leaves spring forth.'

12. Satyakâma Gâbâla told the same to his pupils, and said: ' If a man were to pour it on a dry stick; branches would grow, and leaves spring forth.'

Let no one tell this [1] to any one, except to a son or to a pupil [2].

13. Four things are made of the wood of the Udumbara tree, the sacrificial ladle (sruva), the cup (kamasa), the fuel, and the two churning sticks.

There are ten kinds of village (cultivated) seeds, viz. rice and barley (brîhiyavâs), sesamum and kidney-beans (tilamâshâs), millet and panic seed (anupriyaṅ-gavas), wheat (godhûmâs), lentils (masûrâs), pulse (khalvâs), and vetches (khalakulâs [3]).   After having

---

[1] The Mantha-doctrine with the prânadarsana.   Comm.

[2] It probably means to no one except to one's own son and to one's own disciple. Cf. Svet. Up. VI, 22.

[3] I have given the English names after Roer, who, living in India, had the best opportunity of identifying the various kinds of plants here mentioned. The commentators do not help us much. Saṅkara

ground these he sprinkles them with curds (dadhi), honey, and ghee, and then offers (the proper portions) of clarified butter [1] (â*g*ya).

FOURTH BRÂHMAⁿA [2].

1. The earth is the essence of all these things, water is the essence of the earth, plants of water, flowers of plants, fruits of flowers, man of fruits, seed of man.

2. And Pra*g*âpati thought, let me make an abode for him, and he created a woman (*S*atarûpâ).

Tâ*m* [3] s*ri*sh*t*vâdha upâsta, tasmât striyam adha upâsîta. Sa etam prâ*ñk*am grâvâ*n*am âtmana eva samudapârayat, tenainâm abhyas*ri*gat.

---

says that in some places Priyaṅgu (panic seed or millet) is called Kaṅgu; that Khalva, pulse, is also called Nishpâva and Valla, and Khalakula, vetches, commonly Kulattha. Dvivedagaṅga adds that A*n*u is called in Guzerat Moriya, Priyaṅgu Kaṅgu, Khalva, as nishpâva, Valla, and Khalakula Kulattha.

[1] According to the rules laid down in the proper G*ri*hya-sûtras.

[2] This Brâhma*n*a is inserted here because there is supposed to be some similarity between the preparation of the *S*rîmantha and the Putramantha, or because a person who has performed the *S*rîmantha is fit to perform the Putramantha. Thus *S*aṅkara says: Prâ*n*adar*s*ina*h* *s*rîmantha*m* karma k*ri*tavata*h* putramanthe 'dhikâra*h*. Yadâ putramantha*m* *k*ikîrshati tadâ *s*rîmantha*m* k*ri*tvâ *ri*tukâla*m* patnyâ*h* (brahma*k*arye*n*a) pratîkshata iti.

[3] I have given those portions of the text which did not admit of translation into English, in Sanskrit. It was not easy, however, to determine always the text of the Kâ*n*va-sâkhâ. Poley's text is not always correct, and Roer seems simply to repeat it. *S*aṅkara's commentary, which is meant for the Kâ*n*va text, becomes very short towards the end of the Upanishad. It is quite sufficient for the purpose of a translation, but by no means always for restoring a correct text. MS. Wilson 369, which has been assigned to the Kâ*n*va-sâkhâ, and which our Catalogue attributes to the same school, gives the Mâdhyandina text, and so does MS. Mill 108. I have therefore collated two MSS. of the India Office, which Dr. Rost had the kindness to select for me, MS. 375 and MS. 1973, which I call A. and B.

3. Tasyâ vedir upastho, lomâni barhis, karmâ-dhishavane, samiddho¹ madhyatas, tau mushkau. Sa yâvân ha vai vâgapeyena yagamânasya loko bhavati tâvân asya loko bhavati ya evam vidvân adhopahâsam karaty â sa² strînâm sukritam vriṅkte 'tha ya idam avidvân adhopahâsam karaty âsya striyah sukritam vriṅgate.

4. Etad dha sma vai tadvidvân Uddâlaka Ârunir âhaitad dha sma vai tadvidvân Nâko Maudgalya âhaitad dha sma vai tadvidvân Kumârahârita âha, bahavo maryâ brâhmanâyanâ³ nirindriyâ visukrito'smâl lokât prayanti⁴ ya idam avidvâmso 'dhopahâsam karantîti. Bahu vâ⁵ idam suptasya vâ gâgrato vâ retah skandati,

5. Tad abhimrised anu vâ mantrayeta yan me 'dya retah prithivîm askântsîd yad oshadhîr apy asarad yad apah, idam aham tad reta âdade punar mâm aitv indriyam punas tegah punar bhagah, punar agnayo⁶ dhishnyâ yathâsthânam kalpantâm, ity anâmikâṅgushthâbhyâm âdâyântarena stanau vâ bhruvau vâ nimriṅgyât⁷.

6. If a man see himself in the water⁸, he should

---

¹ Roer reads samidho, but Sankara and Dvivedaganga clearly presuppose samiddho, which is in A. and B.

² Roer has âsâm sa strînâm, Poley, A. and B. have âsâm strînâm. Sankara (MS. Mill 64) read â sa strînâm, and later on âsya striyah, though both Roer and Poley leave out the â here too (â asyeti khedah).

³ Brâhmanâyanâh, the same as brahmabandhavah, i. e. Brâhmans by descent only, not by knowledge.

⁴ Narakam gakkhantîtyarthah. Dvivedaganga.

⁵ Bahu vâ svalpam vâ.

⁶ The Mâdhyandina text has agnayo, and Dvivedaganga explains it by dhîshnyâ agnayah sarîrasthitâh. Poley and Roer have punar agnir dhishnyâ, and so have A. and B.

⁷ Nirmrigyât, A.; nimriṅgyât, B.

⁸ Dvivedaganga adds, retoyonâv udake retahsikas tatra svakkhâyâdarsane prâyaskittam âha.

recite the following verse: 'May there be in me splendour, strength, glory, wealth, virtue.'

She is the best of women whose garments are pure [1]. Therefore let him approach a woman whose garments are pure, and whose fame is pure, and address her.

7. If she do not give in [2], let him, as he likes, bribe her (with presents). And if she then do not give in, let him, as he likes, beat her with a stick or with his hand, and overcome her [3], saying: 'With manly strength and glory I take away thy glory,'—and thus she becomes unglorious [4].

8. If she give in, he says: 'With manly strength and glory I give thee glory,'—and thus they both become glorious.

9. Sa yâm ikkhet kâmayeta meti tasyâm artham nishtâya [5] mukhena mukham sandhâyopastham asyâ abhimrisya gaped angâdangât sambhavasi hridayâd adhi gâyase, sa tvam angakashâyo [6] 'si digdhaviddhâm [7] iva mâdayemâm amûm mayîti [8].

10. Atha yâm ikkhen na garbham dadhîteti [9] tasyâm artham nishtâya mukhena mukham sandhâyâbhiprânyâpânyâd indriyena te retasâ reta âdada ity aretâ [10] eva bhavati.

---

[1] Trirâtravratam kritvâ katurtha 'hni snâtâm.

[2] Instead of connecting kâmam with dadyât, Dvivedaganga explains it by yathâsakti.

[3] Atikram, scil. maithunâya.   [4] Bandhyâ durbhagâ.

[5] Nishtâya, A. B.; nishthâya, Roer, Poley; the same in § 10.

[6] Sa tvam angânam kashâyo raso 'si.

[7] Vishaliptasaraviddhâm mrigîm iva.

[8] Mâdayeti is the reading of the Mâdhyandina text. Poley, Roer, A. and B. read mâdayemâm amûm mayîti. Ânandagiri has mrigîm ivâmûm madîyâm striyam me mâdaya madvasâm kurv ityarthah. Dvivedaganga explains mâdayeti.

[9] Rûpabhramsayauvanahânibhayât.   [10] Agarbhinî.

11. Atha yâm i*kkh*ed garbha*m* dadhîteti tasyâm artha*m* nish*t*âya mukhena mukha*m* sandhâyâpânyâbhiprâ*n*yâd indriye*n*a te retasâ reta âdadhâmîti garbhi*n*y eva bhavati.

12. Now again, if a man's wife has a lover and the husband hates him, let him (according to rule)[1] place fire by an unbaked jar, spread a layer of arrows in inverse order[2], anoint these three arrow-heads[3] with butter in inverse order, and sacrifice, saying: 'Thou hast sacrificed in my fire, I take away thy up and down breathing, I here[4].'

'Thou hast sacrificed in my fire, I take away thy sons and cattle, I here.'

'Thou hast sacrificed in my fire, I take away thy sacred and thy good works, I here.'

'Thou hast sacrificed in my fire, I take away thy hope and expectation, I here.'

He whom a Brâhma*n*a who knows this curses, departs from this world without strength and without good works. Therefore let no one wish even for sport with the wife of a *S*rotriya[5] who knows this, for he who knows this, is a dangerous enemy.

13. When the monthly illness seizes his wife, she

---

[1] Âvasathyâgnim eva pra*g*vâlya.

[2] Pa*sk*imâgra*m* dakshi*n*âgra*m* vâ yathâ syât tathâ.

[3] Tisra*h* is left out by Roer and Poley, by A. and B.

[4] I have translated according to the Kâ*n*va text, as far as it could be made out. As there are four imprecations, it is but natural that tisra*h* should be left out in the Kâ*n*va text. It is found in the Mâdhyandina text, because there the imprecations are only three in number, viz. the taking away of hope and expectation, of sons and cattle, and of up and down breathing. Instead of asâv iti, which is sufficient, the Mâdhyandina text has asâv iti nâma g*ri*h*n*âti, and both Ânandagiri and Dvivedaga*n*ga allow the alternative, âtmana*h* *s*atror vâ nâma g*ri*h*n*âti, though asau can really refer to the speaker only.

[5] Roer reads dvâre*n*a; Poley, A. and B. dâre*n*a; the Mâdhyan-

should for three days not drink from a metal vessel, and wear a fresh dress. Let no V*ri*shala or V*ri*shalî (a *S*ûdra man or woman) touch her. At the end of the three days, when she has bathed, the husband should make her pound rice [1].

14. And if a man wishes that a white son should be born to him, and that he should know one Veda, and live to his full age, then, after having prepared boiled rice with milk and butter, they should both eat, being fit to have offspring.

15. And if a man wishes that a reddish [2] son with tawny eyes should be born to him, and that he should know two Vedas, and live to his full age, then, after having prepared boiled rice with coagulated milk and butter, they should both eat, being fit to have offspring.

16. And if a man wishes that a dark son should be born to him with red eyes, and that he should know three Vedas, and live to his full age, then, after having prepared boiled rice with water and butter, they should both eat, being fit to have offspring.

17. And if a man wishes that a learned daughter should be born to him, and that she should live to her full age, then, after having prepared boiled rice with sesamum and butter, they should both eat, being fit to have offspring.

18. And if a man wishes that a learned son should be born to him, famous, a public man, a popular speaker, that he should know all the Vedas, and that

---

dinas *g*âyâyâ. *S*ankara, according to Roer, interprets dvâre*n*a, but it seems that dâre*n*a is used here in the singular, instead of the plural. See Pâraskara G*ri*hya-sûtras I, 11.

[1] To be used for the ceremony described in § 14 seq.

[2] Kapilo var*n*ata*h* pingala*h* pingâksha*h*.

he should live to his full age, then, after having prepared boiled rice with meat and butter, they should
both eat, being fit to have offspring. The meat
should be of a young or of an old bull.

19. And then toward morning, after having, according to the rule of the Sthâlîpâka (pot-boiling),
performed the preparation of the Âgya (clarified
butter[1]), he sacrifices from the Sthâlîpâka bit by bit,
saying : ' This is for Agni, Svâhâ ! This is for Anu-
mati, Svâhâ ! This is for the divine Savitri, the true
creator, Svâhâ !' Having sacrificed, he takes out the
rest of the rice and eats it, and after having eaten,
he gives it to his wife. Then he washes his hands,
fills a water-jar, and sprinkles her thrice with it,
saying : ' Rise hence, O Visvâvasu[2], seek another
blooming girl, a wife with her husband.'

20. Then he embraces her, and says : 'I am Ama
(breath), thou art Sâ (speech)[3]. Thou art Sâ (speech),
I am Ama (breath). I am the Sâman, thou art the
Rik[4]. I am the sky, thou art the earth. Come, let
us strive together, that a male child may be
begotten[5].'

---

[1] Karum srapayitvâ.
[2] Name of a Gandharva, as god of love. See Rig-veda X, 85, 22.
Dvivedaganga explains the verse differently, so that the last words
imply, I come together with my own wife.
[3] Because speech is dependent on breath, as the wife is on the
husband. See Khând. Up. I, 6, 1.
[4] Because the Sâma-veda rests on the Rig-veda.
[5] This is a verse which is often quoted and explained. It occurs
in the Atharva-veda XIV, 71, as ' amo 'ham asmi sâ tvam, sâmâ-
ham asmy rik tvam, dyaur aham prithivî tvam; tâv iha sam
bhavâva pragâm â ganayâvahai.'
Here we have the opposition between amah and sâ, while in
the Ait. Brâhmana VIII, 27, we have amo 'ham asmi sa tvam,
giving amah in opposition to sa. It seems not unlikely that this

21. Athâsyâ ûrû vihâpayati, vi*g*ihîthâ*m* dyâvâp*ri*-thivî iti tasyâm artha*m* nish*t*âya mukhena mukha*m* sandhâya trir enâm anulomâm [1] anumârsh*t*i, Vish*n*ur yoni*m* kalpayatu, Tvash*t*â rûpâ*n*i pi*m*satu, âsi*ñk*atu Pra*g*âpatir Dhâtâ garbha*m* dadhatu te. Garbha*m* dhehi Sinîvâli, garbha*m* dhehi p*ri*thush*t*uke, garbha*m* te A*s*vinau devâv âdhattâm pushkarasra*g*au.

22. Hira*n*mayî ara*n*î yâbhyâ*m* nirmanthatâm [2] a*s*vi-nau [3], ta*m* te garbha*m* havâmahe [4] da*s*ame mâsi sûtave. Yathâgnigarbhâ p*ri*thivî, yathâ dyaur in-dre*n*a garbhi*n*î, vâyur di*s*â*m* yathâ garbha eva*m* garbha*m* dadhâmi te 'sâv iti [5].

23. Soshyantîm [6] adbhir abhyukshati. Yathâ vâyu*h* [7] pushkari*n*î*m* sami*ñg*ayati sarvata*h*, evâ te garbha e*g*atu sahâvaitu *g*arâyu*n*â. Indrasyâya*m* vra*g*a*h* k*ri*ta*h* sârga*l*a*h* [8] sapari*s*raya*h* [9], tam indra nir*g*ahi garbhe*n*a sâvarâ*m* [10] saheti.

was an old proverbial formula, and that it meant originally no more than 'I am he, and thou art she.' But this meaning was soon for-gotten. In the *Kh*ând. Up. I, 6, 1, we find sâ explained as earth, ama as fire (Sacred Books of the East, vol. i, p. 13). In the Ait. Brâhma*n*a sâ is explained as *Ri*k, ama as Sâman. I have therefore in our passage also followed the interpretation of the commentary, instead of rendering it, 'I am he, and thou art she ; thou art she, and I am he.'

[1] Anulomam, mûrdhânam ârabhya pâdântam.

[2] Nirmathitavantau. [3] A*s*vinau devau, Mâdhyandina text.

[4] Dadhâmahe, Mâdhyandina text. Instead of sûtave, A. has sûyate, B. sûtaye.

[5] Iti nâma g*ri*hnâti, Mâdhyandina text. *S*ankara says, asâv iti tasyâ*h*. Ânandagiri says, asâv iti patyur vâ nirde*s*a*h* ; tasyâ nâma g*ri*hnâtîti pûrve*n*a sambandha*h*. Dvivedaganga says, ante bhartâ-sâv aham iti svâtmano nâma g*ri*hnâti, bhâryâyâ vâ.

[6] See Pâraskara G*ri*hya-sûtra I, 16 seq. [7] Vâta*h*, M.

[8] Arga*d*ayâ nirodhena saha vartamâna*h* sârga*d*a*h*, Dvivedaganga.

[9] Sapari*s*raya*h*, pari*s*raye*n*a parivesh*t*anena *g*arâyu*n*â sahita*h*, Dvivedaganga.

[10] Sâvarâm is the reading given by Poley, Roer, A. and B.

24 [1]. When the child is born, he prepares the fire, places the child on his lap, and having poured p*ri*-shad*â*gya, i. e. dadhi (thick milk) mixed with gh*ri*ta (clarified butter) into a metal jug, he sacrifices bit by bit of that p*ri*shad*â*gya, saying : ' May I, as I increase in this my house, nourish a thousand ! May fortune never fail in his race, with offspring and cattle, Svâhâ !'

' I offer to thee· in my mind the vital breaths which are in me, Svâhâ !'

' Whatever [2] in my work I have done too much, or whatever I have here done too little, may the wise Agni Svish*t*ak*ri*t make this right and proper for us, Svâhâ !'

25. Then putting his mouth near the child's right ear, he says thrice, Speech, speech [3]! After

---

Ânandagiri explains : garbhani*h*sara*n*ânantara*m* yâ mâ*m*sape*s*î nirga*kkh*ati sâvarâ, tâ*m* *k*a nirgamayety artha*h*. Dvivedaga*n*ga (ed. Weber) writes : nirgamyamânamâ*m*sape*s*î sâ-avara*s*abd*d*avâ*ky*â, ta*m* sâvara*m* *k*a nirgamaya.

[1] These as well as the preceding rules refer to matters generally treated in the Gr*i*hya-sûtras ; see Â*s*valâyana, Gr*i*hya-sûtras I, 13 seq. ; Pâraskara, Gr*i*hya-sûtras I, 11 seq. ; *S*ânkhâyana, Gr*i*hya-sûtras I, 19 seq. It is curious, however, that Â*s*valâyana I, 13, 1, refers distinctly to the Upanishad as the place where the pu*m*savana and similar matters were treated. This shows that the Upanishads were known before the composition of the Gr*i*hya-sûtras, and explains perhaps, at least partially, why the Upanishads were considered as rahasya. Â*s*valâyana says, ' Conception, begetting of a boy, and guarding the embryo are to be found in the Upanishad. But if a man does not read the Upanishad, let him know that he should feed his wife,' &c. Nârâya*n*a explains that Â*s*valâyana here refers to an Upanishad which does not exist in his own *S*âkhâ, but he objects to the conclusion that therefore the garbhâdhâna and other ceremonies need not be performed, and adds that some hold it should be performed, as prescribed by *S*aunaka and others.

[2] Â*s*valâyana, Gr*i*hya-sûtra I, 10, 23.

[3] Trayîlaksha*n*â vâk tvayi pravi*s*atv iti *g*apato 'bhiprâya*h*.

that he pours together thick milk, honey, and clarified butter, and feeds the child with (a ladle of)
pure gold [1], saying : 'I give thee Bhû*h*, I give thee
Bhuva*h*, I give thee Sva*h* [2]. Bhûr, Bhuva*h*, Sva*h*, I
give thee all [3].'

26 [4]. Then he gives him his name, saying: 'Thou
art Veda ;' but this is his secret name [5].

27. Then he hands the boy to his mother and
gives him her breast, saying : 'O Sarasvatî, that
breast of thine which is inexhaustible, delightful,
abundant, wealthy, generous, by which thou cherish-
est all blessings, make that to flow here [6].'

28 [7]. Then he addresses the mother of the boy :

---

[1] Cf. Pâraskara Gr*i*hya-sûtras I, 16, 4, anâmikayâ suvar*n*ântar-
hitayâ ; *S*ânkhâyana, Gr*i*hya-sûtras I, 24, prâ*s*aye*g* *g*âtarupe*n*a.

[2] Bhûr bhuva*h* sva*h* are explained by Dvivedaganga as the *R*ig-
veda, Ya*g*ur-veda, and Sâma-veda. They might also be earth, air,
and heaven. See *S*ânkhâyana, Gr*i*hya-sûtras I, 24; Bhur *r*igveda*m*
tvayi dadhâmi, &c.

[3] The Mâdhyandinas add here another verse, which the father
recites while he strokes his boy: 'Be a stone, be an axe, be pure
gold. Thou art my Self, called my son ; live a hundred harvests.'
The same verse occurs in the Â*s*valâyana Gr*i*hya-sûtras I, 15, 3.

[4] The two ceremonies, here described, are the âyushya-karman
and the medhâ*g*anana. They are here treated rather confusedly.
Pâraskara (Gr*i*hya-sûtras I, 16, 3) distinguishes the medhâ*g*anana
and the âyushya. He treats the medhâ*g*anana first, which consists
in feeding the boy with honey and clarified butter, and saying to
him bhûs tvayi dadhâmi, &c. The âyushya consists in repeating
certain verses in the boy's ear, wishing him a long life, &c. In
Â*s*valâyana's Gr*i*hya-sûtras, I, 15, 1 contains the âyushya, I, 15, 2
the medhâ*g*anana. *S*ânkhâyana also (I, 24) treats the âyushya first,
and the medhâ*g*anana afterwards, and the same order prevails in
the Mâdhyandina text of the Br*i*hadâra*n*yaka-upanishad.

[5] In the Mâdhyandina text these acts are differently arranged.

[6] Rig-veda I, 164, 49.

[7] These verses are differently explained by various commentators.
Ânandagiri explains i*l*â as stutyâ, bhogyâ. He derives Maitrâvaru*n*î

'Thou art I*l*â Maitrâvaru*n*î : thou strong woman
hast born a strong boy. Be thou blessed with
strong children thou who hast blessed me with a
strong child.'

And they say of such a boy: 'Ah, thou art better
than thy father ; ah, thou art better than thy grandfather. Truly he has reached the highest point in
happiness, praise, and Vedic glory who is born as
the son of a Brâhma*n*a that knows this.'

Fifth Brâhma*n*a.

1. Now follows the stem [1] :

   1. Pautimâshîputra from Kâtyâyanîputra,

---

from Maitrâvaru*n*a, i. e. Vasish*th*a, the son of Mitrâvaru*n*au, and
identifies her with Arundhatî.   Dvivedaga*n*ga takes i*d*â as bhogyâ,
or i*d*âpâtrî, or pr*i*thivîrûpâ, and admits that she may be called
Maitrâvaru*n*î, because born of Mitrâvaru*n*au.   Vîre is rightly taken
as a vocative by Dvivedaga*n*ga, while Ânandagiri explains it as a
locative, mayi nimittabhûte.   One expects ag*î*gana*h* instead of
ag*î*ganat, which is the reading of A. and B.   The reading of the
Mâdhyandinas, âg*î*ganathâ*h*, is right grammatically, but it offends
against the metre, and is a theoretical rather than a real form.
If we read ag*î*gana*h*, we must also read akara*h*, unless we are
prepared to follow the commentator, who supplies bhavatî.

   [1] The Mâdhyandinas begin with vayam, we, then 1. Bhâradvâg*î*-
putra, 2. Vâtsîma*nd*avîputra, 3. Pâra*s*arîputra, 4. Gârgîputra, 5. Pârâ*s*arî-kau*nd*inîputra, 6. Gârgîputra, 7. Gârgîputra, 8. Bâ*d*eyîputra,
9. Maushikîputra, 10. Hârikar*n*îputra, 11. Bhâradvâg*î*putra, 12.
Paing*î*putra, 13. *S*aunakîputra, 14. Kâ*s*yapî-bâlâkyâ-mâ*th*arîputra,
15. Kautsîputra, 16. Baudhîputra, 17. *S*âla*n*kâyanîputra, 18. Vârshaga*n*îputra, 19. Gautamîputra, 20. Âtreyîputra, 21. Gautamîputra,
22. Vâtsîputra, 23. Bhâradvâg*î*putra, 24. Pârâ*s*arîputra, 25. Vârkâ-
ru*n*îputra ; then from No. 20 as in the Kâ*n*va text.

   This stem is called by *S*ankara, Samastaprava*k*anavamsah, and
Ânandagiri adds, pûrvau va*m*sau purushaviseshitau, tr*i*tîyas tu
strîviseshita*h*, strîprâdhânyât.   Dvivedaga*n*ga writes, putramantha-
karma*n*a*h* strîsa*m*skârârthatvenoktatvât tatsannidhânâd aya*m* va*m*sa*h*
strîprâdhânyeno*k*yate.

2. Kâtyâyanîputra from Gotamîputra,

3. Gotamîputra from Bhâradvâgîputra,

4. Bhâradvâgîputra from Pârâsarîputra,

5. Pârâsarîputra from Aupasvatîputra,

6. Aupasvatîputra from Pârâsarîputra,

7. Pârâsarîputra from Kâtyâyanîputra,

8. Kâtyâyanîputra from Kausikîputra,

9. Kausikîputra from Âlambîputra and Vaiyâghrapadîputra,

10. Âlambîputra and Vaiyâghrapadîputra from
Kânvîputra,

11. Kânvîputra from Kâpîputra,

12. Kâpîputra

2. from Âtreyîputra,

13. Âtreyîputra from Gautamîputra,

14. Gautamîputra from Bhâradvâgîputra,

15. Bhâradvâgîputra from Pârâsarîputra,

16. Pârâsarîputra from Vâtsîputra,

17. Vâtsîputra from Pârâsarîputra,

18[1]. Pârâsarîputra from Vârkâruñîputra,

19. Vârkâruñîputra from Vârkâruñîputra,

20. Vârkâruñîputra from Ârtabhâgîputra,

21. Ârtabhâgîputra from Saungîputra,

22. Saungîputra from Sânkritîputra,

23[2]. Sânkritîputra from Âlambâyanîputra,

24. Âlambâyanîputra from Âlambîputra,

25. Âlambîputra from Gâyantîputra,

26. Gâyantîputra from Mândûkâyanîputra,

27. Mândûkâyanîputra from Mândûkîputra,

28. Mândûkîputra from Sândilîputra,

29. Sândilîputra from Râthîtarîputra,

30[3]. Râthîtarîputra from Bhâlukîputra,

---

[1] M. has only one.   [2] M. inverts 23 and 24.

[3] Deest in M.

31. Bhâluk*î*putra from Krau*ñkî*ik*î*putrau,

32. Krau*ñkî*ik*î*putrau from Vai*tt*abhat*î*putra [1],

33. Vai*tt*abhat*î*putra from Kârsakey*î*putra [2],

34. Kârsakey*î*putra from Prâ*k*înayog*î*putra,

35. Prâ*k*înayog*î*putra from Sâ*ñ*gîv*î*putra [3],

36. Sâ*ñ*gîv*î*putra from Prâs*ñî*putra Âsurivâsin,

37. Prâs*ñî*putra Âsurivâsin from Âsurâya*n*a,

38. Âsurâya*n*a from Âsuri,

39. Âsuri

3. from Yâg*ñ*avalkya,

40. Yâg*ñ*avalkya from Uddâlaka,

41. Uddâlaka from Aru*n*a,

42. Aru*n*a from Upave*s*i,

43. Upave*s*i from Ku*s*ri,

44. Ku*s*ri from Vâ*g*a*s*ravas,

45. Vâ*g*a*s*ravas from *G*ihvâvat Vâdhyoga,

46. *G*ihvâvat Vâdhyoga from Asita Vârshaga*n*a,

47. Asita Vârshaga*n*a from Harita Ka*s*yapa,

48. Harita Ka*s*yapa from *S*ilpa Ka*s*yapa,

49. *S*ilpa Ka*s*yapa from Ka*s*yapa Naidhruvi,

50. Ka*s*yapa Naidhruvi from Vâ*k*,

51. Vâ*k* from Ambhi*n*î,

52. Ambhi*n*î from Âditya, the Sun.

As coming from Âditya, the Sun, these pure [4] Ya*g*us verses have been proclaimed by Yâg*ñ*avalkya Vâ*g*asaneya.

---

[1] Vaidabh*ri*î*î*putra, M.   [2] Bhâluk*î*putra, M.

[3] Kârsakey*î*putra after 35 in M.

[4] They are called *s*uklâni, white or pure, because they are not mixed with Brâhma*n*as, avyâmi*s*râ*n*i brâhma*n*ena (doshair asankîr-*n*âni, paurusheyatvadoshadvârâbhâvâd ityartha*h*). Or they are ayâtayâmâni, unimpaired. Ânandagiri adds, Pra*g*âpatim ârabhya Sâ*ñ*gîv*î*putraparyanta*m* (No. 36) Vâ*g*asaneyi*s*âkhâsu sarvâsv eko va*m*sa ityâha samânam iti. Dvivedaga*ñ*ga says: Vâ*g*i*s*âkhâva*kkh*in-

4 [1]. The same as far as Sâ*ng*îvîputra (No. 36), then

36. Sâ*ng*îvîputra from Mâ*nd*ûkâyani,

37. Mâ*nd*ûkâyani from Mâ*nd*avya,

38. Mâ*nd*avya from Kautsa,

39. Kautsa from Mâhitthi,

40. Mâhitthi from Vâmakakshâya*n*a,

41. Vâmakakshâya*n*a from *S*â*nd*ilya,

42. *S*â*nd*ilya from Vâtsya,

43. Vâtsya from Ku*s*ri,

44. Ku*s*ri from Ya*gñ*ava*k*as Râ*g*astambâyana,

45. Ya*gñ*ava*k*as Râ*g*astambâyana from Tura Kâvasheya,

46. Tura Kâvasheya from Pra*g*âpati,

47. Pra*g*âpati from Brahman,

48. Brahman is Svayambhu, self-existent.

Adoration to Brahman!

---

nânâ*m* ya*g*ushâ*m* Sûrye*n*opadish*t*atva*m* Yâ*gñ*avalkyena prâptatvam *k*a purâ*n*eshu prasiddham.

[1] This last paragraph is wanting in the Mâdhyandina text, but a very similar paragraph occurs in *S*atapatha-brâhma*n*a X, 6, 5, 9, where, however, Vâtsya comes before *S*â*nd*ilya.

SVETÂSVATARA-
UPANISHAD.

SVETÂSVATARA-
UPANISHAD.

FIRST ADHYÂYA.

1. The Brahma-students say: Is Brahman the cause[1]? Whence are we born? Whereby do we live, and whither do we go? O ye who know Brahman, (tell us) at whose command we abide, whether in pain or in pleasure?

---

[1] This translation seems the one which Sankara himself prefers, for on p. 277, when recapitulating, he says, kim brahma kâra*n*am âhosvit kâlâdi. In comparing former translations, whether by Weber, Roer, Gough, and others, it will be seen that my own differs considerably from every one of them, and differs equally from Sankara's interpretation. It would occupy too much space to criticise former translations, nor would it seem fair, considering how long ago they were made, and how imperfect were the materials which were then accessible. All I wish my readers to understand is that, if I differ from my predecessors, I do so after having carefully examined their renderings. Unfortunately, Roer's edition of both the text and the commentary is often far from correct. Thus in the very first verse of the Svetâsvatara-upanishad, I think we ought to read sampratish*thâh*, instead of sampratish*thitâh*. In the commentary the reading is right. Vyavasyâm is a misprint for vyavasthâm. In the second verse we must separate kâla*h* and svabhâva*h*. Yad*rikkh*â, no very unusual word, meaning chance, was formerly taken for a name of the moon! Instead of na tvâtma-bhâvât, both sense and metre require that we should read anâtmabhâvât, though the commentators take a different view. They say, because there is a self, and then go on to say that even that would not suffice. Such matters, however, belong to a critical commentary on the Upanishads rather than to a translation, and I can refer to them in cases of absolute necessity only, and where the readings of the two MSS., A. and B, seem to offer some help.

2. Should time, or nature[1], or necessity, or chance, or the elements be considered as the cause, or he who is called the person (purusha, vig*ñ*ânâtmâ)? It cannot be their union either, because that is not self-dependent[2], and the self also is powerless, because there is (independent of him) a cause of good and evil[3].

3. The sages, devoted to meditation and concentration, have seen the power belonging to God himself[4], hidden in its own qualities (gu*n*a). He, being one, superintends all those causes, time, self, and the rest[5].

4[6]. We meditate on him who (like a wheel) has one felly with three tires, sixteen ends, fifty spokes, with twenty counter-spokes, and six sets of eight;

---

[1] Svabhâva, their own nature or independent character.

[2] Union presupposes a uniter.

[3] Âtmâ is explained by *S*ankara as the g*î*va*h*, the living self, and as that living self is in his present state determined by karman, work belonging to a former existence, it cannot be thought of as an independent cause.

[4] Devâtma*s*akti is a very important term, differently explained by the commentators, but meaning a power belonging to the Deva, the Î*s*vara, the Lord, not independent of him, as the Sânkhyas represent Prak*ri*ti or nature. Herein lies the important distinction between Vedânta and Sânkhya.

[5] Kâlâtmabhyâ*m* yuktâni, kâlapurushasa*m*yuktâni svabhâvâdîni. Âtman is here taken as synonymous with purusha in verse 2.

[6] It is difficult to say whether this verse was written as a summing up of certain technicalities recognised in systems of philosophy existing at the time, or whether it is a mere play of fancy. I prefer the former view, and subjoin the explanation given by *S*ankara, though it is quite possible that on certain points he may be mistaken. The î*s*vara or deva is represented as a wheel with one felly, which would seem to be the phenomenal world. It is called triv*ri*t, threefold, or rather having three tires, three bands or hoops to bind the felly, these tires being intended for the three gu*n*as of the prak*ri*ti, the Sattva, Ra*g*as, and Tamas. In the Brahmopanishad (Bibl. Ind.

whose one rope is manifold, who proceeds on three different roads, and whose illusion arises from two causes.

---

p. 251) the trivr*i*t sûtram is mentioned. Next follows sho*d*a*s*ântam, ending in the sixteen. These sixteen are differently explained. They may be meant for the five elements and the eleven indriyas or organs (the five receptive and the five active senses, together with manas, the common sensory); or for the sixteen kalâs, mentioned in the Pra*s*ñopanishad, VI, 1, p. 283. Then follows a new interpretation. The one felly may be meant for the chaos, the undeveloped state of things, and the sixteen would then be the two products in a general form, the Virâ*g* and the Sûtrâtman, while the remaining fourteen would be the individual products, the bhuvanas or worlds beginning with Bhû*h*.

Next follows *s*atârdhâram, having fifty spokes. These fifty spokes are supposed to produce the motion of the mundane wheel, and are explained by *S*ankara as follows:

1. The five Viparyayas, misconceptions, different kinds of ignorance or doubt, viz. Tamas, Moha, Mahâmoha, Tâmisra, Andhatâmisra, or, according to Pata*ñg*ali, ignorance, self-love, love, hatred, and fear (Yoga-sûtras I, 8; II, 2; Sânkhya-sûtras III, 37).

2. The twenty-eight A*s*aktis, disabilities, causes of misconception. (See Sânkhya-sûtras III, 38.)

3. The nine inversions of the Tush*t*is, satisfactions. (Sânkhya-sûtras III, 39.)

4. The eight inversions of the Siddhis, perfections. (Sânkhya-sûtras III, 40.)

These are afterwards explained singly. There are 8 kinds of Tamas, 8 kinds of Moha, 10 kinds of Mahâmoha, 18 kinds of Tâmisra, and 18 kinds of Andhatâmisra, making 62 in all. More information on the A*s*aktis, the Tush*t*is, and Siddhis may be found in the Sânkhya-sûtras III, 37–45; Sânkhya-kârikâ 47 seq.; Yoga-sûtras II, 2 seq.

Then follow the 20 pratyaras, the counter-spokes, or wedges to strengthen the spokes, viz. the 10 senses and their 10 objects.

The six ash*t*akas or ogdoads are explained as the ogdoads of Prak*ri*ti, of substances (dhâtu), of powers (ai*s*varya), of states (bhâva), of gods (deva), of virtues (âtmagu*n*a).

The one, though manifold cord, is love or desire, Kâma, whether of food, children, heaven or anything else.

The three paths are explained as righteousness, unrighteousness,

5[1]. We meditate on the river whose water consists of the five streams, which is wild and winding with its five springs, whose waves are the five vital breaths, whose fountain head is the mind, the course of the five kinds of perceptions. It has five whirlpools, its rapids are the five pains; it has fifty kinds of suffering, and five branches.

6. In that vast Brahma-wheel, in which all things live and rest, the bird flutters about, so long as he thinks that the self (in him) is different from the mover (the god, the lord). When he has been blessed by him, then he gains immortality[2].

7. But what is praised (in the Upanishads) is the

---

and knowledge, and the one deception arising from two causes is ignorance of self, produced by good or bad works.

[1] Here again, where the îsvara is likened to a stream, the minute coincidences are explained by *S*ankara in accordance with certain systems of philosophy. The five streams are the five receptive organs, the five springs are the five elements, the five waves are the five active organs. The head is the manas, the mind, or common sensory, from which the perceptions of the five senses spring. The five whirlpools are the objects of the five senses, the five rapids are the five pains of being in the womb, being born, growing old, growing ill, and dying. The next adjective pañ*k*â-*s*adbhedâm is not fully explained by *S*ankara. He only mentions the five divisions of the kle*s*a (see Yoga-sûtras II,.2), but does not show how their number is raised to fifty. Dr. Roer proposes to read pañ*k*akle*s*a-bhedâm, but that would not agree with the metre. The five parvans or branches are not explained, and may refer to the fifty kinds of suffering (kle*s*a). The whole river, like the wheel in the preceding verse, is meant for the Brahman as kârya-kâra*n*âtmaka, in the form of cause and effect, as the phenomenal, not the absolutely real world.

[2] If he has been blessed by the Îsvara, i. e. when he has been accepted by the Lord, when he has discovered his own true self in the Lord. It must be remembered, however, that both the Îsvara, the Lord, and the purusha, the individual soul, are phenomenal only, and that the Brahma-wheel is meant for the prapañ*k*a, the manifest, but unreal world.

Highest Brahman, and in it there is the triad[1]. The
Highest Brahman is the safe support, it is imperishable. The Brahma-students[2], when they have known
what is within this (world), are devoted and merged
in the Brahman, free from birth[3].

8. The Lord (îsa) supports all this together, the
perishable and the imperishable, the developed and
the undeveloped. The (living) self, not being a lord,
is bound[4], because he has to enjoy (the fruits of
works); but when he has known the god (deva), he
is freed from all fetters.

9. There are two, one knowing (îsvara), the other
not-knowing (gîva), both unborn, one strong, the
other weak[5]; there is she, the unborn, through
whom each man receives the recompense of his
works[6]; and there is the infinite Self (appearing)
under all forms, but himself inactive. When a man
finds out these three, that is Brahma[7].

10. That which is perishable[8] is the Pradhâna[9]
(the first), the immortal and imperishable is Hara[10].

---

[1] The subject (bhoktri), the object (bhogya), and the mover
(preritri), see verse 12.

[2] B. has Vedavido, those who know the Vedas.

[3] Tasmin pralîyate tv âtmâ samâdhih sa udâhritah.

[4] Read badhyate for budhyate.

[5] The form îsanîsau is explained as khândasa; likewise brahmam for brahma.

[6] Cf. Svet. Up. IV, 5, bhuktabhogyâm.

[7] The three are (1) the lord, the personal god, the creator and
ruler; (2) the individual soul or souls; and (3) the power of creation,
the devâtmasakti of verse 3. All three are contained in Brahman;
see verses 7, 12. So 'pi mâyî paramesvaro mâyopâdhisannidhes
tadvân iva.

[8] See verse 8.

[9] The recognised name for Prakriti, or here Devâtmasakti, in
the later Sânkhya philosophy.

[10] Hara, one of the names of Siva or Rudra, is here explained as

The one god rules the perishable (the pradhâna) and the (living) self[1]. From meditating on him, from joining him, from becoming one with him there is further cessation of all illusion in the end.

11. When that god is known, all fetters fall off, sufferings are destroyed, and birth and death cease. From meditating on him there arises, on the dissolution of the body, the third state, that of universal lordship[2]; but he only who is alone, is satisfied[3].

12. This, which rests eternally within the self, should be known; and beyond this not anything has to be known. By knowing the enjoyer[4], the enjoyed, and the ruler, everything has been declared to be threefold, and this is Brahman.

13. As the form of fire, while it exists in the under-wood[5], is not seen, nor is its seed destroyed,

---

avidyâder harañât, taking away ignorance. He would seem to be meant for the îsvara or deva, the one god, though immediately afterwards he is taken for the true Brahman, and not for its phenomenal divine personification only.

[1] The self, âtman, used here, as before, for purusha, the individual soul, or rather the individual souls.

[2] A blissful state in the Brahma-world, which, however, is not yet perfect freedom, but may lead on to it. Thus it is said in the Sivadharmottara:

Dhyânâd aisvaryam atulam aisvaryât sukham uttamam,
Gñânena tat parityagya videho muktim âpnuyât.

[3] This alone-ness, kevalatvam, is produced by the knowledge that the individual self is one with the divine self, and that both the individual and the divine self are only phenomenal forms of the true Self, the Brahman.

[4] Bhoktâ, possibly for bhoktrâ, unless it is a Khândasa form. It was quoted before, Bibl. Ind. p. 292, l. 5. The enjoyer is the purusha, the individual soul, the subject; the enjoyed is prakriti, nature, the object; and the ruler is the îsvara, that is, Brahman, as god. I take brahmam etat in the same sense here as in verse 9.

[5] This metaphor, like most philosophical metaphors in Sanskrit,

but it has to be seized again and again by means of the stick and the under-wood, so it is in both cases, and the Self has to be seized in the body by means of the pra*n*ava (the syllable Om).

14. By making his body the under-wood, and the syllable Om the upper-wood, man, after repeating the drill of meditation, will perceive the bright god, like the spark hidden in the wood[1].

15. As oil in seeds, as butter in cream, as water in (dry) river-beds[2], as fire in wood, so is the Self seized within the self, if man looks for him by truthfulness and penance[3];

16. (If he looks) for the Self that pervades everything, as butter is contained in milk, and the roots whereof are self-knowledge and penance. That is the Brahman taught by the Upanishad.

---

is rather obscure at first sight, but very exact when once understood. Fire, as produced by a fire drill, is compared to the Self. It is not seen at first, yet it must be there all the time ; its li*n*ga or subtle body cannot have been destroyed, because as soon as the stick, the indhana, is drilled in the under-wood, the yoni, the fire becomes visible. In the same way the Self, though invisible during a state of ignorance, is there all the time, and is perceived when the body has been drilled by the Pra*n*ava, that is, after, by a constant repetition of the sacred syllable Om, the body has been subdued, and the ecstatic vision of the Self has been achieved.

Indhana, the stick used for drilling, and yoni, the under-wood, in which the stick is drilled, are the two ara*n*is, the fire-sticks used for kindling fire. See Tylor, Anthropology, p. 260.

[1] Cf. Dhyânavindûpan. verse 20; Brahmopanishad, p. 256.

[2] Srotas, a stream, seems to mean here the dry bed of a stream, which, if dug into, will yield water.

[3] The construction is correct, if we remember that he who is seized is the same as he who looks for the hidden Self. But the metre would be much improved if we accepted the reading of the Brahmopanishad, evam âtmâ âtmani gr*i*hyate 'sau, which is confirmed by B. The last line would be improved by reading, satyenaina*m* ye 'nupa*s*yanti dhîrâ*h*.

SECOND ADHYÂYA.

1[1]. Savit*ri* (the sun), having first collected his mind and expanded his thoughts, brought Agni (fire), when he had discovered his light, above the earth.

2[2]. With collected minds we are at the command of the divine Savit*ri*, that we may obtain blessedness.

---

[1] The seven introductory verses are taken from hymns addressed to Savit*ri* as the rising sun. They have been so twisted by *S*ankara, in order to make them applicable to the teachings of the Yoga philosophy, as to become almost nonsensical. I have given a few specimens of *S*ankara's renderings in the notes, but have translated the verses, as much as possible, in their original character. As they are merely introductory, I do not understand why the collector of the Upanishad should have seen in them anything but an invocation of Savit*ri*.

These verses are taken from various Sa*m*hitâs. The firs*t* yu*ñ*gâna*h* prathamam is from Taitt. Sa*m*h. IV, 1, 1, 1, 1 ; Vâ*g*. Sa*m*h. XI, 1; see also *S*at. Br. VI, 3, 1, 12. The Taittirîya-text agrees with the Upanishad, the Vâ*g*asaneyi-text has dhiyam for dhiya*h*, and agne*h* for agnim. Both texts take tatvâya as a participle of tan, while the Upanishad reads tattvâya, as a dative of tattva, truth. I have translated the verse in its natural sense. *S*ankara, in explaining the Upanishad, translates : ' At the beginning of our meditation, joining the mind with the Highest Self, also the other prâ*n*as, or the knowledge of outward things, for the sake of truth, Savit*ri*, out of the knowledge of outward things, brought Agni, after having discovered his brightness, above the earth, in this body.' He explains it : ' May Savit*ri*, taking our thoughts away from outward things, in order to concentrate them on the Highest Self, produce in our speech and in our other senses that power which can lighten all objects, which proceeds from Agni and from the other favourable deities.' He adds that ' by the favour of Savit*ri*, Yoga may be obtained.'

[2] The second verse is from Taitt. Sa*m*h. IV, 1, 1, 1, 3 ; Vâ*g*. Sa*m*h. XI, 2. The Vâ*g*asaneyi-text has svargyâya for svargeyâya, and *s*aktyâ for *s*aktyai. *S*ankara explains : ' With a mind that has been joined

3[1]. May Savit*ri*, after he has reached with his mind the gods as they rise up to the sky, and with his thoughts (has reached) heaven, grant these gods to make a great light to shine.

4[2]. The wise sages of the great sage collect their mind and collect their thoughts. He who alone knows the law (Savit*ri*) has ordered the invocations; great is the praise of the divine Savit*ri*.

by Savit*ri* to the Highest Self, we, with the sanction of that Savit*ri*, devote ourselves to the work of meditation, which leads to the obtainment of Svarga, according to our power.' He explains Svarga by Paramâtman. Sâya*n*a in his commentary on the Taittirîya-sa*m*hitâ explains svargeyâya by svargaloke gîyamânasyâgne*h* sampâdanâya; *S*ankara, by svargaprâptihetubhûtâya dhyânakarma*n*e. *S*aktyai is explained by *S*ankara by yathâsâmarthyam; by Sâya*n*a, by *s*aktâ bhûyâsma. Mahîdhara explains *s*aktyâ by svasâmarthyena. I believe that the original reading was svargyâya *s*aktyai, and that we must take *s*aktyai as an infinitive, like ityai, construed with a dative, like dr*i*saye sûryâya, for the seeing of the sun. The two attracted datives would be governed by save, 'we are under the command of Savit*ri*,' svargyâya *s*aktyai, 'that we may obtain svargya, life in Svarga or blessedness.'

[1] The third verse is from Taitt. Sa*m*h. IV, 1, 1, 1, 2; Vâ*g*. Sa*m*h. XI, 3. The Taittirîyas read yuktvâya manasâ; the Vâ*g*asaneyins, yuktvâya savitâ. *S*ankara translates: 'Again he prays that Savit*ri*, having directed the devas, i. e. the senses, which are moving towards Brahman, and which by knowledge are going to brighten up the heavenly light of Brahman, may order them to do so; that is, he prays that, by the favour of Savit*ri*, our senses should be turned away from outward things to Brahman or the Self.' Taking the hymn as addressed to Savit*ri*, I have translated deva by gods, not by senses, suvaryata*h* by rising to the sky, namely, in the morning. The opposition between manasâ and dhiyâ is the same here as in verse 1, and again in verse 4.

[2] This verse is from Taitt. Sa*m*h. IV, 1, 1, 1, 4; 1, 2, 13, 1, 1; Vâ*g*. Sa*m*h. V, 14; XI, 4; XXXVII, 2; Rig-veda V, 81, 1; *S*at. Br. III, 5, 3, 11; VI, 3, 1, 16. *S*ankara explains this verse again in the same manner as he did the former verses, while the *S*atapatha-brâhma*n*a supplies two different ritual explanations.

5[1]. Your old prayer has to be joined[2] with praises. Let my song go forth like the path of the sun! May all the sons of the Immortal listen, they who have reached their heavenly homes.

6. Where the fire is rubbed[3], where the wind is checked, where the Soma flows over, there the mind is born.

---

[1] For this verse, see Taitt. Samh. IV, 1, 1, 2, 1; Vâg. Samh. XI, 5; Atharva-veda XVIII, 3, 39; Rig-veda X, 13, 1. The Vâgasaneyins read vi sloka etu for vi slokâ yanti; sûreh for sûrâh; srinvantu for srinvanti; and the Rig-veda agrees with them. The dual vâm is accounted for by the verse belonging to a hymn celebrating the two sakatas, carts, bearing the offerings (havirdhâne); most likely, however, the dual referred originally to the dual deities of heaven and earth. I prefer the text of the Rig-veda and the Vâgasaneyins to that of the Taittirîyas, and have translated the verse accordingly. In the Atharva-veda XVIII, 39, if we may trust the edition, the verse begins with svâsasthe bhavatam indave nah, which is really the end of the next verse (Rv. X, 13, 2), while the second line is, vi sloka eti pathyeva sûrih srinvantu visve amritâsa etat. I see no sense in pathyeva sûrâh. Sankara explains pathyeva by pathi sanmârge, athavâ pathyâ kîrtih, while his later commentary, giving srinvantu and putrâh sûrâtmano hiranyagarbhasya, leads one to suppose that he read sûreh srinvantu. Sâyana (Taitt. Samh. IV, 1, 1, 2) explains pathyâ sûrâ iva by gîrvânamârga antarikshe sûryarasmayo yathâ prasaranti tadvat. The same, when commenting on the Rig-veda (X, 13, 1), says: pathyâ-iva sûreh, yathâ stotuh svabhûtâ pathyâ parinâmasukhâvahâhutir visvân devân prati vividham gakkhati tadvat. Mahîdhara (Vâg. Samh. XI, 5) refers sûreh (panditasya) to slokah, and explains pathyeva by patho 'napetâ pathyâ yagñamârgapravrittâhutih.

[2] Yugé cannot stand for yuñge, as all commentators and translators suppose, but is a datival infinitive. Neither can yuñgate in the following verse stand for yunkte (see Boehtlingk, s. v.), or be explained as a subjunctive form. A. reads adhirudhyate, B. abhirudhyate, with a marginal note abhinudyate. It is difficult to say whether in lighting the fire the wind should be directed towards it, or kept from it.

[3] That is, at the Soma sacrifice, after the fire has been kindled and stirred by the wind, the poets, on partaking of the juice, are

7. Let us love the old Brahman by the grace of Savit*ri*; if thou make thy dwelling there, the path will not hurt thee[1].

8. If a wise man hold his body with its three erect parts (chest, neck, and head) even[2], and turn his senses with the mind towards the heart, he will then in the boat of Brahman[3] cross all the torrents which cause fear.

9. Compressing his breathings let him, who has subdued all motions, breathe forth through the nose with gentle breath[4]. Let the wise man without fail restrain his mind, that chariot yoked with vicious horses[5].

10. Let him perform his exercises in a place[6]

---

inspirited for new songs. *S*ankara, however, suggests another explanation as more appropriate for the Upanishad, namely, 'Where the fire, i.e. the Highest Self, which burns all ignorance, has been kindled (in the body, where it has been rubbed with the syllable Om), and where the breath has acted, i. e. has made the sound peculiar to the initial stages of Yoga, there Brahman is produced.' In fact, what was intended to be taught was this, that we must begin with sacrificial acts, then practise yoga, then reach samâdhi, perfect knowledge, and lastly bliss.

[1] We must read k*ri*navase, in the sense of ' do this and nothing will hurt thee,' or, if thou do this, thy former deeds will no longer hurt thee.

[2] Cf. Bhagavadgîtâ VI, 13. Sama*m* kâya*s*irogrîva*m* dhârayan. *S*ankara says: trî*n*y unnatâny urogrîva*s*irâ*m*sy unnatâni yasmin *s*arîre.

[3] Explained by *S*ankara as the syllable Om.

[4] Cf. Bhagavadgîtâ V, 27. Prâ*n*âpânau samau k*ri*tvâ nâsâbhyantara *k*âri*n*au. See Telang's notes, Sacred Books of the East, vol. viii, p. 68 seq.

[5] A similar metaphor in Ka*th*. Up. III, 4–6 ; Sacred Books of the East, vol. xv, p. 13.

[6] The question is whether *s*abda*g*alâ*s*rayâdibhi*h* should be referred to mano 'nukûle, as I have translated it, or to vivar*g*ite, as *S*ankara seems to take it, because he renders *s*abda, sound, by noise, and

level, pure, free from pebbles, fire, and dust, delightful by its sounds, its water, and bowers, not painful to the eye, and full of shelters and caves.

11. When Yoga is being performed, the forms which come first, producing apparitions in Brahman, are those of misty smoke, sun, fire, wind, fire-flies, lightnings, and a crystal moon [1].

12. When, as earth, water, light, heat, and ether arise, the fivefold quality of Yoga takes place [2], then there is no longer illness, old age, or pain [3] for him who has obtained a body, produced by the fire of Yoga.

13. The first results of Yoga they call lightness, healthiness, steadiness, a good complexion, an easy pronunciation, a sweet odour, and slight excretions.

14. As a metal disk (mirror), tarnished by dust, shines bright again after it has been cleaned, so is the one incarnate person satisfied and free from grief, after he has seen the real nature of the self [4].

âsraya by mandapa, a booth. See Bhagavadgîtâ VI, 11. In the Maitr. Up. VI, 30, Râmatîrtha explains sukau dese by girinadî-pulinaguhâdisuddhasthâne. See also Âsv. Grihya-sûtras III, 2, 2.

[1] Or, it may be, a crystal and the moon.

[2] The Yogaguna is described as the quality of each element, i. e. smell of the earth, taste of water, &c. It seems that the perception of these gunas is called yogapravritti. Thus by fixing the thought on the tip of the nose, a perception of heavenly scent is produced; by fixing it on the tip of the tongue, a perception of heavenly taste; by fixing it on the point of the palate, a heavenly colour; by fixing it on the middle of the tongue, a heavenly touch; by fixing it on the roof of the tongue, a heavenly sound. By means of these perceptions the mind is supposed to be steadied, because it is no longer attracted by the outward objects themselves. See Yoga-sûtras I, 35.

[3] Or no death, na mrityuh, B.

[4] Pareshâm pâthe tadvat sa tattvam prasamîkshya dehîti.

15. And when by means of the real nature of his self he sees, as by a lamp, the real nature of Brahman, then having known the unborn, eternal god, who is beyond all natures [1], he is freed from all fetters.

16. He indeed is the god who pervades all regions: he is the first-born (as Hiranyagarbha), and he is in the womb. He has been born, and he will be born [2]. He stands behind all persons, looking everywhere.

17. The god [3] who is in the fire, the god who is in the water, the god who has entered into the whole world, the god who is in plants, the god who is in trees, adoration be to that god, adoration!

---

[1] Sarvatattvair avidyâtatkâryair visuddham asamsprishtam.

[2] This verse is found in the Vâg. Samh. XXXII, 4; Taitt. Âr. X, 1, 3, with slight modifications. The Vâgasaneyins read esho ha (so do A. B.) for esha hi; sa eva gâtah (A. B.) for sa vigâtah; ganâs (A.B.) for ganâms. The Âranyaka has sa vigâyamânah for sa vigâtah, pratyanmukhâs for pratyanganâms, and visvatomukhah for sarvatomukhah. Colebrooke (Essays, I, 57) gives a translation of it. If we read ganâh, we must take it as a vocative.

[3] B. (not A.) reads yo rudro yo 'gnau.

THIRD ADHYÂYA[1].

1. The snarer[2] who rules alone by his powers, who rules all the worlds by his powers, who is one and the same, while things arise and exist[3],—they who know this are immortal.

2. For there is one Rudra only, they do not allow a second, who rules all the worlds by his powers. He stands behind all persons[4], and after having created all worlds he, the protector, rolls it up[5] at the end of time.

3[6]. That one god, having his eyes, his face, his arms, and his feet in every place, when producing heaven and earth, forges them together with his arms and his wings[7].

---

[1] This Adhyâya represents the Highest Self as the personified deity, as the lord, îsa, or Rudra, under the sway of his own creative power, prakriti or mâyâ.

[2] Sankara explains gâla, snare, by mâyâ. The verse must be corrected, according to Sankara's commentary:

ya eko gâlavân îsata îsanîbhih
sarvâñ llokân îsata îsanîbhih.

[3] Sambhava, in the sense of Vergehen, perishing, rests on no authority.

[4] Here again the MSS. A. B. read ganâs, as a vocative.

[5] I prefer samkukoka to samkukopa, which gives us the meaning that Rudra, after having created all things, draws together, i. e. takes them all back into himself, at the end of time. I have translated samsrigya by having created, because Boehtlingk and Roth give other instances of samsrig with that sense. Otherwise, 'having mixed them together again,' would seem more appropriate. A. and B. read samkukoka.

[6] This is a very popular verse, and occurs Rig-veda X, 81, 3; Vâg. Samh. XVII, 19; Ath.-veda XIII, 2, 26; Taitt. Samh. IV, 6, 2, 4; Taitt. Âr. X, 1, 3.

[7] Sankara takes dhamati in the sense of samyogayati, i. e. he joins men with arms, birds with wings.

4. He[1], the creator and supporter of the gods, Rudra, the great seer, the lord of all, he who formerly gave birth to Hira*n*yagarbha, may he endow us with good thoughts.

5[2]. O Rudra, thou dweller in the mountains, look upon us with that most blessed form of thine which is auspicious, not terrible, and reveals no evil!

6[3]. O lord of the mountains, make lucky that arrow which thou, a dweller in the mountains, holdest in thy hand to shoot. Do not hurt man or beast!

7. Those who know beyond this the High Brahman, the vast, hidden in the bodies of all creatures, and alone enveloping everything, as the Lord, they become immortal[4].

8[5]. I know that great person (purusha) of sunlike lustre beyond the darkness[6]. A man who knows him truly, passes over death; there is no other path to go[7].

9. This whole universe is filled by this person (purusha), to whom there is nothing superior, from whom there is nothing different, than whom there is

---

[1] See IV, 12.

[2] See Vâg. Sa*m*h. XVI, 2; Taitt. Sa*m*h. IV, 5, 1, 1.

[3] See Vâg. Sa*m*h. XVI, 3; Taitt. Sa*m*h. IV, 5, 1, 1; Nîlarudropan. p. 274.

[4] The knowledge consists in knowing either that Brahman is Îsa or that Îsa is Brahman. But in either case the gender of the adjectives is difficult. The *S*vetâ*s*vatara-upanishad seems to use br*i*-hanta as an adjective, instead of br*i*hat. I should prefer to translate: Beyond this is the High Brahman, the vast. Those who know Îsa, the Lord, hidden in all things and embracing all things to be this (Brahman), become immortal. See also Muir, Metrical Translations, p. 196, whose translation of these verses I have adopted with few exceptions.

[5] Cf. Vâg. Sa*m*h. XXX, 18; Taitt. Âr. III, 12, 7; III, 13, 1.

[6] Cf. Bhagavadgîtâ VIII, 9.   [7] Cf. *S*vet. Up. VI, 15.

nothing smaller or larger, who stands alone, fixed
like a tree in the sky[1].

10. That which is beyond this world is without
form and without suffering. They who know it,
become immortal, but others suffer pain indeed[2].

11. That Bhagavat[3] exists in the faces, the heads,
the necks of all, he dwells in the cave (of the heart)
of all beings, he is all-pervading, therefore he is the
omnipresent Śiva.

12. That person (purusha) is the great lord; he
is the mover of existence[4], he possesses that purest
power of reaching everything[5], he is light, he is
undecaying.

13[6]. The person (purusha), not larger than a thumb,

---

[1] Divi, the sky, is explained by Śankara as dyotanâtmani sva-
mahimni.

[2] The pain of samsâra, or transmigration. See Brihad. Up. IV,
3, 20 (p. 178).

[3] I feel doubtful whether the two names Bhagavat and Śiva should
here be preserved, or whether the former should be rendered by
holy, the latter by happy. The commentator explains Bhagavat by
    aisvaryasya samagrasya vîryasya yasasah sriyah
    Gñânavairâgyayos kaiva shannâm bhaga itîranâ.
Wilson, in his Essay on the Religious Sects of the Hindus,
published in 1828, in the Asiatic Researches, XVI, p. 11, pointed
out that this verse and another (Śvet. Up. II, 2) were cited by the
Śaivas as Vedic authorities for their teaching. He remarked that
these citations would scarcely have been made, if not authentic, and
that they probably did occur in the Vedas. In the new edition of
this Essay by Dr. Rost, 1862, the references should have been added.

[4] Śankara explains sattvasya by antahkaranasya.

[5] I take prâpti, like other terms occurring in this Upanishad, in
its technical sense. Prâpti is one of the vibhûtis or aisvaryas, viz.
the power of touching anything at will, as touching the moon with
the tip of one's finger. See Yoga-sûtras, ed. Rajendralal Mitra,
p. 121.

[6] Cf. Taitt. Âr. X, 71 (Anuv. 38, p. 858). Kath. Up. IV, 12–13;
above, p. 16.

dwelling within, always dwelling in the heart of man,
is perceived by the heart, the thought[1], the mind;
they who know it become immortal.

14[2]. The person (purusha) with a thousand heads,
a thousand eyes, a thousand feet, having compassed
the earth on every side, extends beyond it by ten
fingers' breadth.

15. That person alone (purusha) is all this, what
has been and what will be; he is also the lord of
immortality; he is whatever grows by food[3].

16. Its[4] hands and feet are everywhere, its eyes
and head are everywhere, its ears are everywhere,
it stands encompassing all in the world[5].

17. Separate from all the senses, yet reflecting
the qualities of all the senses, it is the lord and ruler
of all, it is the great refuge of all.

18. The embodied spirit within the town with
nine gates[6], the bird, flutters outwards, the ruler of

---

[1] The text has manvîsa, which Sankara explains by gñânesa.
But Weber has conjectured rightly, I believe, that the original text
must have been manîshâ. The difficulty is to understand how so
common a word as manîshâ could have been changed into so unusual a word as manvîsa. See IV, 20.

[2] This is a famous verse of the Rig-veda, X, 90, 1; repeated in
the Atharva-veda, XIX, 6, 1; Vâg. Samh. XXXI, 1; Taitt. Âr. III,
12, 1. Sankara explains ten fingers' breadth by endless; or, he
says, it may be meant for the heart, which is ten fingers above
the navel.

[3] Sâyana, in his commentary on the Rig-veda and the Taitt. Âr.,
gives another explanation, viz. he is also the lord of all the immortals, i. e. the gods, because they grow to their exceeding state
by means of food, or for the sake of food.

[4] The gender changes frequently, according as the author thinks
either of the Brahman, or of its impersonation as Îsa, Lord.

[5] Sankara explains loka by nikâya, body.

[6] Cf. Kath. Up. V, 1.

the whole world, of all that rests and of all that moves.

19. Grasping without hands, hasting without feet, he sees without eyes, he hears without ears. He knows what can be known, but no one knows him; they call him the first, the great person (purusha).

20[1]. The Self, smaller than small, greater than great, is hidden in the heart of the creature. A man who has left all grief behind, sees the majesty, the Lord, the passionless, by the grace of the creator (the Lord).

21[2]. I know[3] this undecaying, ancient one, the self of all things, being infinite and omnipresent. They declare that in him all birth is stopped, for the Brahma-students proclaim him to be eternal[4].

---

[1] Cf. Taitt. Âr. X, 12 (10), p. 800; Ka*th*. Up. II, 20; above, p. 11. The translation had to be slightly altered, because the *S*vetâsvataras, as Taittirîyas, read akratum for akratu*h*, and îsam for âtmana*h*.

[2] Cf. Taitt. Âr. III, 13, 1; III, 12, 7.

[3] A. reads vedârû*dh*am, not B.

[4] A. and B. read brahmavâdino hi pravadanti.

FOURTH ADHYÂYA.

1. He, the sun, without any colour, who with set purpose[1] by means of his power (*s*akti) produces endless colours[2], in whom all this comes together in the beginning, and comes asunder in the end—may he, the god, endow us with good thoughts[3].

2. That (Self) indeed is Agni (fire), it is Âditya (sun), it is Vâyu (wind), it is *K*andramas (moon); the same also is the starry firmament[4], it is Brahman (Hira*n*yagarbha), it is water, it is Pra*g*âpati (Virâ*g*).

3. Thou art woman, thou art man; thou art youth, thou art maiden; thou, as an old man, totterest[5] along on thy staff; thou art born with thy face turned everywhere.

4. Thou art the dark-blue bee, thou art the green

---

[1] Nihitârtha, explained by *S*ankara as g*ri*hîtaprayo*g*ana*h* svârtha-nirapeksha*h*. This may mean with set purpose, but if we read ag*ri*hîtaprayo*g*ana*h* it would mean the contrary, namely, without any definite object, irrespective of his own objects. This is possible, and perhaps more in accordance with the idea of creation as propounded by those to whom the devâtma*s*akti is mâyâ. Nihita would then mean hidden.

[2] Colour is intended for qualities, differences, &c.

[3] This verse has been translated very freely. As it stands, vi *k*aiti *k*ânte vi*s*vam âdau sa deva*h*, it does not construe, in spite of all attempts to the contrary, made by *S*ankara. What is intended is yasminn ida*m* sa*m* *k*a vi *k*aiti sarvam (IV, 11); but how so simple a line should have been changed into what we read now, is difficult to say.

[4] This is the explanation of *S*ankara, and probably that of the Yoga schools in India at his time. But to take *s*ukram for dîptiman nakshatrâdi, brahma for Hira*n*yagarbha, and Pra*g*âpati for Virâ*g* seems suggested by this verse only.

[5] Va*ñk*ayasi, an exceptional form, instead of va*ñk*asi (A. B.)

parrot with red eyes, thou art the thunder-cloud, the
seasons, the seas. Thou art without beginning[1],
because thou art infinite, thou from whom all worlds
are born.

5 [2]. There is one unborn being (female), red, white,
and black, uniform, but producing manifold offspring.
There is one unborn being (male) who loves her
and lies by her; there is another who leaves her,
while she is eating what has to be eaten.

---

[1] We see throughout the constant change from the masculine
to the neuter gender, in addressing either the lord or his true
essence.

[2] This is again one of the famous verses of our Upanishad,
because it formed for a long time a bone of contention between
Vedânta and Sânkhya philosophers. The Sânkhyas admit two
principles, the Purusha, the absolute subject, and the Prakriti,
generally translated by nature. The Vedânta philosophers admit
nothing but the one absolute subject, and look upon nature as due
to a power inherent in that subject. The later Sânkhyas therefore,
who are as anxious as the Vedântins to find authoritative passages
in the Veda, confirming their opinions, appeal to this and other
passages, to show that their view of Prakriti, as an independent
power, is supported by the Veda. The whole question is fully
discussed in the Vedânta-sûtras I, 4, 8. Here we read rohita-
krishna-suklâm, which seems preferable to lohita-krishna-varnâm,
at least from a Vedânta point of view, for the three colours, red,
black, and white, are explained as signifying either the three gunas,
ragas, sattva, and tamas, or better (Khând. Up. VI, 3, 1), the three
elements, tegas (fire), ap (water), and anna (earth). A. reads
rohitasuklakrishnâm; B. lohitasuklakrishnâ (sic). We also find
in A. and B. bhuktabhogâm for bhuktabhogyâm, but the latter
seems technically the more correct reading. It would be quite
wrong to imagine that aga and agâ are meant here for he-goat
and she-goat. These words, in the sense of unborn, are recognised
as early as the hymns of the Rig-veda, and they occurred in our
Upanishad I, 9, where the two agas are mentioned in the same
sense as here. But there is, no doubt, a play on the words, and
the poet wished to convey the second meaning of he-goat and
she-goat, only not as the primary, but as the secondary intention.

6 [1]. Two birds, inseparable friends, cling to the same tree. One of them eats the sweet fruit, the other looks on without eating.

7. On the same tree man sits grieving, immersed, bewildered, by his own impotence (an-îsâ). But when he sees the other lord (îsa) contented, and knows his glory, then his grief passes away.

8 [2]. He who does not know that indestructible being of the *Rig*-veda, that highest ether-like (Self) wherein all the gods reside, of what use is the *Rig*-veda to him? Those only who know it, rest contented.

9. That from which the maker (mâyin [3]) sends forth all this—the sacred verses, the offerings, the sacrifices, the panaceas, the past, the future, and all

---

[1] The same verses occur in the Mu*nd*aka Up. III, 1.

[2] It is difficult to see how this verse comes in here. In the Taitt. Âr. II, 11, 6, it is quoted in connection with the syllable Om, the Akshara, in which all the Vedas are comprehended. It is similarly used in the N*ri*sim*ha-pûrva-tâpanî, IV, 2 ; V, 2. In our passage, however, akshara is referred by *S*ankara to the paramât-man, and I have translated it accordingly. *Rikah* is explained as a genitive singular, but it may also be taken as a nom. plur., and in that case both the verses of the Veda and the gods are said to reside in the Akshara, whether we take it for the Paramâtman or for the Om. In the latter case, parame vyoman is explained by utk*ri*sh*t*e and rakshake.

[3] It is impossible to find terms corresponding to mâyâ and mâyin. Mâyâ means making, or art, but as all making or creating, so far as the Supreme Self is concerned, is phenomenal only or mere illusion, mâyâ conveys at the same time the sense of illusion. In the same manner mâyin is the maker, the artist, but also the magician or juggler. What seems intended by our verse is that from the akshara, which corresponds to brahman, all proceeds, whatever exists or seems to exist, but that the actual creator or the author of all emanations is Îsa, the Lord, who, as creator, is acting through mâyâ or devâtma*s*akti. Possibly, however, anya, the other, may be meant for the individual purusha.

that the Vedas declare—in that the other is bound up through that mâyâ.

10. Know then Prakr*i*ti (nature) is Mâyâ (art), and the great Lord the Mâyin (maker); the whole world is filled with what are his members.

11. If a man has discerned him, who being one only, rules over every germ (cause), in whom all this comes together and comes asunder again, who is the lord, the bestower of blessing, the adorable god, then he passes for ever into that peace.

12 [1]. He, the creator and supporter of the gods, Rudra, the great seer, the lord of all, who saw [2] Hira*n*yagarbha being born, may he endow us with good thoughts.

13. He who is the sovereign of the gods, he in whom all the worlds [3] rest, he who rules over all two-footed and four-footed beings, to that god [4] let us · sacrifice an oblation.

14. He who has known him who is more subtile than subtile, in the midst of chaos, creating all things, having many forms, alone enveloping everything [5], the happy one (*S*iva), passes into peace for ever.

---

[1] See before, III, 4.

[2] *S*ankara does not explain this verse again, though it differs from III, 4. Vig*ñ*ânâtman explains pa*s*yata by apa*s*yata, and qualifies the Âtmanepada as irregular.

[3] B. reads yasmin devâ*h*, not A.

[4] I read tasmai instead of kasmai, a various reading mentioned by Vig*ñ*ânâtman. It was easy to change tasmai into kasmai, because of the well-known line in the Rig-veda, kasmai devâya havishâ vidhema. Those who read kasmai, explain it as a dative of Ka, a name of Pra*g*âpati, which in the dative should be kâya, and not kasmai. It would be better to take kasmai as the dative of the interrogative pronoun. See M. M., History of Ancient Sanskrit Literature, p. 433; and Vitâna-sutras IV, 22.

[5] Cf. III, 7.

15. He also was in time [1] the guardian of this world, the lord of all, hidden in all beings. In him the Brahmarshis and the deities are united [2], and he who knows him cuts the fetters of death asunder.

16. He who knows Siva (the blessed) hidden in all beings, like the subtile film that rises from out the clarified butter [3], alone enveloping everything,— he who knows the god, is freed from all fetters.

17. That god, the maker of all things, the great Self [4], always dwelling in the heart of man, is perceived by the heart, the soul, the mind [5];—they who know it become immortal.

18. When the light has risen [6], there is no day, no night, neither existence nor non-existence [7]; Siva (the blessed) alone is there. That is the eternal, the adorable light of Savitri [8],—and the ancient wisdom proceeded thence.

19. No one has grasped him above, or across, or in the middle [9]. There is no image of him whose name is Great Glory.

20. His form cannot be seen, no one perceives him with the eye. Those [10] who through heart and

---

[1] In former ages, Sankara.

[2] Because both the Brahmarshis, the holy seers, and the deities find their true essence in Brahman.

[3] We should say, like cream from milk.

[4] Or the high-minded.

[5] See III, 13.

[6] Atamas, no darkness, i. e. light of knowledge.

[7] See on the difficulty of translating sat and asat, τὸ ὄν and τὸ μὴ ὄν, the remarks in the Preface.

[8] Referring to the Gâyatrî, Rig-veda III, 62, 10; see also Svet. Up. V, 4.

[9] See Muir, Metrical Translations, p. 198; Maitr. Up. VI, 17.

[10] B. reads hridâ manîshâ manasâbhiklipto, yat tad vidur; A. hridi hridistham manasâya enam evam vidur.

mind know him thus abiding in the heart, become immortal.

21. 'Thou art unborn,' with these words some one comes near to thee, trembling. O Rudra, let thy gracious[1] face protect me for ever!

22[2]. O Rudra! hurt us not in our offspring and descendants, hurt us not in our own lives, nor in our cows, nor in our horses! Do not slay our men in thy wrath, for, holding oblations, we call on thee always.

---

[1] Dakshina is explained either as invigorating, exhilarating, or turned towards the south.

[2] See Colebrooke, Miscellaneous Essays, I, p. 141; Rig-veda I, 114, 8; Taitt. Samh. IV, 5, 10, 3; Vâg. Samh. XVI, 16. The various readings are curious. Âyushi in the Svet. Up., instead of âyau in the Rig-veda, is supported by the Taitt. Samh. and the Vâg. Samh.; but Vignânâtman reads âyau. As to bhâmito, it seems the right reading, being supported by the Rig-veda, the Taitt. Samh., and the Svet. Up., while bhâvito in Roer's edition is a misprint. The Vâg. Samh. alone reads bhâmino, which Mahîdhara refers to vîrân. The last verse in the Rig-veda and Vâg. Samh. is havishmantah sadam it tvâ havâmahe; in the Taitt. Samh. havishmanto namasâ vidhema te. In the Svet. Up. havishmantah sadasi tvâ havâmahe, as printed by Roer, seems to rest on Sankara's authority only. The other commentators, Sankarânanda and Vignânâtman, read and interpret sadam it.

FIFTH ADHYÂYA.

1. In the imperishable and infinite Highest Brahman[1], wherein the two, knowledge and ignorance, are hidden[2], the one, ignorance, perishes[3], the other, knowledge, is immortal; but he who controls both, knowledge and ignorance, is another[4].

2. It is he who, being one only, rules over every germ (cause), over all forms, and over all germs; it is he who, in the beginning, bears[5] in his thoughts the wise son, the fiery, whom he wishes to look on[6] while he is born[7].

3[8]. In that field[9] in which the god, after spreading out one net after another[10] in various ways, draws it together again, the Lord, the great Self[11], having

---

[1] Sankara explains Brahmapare by brahmano hiranyagarbhât pare, or by parasmin brahmani, which comes to the same. Vignâ-nâtman adds khândasah paranipâtah. As the termination e may belong to the locative singular or to the nom. dual, commentators vary in referring some of the adjectives either to brahman or to vidyâvidye.

[2] Gûdhe, lokair gñâtum asakye, Sankarânanda.

[3] Sankara explains ksharam by samsritikâranam, amritam by mokshahetuh.

[4] Sankara explains that he is different from them, being only the sâkshin, or witness. Sankarânanda seems to have read Somya, i. e. Somavatpriyadarsana, as if Svetâsvatvara addressed his pupil.

[5] Like a mother, see I, 9.   [6] Like a father.

[7] See on this verse the remarks made in the Introduction.

[8] The MSS. read yasmin for asmin, and patayas for yatayas, which the commentator explains by patîn.

[9] The world, or the mûlaprakriti, the net being the samsâra.

[10] Sankara explains ekaikam by pratyekam, i. e. for every creature, such as gods, men, beasts, &c.

[11] I doubt whether mahâtmâ should be translated by the great

further created the lords[1], thus carries on his lordship over all.

4. As the car (of the sun) shines, lighting up all
quarters, above, below, and across, thus does that
god, the holy, the adorable, being one, rule over all
that has the nature of a germ[2].

5. He, being one, rules over all and everything,
so that the universal germ ripens its nature, diversi-
fies all natures that can be ripened[3], and determines
all qualities[4].

6[5]. Brahmâ (Hira*n*yagarbha) knows this, which
is hidden in the Upanishads, which are hidden in
the Vedas, as the Brahma-germ.   The ancient gods

Self, or whether great would not be sufficient.   The whole verse is
extremely difficult.

[1] From Hira*n*yagarbha to insects; or beginning with Mari*k*i.

[2] Cf. IV, 11; V, 2.

[3] MS. B. has prâ*k*yân, and explains it by pûrvotpannân.

[4] This is again a very difficult verse.   I have taken vi*s*vayoni*h*
as a name for Brahman, possessed of that devâtma*s*akti which was
mentioned before, but I feel by no means satisfied.   The commentators do not help, because they do not see the difficulty of the
construction.   If one might conjecture, I should prefer pa*k*et for
pa*k*ati, and should write pari*n*âmayed yat, and viniyo*g*ayed yat,
unless we changed ya*kk*a into ya*s* *k*a.

[5] This verse admits of various translations, and requires also
some metrical emendations.   Thus Vi*gñ*ânâtman explains vedagu-
hyopanishatsu very ingeniously by the Veda, i. e. that part of it
which teaches sacrifices and their rewards; the Guhya, i. e. the
Âra*n*yaka, which teaches the worship of Brahman under various
legendary aspects; and the Upanishads, which teach the knowledge
of Brahman without qualities.   These three divisions would correspond to the karmakâ*nd*a, yogakâ*nd*a, and *gñ*ânakâ*nd*a (*G*aimini,
Pata*ñg*ali, Bâdarâya*n*a).   See Deussen, Vedânta, p. 20.   Mr. Gough
and Dr. Roer take Brahmayoni as 'the source of the Veda,' or as
the source of Hira*n*yagarbha.   The irregular form vedate may be
due to a corruption of vedânte.

and poets who knew it, they became it and were
immortal.

7 [1]. But he who is endowed with qualities, and
performs works that are to bear fruit, and enjoys
the reward of whatever he has done, migrates
through his own works, the lord of life, assuming
all forms, led by the three Gu*n*as, and following the
three paths [2].

8 [3]. That lower one also, not larger than a thumb,
but brilliant like the sun, who is endowed with personality and thoughts, with the quality of mind and
the quality of body, is seen small even like the point
of a goad.

9. That living soul is to be known as part of the
hundredth part of the point of a hair [4], divided a
hundred times, and yet it is to be infinite.

10. It is not woman, it is not man, nor is it
neuter; whatever body it takes, with that it is
joined [5] (only).

11 [6]. By means of thoughts, touching, seeing, and

---

[1] Here begins the description of what is called the tvam (thou),
as opposed to the tat (that), i. e. the living soul, as opposed to the
Highest Brahman.

[2] The paths of vice, virtue, and knowledge.

[3] Both MSS. (A. and B.) read ârâgramâtro hy avaro 'pi d*ri*-
sh*ta*h.

[4] An expression of frequent occurrence in Buddhist literature.

[5] A. and B. read yu*g*yate. A. explains yu*g*yate by sambadh-
yate. B. explains adyate bhakshyate tirobhûta*h* kriyate. *S*ankara
explains rakshyate, sa*m*rakshyate, tattaddharmân âtmany adhyasyâ-
bhimanyate.

[6] The MSS. vary considerably. Instead of mohair, A. and B.
read homair. They read grâsâmbuv*ri*sh*t*yâ *k*âtma. A. reads
âtmaviv*ri*ddhi*g*anma, B. âtmaniv*ri*ddha*g*anmâ. A. has abhisam-
prapadye, B. abhisamprapadyate. My translation follows *S*ankara,
who seems to have read âtmaviv*ri*ddhi*g*anma, taking the whole line

passions the incarnate Self assumes successively in
various places various forms[1], in accordance with his
deeds, just as the body grows when food and drink
are poured into it.

12. That incarnate Self, according to his own
qualities, chooses (assumes) many shapes, coarse or
subtile, and having himself caused his union with
them, he is seen as another and another[2], through
the qualities of his acts, and through the qualities of
his body.

13[3]. He who knows him who has no beginning
and no end, in the midst of chaos, creating all things,
having many forms, alone enveloping everything, is
freed from all fetters.

14. Those who know him who is to be grasped
by the mind, who is not to be called the nest (the
body[4]), who makes existence and non-existence, the

---

as a simile and in an adverbial form. Vigñânâtman, however, differs
considerably. He reads homaih, and explains homa as the act of
throwing oblations into the fire, as in the Agnihotra. This action
of the hands, he thinks, stands for all actions of the various members of the body. Grâsâmbuvrishti he takes to mean free distribution of food and drink, and then explains the whole sentence by
'he whose self is born unto some states or declines from them
again, namely, according as he has showered food and drink, and
has used his hands, eyes, feelings, and thoughts.' Ṣankarânanda
takes a similar view, only he construes sankalpanam and sparṣanam
as two drishtis, te eva drishtî, tayor âtmâgnau prakshepâ homâh;
and then goes on, na kevalam etaih, kim tv asmin sthâne ṣarire
grâsâmbuvrishtyâ ka. He seems to read âtmavivriddhaganmâ, but
afterwards explains vivriddhi by vividhâ vriddhih.

[1] Forms as high as Hiranyagarbha or as low as beasts.
[2] Instead of aparo, B. reads avaro, but explains aparo.
[3] Cf. III, 7; IV, 14, 16.
[4] Nida is explained as the body, but Ṣankarânanda reads anilâ-
khyam, who is called the wind, as being prânasya prânam, the
breath of the breath.

happy one (*S*iva), who also creates the elements[1], they have left the body.

---

[1] *S*ankara explains kalâsargakaram by he who creates the sixteen kalâs, mentioned by the Âtharva*n*ikas, beginning with prâ*n*a, and ending with nâman; see Pras*ñ*a Up. VI, 4. Vig*ñ*ânâtman suggests two other explanations, 'he who creates by means of the kalâ, i. e. his inherent power;' or 'he who creates the Vedas and other sciences.' The sixteen kalâs are, according to *S*ankarânanda, prâ*n*a, *s*raddhâ, kha, vâyu, gyoti*h*, ap, pr*i*thivî, indriya, mana*h*, anna, vîrya, tapa*h*, mantra, karman, kâla (?), nâman. See also before, I, 4.

SIXTH ADHYÂYA.

1[1]. Some wise men, deluded, speak of Nature, and others of Time (as the cause of everything[2]); but it is the greatness of God by which this Brahma-wheel is made to turn.

2. It is at the command of him who always covers this world, the knower, the time of time[3], who assumes qualities and all knowledge[4], it is at his command that this work (creation) unfolds itself, which is called earth, water, fire, air, and ether;

3[5]. He who, after he has done that work and rested again, and after he has brought together one essence (the self) with the other (matter), with one, two, three, or eight, with time also and with the subtile qualities of the mind,

4. Who, after starting[6] the works endowed with (the three) qualities, can order all things, yet when, in the absence of all these, he has caused the destruction of the work, goes on, being in truth[7] different (from all he has produced);

---

[1] See Muir, Metrical Translations, p. 198.

[2] See before, I, 2.

[3] The destroyer of time. Vignânâtman reads kâlakâlo, and explains it by kâlasya niyantâ, upahartâ. Sankarânanda explains kâlah sarvavinâsakârî, tasyâpi vinâsakarah. See also verse 16.

[4] Or sarvavid yah.

[5] Instead of vinivartya, Vignânâtman and Sankarânanda read vinivrityâ.

[6] Âruhya for ârabhya, Sankarânanda.

[7] These two verses are again extremely obscure, and the explanations of the commentators throw little light on their real, original meaning. To begin with Sankara, he assumes the subject to be the same as he at whose command this work unfolds itself, and explains

5. He is the beginning, producing the causes which unite (the soul with the body), and, being

tattvasya tattvena sametya yogam by âtmano bhûmyâdinâ yogam samgamayya. As the eight Tattvas he gives earth, water, fire, air, ether, mind, thought, personality, while the Âtmagunas are, according to him, the affections of the mind, love, anger, &c. In the second verse, however, Sankara seems to assume a different subject. 'If a man,' he says, 'having done works, infected by qualities, should transfer them on Îsvara, the Lord, there would be destruction of the works formerly done by him, because there would be no more connection with the self.' Something is left out, but that this is Sankara's idea, appears from the verses which he quotes in support, and which are intended to show that Yogins, transferring all their acts, good, bad, or indifferent, on Brahman, are no longer affected by them. 'That person,' Sankara continues, 'his works being destroyed and his nature purified, moves on, different from all things (tattva), from all the results of ignorance, knowing himself to be Brahman.' 'Or,' he adds, 'if we read anyad, it means, he goes to that Brahman which is different from all things.'

Sankarânanda takes a different view. He says: 'If a man has performed sacrifices, and has finished them, or, has turned away from them again as vain, and if he has obtained union with that which is the real of the (apparently) real, &c.' The commentator then asks what is that with which he obtains union, and replies, 'the one, i. e. ignorance; the two, i. e. right and wrong; the three, i. e. the three colours, red, white, and black; and the eight, i. e. the five elements, with mind, thought, and personality; also with time, and with the subtile affections of the mind.' He then goes on, 'If that man, after having begun qualified works, should take on himself all states (resulting from ignorance), yet, when these states cease, there would be an end of the work, good or bad, done by him, and when his work has come to an end, he abides in truth (according to the Veda); while the other, who differs from the Veda, is wrong.' Sankarânanda, however, evidently feels that this is a doubtful interpretation, and he suggests another, viz. 'If the Lord himself,' he says, 'determined these states (bhâva), it would seem that there would be no end of samsâra. He therefore says, that when these states, ignorance &c., cease, the work done by man ceases; and when the work done ceases, the living soul gets free of samsâra, being in truth another, i. e. different from ignorance and its products.'

Vignânâtman says: 'If a man, having done work, turns away

above the three kinds of time (past, present, future),
he is seen as without parts [1], after we have first worshipped that adorable god, who has many forms,
and who is the true source (of all things), as dwelling
in our own mind.

6. He is beyond all the forms of the tree [2] (of the
world) and of time, he is the other, from whom this
world moves round, when [3] one has known him who

from it, and obtains union of one tattva (the tvam, or self) with the
real tattva (the tat, or the Lord);—and how? By means of the one,
i. e. the teaching of the Guru; the two, i. e. love of the Guru and of the
Lord; the three, i. e. hearing, remembering, and meditating; the eight,
i. e. restraint, penance, postures, regulation of the breath, abstrac-
tion, devotion, contemplation, and meditation (Yoga-sûtras II, 29);
by time, i. e. the right time for work; by the qualities of the self, i. e.
pity, &c.; by the subtile ones, i. e. the good dispositions for knowledge, then (we must supply) he becomes free.' And this he explains more fully in the next verse. 'If, after having done qualified
works, i. e. works to please the Lord, a Yati discards all things,
and recognises the phenomenal character of all states, and traces
them back to their real source in Mûlaprak*ri*ti and, in the end,
in the Sa*kk*idânanda, he becomes free. If they (the states) cease,
i. e. are known in their real source, the work done ceases also in its
effects, and when the work has been annihilated, he goes to freedom, being another in truth; or, if we read anyat, he goes to what
is different from all these things, namely, to the Lord; or, he goes
to a state of perfect lordship in truth, having discovered the highest
truth, the oneness of the self with the Highest Self.'

I think that, judging from the context, the subject is really the same
in both verses, viz. the Lord, as passing through different states, and
at last knowing himself to be above them all. Yet, the other explanations may be defended, and if the subject were taken to be different
in each verse, some difficulties would disappear.

[1] Vig*ñâ*nâtman and *S*ankarânanda read akalo 'pi, without parts,
and *S*ankara, too, presupposes that reading, though the text is
corrupt in Roer's edition.

[2] Explained as sa*m*sârav*ri*ksha, the world-tree, as described in
the Ka*th*a Up. VI, 1.

[3] It seems possible to translate this verse in analogy with the
former, and without supplying the verb either from yâti, in verse 4,

brings good and removes evil, the lord of bliss, as
dwelling within the self, the immortal, the support
of all.

7. Let us know that highest great lord of lords[1],
the highest deity of deities, the master of masters,
the highest above, as god, the lord of the world, the
adorable.

8. There is no effect and no cause known of him,
no one is seen like unto him or better; his high
power is revealed as manifold, as inherent, acting
as force and knowledge.

9. There is no master of his in the world, no ruler
of his, not even a sign of him[2]. He is the cause,
the lord of the lords of the organs[3], and there is of
him neither parent nor lord.

10. That only god who spontaneously covered
himself, like a spider, with threads drawn from
the first cause (pradhâna), grant us entrance into
Brahman[4].

11. He is the one God, hidden in all beings, all-

---

or from vidâma, in verse 7. The poet seems to have said, he is
that, he is seen as that, when one has worshipped him, or when
one has known him within oneself.

[1] Sankara thinks that the lords are Vaivasvata &c.; the deities,
Indra &c.; the masters, the Pragâpatis. Vignânâtman explains the
lords as Brahman, Vishnu, Rudra, &c.; the deities as Indra, &c.;
the masters as Hiranyagarbha, &c. Sankarânanda sees in the lords
Hiranyagarbha &c., in the deities Agni &c., in the masters the
Pragâpatis, such as Kasyapa.

[2] If he could be inferred from a sign, there would be no necessity for the Veda to reveal him.

[3] Karana, instrument, is explained as organ of sense. The lords
of such organs would be all living beings, and their lord the true
Lord.

[4] Besides brahmâpyayam, i. e. brahmany apyayam, ekîbhâvam,
another reading is brahmâvyayam, i. e. brahma kâvyayam ka.

pervading, the self within all beings, watching over all works, dwelling in all beings, the witness, the perceiver[1], the only one, free from qualities.

12[2]. He is the one ruler of many who (seem to act, but really do) not act[3]; he makes the one seed manifold. The wise who perceive him within their self, to them belongs eternal happiness, not to others.

13[4]. He is the eternal among eternals, the thinker among thinkers, who, though one, fulfils the desires of many. He who has known that cause which is to be apprehended by Sânkhya (philosophy) and Yoga (religious discipline), he is freed from all fetters.

---

[1] All the MSS. seem to read ketâ, not kettâ.

[2] See Katha-upanishad V, 12–15.

[3] Sankara explains that the acts of living beings are due to their organs, but do not affect the Highest Self, which always remains passive (nishkriya).

[4] I have formerly translated this verse, according to the reading nityo 'nityânâm ketanas ketanânâm, the eternal thinker of non-eternal thoughts. This would be a true description of the Highest Self who, though himself eternal and passive, has to think (gîvât-man) non-eternal thoughts. I took the first ketanah in the sense of kettâ, the second in the sense of ketanam. The commentators, however, take a different, and it may be, from their point, a more correct view. Sankara says: 'He is the eternal of the eternals, i. e. as he possesses eternity among living souls (gîvas), these living souls also may claim eternity. Or the eternals may be meant for earth, water, &c. And in the same way he is the thinker among thinkers.'

Sankarânanda says: 'He is eternal, imperishable, among eternal, imperishable things, such as the ether, &c. He is thinking among thinkers.'

Vignânâtman says: 'The Highest Lord is the cause of eternity in eternal things on earth, and the cause of thought in the thinkers on earth.' But he allows another construction, namely, that he is the eternal thinker of those who on earth are endowed with eter-nity and thought. In the end all these interpretations come to

14. The[1] sun does not shine there, nor the moon and the stars, nor these lightnings, and much less this fire. When he shines, everything shines after him; by his light all this is lightened.

15. He is the one bird[2] in the midst of the world; he is also (like) the fire (of the sun) that has set in the ocean. A man who knows him truly, passes over death[3]; there is no other path to go.

16. He makes all, he knows all, the self-caused, the knower[4], the time of time (destroyer of time), who assumes qualities and knows everything, the master of nature and of man[5], the lord of the three qualities (guna), the cause of the bondage, the existence, and the liberation of the world[6].

17. He who has become that[7], he is the immortal, remaining the lord, the knower, the ever-present guardian of this world, who rules this world for ever, for no one else is able to rule it.

18. Seeking for freedom I go for refuge to that God who is the light of his own thoughts[8], he who

the same, viz. that there is only one eternal, and only one thinker, from whom all that is (or seems to be) eternal and all that is thought on earth is derived.

[1] See Ka*th*. Up. V, 15; Mu*nd*. Up. II, 2, 10; Bhagavadgîtâ XV, 6.

[2] Ha*m*sa, frequently used for the Highest Self, is explained here as hanty avidyâdibandhakâra*n*am iti ha*m*sa*h*.

[3] Cf. III, 8.

[4] Again the MSS. read kâlakâlo, as in verse 2. They also agree in putting g*ñ*a*h* before kâlakâlo, as in verse 2.

[5] Pradhânam avyaktam, kshetrag*ñ*o vig*ñ*ânâtmâ.

[6] He binds, sustains, and dissolves worldly existence.

[7] He who seems to exist for a time in the form of kshetrag*ñ*a and pradhâna.

[8] The MSS. vary between âtmabuddhiprakâ*s*am and âtmabuddhiprasâdam. The former reading is here explained by *S*ankarânanda as svabuddhisâkshi*n*am.

first creates Brahman (m.)[1] and delivers the Vedas
to him ;

19. Who is without parts, without actions, tranquil, without fault, without taint[2], the highest bridge
to immortality—like a fire that has consumed its
fuel.

20. Only when men shall roll up the sky like
a hide, will there be an end of misery, unless God
has first been known[3].

21. Through the power of his penance and
through the grace of God[4] has the wise Svetâsvatara truly[5] proclaimed Brahman, the highest and
holiest, to the best of ascetics[6], as approved by
the company of Rishis.

---

[1] Explained as Hiranyagarbha.

[2] Niranganam nirlepam.

[3] Sankarânanda reads tadâ sivam avignâya duhkhasyânto bhavishyati; Vignânâtman retains devam, but mentions sivam as a various
reading. Both have anto, not antam, like Roer. Sankara seems
to have found na before bhavishyati, or to have read duhkhânto na
bhavishyati, for he explains that there will be no end of misery,
unless God has first been known. It is possible, however, that the
same idea may be expressed in the text as we read it, so that it
should mean, Only when the impossible shall happen, such as the
sky being rolled up by men, will misery cease, unless God has been
discovered in the heart.

[4] The MSS. read devaprasâdât, which is more in keeping with
the character of this Upanishad.

[5] Samyak may be both adverb and adjective in this sentence,
kâkâkshinyâyena.

[6] Atyâsramin is explained by Sankara as atyantam pûgyatamâ-
sramibhyah; and he adds, katurvidhâ bhikshavas ka bahûdakakuti-
kakau, Hamsah paramahamsas ka yo yah paskât sa uttamah. Weber
(Indische Studien, II, 109) has himself corrected his mistake of
reading antyâsramibhyah, and translating it by neighbouring
hermits.

These four stages in the life of a Sannyâsin are the same to-day as
they were in the time of the Upanishads, and Dayânanda Sarasvatî

22. This highest mystery in the Vedânta, delivered in a former age, should not be given to one whose passions have not been subdued, nor to one who is not a son, or who is not a pupil[1].

23. If these truths have been told to a high-minded man, who feels the highest devotion for God, and for his Guru as for God, then they will shine forth,—then they will shine forth indeed.

describes them in his autobiography, though in a different order : 1. Kuṭîkaka, living in a hut, or in a desolate place, and wearing a red-ochre coloured garment, carrying a three-knotted bamboo rod, and wearing the hair in the centre of the crown of the head, having the sacred thread, and devoting oneself to the contemplation of Parabrahma. 2. Bahûdaka, one who lives quite apart from his family and the world, maintains himself on alms collected at seven houses, and wears the same kind of reddish garment. 3. Haṃsa, the same as in the preceding case, except the carrying of only a one-knotted bamboo. 4. Paramahaṃsa, the same as the others ; but the ascetic wears the sacred thread, and his hair and beard are quite long. This is the highest of all orders. A Paramahaṃsa who shows himself worthy is on the very threshold of becoming a Dîkshita.

[1] Cf. Brïh. Up. VI, 3, 12 ; Maitr. Up. VI, 29.

PRASÑA-UPANISHAD.

PRAS*Ñ*A-UPANISHAD.

FIRST QUESTION.

Adoration to the Highest Self! Hari*h*, Om!

1. Suke*s*as [1] Bhâradvâ*g*a [2], and *S*aivya Satyakâma, and Sauryâya*n*in [3] Gârgya, and Kausalya [4] Â*s*valâyana, and Bhârgava Vaidarbhi [5], and Kabandhin Kâtyâyana, these were devoted to Brahman, firm in Brahman, seeking for the Highest Brahman. They thought that the venerable Pippalâda could tell them all that, and they therefore took fuel in their hands (like pupils), and approached him.

2. That *R*ishi said to them: 'Stay here a year longer, with penance, abstinence, and faith; then you may ask questions according to your pleasure, and if we know them, we shall tell you all.'

3. Then [6] Kabandhin Kâtyâyana approached him and asked: 'Sir, from whence may these creatures be born?'

---

[1] Suke*s*as seems better than Suke*s*an, and he is so called in the sixth Pras*ña*, in MS. Mill 74.

[2] Bhâradvâga, *S*aivya, Gârgya, Â*s*valâyana, Bhârgava, and Kâtyâyana are, according to *S*ankara, names of gotras or families.

[3] Sûryasyâpatya*m* Saurya*h*, tadapatya*m* *S*auryâya*n*i*h*. Dîrgha*h* sulopa*s* *k*a *kh*ândasa iti sa eva Sauryâya*n*î.

[4] Kausalyo nâmata*h*, kosalâyâm bhavo vâ.

[5] Vaidarbhi is explained as vidarbhe*h* prabhava*h*, or Vidarbheshu prabhava*h*. Vidarbha, a country, south of the Vindhya mountains, with Ku*nd*ina as its capital. Vaidarbha, a king of the Vidarbhas, is mentioned in the Ait. Brâhm. VII, 34. Vaidarbhi is a patronymic of Vidarbha. See B. R. s. v.

[6] After the year was over.

4. He replied: 'Pragâpati (the lord of creatures) was desirous of creatures (pragâh). He performed penance[1], and having performed penance, he produces a pair, matter (rayi) and spirit (prâna), thinking that they together should produce creatures for him in many ways.

5[2]. The sun is spirit, matter is the moon. All this, what has body and what has no body, is matter, and therefore body indeed is matter.

6. Now Âditya, the sun, when he rises, goes toward the East, and thus receives the Eastern spirits into his rays. And when he illuminates the South, the West, the North, the Zenith, the Nadir, the intermediate quarters, and everything, he thus receives all spirits into his rays.

7. Thus he rises, as Vaisvânara, (belonging to all men,) assuming all forms, as spirit, as fire. This has been said in the following verse:

8[3]. (They knew) him who assumes all forms, the golden[4], who knows all things, who ascends highest, alone in his splendour, and warms us; the thousand-rayed, who abides in a hundred places, the spirit of all creatures, the Sun, rises.

9. The year indeed is Pragâpati, and there are two paths thereof, the Southern and the Northern. Now those who here believe in sacrifices and pious gifts as work done, gain the moon only as their

---

[1] Or he meditated; see Upanishads, vol. i, p. 238, n. 3.

[2] Sankara explains, or rather obscures, this by saying that the sun is breath, or the eater, or Agni, while matter is the food, namely, Soma.

[3] Cf. Maitr. Up. VI, 8.

[4] Harinam is explained as rasmimantam, or as harati sarveshâm prâninâm âyûmshi bhaumân vâ rasân iti harinah. I prefer to take it in the sense of yellow, or golden.

(future) world, and return again. Therefore the
*Ri*shis who desire offspring, go to the South, and
that path of the Fathers is matter (rayi).

10. But those who have sought the Self by
penance, abstinence, faith, and knowledge, gain by
the Northern path Âditya, the sun. This is the
home of the spirits, the immortal, free from danger,
the highest. From thence they do not return, for
it is the end. Thus says the *S*loka [1]:

11. Some call him the father with five feet (the
five seasons), and with twelve shapes (the twelve
months), the giver of rain in the highest half of
heaven; others again say that the sage is placed in
the lower half, in the chariot [2] with seven wheels
and six spokes.

12. The month is Pra*g*âpati; its dark half is
matter, its bright half spirit. Therefore some *Ri*shis
perform sacrifice in the bright half, others in the
other half.

13. Day and Night [3] are Pra*g*âpati; its day is
spirit, its night matter. Those who unite in love
by day waste their spirit, but to unite in love by
night is right.

14. Food is Pra*g*âpati. Hence proceeds seed,
and from it these creatures are born.

15. Those therefore who observe this rule of
Pra*g*âpati (as laid down in § 13), produce a pair,
and to them belongs this Brahma-world here [4]. But

---

[1] Rig-veda I, 164, 12. We ought to read upare vi*k*aksha*n*am.

[2] Sapta*k*akre, i. e. rathe. The seven wheels are explained as the
rays or horses of the sun; or as half-years, seasons, months, half-
months, days, nights, and muhûrtas.

[3] Taken as one, as a Nychthemeron.

[4] In the moon, reached by the path of the Fathers.

those in whom dwell penance, abstinence, and truth,

16. To them belongs that pure Brahma-world, to them, namely, in whom there is nothing crooked, nothing false, and no guile.'

SECOND QUESTION.

1. Then Bhârgava Vaidarbhi asked him: 'Sir, How many gods[1] keep what has thus been created, how many manifest this[2], and who is the best of them?'

2. He replied: 'The ether is that god, the wind, fire, water, earth, speech, mind, eye, and ear. These, when they have manifested (their power), contend and say: We (each of us) support this body and keep it[3].

3[4]. Then Prâ͟na (breath, spirit, life), as the best, said to them: Be not deceived, I alone, dividing myself fivefold, support this body and keep it.

4. They were incredulous; so he, from pride, did as if he were going out from above. Thereupon,

---

[1] Devâ͟h, powers, organs, senses.

[2] Their respective power.

[3] This is ͟Sankara's explanation, in which bâ͟na is taken to mean the same as ͟sarîra, body. But there seems to be no authority for such a meaning, and Ânandagiri tries in vain to find an etymological excuse for it. Bâ͟na or Vâ͟na generally means an arrow, or, particularly in Brâhma͟na writings, a harp with many strings. I do not see how an arrow could be used as an appropriate simile here, but a harp might, if we take avash͟tabhya in the sense of holding the frame of the instrument, and vidhârayâma͟h in the sense of stretching and thereby modulating it.

[4] On this dispute of the organs of sense, see Br͟ih. Up. VI, 1, p. 201; ͟Kh͟ând. Up. V, 1 (S. B. E., vol. i, p. 72).

as he went out, all the others went out, and as he
returned, all the others returned. As bees go out
when their queen[1] goes out, and return when she
returns, thus (did) speech, mind, eye, and ear; and,
being satisfied, they praise Prâna, saying:

5. He is Agni (fire), he shines as Sûrya (sun),
he is Parganya (rain), the powerful (Indra), he is
Vâyu (wind), he is the earth, he is matter, he is
God—he is what is and what is not, and what
is immortal.

6. As spokes in the nave of a wheel, everything
is fixed in Prâna, the verses of the Rig-veda, Yagur-
veda, Sâma-veda, the sacrifice, the Kshatriyas, and
the Brâhmans.

7. As Pragâpati (lord of creatures) thou movest
about in the womb, thou indeed art born again.
To thee, the Prâna, these creatures bring offerings,
to thee who dwellest with the other prânas (the
organs of sense).

8. Thou art the best carrier for the Gods, thou
art the first offering[2] to the Fathers. Thou art the
true work of the Rishis[3], of the Atharvângiras.

9. O Prâna, thou art Indra by thy light, thou art
Rudra, as a protector; thou movest in the sky, thou
art the sun, the lord of lights.

10. When thou showerest down rain, then, O Prâna,
these creatures of thine are delighted[4], hoping that
there will be food, as much as they desire.

---

[1] In Sanskrit it is madhukararâga, king of the bees.

[2] When a srâddha is offered to the Pitris.

[3] Explained as the eye and the other organs of sense which the
chief Prâna supports; but it is probably an old verse, here applied
to a special purpose.

[4] Another reading is prânate, they breathe.

11. Thou art a Vrâtya [1], O Prâ*n*a, the only *Ri*shi [2], the consumer of everything, the good lord. We are the givers of what thou hast to consume, thou, O Mâtari*s*va [3], art our father.

12. Make propitious that body of thine which dwells in speech, in the ear, in the eye, and which pervades the mind; do not go away!

13. All this is in the power of Prâ*n*a, whatever exists in the three heavens. Protect us like a mother her sons, and give us happiness and wisdom.'

THIRD QUESTION.

1. Then Kausalya Â*s*valâyana asked: 'Sir, whence is that Prâ*n*a (spirit) born? How does it come into this body? And how does it abide, after it has divided itself? How does it go out? How does it support what is without [4], and how what is within?'

2. He replied: 'You ask questions more difficult, but you are very fond of Brahman, therefore I shall tell it you.

3. This Prâ*n*a (spirit) is born of the Self. Like the shadow thrown on a man, this (the prâ*n*a) is

---

[1] A person for whom the sa*m*skâras, the sacramental and initiatory rites, have not been performed. *S*ankara says that, as he was the first born, there was no one to perform them for him, and that he is called Vrâtya, because he was pure by nature. This is all very doubtful.

[2] Agni is said to be the *Ri*shi of the Âtharva*n*as.

[3] Instead of the irregular vocative Mâtari*s*va, there is another reading, Mâtari*s*vana*h*, i.e. thou art the father of Mâtari*s*van, the wind, and therefore of the whole world.

[4] All creatures and the gods.

spread out over it (the Brahman) [1]. By the work of the mind [2] does it come into this body.

4. As a king commands officials, saying to them : Rule these villages or those, so does that Prâ*n*a (spirit) dispose the other prâ*n*as, each for their separate work.

5. The Apâna (the down-breathing) in the organs of excretion and generation; the Prâ*n*a himself dwells in eye and ear, passing through mouth and nose. In the middle is the Samâna [3] (the on-breathing); it carries what has been sacrificed as food equally (over the body), and the seven lights proceed from it.

6. The Self [4] is in the heart. There are the 101 arteries, and in each of them there are a hundred (smaller veins), and for each of these branches there are 72,000 [5]. In these the Vyâna (the back-breathing) moves.

---

[1] Over Brahman, i. e. the Self, the parama purusha, the akshara, the satya. The prâ*n*a being called a shadow, is thereby implied to be unreal (anr*i*ta). *S*ankara.

[2] Manok*ri*ta is explained as an ârsha sandhi. It means the good or evil deeds, which are the work of the mind.

[3] I keep to the usual translation of Samâna by on-breathing, though it is here explained in a different sense. Samâna is here supposed to be between prâ*n*a and apâna, and to distribute the food equally, samam, over the body. The seven lights are explained as the two eyes, the two ears, the two nostrils, and the mouth.

[4] Here the Lingâtmâ or *G*îvâtmâ.

[5] A hundred times 101 would give us 10,100, and each multiplied by 72,000 would give us a sum total of 727,200,000 veins, or, if we add the principal veins, 727,210,201. Ânandagiri makes the sum total, 72 *k*o*t*is, 72 lakshas, six thousands, two hundred and one, where the six of the thousands seems to be a mistake for da*s*asa-hasram. In the Br*i*hadâr. Upanishad II, 1, 19, we read of 72,000 arteries, likewise in Yâg*ñ*avalkya III, 108. See also Br*i*h. Up. IV,

7. Through one of them, the Udâna (the out-breathing) leads (us) upwards to the good world by good work, to the bad world by bad work, to the world of men by both.

8. The sun rises as the external Prâ*n*a, for it assists the Prâ*n*a in the eye [1]. The deity that exists in the earth, is there in support of man's Apâna (down-breathing). The ether between (sun and earth) is the Samâna (on-breathing), the air is Vyâna (back-breathing).

9. Light is the Udâna (out-breathing), and therefore he whose light has gone out comes to a new birth with his senses absorbed in the mind.

10. Whatever his thought (at the time of death) with that he goes back to Prâ*n*a, and the Prâ*n*a, united with light [2], together with the self (the *g*îvâtmâ) leads on to the world, as deserved.

11. He who, thus knowing, knows Prâ*n*a, his offspring does not perish, and he becomes immortal. Thus says the *S*loka:

12. He who has known the origin [3], the entry, the place, the fivefold distribution, and the internal state [4] of the Prâ*n*a, obtains immortality, yes, obtains immortality.'

3, 20; *Kh*ând. Up. VI, 5, 3, comm.; Kaush. Up. IV, 20; Ka*th*a Up. VI, 16.

[1] Without the sun the eye could not see.

[2] With Udâna, the out-breathing.

[3] This refers to the questions asked in verse 1, and answered in the verses which follow.

[4] The adhyâtma, as opposed to the vâhya, mentioned in verse 1. Ayati instead of âyâti is explained by *kh*ândasa*m* hrasvatvam.

FOURTH QUESTION.

1. Then Sauryâya*n*in Gârgya asked: 'Sir, What are they that sleep in this man, and what are they that are awake in him? What power (deva) is it that sees dreams? Whose is the happiness? On what do all these depend?'

2. He replied: 'O Gârgya, As all the rays of the sun, when it sets, are gathered up in that disc of light, and as they, when the sun rises again and again, come forth, so is all this (all the senses) gathered up in the highest faculty (deva)[1], the mind. Therefore at that time that man does not hear, see, smell, taste, touch, he does not speak, he does not take, does not enjoy, does not evacuate, does not move about. He sleeps, that is what people say.

3. The fires of the prâ*n*as are, as it were[2], awake in that town (the body). The Apâna is the Gârhapatya fire, the Vyâna the Anvâhâryapa*k*ana fire; and because it is taken out of the Gârhapatya fire, which is fire for taking out[3], therefore the Prâ*n*a is the Âhavanîya fire[4].

---

[1] See note to verse 5.   [2] We ought to read agnaya iva.

[3] Pra*n*ayana, pra*n*îyate 'smâd iti pra*n*ayano gârhapatyo 'gni*h*.

[4] The comparison between the prâ*n*as and the fires or altars is not very clear. As to the fires or altars, there is the Gârhapatya, placed in the South-west, the household fire, which is always kept burning, from which the fire is taken to the other altars. The Anvâhâryapa*k*ana, commonly called the Dakshi*n*a fire, placed in the South, used chiefly for oblations to the forefathers. The Âhavanîya fire, placed in the East, and used for sacrifices to the gods.

Now the Apâna is identified with the Gârhapatya fire, no reason being given except afterwards, when it is said that the Prâ*n*a is the Âhavanîya fire, being taken out of the Gârhapatya, here called

4. Because it carries equally these two oblations, the out-breathing and the in-breathing, the Samâna is he (the Hot*ri* priest)[1]. The mind is the sacrificer, the Udâna is the reward of the sacrifice, and it leads the sacrificer every day (in deep sleep) to Brahman.

5. There that god[2] (the mind) enjoys in sleep greatness. What has been seen, he[2] sees again; what has been heard, he hears again; what has been enjoyed in different countries and quarters, he enjoys again; what has been seen and not seen, heard and not heard, enjoyed and not enjoyed, he sees it all; he, being all, sees.

6. And when he is overpowered by light[3], then that god sees no dreams, and at that time that happiness arises in his body.

7. And, O friend, as birds go to a tree to roost, thus all this rests in the Highest Âtman,—

8. The earth and its subtile elements, the water and its subtile elements, the light and its subtile elements, the air and its subtile elements, the ether and its subtile elements; the eye and what can be

---

pra*n*ayana, in the same manner as the prâ*n*a proceeds in sleep from the apâna. The Vyâna is identified with the Dakshinâgni, the Southern fire, because it issues from the heart through an aperture on the right.

[1] The name of the Hot*ri* priest must be supplied. He is supposed to carry two oblations equally to the Âhavanîya, and in the same way the Vyâna combines the two breathings, the in and out breathings.

[2] The *g*îvâtman under the guise of manas. The Sanskrit word is deva, god, used in the sense of an invisible power, but as a masculine. The commentator uses manodeva*h*, p. 212, l. 5. I generally translate deva, if used in this sense, by faculty, but the context required a masculine. See verse 2.

[3] In the state of profound sleep or sushu*p*ti.

seen, the ear and what can be heard, the nose and
what can be smelled, the taste and what can be
tasted, the skin and what can be touched, the voice
and what can be spoken, the hands and what can
be grasped, the feet and what can be walked, the
mind and what can be perceived, intellect (buddhi)
and what can be conceived, personality and what
can be personified, thought and what can be thought,
light and what can be lighted up, the Prâ*n*a and
what is to be supported by it.

9. For he it is who sees, hears, smells, tastes,
perceives, conceives, acts, he whose essence is knowledge [1], the person, and he dwells in the highest,
indestructible Self,—

10. He who knows that indestructible being, obtains
(what is) the highest and indestructible, he without
a shadow, without a body, without colour, bright,—
yes, O friend, he who knows it, becomes all-knowing,
becomes all.   On this there is this *S*loka:

11. He, O friend, who knows that indestructible
being wherein the true knower, the vital spirits
(prâ*n*as), together with all the powers (deva), and
the elements rest, he, being all-knowing, has pene-
trated all.'

FIFTH QUESTION.

1. Then *S*aivya Satyakâma asked him: 'Sir, if some
one among men should meditate here until death
on the syllable Om, what would he obtain by it?'

2. He replied: 'O Satyakâma, the syllable Om
(AUM) is the highest and also the other Brahman;

---

[1] Buddhi and the rest are the instruments of knowledge, but
there is the knower, the person, in the Highest Self.

therefore he who knows it arrives by the same means [1] at one of the two.

3. If he meditate on one Mâtrâ (the A)[2], then, being enlightened by that only, he arrives quickly at the earth [3]. The *Rik*-verses lead him to the world of men, and being endowed there with penance, abstinence, and faith, he enjoys greatness.

4. If he meditate with [4] two Mâtrâs (A + U) he arrives at the Manas [5], and is led up by the Ya*g*us-verses to the sky, to the Soma-world. Having enjoyed greatness in the Soma-world, he returns again.

5. Again, he who meditates with this syllable AUM of three Mâtrâs, on the Highest Person, he comes to light and to the sun. And as a snake is freed from its skin, so is he freed from evil. He is led up by the Sâman-verses to the Brahma-world [6]; and from him, full of life (Hira*n*yagarbha, the lord of the Satya-loka [7]), he learns [8] to see the all-pervading, the Highest Person. And there are these two *S*lokas :

6. The three Mâtrâs (A + U + M), if employed separate, and only joined one to another, are mortal [9];

---

[1] Âyatanena, âlambanena.

[2] Dîpikâyâ*m* Vâ*k*aspatinaivâkâramâtram ityeva vyâkhyâtam.

[3] Sampadyate prâpnoti *g*anmeti *s*esha*h*.

[4] *S*rutau tr*i*tîyâ dvitîyârthe.

[5] Literally the mind, but here meant for the moon, as before. It is clear that manasi belongs to sampadyate, not, as the Dîpikâ and Roer think, to dhyâyîta. Some take it for svapnâbhimânî Hira*n*yagarbha*h*.

[6] The world of Hira*n*yagarbha*h*, called the Satyaloka.

[7] On a later addition, bringing in the Om as consisting of three Mâtrâs and a half, see Weber, Ind. Stud. I, p. 453; Roer, p. 138.

[8] Tadupade*s*eneti yâvat.

[9] Because in their separate form, A, U, M, they do not mean the Highest Brahman.

but in acts, external, internal, or intermediate, if
well performed, the sage trembles not [1].

7. Through the *Rik*-verses he arrives at this
world, through the Ya*g*us-verses at the sky, through
the Sâman-verses at that which the poets teach,—he
arrives at this by means of the Oṅkâra; the wise
arrives at that which is at rest, free from decay, from
death, from fear,—the Highest.'

SIXTH QUESTION.

1. Then Suke*s*as Bhâradvâ*g*a asked him, saying:
'Sir, Hira*n*yanâbha, the prince of Kosalâ [2], came to
me and asked this question: Do you know the
person of sixteen parts, O Bhâradvâ*g*a? I said to
the prince: I do not know him; if I knew him,
how should I not tell you? Surely, he who speaks
what is untrue withers away to the very root;
therefore I will not say what is untrue. Then he
mounted his chariot and went away silently. Now
I ask you, where is that person?'

2. He replied: 'Friend, that person is here within
the body, he in whom these sixteen parts arise.

3. He reflected: What is it by whose departure
I shall depart, and by whose staying I shall stay?

4. He sent forth (created) Prâ*n*a (spirit) [3]; from

---

[1] The three acts are explained as waking, slumbering, and deep
sleep; or as three kinds of pronunciation, târa-mandra-madhyama.
They are probably meant for Yoga exercises in which the three
Mâtrâs of Om are used as one word, and as an emblem of the
Highest Brahman.

[2] *S*aṅkara explains Kausalya by Kosalâyâm bhava*h*. Ânandatîrtha gives the same explanation. Kosalâ is the capital, generally
called Ayodhyâ. There is no authority for the palatal *s*.

[3] *S*aṅkara explains prâ*n*a by sarvaprâ*n*o Hira*n*yagarbha (sarvaprâ*n*ikara*n*âdhâram antarâtmânam).

Prâ*n*a *S*raddhâ (faith)[1], ether, air, light, water, earth, sense, mind, food; from food came vigour, penance, hymns, sacrifice, the worlds, and in the worlds the name[2] also.

5. As these flowing rivers[3] that go towards the ocean, when they have reached the ocean, sink into it, their name and form are broken, and people speak of the ocean only, exactly thus these sixteen parts of the spectator that go towards the person (purusha), when they have reached the person, sink into him, their name and form are broken, and people speak of the person only, and he becomes without parts and immortal. On this there is this verse:

6. That person who is to be known, he in whom these parts rest, like spokes in the nave of a wheel, you know him, lest death should hurt you.'

7. Then he (Pippalâda) said to them: 'So far do I know this Highest Brahman, there is nothing higher than it.'

8. And they praising him, said: 'You, indeed, are our father, you who carry us from our ignorance to the other shore.'

Adoration to the highest *Ri*shis!
Adoration to the highest *Ri*shis!
Tat sat. Hari*h*, Om!

---

[1] Faith is supposed to make all beings act rightly.
[2] Nâma stands here for nâmarûpe, name (concept) and form. See before, p. 259.
[3] Cf. Mu*nd*. Up. IV, 2, 8; *Kh*ând. Up. VIII, 10.

MAITRÂYANA-BRÂHMANA-
UPANISHAD.

MAITRÂYANA-BRÂHMANA-UPANISHAD.

FIRST PRAPÂTHAKA.

1. The laying of the formerly-described sacrificial fires [1] is indeed the sacrifice of Brahman. Therefore let the sacrificer, after he has laid those fires, meditate on the Self. Thus only does the sacrificer become complete and faultless.

But who is to be meditated on? He who is called Prâna (breath). Of him there is this story:

2. A King, named Brihadratha, having established his son in his sovereignty [2], went into the forest, because he considered this body as transient, and had obtained freedom from all desires. Having performed the highest penance, he stands there, with uplifted arms, looking up to the sun. At the end of a thousand (days) [3], the Saint Sâkâyanya [4], who knew the Self, came near [5], burning with splendour,

---

[1] The performance of all the sacrifices, described in the Maitrâyana-brâhmana, is to lead up in the end to a knowledge of Brahman, by rendering a man fit for receiving the highest knowledge. See Manu VI, 82: 'All that has been declared (above) depends on meditation; for he who is not proficient in the knowledge of the Self reaps not the full reward of the performance of rites.'

[2] Instead of virâgye, a doubtful word, and occurring nowhere else, m. reads vairâgye.

[3] Or years, if we read sahasrasya instead of sahasrâhasya.

[4] The descendant of Sâkâyana. Saint is perhaps too strong; it means a holy, venerable man, and is frequently applied to a Buddha.

[5] Both M. and m. add muneh before antikam, whereas the commentary has râgñah.

like a fire without smoke. He said to the King :
' Rise, rise ! Choose a boon !'

The King, bowing before him, said : ' O Saint, I
know not the Self, thou knowest the essence (of the
Self). We have heard so. Teach it us.'

Sâkâyanya replied : ' This was achieved of yore;
but what thou askest is difficult to obtain[1]. O
Aikshvâka, choose other pleasures.'

The King, touching the Saint's feet with his head,
recited this Gâthâ :

3. 'O Saint, What is the use of the enjoyment of
pleasures in this offensive, pithless body—a mere
mass of bones, skin, sinews, marrow[2], flesh, seed,
blood, mucus, tears, phlegm, ordure, water[3], bile,
and slime! What is the use of the enjoyment of
pleasures in this body which is assailed by lust,
hatred, greed, delusion, fear, anguish, jealousy, separation from what is loved, union with what is not
loved[4], hunger, thirst, old age, death, illness, grief,
and other evils!

4. And we see that all this is perishable, as these
flies, gnats, and other insects, as herbs and trees[5],

---

[1] Though the commentator must have read etad vrittam purastâd
duhsakyam etat prasñam, yet prasñam as a neuter is very strange.
M. reads etad vrittam purastât, dussakama prikkha prasñam;
m. reads etad vratam purastâd asakyam mâ prikha prasñam
aikshvâka, &c. This suggests the reading, etad vrittam purastâd
duhsakam mâ prikkha prasñam, i. e. this was settled formerly, do
not ask a difficult or an impossible question.

[2] Read maggâ.   [3] M. adds vâta before pitta ; not m.

[4] An expression that often occurs in Buddhist literature. See
also Manu VI, 62 : 'On their separation from those whom they
love, and their union with those whom they hate; on their strength
overpowered by old age, and their bodies racked with disease.'

[5] The Sandhi vanaspatayodbhûta for vanaspataya udbhûta is
anomalous. M. reads vanaspatayo bhûtapradhvamsinah.

growing and decaying. And what of these? There
are other great ones, mighty wielders of bows, rulers
of empires, Sudyumna, Bhûridyumna, Indradyumna,
Kuvalayâ*s*va, Yauvanâ*s*va, Vadhrya*s*va, A*s*vapati[1],
*S*a*s*abindu, Hari*sk*andra, Ambarîsha[2], Nahusha,
Anânata, *S*aryâti, Yayâti, Anara*n*ya[3], Ukshasena[4],
&c., and kings such as Marutta, Bharata (Daush-
yanti), and others, who before the eyes of their whole
family surrendered the greatest happiness, and
passed on from this world to that. And what of
these? There are other great ones. We see the
destruction[5] of Gandharvas, Asuras[6], Yakshas, Râkshasas, Bhûtas, Ga*n*as, Pisâ*k*as, snakes, and vam-
pires. And what of these? There is the drying
up of other great oceans, the falling of mountains,
the moving of the pole-star, the cutting of the wind-
ropes (that hold the stars), the submergence of the
earth, and the departure of the gods (suras) from
their place. In such a world as this, what is the
use of the enjoyment of pleasures, if he who has
fed[7] on them is seen[8] to return (to this world) again

---

[1] M. carries on a*s*vapati*s*a*s*abinduhari*sk*andrâmbarîsha.

[2] After Ambarîsha, M. reads Nabhushânanutu*s*ayyâtiyayâtyanara-
*n*yâkshasenâdayo. Nahusha (Naghusha?) is the father of *S*aryâti;
Nâbhâga, the father of Ambarîsha. These names are so care-
lessly written that even the commentator says that the text is
either *khâ*ndasa or prâmâdika. Anânata is a mere conjecture. It
occurs as the name of a *R*i*s*hi in Rig-veda IX, 111.

[3] Anara*n*ya, mentioned in the Mahâbhârata, I, 230.

[4] M. reads anara*n*yâkshasena.

[5] M. and m. read nirodhanam.   [6] M. adds Apsarasas.

[7] M. and m. read â*s*ritasya, but the commentator explains a*s*i-
tasya.

[8] Here we have the Maitrâya*n*a Sandhi, dr*i*syatâ iti, instead
of dr*i*syata iti; see von Schroeder, Maitrâya*n*î Sa*m*hitâ, p. xxviii.
M. and m. read dr*i*syata.

and again! Deign therefore to take me out! In this world I am like a frog in a dry well. O Saint, thou art my way, thou art my way.'

SECOND PRAPÂTHAKA.

1. Then the Saint Sâkâyanya, well pleased, said to the King: 'Great King Brihadratha, thou banner of the race of Ikshvâku, quickly obtaining a knowledge of Self, thou art happy, and art renowned by the name of Marut, the wind[1]. This indeed is thy Self[2].'

'Which[3], O Saint,' said the King.

Then the Saint said to him:

2. 'He[4] who, without stopping the out-breathing[5], proceeds upwards (from the sthûla to the sûkshma sarîra), and who, modified (by impressions), and yet not modified[6], drives away the darkness (of error), he is the Self. Thus said the Saint Maitri[7].' And Sâkâyanya said to the King Brihadratha: 'He who in perfect rest, rising from this body (both from the sthûla and sûkshma), and reaching the highest

---

[1] Prishadasva in the Veda is another name of the Maruts, the storm gods. Afterwards the king is called Marut, VI, 30.

[2] This sentence is called a Sûtra by the commentator to VI, 32.

[3] M. reads Kathaya me katamo bhavân iti.

[4] M. leaves out atha.

[5] One might read âvish/ambhanena, in the sense of while preventing the departure of the vital breath, as in the Brih. Âr. VI, 3, prânena rakshann avaram kulâyam.

[6] M. reads vyathamâno 'vyathamânas.

[7] M. leaves out Maitrih-ity evam hyâha. The commentator explains Maitrir by mitrâyâ apatyam rishir maitrir maitreya. In a later passage (II, 3) M. reads Bhagavatâ Maitrena, likewise the Anubhûti-prakâsa.

light[1], comes forth in his own form, he is the Self[2] (thus said *S*âkâyanya); this is the immortal, the fearless, this is Brahman.'

3. 'Now then this is the science of Brahman, and the science of all Upanishads, O King, which was told us by the Saint Maitri[3]. I shall tell it to thee:

'We hear (in the sacred records) that there were once the Vâlakhilyas[4], who had left off all evil, who were vigorous and passionless. They said to the Pra-*g*âpati Kratu: "O Saint, this body is without intelligence, like a cart. To what supernatural being belongs this great power by which such a body has been made intelligent? Or who is the driver? What thou knowest, O Saint, tell us that[5]."' Pra*g*â-pati answered and said:

4. 'He who in the *S*ruti is called "Standing above," like passionless ascetics[6] amidst the objects of the world, he, indeed, the pure, clean, undeveloped, tranquil, breathless, bodiless[7], endless, imperishable, firm, everlasting, unborn, independent one, stands in his own greatness, and by him has this body been made intelligent, and he is also the driver of it.'

---

[1] M. adds svaya*m g*yotir upasampadya.

[2] M. reads esha for ity esha, which seems better.

[3] M. reads Maitre*na* vyâkhyâtâ.

[4] M. M., Translation of Rig-veda, Preface, p. xxxiv.

[5] M. adds: brûhîti te ho*k*ur Bhagavan katham anena vâsya*m* yat Bhagavan vetsy etad asmâka*m* brûhîti tân hovâ*k*eti.

[6] The commentator allows ûrdhvaretasasa*h* to be taken as a vocative also.

[7] Nirâtmâ is explained by the commentator as thoughtless, without volition, &c. But âtmâ is frequently used for body also, and this seems more appropriate here. M., however, reads anî*s*âtmâ, and this is the reading explained in the Anubhûtiprakâ*s*a, p. 228, ver. 60. This might mean the Âtman which has not yet assumed the quality of a personal god. See VI, 28; VI, 31.

They said: 'O Saint, How has this been made intelligent by such a being as this which has no desires[1], and how is he its driver?' He answered them and said:

5. 'That Self which is very small, invisible, incomprehensible, called Purusha, dwells of his own will here in part[2]; just as a man who is fast asleep awakes of his own will[3]. And this part (of the Self) which is entirely intelligent, reflected in man (as the sun in different vessels of water), knowing the body (kshetragña), attested by his conceiving, willing, and believing[4], is Pragâpati (lord of creatures), called Visva. By him, the intelligent, is this body made intelligent, and he is the driver thereof.'

They said to him: 'O Saint[5], if this has been made intelligent by such a being as this, which has no desires, and if he is the driver thereof, how was it?' He answered them and said:

6. 'In the beginning Pragâpati (the lord of creatures) stood alone. He had no happiness, when alone. Meditating[6] on himself, he created many

---

[1] The reading anishthena is explained by the commentator as free from any local habitation or attachment. He also mentions the various readings anishtena, free from wishes, and anishthena, the smallest. M. reads anikkhena, and this seems better than anishtena. The Anubhûtiprakâsa reads likewise anikkhasya.

[2] I read buddhipûrvam, and again with M. suptasyeva buddhipûrvam. I also read amsena without iti, as in M. The simile seems to be that a man, if he likes, can wake himself at any time of night, and this 'if he likes' is expressed by buddhipûrvam. See Anubhûtiprakâsa, vv. 67, 68.

[3] M. reads vibodhayati, atha.

[4] See Maitr. Up. V, 2; Cowell's Translation, pp. 246, 256; Vedântaparibhâshâ, ed. A. Venis, in the Pandit, IV, p. 110.

[5] M. adds: bhagavann îdrisasya katham amsena vartanam iti tân hovâka.

[6] M. reads abhidhyâyan.

creatures. He looked on them and saw they were,
like a stone, without understanding, and standing
like a lifeless post. He had no happiness. He
thought, I shall enter[1] within, that they may awake.
Making himself like air (vâyu)[2] he entered within.
Being one, he could not do it. Then dividing himself fivefold, he is called Prâ*n*a, Apâna, Samâna,
Udâna, Vyâna. Now that[3] air which rises upwards, is Prâ*n*a. That which moves downwards,
is Apâna. That by which these two are supposed
to be held, is Vyâna. That[4] which carries the
grosser material of food to the Apâna, and brings
the subtler material to each limb, has the name
Samâna. [After these (Prâ*n*a, Apâna, Samâna) comes
the work of the Vyâna, and between them (the Prâ*n*a,
Apâna, and Samâna on one side and the Vyâna on
the other) comes the rising of the Udâna.] That
which brings up or carries down[5] what has been
drunk and eaten, is the Udâna[6].

Now the Upâ*m*su-vessel (or prâ*n*a) depends on
the Antaryâma-vessel (apâna) and the Antaryâma-

---

[1] It is better to read with M. vi*s*ânîti.

[2] M. vâyum iva.   [3] M. Atha yo 'yam.

[4] M. reads: yo 'ya*m* sthavish*th*am anna*m* dhâtum annasyâpâne
sthâpayaty a*n*ish*th*am *k*âṅge 'ṅge sa*m*nayati esha vâva sa samâno
'tha yo 'yam. Leaving out annam, this seems the right reading.
The whole sentence from uttaram to udânasya is left out in M.

[5] M. nigirati *k*aisho vâva sa udâno 'tha yenaitâs sirâ anuvyâptâ
esha vâva sa vyâna*h*.

[6] The views of these five kinds of wind differ considerably.
Here the commentator explains that the prâ*n*a and apâna, the up-
breathing and down-breathing, keep the bodily warmth alive, as
bellows keep up a fire. The food cooked in it is distributed by
the Samâna, so that the coarse material becomes ordure, the middle
flesh, the subtle material mind (manas). The udâna brings up
phlegm, &c., while the Vyâna gives strength to the whole body.

vessel (apâna) on the Upâmsu-vessel[1] (prâna), and
between these two the self-resplendent (Self) produced heat[2]. This heat is the purusha (person),
and this purusha is Agni Vaisvânara. And thus
it is said elsewhere[3]: "Agni Vaisvânara is the fire
within man by which the food that is eaten is cooked,
i.e. digested. Its noise is that which one hears, if
one covers one's ears. When a man is on the point
of departing this life, he does not hear that noise."

Now he[4], having divided himself fivefold, is
hidden in a secret place (buddhi), assuming the
nature of mind, having the prânas as his body, resplendent, having true concepts, and free like ether[5].
Feeling even thus that he has not attained his object,
he thinks from within the interior of the heart[6],
"Let me enjoy objects." Therefore, having first
broken open these five apertures (of the senses), he
enjoys the objects by means of the five reins. This
means that these perceptive organs (ear, skin,
eye, tongue, nose) are his reins; the active organs
(tongue (for speaking), hands, feet, anus, generative
organ) his horses; the body his chariot, the mind
the charioteer, the whip being the temperament.
Driven by that whip, this body goes round like the

---

[1] Two sacrificial vessels (graha) placed on either side of the stone
on which the Soma is squeezed, and here compared to the Prâna
and Apâna, between which the Self (kaitanyâtmâ) assumes heat.

[2] M. reads tayor antarâle kaushnyam prâsuvat.

[3] See Brihadâranyaka Up. V, 9; Khând. Up. III, 13, 8.

[4] The Vaisvânara or purusha, according to the commentator, but
originally the Pragâpati, who had made himself like air, and divided
himself into five vital airs.

[5] Thus the âtmâ, with his own qualities and those which he
assumes, becomes a living being.

[6] M. reads esho 'sya hridantare tishthann.

wheel driven by the potter. This body is made intelligent, and he is the driver thereof.

This[1] is indeed the Self, who seeming to be filled with desires, and seeming to be overcome[2] by bright or dark fruits of action, wanders about in every body (himself remaining free). Because he is not manifest, because he is infinitely small, because he is invisible, because he cannot be grasped, because he is attached to nothing, therefore he, seeming to be changing, an agent in that which is not (prak*ri*ti), is in reality not an agent and unchanging. He is pure, firm, stable, undefiled[3], unmoved, free from desire, remaining a spectator, resting in himself. Having concealed himself in the cloak of the three qualities he appears as the enjoyer of *ri*ta, as the enjoyer of *ri*ta (of his good works).'

THIRD PRAPÂ*TH*AKA.

1. The Vâlakhilyas said to Pra*g*âpati Kratu: 'O Saint, if thou thus showest the greatness of that Self, then who is that other different one, also called Self[4], who really overcome by bright and dark fruits of action, enters on a good or bad birth?

---

[1] M. reads: Sa vâ esha âtmeti ho*s*ann iva sitâsitai*h*. This seems better than u*s*anti kavaya*h*, which hardly construes.

[2] M. reads abhibhûyamânay iva, which again is better than ana-bhibhûta iva, for he seems to be overcome, but is not, just as he seems to be an agent, but is not. See also III, 1.

[3] M. has alepo.

[4] The pure Self, called âtmâ, brahma, *k*inmâtram, pra*gñ*ânaghanam, &c., after entering what he had himself created, and no longer distinguishing himself from the created things (bhûta), is called Bhûtâtmâ.

Downward or upward is his course[1], and overcome
by the pairs (distinction between hot and cold, pleasure and pain, &c.) he roams about[2].'

2. Pragâpati Kratu replied : 'There is indeed that
other[3] different one, called the elemental Self (Bhûtâtmâ), who, overcome by bright and dark fruits of
action, enters on a good or bad birth : downward or
upward is his course, and overcome by the pairs he
roams about. And this is his explanation : The five
Tanmâtrâs[4] (sound, touch, form, taste, smell) are
called Bhûta ; also the five Mahâbhûtas (gross elements) are called Bhûta. Then the aggregate[5] of all
these is called *sarîra*, body[6]. And lastly he of whom
it was said that he dwelt in the body[7], he is called
Bhûtâtmâ, the elemental Self. Thus his immortal
Self[8] is like a drop of water on a lotus leaf[9], and
he himself is overcome by the qualities of nature.
Then[10], because he is thus overcome, he becomes
bewildered, and because he is bewildered, he saw
not the creator, the holy Lord, abiding within
himself. Carried along by the waves of the qualities[11], darkened in his imaginations, unstable, fickle,

---

[1] M. reads here and afterwards avâkam ûrdhva*m* vâ gatidvandvai*h*.

[2] M. adds at the end, paribhramatîti katama esha iti, tân hovâ*k*eti,
and leaves it out at the end of § 2.

[3] M. here reads avara.   [4] M. reads tanmâtrâ*n*i.

[5] M. reads teshâ*m* samudayas ta*kkh*arîram.

[6] The commentator distinguishes.between linga-*sarîra*, consisting
of prâ*n*as, indriyas, the anta*h*kara*n*a, and the sûkshmabhûtas ; and
the sthûla-*sarîra*, consisting of the five Mahâbhûtas.

[7] M. reads *sarîram* ity uktam.

[8] M. reads athâsti tasyâ*h* bindur iva.

[9] It sticks to it, yet it can easily run off again.

[10] M. reads Ato, and the commentator explains atho by ata*h*
kâra*n*ât, adding sandhi*h* *kh*ândasa*h*.

[11] See VI, 30.

crippled, full of desires, vacillating, he enters into
belief, believing "I am he," "this is mine[1];" he binds
his Self by his Self, as a bird with a net, and overcome afterwards by the fruits of what he has done,
he enters on a good and bad birth; downward or
upward is his course, and overcome by the pairs he
roams about.'

They asked: 'Which is it?' And he answered
them:

3. 'This also has elsewhere been said: He who
acts, is the elemental Self; he who causes to act by
means of the organs[2], is the inner man (anta*h*purusha). Now as even a ball of iron, pervaded (overcome) by fire, and hammered by smiths, becomes
manifold (assumes different forms, such as crooked,
round, large, small[3]), thus the elemental Self, pervaded (overcome) by the inner man, and hammered
by the qualities, becomes manifold[4]. And the four
tribes (mammals, birds, &c.), the fourteen worlds
(Bhûr, &c.), with all the number of beings, multiplied eighty-four times[5], all this appears as manifold-
ness. And those multiplied things are impelled by
man (purusha) as the wheel by the potter[6]. And as
when the ball of iron is hammered, the fire is not
overcome, so the (inner) man is not overcome, but
the elemental Self is overcome, because it has united
itself (with the elements).

---

[1] M. reads aha*m* so mamedam.   [2] M. anta*h*kara*n*ai*h*.

[3] See commentary, p. 48, l. 7.

[4] M. reads upety atha trigu*n*am *k*aturg*â*lam.

[5] M. reads *k*atura*s*îtilakshayonipari*n*atam. See also Anubhûtiprakâ*s*a, ver. 118.

[6] M*ri*tyava seems an impossible word, though the commentator
twice explains it as kulâla, potter. M. reads *k*akri*n*eti, which seems
preferable. Weber conjectures m*ri*tpa*k*a.

4. And it has been said elsewhere[1] : This body produced from marriage, and endowed with growth[2] in darkness, came forth by the urinary passage, was built up with bones, bedaubed with flesh, thatched with skin, filled with ordure, urine, bile, slime, marrow, fat, oil[3], and many impurities besides, like a treasury full of treasures[4].

5. And it has been said elsewhere: Bewilderment, fear, grief, sleep, sloth, carelessness, decay, sorrow, hunger, thirst, niggardliness, wrath, infidelity, ignorance, envy, cruelty[5], folly, shamelessness, meanness[6], pride, changeability[7], these are the results of the quality of darkness (tama$h$)[8].

---

[1] Part of this passage has been before the mind of the author of the Mânava-dharmasâstra, when writing, VI, 76, 77 : asthisthûnam snâyuyutam mâmsasonitalepanam, karmâvanaddham durgandhi pûrnam mûtrapurîshayoh, garâsokasamâvishtam rogâyatanam âturam ragasvalam anityam ka bhûtâvâsam imam tyaget. The same verses occur in the Mahâbhârata XII, 12463-4, only with tyaga at the end, instead of tyaget. The rendering of asthibhis kitam by asthisthûnam shows that kita was understood to mean piled or built up, i. e. supported by bones.

[2] Instead of samvriddhyupetam M. reads samviddhyapetam.

[3] M. adds snâyu after vasâ, and instead of âmayaih reads malaih. This reading, malaih, would seem preferable, though Manu's rogâyatanam might be quoted in support of âmayaih. The exact meaning of vasâ is given in the Âryavidyâsudhâkara, p. 82, l. 9.

[4] Therefore should wise people not identify their true Self with the body. M. reads vasuneti.

[5] M. reads vaikârunyam.

[6] Instead of nirâkrititvam M. reads nikritatvam, which is decidedly preferable. We may take it to mean either meanness, as opposed to uddhatatvam, overbearing, or knavery, the usual meaning of nikriti.

[7] M. reads asatvam, possibly for asattvam.

[8] M. reads tâmasânvitaih, and afterwards râgasânvitaih; also trishnâ instead of antastrishnâ.

Inward thirst, fondness, passion, covetousness, unkindness, love, hatred, deceit[1], jealousy, vain restlessness, fickleness[2], unstableness, emulation, greed, patronising of friends, family pride, aversion to disagreeable objects, devotion to agreeable objects, whispering[3], prodigality, these are the results of the quality of passion (ra*g*as).

By these he is filled, by these he is overcome, and therefore this elemental Self assumes manifold forms, yes, manifold forms.'

Fourth Prapâ*th*aka.

1. The Vâlakhilyas, whose passions were subdued, approached him full of amazement and said: 'O Saint, we bow before thee; teach thou, for thou art the way, and there is no other for us. What process is there for the elemental Self, by which, after leaving this (identity with the elemental body), he obtains union[4] with the (true) Self?' Pra*g*âpati Kratu said to them:

2. 'It has been said elsewhere: Like the waves in large rivers, that which has been done before, cannot be turned back, and, like the tide of the sea, the approach of death is hard to stem. Bound[5] by the fetters of the fruits of good and evil, like a cripple; without freedom, like a man in prison; beset by many fears, like one standing before Yama (the judge of

---

[1] M. reads vyavartatvam.   [2] It should be *kañk*alatvam.

[3] M. reads mattasvaro.

[4] Instead of the irregular sâyo*g*yam, M. always reads sâyu*g*yam.

[5] It is not quite clear what is the subject to which all these adjectives refer.   M. reads baddho for baddham, but afterwards agrees with the text as published by Cowell.

the dead); intoxicated by the wine of illusion, like one intoxicated by wine; rushing about, like one possessed by an evil spirit; bitten by the world, like one bitten by a great serpent; darkened by passion, like the night; illusory, like magic; false, like a dream; pithless, like the inside of the Kadalî; changing its dress in a moment, like an actor[1]; fair in appearance, like a painted wall, thus they call him; and therefore it is said:

Sound[2], touch, and other things are like nothings; if the elemental Self is attached to them, it will not remember the Highest Place[3].

3. This is indeed the remedy for the elemental Self: Acquirement of the knowledge of the Veda, performance of one's own duty, therefore conformity on the part of each man to the order to which he happens to belong. This[4] is indeed the rule for one's own duty, other performances are like the mere branches of a stem[5]. Through it one obtains the Highest above, otherwise one falls downward[6]. Thus is one's own duty declared, which is to be found in the Vedas. No one belongs truly to an order (âsrama) who transgresses his own law[7]. And if people say, that a man does not belong to any of the orders, and that he is an ascetic[8], this is wrong, though, on

---

[1] M. reads naḷavat.

[2] M. reads ye 'rthâ anarthâ iva te sthitâḥ, esham.

[3] M. reads na smaret paramam padam.

[4] M. reads svadharma eva sarvaṃ dhatte, stambhaṣâkhevetarâṇi.

[5] The commentator considers the other sacrificial performances as hurtful, and to be avoided.

[6] M. reads anyathâdhaḥ pataty, esha.

[7] The rules of the order to which he belongs.

[8] A Tapasvin is free from the restrictions of the preceding âsra-

the other hand, no one who is not an ascetic brings his sacrificial works to perfection or obtains knowledge of the Highest Self[1]. For thus it is said:

By ascetic penance goodness is obtained, from goodness understanding is reached, from understanding the Self is obtained, and he who has obtained that, does not return[2].

4. "Brahman is," thus said one who knew the science of Brahman; and this penance is the door to Brahman, thus said one who by penance had cast off all sin. The syllable Om is the manifest greatness of Brahman, thus said one who well grounded (in Brahman) always meditates on it. Therefore by knowledge, by penance, and by meditation is Brahman gained. Thus one goes beyond[3] Brahman (Hiranyagarbha), and to a divinity higher than the gods; nay, he who knows this, and worships Brahman by these three (by knowledge, penance, and meditation), obtains bliss imperishable, infinite, and unchangeable. Then freed from those things (the senses of the body, &c.) by which he was filled and overcome, a mere charioteer[4], he obtains union with the Self.'

---

mas, but he must have obeyed them first, before he can become a real Tapasvin.

[1] M. reads âsrameshv evâvasthitas tapasvî kety ukyata ity, etad apy uktam, &c. This would mean, 'For it is said that he only who has dwelt in the âsramas is also called a Tapasvin, a real ascetic; and this also has been said, that no one obtains self-knowledge except an ascetic.' This is not impossible, but the commentator follows the text as printed by Cowell. M. reads âtmagñânenâdhigamah, karmasuddhi.

[2] M. reads manasâ prâpyate tv âtmâ hy âtmâptyâ na nivartata iti.

[3] M. reads pura eta, which may be right.

[4] Rathitah is a very strange word, but, like everything else, it is

5. The Vâlakhilyas said : ' O Saint, thou art the
teacher, thou art the teacher [1]. What thou hast said,
has been properly laid up in our mind. Now answer
us a further question : Agni, Vâyu, Âditya, Time
(kâla)which is Breath (prâna[2]), Food (anna), Brahmâ [3],
Rudra, Vishnu, thus do some meditate on one, some
on another. Say which of these is the best for us.'
He said to them :

6. 'These are but the chief manifestations of the
highest, the immortal, the incorporeal Brahman. He
who is devoted to one, rejoices here in his world
(presence), thus he said. Brahman indeed is all this,
and a man may meditate on, worship, or discard also
those which [4] are its chief manifestations. With these
(deities) he proceeds to higher and higher worlds,
and when all things perish, he becomes one with the
Purusha, yes, with the Purusha.'

---

explained by the commentator, viz. as ratham prâpito rathitvam ka
prâpita iti yâvat. Nevertheless the reading of M. seems to me preferable, viz. atha yaih paripûrno 'bhibhûto 'yam tathaitais ka, taih
sarvair vimukta svâtmany eva sâyugyam upaiti. I should prefer
vimuktas tv âtmany eva, and translate, 'But then, freed from all
those things by which he was filled and likewise was overcome by
them, he obtains union with the Self.'

[1] M. reads the second time abhivâdy asmîti, which is no improvement. It might have been ativâdyasîti.

[2] M. reads Yamah prâno.

[3] This is, of course, the personal Brahmâ of the Hindu triad. To
distinguish this personal Brahmâ from the impersonal, I sometimes
give his name in the nom. masc., Brahmâ, and not the grammatical
base, Brahman.

[4] M. reads yâ vâ asyâ. The commentator explains yâ vâsyâh by
vâsayogyâh; or yâ vâ yâh by kaskit, admitting a Vedic irregularity
which is not quite clear.

FIFTH PRAPÂ*TH*AKA [1].

1. Next follows Kutsâyana's hymn of praise :
'Thou art Brahmâ, and thou art Vish*n*u, thou
art Rudra, thou Pra*g*âpati [2], thou art Agni, Varu*n*a,
Vâyu, thou art Indra, thou the Moon.

Thou art Anna [3] (the food or the eater), thou art
Yama, thou art the Earth, thou art All, thou art
the Imperishable. In thee all things exist in many
forms, whether for their natural or for their own
(higher) ends.

Lord of the Universe, glory to thee! Thou art
the Self of All, thou art the maker of All, the
enjoyer of All; thou art all life, and the lord of all
pleasure and joy [4]. Glory to thee, the tranquil, the
deeply hidden, the incomprehensible, the immeasurable, without beginning and without end.'

---

2. 'In the beginning [5] darkness (tamas) alone was
this. It was in the Highest, and, moved by the Highest, it becomes uneven. Thus it becomes obscurity

---

[1] At the beginning of the fifth Prapâ*th*aka my MS. gives the
*S*lokas which in the printed edition are found in VI, 34, p. 178,
Atreme *s*lokâ bhavanti, yathâ nirindhano vahnir, &c., to nirvishaya*m*
smr*i*tam. Then follows as § 2, Atha yatheda*m* Kautsyâyanistutis,
tvam, &c.

[2] The commentator explains Brahmâ by Hira*n*yagarbha and
Pra*g*âpati by Virâ*g*.

[3] M. reads tvam Manus, tva*m* Yama*s* *k*a tvam, pr*i*thivî tvam athâ-
*k*yuta*h*, which is so clearly the right reading that it is difficult to
understand how the mistakes arose which are presupposed by the
commentary. See Taitt. Up. II, 2.

[4] M. reads vi*s*vakr*i*d*â*rati*h* prabhu*h*, which seems better.

[5] M. reads tamo vâ idam ekam âsta tat paro syât tat pare*n*eritam.
It may have been tat pare 'sthât.

(ragas)[1]. Then this obscurity, being moved, becomes uneven. Thus it becomes goodness (sattva). Then this goodness, being moved, the essence flowed forth[2]. This is that part (or state of Self) which is entirely intelligent, reflected in man (as the sun is in different vessels of water) knowing the body (kshetragña), attested by his conceiving, willing, and believing, it is Pragâpati, called Visva. His manifestations have been declared before[3]. Now that part of him which belongs to darkness, that, O students[4], is he who is called Rudra. That part of him which belongs to obscurity, that, O students, is he who is called Brahmâ. That part of him which belongs to goodness, that, O students, is he who is called Vishñu. He being one, becomes three, becomes eight[5], becomes eleven[6], becomes twelve, becomes infinite. Because[7] he thus came to be, he is the Being (neut.), he moves about, having entered all beings, he has become the Lord of all beings. He is the Self within and without, yes, within and without.'

---

[1] M. reads etad vai ragaso rûpam, which is better, or, at least, more in accordance with what follows.

[2] M. reads sattvam everitarasas sam prâsrivat.

[3] A reference to Maitr. Up. II, 5, would have saved the commentator much trouble. M. has a better text. It leaves out visveti or visvâkhyas after pragâpati, which may be wrong, but then goes on : tasya proktâ agryâs tanavo brahmâ rudro vishñur iti. In enumerating the three agryâs tanavah, however, M. is less consistent, for it begins with ragas or Brahmâ, then goes on to tamas or Rudra, and ends with sattva or Vishñu. The Anubhûtiprakâsa, verse 142, has the right succession.

[4] This vocative, brahmakârino, is always left out in M.

[5] The five prâñas, the sun, moon, and asterisms.

[6] The eleven organs of sense and action, which, by dividing manas and buddhi, become twelve.

[7] M. reads aparimitadhâ kodbhûtatvâd bhûteshu karati pravishtah sarvabhûtânâm.

Sixth Prapâ*th*aka [1].

1. He (the Self) bears the Self in two ways [2], as he who is Prâ*n*a (breath), and as he who is Âditya (the sun). Therefore there are two paths for him [3], within and without, and they both turn back in a day and night. The Sun is the outer Self, the inner Self is Breath. Hence the motion of the inner Self is inferred from the motion of the outer Self [4]. For thus it is said:

'He who knows, and has thrown off all evil, the overseer of the senses [5], the pure-minded, firmly

---

[1] The commentator describes the sixth and seventh chapters as Khila, supplementary, and does not think that they are closely connected with the chief object of the Upanishad. This chief object was to show that there is only one thinking Self (*k*idâtmâ) to be known, and that the same is to be meditated on as manifested in the different forms of Rudra, Brahmâ, Vish*n*u, &c. Thus the highest object of those who wish for final liberation has been explained before, as well as the proper means of obtaining that liberation. What follows are statements of the greatness of the various manifestations of the Âtman, and advice how to worship them. My MS. gives the beginning of the sixth Prapâ*th*aka, but ends with the end of the eighth paragraph. The verses in paragraph 34, as mentioned before, are given in my MS. at the end of the fourth Prapâ*th*aka. My translation deviates considerably from the commentary. The text is obscure and not always correct. My rule has been throughout to begin a new sentence with eva*m* hy âha, 'for thus it is said,' which introduces proofs of what has been said before. The passages thus quoted as proofs from the Veda are often difficult to understand, nor do they always consist of a complete sentence. My translation therefore is often purely tentative.

[2] M. reads dvitîyâ for dvidhâ.

[3] M. reads dvau vâ etâv asya pa*ñk*adhâ nâmântar bahi*s* *k*âhorâtre tau vyâvartete.

[4] While the sun goes round Meru in a day and a night, the breath performs 21,000 breathings, or, more exactly, 21,600. M. reads bahirâtmagatyâ.

[5] M. reads adhyaksha, not akshâdhyaksha.

grounded (in the Self) and looking away (from all earthly objects), he is the same.' Likewise the motion of the outer Self is inferred from the motion of the inner Self. For thus it is said :

'He who within the sun is the golden person, who looks upon this earth from his golden place, he is the same who, after entering the inner lotus of the heart[1], devours food (perceives sensuous objects, &c.)'

2. And he who having entered the inner lotus of the heart, devours food, the same, having gone to the sky as the fire of the sun, called Time, and being invisible, devours all beings as his food.

What is that lotus and of what is it made ? (the Vâlakhilyas ask [2].)

That lotus is the same as the ether; the four quarters, and the four intermediate points are its leaves [3].

These two, Breath and the Sun, move on near to each other (in the heart and in the ether). Let him worship these two, with the syllable Om, with the Vyâhriti words (bhûh, bhuvah, svar), and with the Sâvitrî hymn.

3. There are two forms of Brahman [4], the material (effect) and the immaterial (cause). The material is false, the immaterial is true. That which is true is Brahman, that which is Brahman is light, and that which is light is the Sun [5]. And this Sun became the Self of that Om.

---

[1] M. reads sa esho 'ntah pushkare hritpushkare vâsrito.

[2] The commentator ascribes the dialogue still to the Vâlakhilyas and Pragâpati Kratu.

[3] M. reads dalasamsthâ âsur vâgnih parata etaih prânâdityâv etâ.

[4] See Brih. Up. II, 3, 1.

[5] Professor Cowell, after giving the various readings of his MSS., says, 'the true reading would seem to be yat satyam tad brahma,

He divided himself threefold, for Om consists of three letters, a + u + m. Through them all this¹ is contained in him as warp and woof. For thus it is said:

'Meditate on that Sun as Om, join your Self (the breath) with the (Self of the) Sun.'

4. And thus it has been said elsewhere: The Udgîtha (of the Sâma-veda) is the Pranava² (of the Rig-veda), and the Pranava is the Udgîtha, and thus the Sun is Udgîtha, and he is Pranava or Om. For thus it is said³:

'The Udgîtha, called Pranava, the leader (in the performance of sacrifices), the bright⁴, the sleepless, free from old age and death, three-footed⁵, consisting of three letters (a + u + m), and likewise to be known as fivefold (five prânas) placed in the cave.' And it is also said:

'The three-footed Brahman has its root upward⁶, the branches are ether, wind, fire, water, earth, &c. This one Asvattha⁷ by name, the world, is Brahman, and of it that is the light which is called the Sun, and it is also the light of that syllable Om. Therefore let him for ever worship that (breath and sun, as manifestations of Brahman) with the syllable Om.'

He alone enlightens us. For thus it is said:

---

yad brahma tag gyotir, yad gyotis sa âdityah.' This is exactly the reading of my own MS.

¹ M. reads kaivâsminn ity evam hyâha.
² The mystic syllable Om.
³ See Khândogyopanishad I, 5; Maitr. Up. VI, 25.
⁴ M. reads nâmarûpam.
⁵ The three feet of the prâna are waking, slumber, and deep sleep; the three feet of the sun, the three worlds, bhûh, bhuvah, svar, as in VII, 11. See also Khând. Up. III, 12.
⁶ Cf. Kath. Up. VI, 1.
⁷ Asvattha, lit. fig-tree, then frequently used metaphorically as a name of the world. Here explained as 'it will not stand till to-morrow.'

'This alone is the pure syllable, this alone is the highest syllable; he who knows that syllable only, whatever he desires, is his[1].'

5. And thus it has been said elsewhere: This Om[2] is the sound-endowed body of him (Prânâdityâtman). This is his gender-endowed body, viz. feminine, masculine, neuter. This is his light-endowed body, viz. Agni, Vâyu, Âditya. This is his lord-endowed body, viz. Brahmâ, Rudra, Vishnu. This is his mouth-endowed body, viz. Gârhapatya, Dakshinâgni, Âhavanîya[3]. This is his knowledge-endowed body, viz. Rik, Yagus, Sâman. This is his world-endowed body, viz. Bhûh, Bhuvah, Svar. This is his time-endowed body, viz. Past, Present, Future. This is his heat-endowed body, viz. Breath, Fire, Sun. This is his growth-endowed body, viz. Food, Water, Moon. This is his thought-endowed body, viz. intellect, mind, personality. This is his breath-endowed body, viz. Prâna, Apâna, Vyâna. Therefore by the aforesaid syllable Om are all these here enumerated bodies praised and identified (with the Prânâdityâtman). For thus it is said[4]:

'O Satyakâma, the syllable Om is the high and the low Brahman.'

6. This[5] (world) was unuttered[6]. Then forsooth Pragâpati, having brooded, uttered it in the words Bhûh, Bhuvah, Svar. This is the grossest body of that Pragâpati, consisting of the three worlds[7]. Of that body Svar is the head, Bhuvah the navel, Bhûh

---

[1] Kath. Up. II, 16.   [2] M. reads tanûr yom iti.

[3] The fires on the three altars.

[4] Prasña Up. V, 2.   [5] M. reads atha vyâttam.

[6] So far the pranava or Om has been explained; now follows the explanation of the Vyâhritis; cf. VI, 2. Vyâhriti is derived from vyâhar, and means an utterance.

[7] Cf. VI, 5.

the feet, the sun the eye. For in the eye is fixed
man's great measure, because with the eye he makes
all measurements. The eye is truth (satyam), for
the person (purusha) dwelling in the eye proceeds to
all things (knows all objects with certainty). Therefore let a man worship with the Vyâhr*i*tis, Bhû*h*,
Bhuva*h*, Svar, for thus Pra*g*âpati, the Self of All, is
worshipped as the (sun, the) Eye of All[1]. For
thus it is said :

'This (the sun) is Pra*g*âpati's all-supporting body, for
in it this all[2] is hid (by the light of the sun); and in this
all it (the light) is hid. Therefore this is worshipped[3].'

7. (The Sâvitrî begins[4]:) Tat Savitur vare*n*yam,
i.e. 'this of Savit*ri*, to be chosen.' Here the Âditya
(sun) is Savit*ri*, and the same is to be chosen by the
love(r) of Self, thus say the Brahma-teachers.

(Then follows the next foot in the Sâvitrî): Bhargo
devasya dhîmahi, i.e. 'the splendour of the god we
meditate on.' Here the god is Savit*ri*, and therefore
he who is called his splendour, him I meditate on,
thus say the Brahma-teachers.

---

[1] M. reads vi*s*vata*s*kakshur.

[2] Pra*g*âpati, according to the commentator, is identified with
Satya, the true, because sat means the three worlds, and these (bhû*h*,
bhuva*h*, svar) are said to be his body. Hence probably the insertion of Satyam before Pra*g*âpati at the beginning of the paragraph.
Then he argues, as the eye has been called satya, and as the eye
is Âditya, therefore Pra*g*âpati also, being Satya, is Âditya, the sun.
And again, if the sun is worshipped (by the vyâhr*i*tis) then, like the
sun, the eye of all, Pra*g*âpati also, the self of all, is worshipped.

[3] Eshopasîta is impossible. We must either read, with the commentator, etâm upâsîta, or with M. eshopasiteti.

[4] He now proceeds to explain the worship of the Sâvitrî verse,
which had been mentioned in VI, 2, after the Om and the Vyâhr*i*tis,
as the third mode of worshipping Prâ*n*a (breath) and Âditya (sun),
these being two correlative embodiments of the Self. The Sâvitrî
is found in Rig-veda III, 62, 10, but it is here explained in a purely
philosophical sense. See also Br*i*h. Up. VI, 3, 6.

(Then follows the last foot) : Dhiyo yo na*h* pra*k*o-dayât, i. e. 'who should stir up our thoughts.' Here the dhiya*h* are thoughts, and he should stir these up for us, thus say the Brahma-teachers.

(He now explains the word bhargas). Now he who is called bhargas is he who is placed in yonder Âditya (sun), or he who is the pupil in the eye[1]. And he is so called, because his going (gati) is by rays (bhâbhi*h*); or because he parches (bhar*g*ayati) and makes the world to shrivel up. Rudra is called Bhargas, thus say the Brahma-teachers. Or bha means that he lights up these worlds; ra, that he delights these beings, ga that these creatures go to him and come from him ; therefore being a bha-ra-ga, he is called Bhargas.

Sûrya[2] (sun) is so called, because Soma is continually squeezed out (su). Savit*ri* (sun) is so called, because he brings forth (su). Âditya (sun) is so called, because he takes up (âdâ, scil. vapour, or the life of man). Pâvana[3] is so called, because he purifies (pu). Âpas, water, is so called, because it nourishes (pyâ).

And it is said:

'Surely the Self (absorbed in Prâ*n*a, breath), which is called Immortal[4], is the thinker, the perceiver, the goer, the evacuator[5], the delighter, the doer, the speaker, the taster, the smeller, the seer, the hearer, and he touches. He is Vibhu (the pervader), who has entered into the body.' And it is said :

---

[1] M. reads târake 'ksh*n*i.

[2] Sûrya is considered as the daily performer of the Prâta*h*savana, &c., the sacrifice at which Soma is squeezed out as an offering.

[3] M. reads pavamânât pavamâna*h*.

[4] M. reads am*ri*tâkhya*s* *k*etâkhya*s* *k*etâ.

[5] M. reads gantâ s*ri*sh*t*â.

' When the knowledge is twofold (subjective and objective), then he hears, sees, smells, tastes, and touches (something), for it is the Self that knows everything.'

But when the knowledge is not twofold (subjective only), without effect, cause, and action[1], without a name, without a comparison, without a predicate[2]— what is that? It cannot be told[3].

8. And the same Self is also called I*s*âna (lord), *S*ambhu, Bhava, Rudra (tâmasa); Pra*g*âpati (lord of creatures), Vi*s*vas*rig* (creator of all), Hira*n*ya-garbha, Satyam (truth), Prâ*n*a (breath), Ha*m*sa (râ*g*asa); *S*âst*ri* (ruler), Vish*n*u, Nârâya*n*a (sâttvika); Arka, Savit*ri*, Dhât*ri* (supporter), Vidhâ-t*ri*[4] (creator), Samrâ*g* (king), Indra, Indu (moon). He is also he who warms, the Sun, hidden by the thousand-eyed golden egg, as one fire by another. He is to be thought after, he is to be sought after. Having said farewell to all living beings, having gone to the forest, and having renounced all sensuous objects, let man perceive the Self[5] from his own body.

' (See him)[6] who assumes all forms, the golden, who knows all things, who ascends highest, alone in his splendour, and warms us; the thousand-rayed,

---

[1] M. reads kâryakâra*n*akarmavinirmuktam.

[2] Nirupâkhyam, rightly translated by Cowell by 'without a predicate,' and rendered by the commentator by apramaya, i. e. not to be measured, not to be classed, i. e. without a predicate.

[3] I have translated this in accordance with a well-known passage, quoted by the commentator from the Br*i*hadâra*n*yaka, rather than in accordance with his own interpretation.

[4] M. leaves out vidhâtâ.

[5] Instead of the peculiar Maitrâya*n*i reading, svâ*ñ* *s*arîrâd, M. reads svâ*s* *kh*arîrâd.

[6] The oneness of the Sun and the Breath is proclaimed in the following verse of the Pra*s*ña Upanishad I, 8.

who abides in a hundred places, the spirit of all
creatures, the Sun, rises[1].'

9. Therefore he who by knowing this has become
the Self of both Breath and Sun, meditates (while
meditating on them) on his Self, sacrifices (while sacrificing to them) to his Self—this meditation, the mind
thus absorbed in these acts, is praised by the wise.

Then let him purify the contamination of the mind
by the verse U*kkh*ish*t*opahatam, &c.[2] : ' Be it food
left, or food defiled by left food, be it food given by
a sinner, food coming from a dead person, or from
one impure from childbirth, may the purifying power
of Vasu, may Agni, and the rays of Savit*ri*, purify
it, and all my sin[3].'

First (before eating) he surrounds (the offered
food) with water (in rincing his mouth[4]). Then
saying, Svâhâ to Prâ*n*a, Svâhâ to Apâna, Svâhâ
to Vyâna, Svâhâ to Samâna, Svâhâ to Udâna, he
offers (the food) with five invocations (in the fire
of the mouth). What is over, he eats in silence,
and then he surrounds (the food) once more afterwards with water (rincing the mouth after his meal).
Having washed let him, after sacrificing to himself,
meditate on his Self with these two verses, Prâ*n*o
'gni*h* and Vi*s*vo 'si, viz. ' May the Highest Self as
breath, as fire (digestive heat), as consisting of the

---

[1] Here ends the M. manuscript, with the following title: iti
*s*rîyagu*ss*âkhâyâm Maitrâya*n*îyabrâhma*n*opanishadi shash*th*a*h* prapâ*th*aka*h*. Samâptâ.

[2] In the following paragraphs the taking of food is represented
as a sacrifice offered by the Self to the Self (âtmaya*g*anarûpam
bho*g*anam, p. 106, l. 13).

[3] Several words have been inserted in this verse, spoiling the
metre.

[4] See *Kh*ând. Up. V, 2.

five vital airs, having entered (the body), himself
satisfied, satisfy all, he who protects all.' 'Thou
art Vi*s*va (all), thou art Vai*s*vânara (fire), all that is
born is upheld by thee; may all offerings enter into
thee; creatures live where thou grantest immortality
to all.' He who eats according to this rule, does
not in turn become food for others.

10. There is something else to be known. There
is a further modification of this Self-sacrifice (the
eating), namely, the food and the eater thereof. This
is the explanation. The thinking Purusha (person),
when he abides within the Pradhâna (nature), is the
feeder who feeds on the food supplied by Prak*ri*ti
(nature). The elemental Self[1] is truly his food, his
maker being Pradhâna (nature[2]). Therefore what
is composed of the three qualities (gu*n*as) is the food,
but the person within is the feeder. And for this the
evidence is supplied by the senses. For animals
spring from seed, and as the seed is the food, therefore it is clear that what is food is Pradhâna (the
seed or cause of everything). Therefore, as has
been said, the Purusha (person) is the eater, Pra-
k*ri*ti, the food; and abiding within it he feeds. All
that begins with the Mahat[3] (power of intellect) and
ends with the Vi*s*eshas (elements[4]), being developed
from the distinction of nature with its three qualities,
is the sign (that there must be a Purusha, an intel-

---

[1] See before, III, 3.

[2] This is very doubtful, in fact, unintelligible. The commentator
says, asya bhûtâtmana*h* kartâ pradhâna*h* pûrvokta*h*, so 'pi bho*g*ya
ity artha*h*.

[3] Technical terms, afterwards adopted by the Sâṅkhya philosophers.

[4] Professor Cowell observes that the term vi*s*esha, as here applied
to the five gross elements, occurs in the Sâṅkhya-kârikâ, ver. 38.

ligent subject). And in this manner the way with
its fourteen steps has been explained[1]. (This is
comprehended in the following verse) : 'This world
is indeed the food, called pleasure, pain, and error
(the result of the three qualities) ; there is no laying
hold of the taste of the seed (cause), so long as there
is no development (in the shape of effect).' And in
its three stages also it has the character of food, as
childhood, youth, and old age ; for, because these
are developed, therefore there is in them the character of food[2].

And in the following manner does the perception
of Pradhâna (nature) take place, after it has become
manifest :—Intellect and the rest, such as determina-
tion, conception, consciousness, are for the tasting (of
the effects of Pradhâna). Then there are the five
(perceptive organs) intended for the (five) objects of
senses, for to taste them. And thus are all acts of
the five active organs, and the acts of the five Prânas
or vital airs (for the tasting of their corresponding
objects). Thus what is manifest (of nature) is food,
and what is not manifest is food. The enjoyer of it
is without qualities, but because he has the quality
of being an enjoyer, it follows that he possesses
intelligence.

As Agni (fire) is the food-eater among the gods,
and Soma the food, so he who knows this eats food
by Agni (is not defiled by food, as little as Agni, the
sacrificial fire). This elemental Self, called Soma
(food), is also called Agni, as having undeveloped
nature for its mouth (as enjoying through nature,
and being independent of it), because it is said, 'The

---

[1] Five receptive, five active organs, and four kinds of consciousness.
[2] Its very development proves it to be food.   Cowell.

Purusha (person) enjoys nature with its three qualities, by the mouth of undeveloped nature.' He who
knows this, is an ascetic, a yogin, he is a performer
of the Self-sacrifice (see before). And he who does
not touch the objects of the senses when they intrude
on him, as no one would touch women intruding into
an empty house, he is an ascetic, a yogin, a performer
of the Self-sacrifice.

11. This is the highest form of Self, viz. food, for
this Prâ*n*a (this body) subsists on food. If it eats
not, it cannot perceive, hear, touch, see, smell, taste,
and it loses the vital airs[1]. For thus it is said :

'If it eats, then in full possession of the vital airs,
it can perceive, hear, touch, speak, taste, smell, see.'
And thus it is said :

'From food are born all creatures that live on
earth; afterwards they live on food, and in the end
(when they die) they return to it[2].'

12. And thus it is said elsewhere: Surely all these
creatures run about day and night, wishing to catch
food. The sun takes food with his rays, and by it
he shines. These vital airs digest, when sprinkled
with food. Fire flares up by food, and by Brahmâ
(Pra*g*âpati), desirous of food, has all this been made.
Therefore let a man worship food as his Self. For
thus it is said :

'From food creatures are born, by food they grow
when born; because it is eaten and because it eats
creatures, therefore it is called food (annam).'

13. And thus it is said elsewhere: This food is
the body of the blessed Vish*n*u, called Vi*s*vabh*ri*t
(all-sustaining). Breath is the essence of food, mind
of breath, knowledge of mind, joy of knowledge. He

---

[1] *Kh*ând. Up. VII, 9, 1.　　　[2] Taitt. Up. II, 2.

who knows this is possessed of food, breath, mind, knowledge, and joy. Whatever creatures here on earth eat food, abiding in them he, who knows this, eats food. Food has been called undecaying, food has been called worshipful; food is the breath of animals, food is the oldest, food has been called the physician.

14. And thus it has been said elsewhere: Food is the cause of all this, time of food, and the sun is the cause of time[1]. The (visible) form of time is the year, consisting of twelve months, made up of Nimeshas (twinklings) and other measures. Of the year one half (when the sun moves northward) belongs to Agni, the other to Varuna (when the sun moves southward). That which belongs to Agni begins with the asterism of Maghâ and ends with half of the asterism of Sravishthâ, the sun stepping down northward. That which belongs to Soma (instead of Varuna) begins with the asterism (of Aslesbâ), sacred to the Serpents, and ends with half of the asterism of Sravishthâ, the sun stepping up southward. And then there (are the months) one by one, belonging to the year, each consisting of nine-fourths of asterisms (two asterisms and a quarter being the twelfth part of the passage of the sun through the twenty-seven Nakshatras), each determined by the sun moving together with the asterisms. Because time is imperceptible by sense, therefore this (the progress of the sun, &c.) is its evidence, and by it alone is time proved to exist. Without proof there is no apprehension of what is to be proved; but even what is to be proved can become proof, for the sake of making itself known,

---

[1] As food depends on time, therefore time is praised, which again depends on the sun, which is a form of the Self.

if the parts (the twinklings, &c.) can be distinguished from the whole (time[1]).   For thus it is said:

'As many portions of time as there are, through them the sun proceeds: he who worships time as Brahman, from him time moves away very far.'   And thus it is said:

'From time all beings flow, from time they grow; in time they obtain rest; time is visible (sun) and invisible (moments).'

15. There are two forms of Brahman, time and non-time.   That which was before the (existence of the) sun is non-time and has no parts.   That which had its beginning from the sun is time and has parts.   Of that which has parts, the year is the form, and from the year are born all creatures; when produced by the year they grow, and go again to rest in the year.   Therefore the year is Pragâ-pati, is time, is food, is the nest of Brahman, is Self. Thus it is said:

'Time ripens and dissolves all beings in the great Self, but he who knows into what time itself is dissolved, he is the knower of the Veda.'

16. This manifest time is the great ocean of creatures.   He who is called Savitri (the sun, as be-getter) dwells in it, from whence the moon, stars, planets, the year, and the rest are begotten.   From them again comes all this, and thus, whatever of good or evil is seen in this world, comes from them. Therefore Brahman is the Self of the sun, and a man should worship the sun under the name of time. Some say the sun is Brahman, and thus it is said:

---

[1] Thus, the commentator says, the existence of the lamp can be proved by the light of the lamp, as the existence of time is proved by what we see, the rising of the sun.   All this is very obscure.

' The sacrificer, the deity that enjoys the sacrifice, the oblation, the hymn, the sacrifice, Vish*n*u, Pra*g*â-pati, all this is the Lord, the witness, that shines in yonder orb.'

17. In the beginning Brahman was all this[1]. He was one, and infinite ; infinite in the East, infinite in the South, infinite in the West, infinite in the North, above and below and everywhere infinite. East and the other regions do not exist for him, nor across, nor below, nor above. The Highest Self is not to be fixed, he is unlimited, unborn, not to be reasoned about, not to be conceived. He is like the ether (everywhere), and at the destruction of the universe, he alone is awake. Thus from that ether he wakes all this world, which consists of thought only, and by him alone is all this meditated on, and in him it is dissolved. His is that luminous form which shines in the sun, and the manifold light in the smokeless fire, and the heat which in the stomach digests the food. Thus it is said :

' He who is in the fire, and he who is in the heart, and he who is in the sun, they are one and the same.'

He who knows this becomes one with the one.

18. This is the rule for achieving it (viz. concentration of the mind on the object of meditation): restraint of the breath, restraint of the senses, meditation, fixed attention, investigation, absorption, these are called the sixfold Yoga[2]. When beholding by

---

[1] Brahman used as neuter, but immediately followed by eko 'nanta*h*, &c.

[2] After having explained the form of what is to be meditated on and the mode of meditation, the Upanishad now teaches the Yoga which serves to keep our thoughts in subjection, and to fix our thoughts on the object of meditation. See Yoga-Sûtras II, 29.

this Yoga, he beholds the gold-coloured maker, the lord, the person, Brahman, the cause, then the sage, leaving behind good and evil, makes everything (breath, organs of sense, body, &c.) to be one in the Highest Indestructible (in the pratyagâtman or Brahman). And thus it is said:

'As birds and deer do not approach a burning mountain, so sins never approach those who know Brahman.'

19. And thus it is said elsewhere: When he who knows has, while he is still Prâ*na* (breath), restrained his mind, and placed all objects of the senses far away from himself, then let him remain without any conceptions. And because the living person, called Prâ*na* (breath), has been produced here on earth from that which is not Prâ*na* (the thinking Self), therefore let this Prâ*na* merge the Prâ*na* (himself) in what is called the fourth[1]. And thus it is said:

'What is without thought, though placed in the centre of thought, what cannot be thought, the hidden, the highest—let a man merge his thought there: then will this living being (li*n*ga) be without attachment[2].'

20. And thus it has been said elsewhere: There is the superior fixed attention (dhâra*nâ*) for him, viz. if he presses the tip of the tongue down the palate and restrains voice, mind, and breath, he sees

---

[1] The fourth stage is meant for the thinking Self, the earlier stages being waking, slumbering, and sleep.

[2] Professor Cowell offers two renderings of this difficult passage: 'This which is called prâ*na*, i.e. the individual soul as characterised by the subtil body, will thus no longer appear in its separate individuality from the absence of any conscious subject; or, this subtil body bearing the name of intellect will thus become void of all objects.'

Brahman by discrimination (tarka). And when, after the cessation of mind[1], he sees his own Self, smaller than small, and shining, as the Highest Self[2], then having seen his Self as the Self, he becomes Self-less, and because he is Self-less, he is without limit, without cause, absorbed in thought. This is the highest mystery, viz. final liberation. And thus it is said :

'Through the serenity of the thought he kills all actions, good or bad; his Self serene, abiding in the Self, obtains imperishable bliss.'

21. And thus it has been said elsewhere : The artery, called Sushumnâ, going upwards (from the heart to the Brahmarandhra), serving as the passage of the Prâna, is divided within the palate. Through that artery, when it has been joined by the breath (held in subjection), by the sacred syllable Om, and by the mind (absorbed in the contemplation of Brahman), let him proceed upwards[3], and after turning the tip of the tongue to the palate, without[4] using any of the organs of sense, let greatness perceive greatness[5]. From thence he goes to selflessness, and through selflessness he ceases to be an enjoyer of pleasure and pain, he obtains aloneness (kevalatva, final deliverance). And thus it is said :

---

[1] The commentator remarks that this process is called Lambikâ-yoga, and the state produced by it Unmanî or Unmanîbhâva ; see amanîbhâva, in VI, 34, ver. 7.

[2] I should have preferred to translate âtmânam âtmanâ pasyati by 'he sees his Self by his Self,' but the commentator takes a slightly different view, and says : itthambhâve tritîyâ ; paramâtmarûpena pasyati.

[3] Cf. Katha Up. VI, 16 ; Prasña Up. III, 6 (p. 277).

[4] If we read samyogya we must follow the commentator in translating by ' uniting the senses with the prâna and the manas.'

[5] Let the Self perceive the Self.

'Having successively fixed the breath, after it had been restrained, in the palate, thence having crossed the limit (the life), let him join himself afterwards to the limitless (Brahman) in the crown of the head.'

22. And thus it has been said elsewhere: Two Brahmans have to be meditated on, the word and the non-word. By the word alone is the non-word revealed. Now there is the word Om. Moving upward by it (where all words and all what is meant by them ceases), he arrives at absorption in the non-word (Brahman). This is the way, this is the immortal, this is union, and this is bliss. And as the spider, moving upward by the thread, gains free space, thus also he who meditates, moving upward by the syllable Om, gains independence.

Other teachers of the word (as Brahman) think otherwise. They listen to the sound of the ether within the heart while they stop the ears with the thumbs. They compare it to seven noises, like rivers, like a bell, like a brazen vessel, like the wheels of a carriage, like the croaking of frogs, like rain, and as if a man speaks in a cavern. Having passed beyond this variously apprehended sound, and having settled in the supreme, soundless (non-word), unmanifested Brahman, they become undistinguished and undistinguishable, as various flavours of the flowers are lost in the taste of honey. And thus it is said:

'Two Brahmans are to be known, the word-Brahman and the highest Brahman; he who is perfect in the word-Brahman attains the highest Brahman[1].'

---

[1] Cf. Mahâbhârata XII, 8540; Sarvadar*s*ana-sa*n*graha, p. 147; Cowell's Translation, p. 271.

23. And thus it has been said elsewhere: The syllable Om is what is called the word. And its end is the silent, the soundless, fearless, sorrowless, joyful, satisfied, firm, unwavering, immortal, immovable, certain (Brahman), called Vishnu. Let him worship these two, that he may obtain what is higher than everything (final deliverance). For thus it is said:

'He who is the high and the highest god[1], by name Om-kâra, he is soundless and free from all distinctions: therefore let a man dwell on him in the crown of his head.'

24. And thus it has been said elsewhere: The body is the bow, the syllable Om is the arrow, its point is the mind. Having cut through the darkness, which consists of ignorance[2], it approaches that which is not covered by darkness[3]. Then having cut through that which was covered (the personal soul), he saw Brahman, flashing like a wheel on fire, bright like the sun, vigorous, beyond all darkness, that which shines forth in yonder sun, in the moon, in the fire, in the lightning[4]. And having seen him, he obtains immortality. And thus it has been said:

'Meditation is directed to the highest Being (Brahman) within, and (before) to the objects (body, Om, mind); thence the indistinct understanding becomes distinct.

And when the works of the mind are dissolved,

---

[1] The commentator takes devâ as devah, though the accent is against it; see Schroeder, Über die Maitrâyanî Samhitâ, p. 9, l. 11.

[2] Should it not be, 'darkness is the mark?'

[3] Atamâvishta, explained as an irregular compound, atama-âvishtam, tama-âvesanarahitam.

[4] Cf. Bhagavadgîtâ XV, 12.

then that bliss which requires no other witness, that
is Brahman (Âtman), the immortal, the brilliant, that
is the way, that is the (true) world.'

25. And thus it has been said elsewhere: He
who has his senses hidden as in sleep, and who,
while in the cavern of his senses (his body), but no
longer ruled by them, sees, as in a dream, with the
purest intellect, Him who is called Pra*n*ava (Om),
the leader [1], the bright, the sleepless, free from old
age, from death, and sorrow, he is himself also
called Pra*n*ava, and becomes a leader, bright, sleepless, free from old age, from death, and sorrow.
And thus it is said:

'Because in this manner he joins the Prâ*n*a
(breath), the Om, and this Universe in its manifold
forms, or because they join themselves (to him),
therefore this (process of meditation) is called Yoga
(joining).

The oneness of breath, mind, and senses, and
then the surrendering of all conceptions, that is
called Yoga.'

26. And thus it has also been said elsewhere:
As a sportsman, after drawing out the denizens of
the waters with a net, offers them (as a sacrifice)
in the fire of his stomach, thus are these Prâ*n*as
(vital airs), after they have been drawn out with the
syllable Om, offered in the faultless fire (Brahman) [2].

Hence he is like a heated vessel (full of clarified
butter); for as the clarified butter in the heated
vessel lights up, when touched with grass and sticks,
thus does this being which is called Not-breath
(Âtman) light up, when touched by the Prâ*n*as (the

---

[1] Cf. VI, 4.   [2] Cf. *S*vetâ*s*vatara-upanishad III, 10.

vital airs)[1]. And that which flares up, that is the manifest form of Brahman, that is the highest place of Vishnu[2], that is the essence of Rudra. And this, dividing his Self in endless ways, fills all these worlds. And thus it is said:

'As the sparks from the fire, and as the rays from the sun, thus do his Prânas and the rest in proper order again and again proceed from him here on earth[3].'

27. And thus it has also been said elsewhere: This is the heat of the highest, the immortal, the incorporeal Brahman, viz. the warmth of the body. And this body is the clarified butter (poured on it, by which the heat of Brahman, otherwise invisible, is lighted up). Then, being manifest, it is placed in the ether (of the heart). Then by concentration they thus remove that ether which is within the heart, so that its light appears, as it were[4]. Therefore the worshipper becomes identified with that light without much delay. As a ball of iron, if placed in the earth, becomes earth without much delay, and as, when it has once become a clod of earth, fire and smiths have nothing more to do with that ball of iron, thus does thought (without delay) disappear, together with its support[5]. And thus it is said:

---

[1] As the fire which exists invisibly in a heated vessel becomes visible when the heated vessel is touched with sticks dipped in butter, thus the Âtman in the body appears only when the Prânas are diffused in it. Or, as the clarified butter, heated together with the vessel, lights up grass that comes in contact with it, so does this Âtman (called Not-breath), by heating its two bodies which are pervaded by the reflections of the thinker, light up everything brought in contact with it, viz. the world.

[2] See Katha Up. III, 9.   [3] See VI, 31; Brih. Up. II, 1, 10.

[4] The light was always there, but it seems then only to appear.

[5] The commentator explains this differently. He says that the

'The shrine which consists of the ether in the
heart, the blissful, the highest retreat, that is our
own, that is our goal, and that is the heat and brightness of the fire and the sun.'

28. And thus it has been said elsewhere: After
having left behind the body, the organs of sense, and
the objects of sense (as no longer belonging to us),
and having seized the bow whose stick is fortitude
and whose string is asceticism, having struck down
also with the arrow, which consists in freedom from
egotism, the first guardian of the door of Brahman—
(for if man looks at the world egotistically, then,
taking the diadem of passion, the earrings of greed
and envy, and the staff of sloth, sleep, and sin, and
having seized the bow whose string is anger, and
whose stick is lust, he destroys with the arrow
which consists of wishes, all beings)—having therefore killed that guardian, he crosses by means of the
boat Om to the other side of the ether within the
heart, and when the ether becomes revealed (as
Brahman), he enters slowly, as a miner seeking
minerals in a mine, into the Hall of Brahman.
After that let him, by means of the doctrine of his
teacher, break through the shrine of Brahman, which
consists of the four nets (of food, breath, mind, knowledge, till he reaches the last shrine, that of blessedness and identity with Brahman). Thenceforth pure,

---

similes are intended to show how, as soon as the impediment is
removed, the worshipper obtains his true form, i.e. becomes Brahman. Afterwards he explains *k*ittam, thought, by the individual
thinker, and declares that he vanishes together with the thought,
which forms the â*s*raya, the place, or the upâdhi, the outward form.
Or again, he says that the *k*itta, the mind, vanishes with its outward
sign, viz. the thoughts and imaginations.

clean, undeveloped, tranquil, breathless, bodiless, endless, imperishable, firm, everlasting, unborn and independent, he stands on his own greatness[1], and having seen (the Self), standing in his own greatness, he looks on the wheel of the world as one (who has alighted from a chariot) looks on its revolving wheel. And thus it is said:

'If a man practises Yoga for six months and is thoroughly free (from the outer world), then the perfect Yoga (union), which is endless, high, and hidden, is accomplished.

But if a man, though well enlightened (by instruction), is still pierced by (the gunas of) passion and darkness, and attached to his children, wife, and house, then perfect Yoga is never accomplished[2].'

29. After he had thus spoken (to Brihadratha), Sâkâyanya, absorbed in thought, bowed before him, and said: 'O King, by means of this Brahma-knowledge have the sons of Pragâpati (the Vâlakhilyas) gone to the road of Brahman. Through the practice of Yoga a man obtains contentment, power to endure good and evil, and tranquillity. Let no man preach this most secret doctrine to any one who is not his son or his pupil[3], and who is not of a serene mind. To him alone who is devoted to his teacher only, and endowed with all necessary qualities, may he communicate it[4].

---

[1] See Maitr. Up. II, 4; VI, 31.

[2] This would seem to have been the end of the dialogue between Pragâpati and the Vâlakhilyas, which, as related by Sâkâyanya to King Brihadratha, began in II, 3. See, however, VII, 8.

[3] Svet. Up. VI, 22 (p. 267); Brih. Up. VI, 3, 12.

[4] Here may have been the end of a chapter, but the story of Sâkâyanya and Brihadratha is continued to VI, 30.

30. Om! Having settled down in a pure place
let him, being pure himself, and firm in goodness,
study the truth, speak the truth, think the truth,
and offer sacrifice to the truth[1]. Henceforth he has
become another; by obtaining the reward of Brahman his fetters are cut asunder, he knows no hope,
no fear from others as little as from himself, he
knows no desires; and having attained imperishable,
infinite happiness, he stands blessed in the true
Brahman, who longs for a true man[2]. Freedom
from desires is, as it were, the highest prize to be
taken from the best treasure (Brahman). For a
man full of all desires, being possessed of will,
imagination, and belief, is a slave; but he who is
the opposite, is free.

Here some say, it is the Gu*n*a[3] (i. e. the so-called
Mahat, the principle of intellect which, according to
the Sânkhyas, is the result of the Gu*n*as or qualities),
which, through the differences of nature (acquired in
the former states of existence), goes into bondage to
the will, and that deliverance takes place (for the Gu*n*a)
when the fault of the will has been removed. (But this
is not our view), because (call it gu*n*a, intellect, buddhi,
manas, mind, ahaṅkâra, egotism, it is not the mind
that acts, but) he sees by the mind (as his instrument), he hears by the mind; and all that we call

---

[1] The truth or the true are explained by, (1) the book which
teaches the Highest Self; (2) by Brahman, who is to be spoken
about; (3) by Brahman, who is to be meditated on; (4) by Brahman, who is to be worshipped in thought.

[2] I have translated this according to the commentary, but I should
prefer to read satyâbhilâshi*n*i.

[3] The passages within brackets had to be added from the commentary in order to make the text intelligible, at least according to
Râmatîrtha's views.

desire, imagination, doubt, belief, unbelief, certainty, uncertainty, shame, thought, fear, all that is but mind (manas). Carried along by the waves of the qualities, darkened in his imaginations, unstable, fickle, crippled, full of desires, vacillating, he enters into belief, believing I am he, this is mine, and he binds his Self by his Self, as a bird with a net[1]. Therefore a man, being possessed of will, imagination, and belief, is a slave, but he who is the opposite is free. For this reason let a man stand free from will, imagination, and belief—this is the sign of liberty, this is the path that leads to Brahman, this is the opening of the door, and through it he will go to the other shore of darkness. All desires are there fulfilled. And for this they quote a verse :

"When the five instruments of knowledge stand still together with the mind, and when the intellect does not move, that is called the highest state[2]."'

Having thus said, Sâkâyanya became absorbed in thought. Then Marut (i. e. the King Brihadratha)[3], having bowed before him and duly worshipped him, went full of contentment to the Northern Path[4], for there is no way thither by any side-road. This is the path to Brahman. Having burst open the solar door, he rose on high and went away. And here they quote :

'There are endless rays (arteries) for the Self who, like a lamp, dwells in the heart : white and black, brown and blue, tawny and reddish[5].

---

[1] See III, 2.   [2] See the same verse in Katha Up. VI, 10.

[3] See before, II, 1.

[4] See Prasña Up. I, 10, 'But those who have sought the Self by penance, abstinence, faith, and knowledge, gain by the Northern Path Âditya, the sun.'

[5] See Khând. Up. VIII, 6, 1.

One of them (the Sushumnâ) leads upwards, piercing the solar orb : by it, having stepped beyond the world of Brahman, they go to the highest path.

The other hundred rays[1] rise upwards also, and on them the worshipper reaches the mansions belonging to the different bodies of gods.

But the manifest rays of dim colour which lead downwards, by them a man travels on and on helplessly, to enjoy the fruits of his actions here.'

Therefore it is said that the holy Âditya (sun) is the cause of new births (to those who do not worship him), of heaven (to those who worship him as a god), of liberty (to those who worship him as Brahman)[2].

31. Some one asks : 'Of what nature are those organs of sense that go forth (towards their objects)? Who sends them out here, or who holds them back?'

Another answers : ' Their nature is the Self; the Self sends them out, or holds them back; also the Apsaras (enticing objects of sense), and the solar rays (and other deities presiding over the senses).'

Now the Self devours the objects by the five rays (the organs of sense); then who is the Self?

He who has been defined by the terms pure, clean, undeveloped, tranquil[3], &c., who is to be apprehended independently by his own peculiar signs. That sign of him who has no signs, is like what the pervading

---

[1] A similar verse, but with characteristic variations, occurs in the *Kh*ând. Up. VIII, 6, 6, and in the Ka*th*a Up. VI, 16.

[2] Here ends the story of *S*âkâyanya, which began I, 2, and was carried on through chap. VI, though that chapter and the seventh are called Khilas, or supplements, and though the MS. M. also ends, as we saw, with the eighth paragraph of the sixth chapter.

[3] See before, II, 4 VI,1 [5]

heat is of fire, the purest taste of water; thus say some[1]. It is speech, hearing, sight, mind, breath; thus say others[2]. It is intellect, retention, remembering, knowledge; thus say others[3]. Now all these are signs of the Self in the same sense in which here on earth shoots are the signs of seed, or smoke, light, and sparks of fire. And for this they quote[4]:

'As the sparks from the fire, and as the rays from the sun, thus do his Prânas and the rest in proper order again and again proceed from him here on earth.'

32. From this very Self, abiding within his Self, come forth all Prânas (speech, &c.), all worlds, all Vedas, all gods, and all beings; its Upanishad (revelation)[5] is that it is 'the true of the true.' Now as from a fire of green wood, when kindled, clouds of smoke come forth by themselves (though belonging to the fire), thus from that great Being has been breathed forth all this which is the Rig-veda, the Yagur-veda, the Sâma-veda, the Atharvângirasas (Atharva-veda), the Itihâsa (legendary stories), the Purâna (accounts of the creation, &c.), Vidyâ (ceremonial doctrines), the Upanishads, the Slokas (verses interspersed in the Upanishads, &c.), the Sûtras (compendious statements), the Anuvyâkhyânas (explanatory notes), the Vyâkhyânas (elucidations)[6]—all these things are his.

---

[1] See Svet. Up. VI, 13.   [2] See Ken. Up. 2.

[3] See Ait. Up. III, 2. Here we find dhriti (holding), smriti (remembering), pragñânam (knowledge), but not buddhi. Pragñânam seems the right reading, and is supported by M.

[4] See before, VI, 26.

[5] Revelation is here the rendering of Upanishad, upanigamayitritvât sâkshâdrahasyam, and the true (sattya) is explained first by the five elements, and then by that which is their real essence.

[6] See Khând. Up. VI, 1. The explanations given of these literary

33. This fire (the Gârhapatya-fire) with five bricks is the year. And its five bricks are spring, summer, rainy season, autumn, winter; and by them the fire has a head, two sides, a centre, and a tail. This earth (the Gârhapatya-fire) here is the first sacrificial pile for Pra*g*âpati, who knows the Purusha (the Virâ*g*). It presented the sacrificer to Vâyu (the wind) by lifting him with the hands to the sky. That Vâyu is Prâ*n*a (Hira*n*yagarbha).

Prâ*n*a is Agni (the Dakshi*n*âgni-fire), and its bricks are the five vital breaths, Prâ*n*a, Vyâna, Apâna, Samâna, Udâna; and by them the fire has a head, two sides, a centre, and a tail. This sky (the Dakshi*n*âgni-fire) here is the second sacrificial pile for Pra*g*âpati, who knows the Purusha. It presented the sacrificer to Indra, by lifting him with the hands to heaven. That Indra is Âditya, the sun.

That (Indra) is the Agni (the Âhavanîya-fire), and its bricks are the *Rik*, the Ya*g*ush, the Sâman, the Atharvângirasas, the Itihâsa, and the Purâ*n*a; and by them the fire has a head, two sides, a tail, and a centre. This heaven (Âhavanîya-fire) is the third sacrificial pile for Pra*g*âpati, who knows the

---

titles are on the whole the same as those we had before in similar passages. What is peculiar to Râmatîrtha is that he explains Upanishad by such passages as we had just now, viz. its Upanishad is that it is the true of the true. The *S*lokas are explained as verses like those in VI, 19, a*k*itta*m k*ittamadhyastham. The Sûtras are explained as comprehensive sentences, such as II, 2, aya*m* vâva khalv âtmâ te. Anuvyâkhyânas are taken as explanations following on the Sûtra in II, 2, beginning with atha ya esho*kkh*vâsâvish*t*ambhanena. The Vyâkhyânas are taken as fuller statements of the meaning contained in the Sûtra, such as the dialogue between the Vâlakhilyas and Kratu.

Purusha. With the hands it makes a present of the sacrificer to the Knower of the Self (Pragâpati); then the Knower of the Self, lifting him up, presented him to Brahman. In him he becomes full of happiness and joy.

34. The earth is the Gârhapatya-fire, the sky the Dakshina-fire, the heaven the Âhavanîya-fire; and therefore they are also the Pavamâna (pure), the Pâvaka (purifying), and the Suki (bright)[1]. By this (by the three deities, Pavamâna, Pâvaka, and Suki) the sacrifice (of the three fires, the Gârhapatya, Dakshina, and Âhavanîya) is manifested. And because the digestive fire also is a compound of the Pavamâna, Pâvaka, and Suki, therefore that fire is to receive oblations, is to be laid with bricks, is to be praised, and to be meditated on. The sacrificer, when he has seized the oblation, wishes[2] to perform his meditation of the deity:

'The gold-coloured bird abides in the heart, and in the sun—a diver bird, a swan, strong in splendour; him we worship in the fire.'

Having recited the verse, he discovers its meaning, viz. the adorable splendour of Savitri (sun) is to be meditated on by him who, abiding within his mind, meditates thereon. Here he attains the place of rest for the mind, he holds it within his own Self. On this there are the following verses:

(1) As a fire without fuel becomes quiet in its

---

[1] Epithets of Agni, the sacrificial-fire, pavamâna applying o the Gârhapatya-fire, pâvaka to the Dakshina-fire, and suki to the Âhavanîya-fire. The construction of the sentence, however, is imperfect.

[2] This means, he ought to perform it.

place[1], thus do the thoughts, when all activity ceases, become quiet[2] in their place.

(2) Even in a mind which loves the truth[3] and has gone to rest in itself there arise, when it is deluded by the objects of sense, wrongs resulting from former acts[4].

(3) For thoughts alone cause the round of births[5]; let a man strive to purify his thoughts. What a man thinks, that he is: this is the old secret[6].

(4) By the serenity of his thoughts a man blots out all actions, whether good or bad. Dwelling within his Self with serene thoughts, he obtains imperishable happiness.

(5) If the thoughts of a man were so fixed on Brahman as they are on the things of this world, who would not then be freed from bondage?

(6) The mind, it is said, is of two kinds, pure or impure; impure from the contact with lust, pure when free from lust[7].

(7) When a man, having freed his mind from sloth, distraction, and vacillation, becomes as it were delivered from his mind[8], that is the highest point.

(8) The mind must be restrained in the heart till it comes to an end;—that is knowledge, that is liberty: all the rest are extensions of the ties[9] (which bind us to this life).

---

[1] Dies in the fireplace. [2] M. reads upa*s*âmyati twice.

[3] M. reads satyakâmina*h*.

[4] The commentator inserts a negative.

[5] M. reads sa*m*sâra*h*.

[6] This is very like the teaching of the Dhammapada, I, 1.

[7] Cf. Ind. Stud. II, 60. Brahmavindu Up. v. 1, where we read kâmasankalpam, as in MS. M.

[8] See note to VI, 20.

[9] M. reads moksha*sk*a and *s*eshâs tu. The commentator says that

(9) That happiness which belongs to a mind which by deep meditation has been washed[1] clean from all impurity and has entered within the Self, cannot be described here by words; it can be felt by the inward power only[2].

(10) Water in water, fire in fire, ether in ether, no one can distinguish them; likewise a man whose mind has entered (till it cannot be distinguished from the Self), attains liberty.

(11) Mind alone is the cause of bondage and liberty for men; if attached to the world, it becomes bound; if free from the world, that is liberty[3].

Therefore those who do not offer the Agnihotra (as described above), who do not lay the fires (with the bricks, as described above), who are ignorant (of the mind being the cause of the round of births), who do not meditate (on the Self in the solar orb) are debarred from remembering the ethereal place of Brahman. Therefore that fire is to receive oblations, is to be laid with bricks, is to be praised, to be meditated on.

35[4]. Adoration to Agni, the dweller on earth, who remembers his world. Grant that world to this thy worshipper!

Adoration to Vâyu, the dweller in the sky, who remembers his world. Grant that world to this thy worshipper!

---

this line is easy, but it is so by no means. Professor Cowell translates granthavistarâ*h* by book-prolixity, but this sounds very strange in an Upanishad. I am not satisfied with my own translation, but it may stand till a better one is found. M. reads gr*i*ndhavistarâ*h*. The granthis are mentioned in *Kh*ând. Up. VII, 26; Ka*th*. Up. VI, 15.

[1] M. reads nirdhûta.   [2] M. reads kara*n*eti.

[3] M. reads vishayâsaktam muktyai.

[4] Next follow invocations to be addressed to the deities.

Adoration to Âditya, the dweller in heaven, who remembers his world. Grant that world to this thy worshipper!

Adoration to Brahman, who dwells everywhere, who remembers all. Grant all to this thy worshipper!

The mouth of the true (Brahman) is covered with a golden lid; open that, O Pûshan (sun), that we may go to the true one, who pervades all (Vish*n*u)[1].

He who is the person in the sun, I am he[2].

And what is meant by the true one is the essence of the sun, that which is bright, personal, sexless[3]; a portion (only) of the light which pervades the ether; which is, as it were, in the midst of the sun, and in the eye, and in the fire. That is Brahman, that is immortal, that is splendour.

That is the true one, a portion (only) of the light which pervades the ether, which is in the midst of the sun, the immortal, of which Soma (the moon) and the vital breaths also are offshoots: that is Brahman, that is immortal, that is splendour.

That is the true one, a portion (only) of the light which pervades the ether, which in the midst of the sun shines as Ya*g*us, viz. as Om, as water, light, essence, immortal, Brahman, Bhû*h*, Bhuva*h*, Svar, Om.

'The eight-footed[4], the bright, the swan, bound

---

[1] The verse occurs in a more original form in Tal. Up. 15.

[2] The commentator adds iti after aham.

[3] *Kh*ând. Up. I, 6, 6; *S*vet. Up. V, 10.

[4] The eight feet are explained as the eight regions, or âroga and the rest. The swan is the sun. The three threads are the three Vedas; see *K*ûl. Up. I, 1; Ind. Stud. IX, 11—ash*t*apâda*m* *s*u*k*ir ha*m*sa*m* trisûtram ma*n*im avyayam, dvivartamâna*m* tai*g*asasiddha*m*

with three threads, the infinitely small, the imperishable, blind for good and evil, kindled with light—he who sees him, sees everything.'

A portion (only) of the light which pervades the ether, are the two rays rising in the midst of the sun. That is the knower[1] (the Sun), the true one. That is the Yagus, that is the heat, that is Agni (fire), that is Vâyu (wind), that is breath, that is water, that is the moon, that is bright, that is immortal, that is the place of Brahman, that is the ocean of light. In that ocean the sacrificers are dissolved[2] like salt, and that is oneness with Brahman, for all desires are there fulfilled. And here they quote :

' Like a lamp, moved by a gentle wind, he who dwells within the gods shines forth. He who knows this, he is the knower, he knows the difference (between the high and the highest Brahman) ; having obtained unity, he becomes identified with it.

They who rise up in endless number, like spray drops (from the sea), like lightnings from the light within the clouds in the highest heaven, they, when they have entered into the light of glory (Brahman), appear like so many flame-crests in the track of fire.'

36. There are two manifestations of the Brahma-light : one is tranquil, the other lively. Of that which is tranquil, the ether is the support; of that which is lively, food. Therefore (to the former) sacrifice must be offered on the house-altar with hymns, herbs, ghee, meat, cakes, sthâlîpâka, and other things ; to the latter, with meat and drinks (belonging to the great sacrifices) thrown into the mouth, for the mouth

---

sarvaḥ paṣyan na paṣyati. Here the eight feet are explained as the five elements, manas, buddhi, and ahaṅkâra.

[1] Savit for savitrí.   [2] Vlîyante for vilîyante.

is the Âhavanîya-fire; and this is done to increase
our bodily vigour, to gain the world of purity, and
for the sake of immortality. And here they quote:

'Let him who longs for heaven, offer an Agnihotra. By an Agnish*t*oma he wins the kingdom
of Yama; by Uktha, the kingdom of Soma; by
a Sho*d*asin-sacrifice, the kingdom of Sûrya; by an
Atirâtra-sacrifice, the kingdom of Indra; by the
sacrifices beginning with the twelve-night sacrifice
and ending with the thousand years' sacrifice, the
world of Pra*g*âpati.

As a lamp burns so long as the vessel that holds
the wick is filled with oil, these two, the Self and the
bright Sun, remain so long as the egg (of the world)
and he who dwells within it hold together.'

37. Therefore let a man perform all these ceremonies with the syllable Om (at the beginning). Its
splendour is endless, and it is declared to be threefold, in the fire (of the altar), in the sun (the deity),
in the breath (the sacrificer). Now this is the channel
to increase the food, which makes what is offered in
the fire ascend to the sun. The sap which flows
from thence, rains down as with the sound of a
hymn. By it there are vital breaths, from them
there is offspring. And here they quote:

'The offering which is offered in the fire, goes to
the sun; the sun rains it down by his rays; thus food
comes, and from food the birth of living beings.'

And thus he said:

'The oblation which is properly thrown on the
fire, goes toward the sun; from the sun comes rain,
from rain food, from food living beings[1].'

---

[1] See Manu III, 76.

38. He who offers the Agnihotra breaks through the net of desire. Then, cutting through bewilderment, never approving of anger, meditating on one desire (that of liberty), he breaks through the shrine of Brahman with its four nets, and proceeds thence to the ether. For having there broken through the (four) spheres of the Sun, the Moon, the Fire, and Goodness, he then, being purified himself, beholds dwelling in goodness, immovable, immortal, indestructible, firm, bearing the name of Vish*n*u, the highest abode, endowed with love of truth and omniscience, the self-dependent Intelligence (Brahman), standing in its own greatness. And here they quote :

'In the midst of the sun stands the moon, in the midst of the moon the fire, in the midst of fire goodness, in the midst of goodness the Eternal.'

Having meditated on him who has the breadth of a thumb within the span (of the heart) in the body, who is smaller than small, he obtains the nature of the Highest; there all desires are fulfilled. And on this they quote:

'Having the breadth of a thumb within the span (of the heart) in the body, like the flame of a lamp, burning twofold or threefold, that glorified Brahman, the great God, has entered into all the worlds. Om! Adoration to Brahman! Adoration!'

Seventh Prapâ*th*aka.

1. Agni, the Gâyatra (metre), the Triv*ri*t (hymn), the Rathantara (song), the spring, the upward breath (prâ*n*a), the Nakshatras, the Vasus (deities)—these rise in the East; they warm, they rain, they praise [1]

---

[1] Other MSS. read sruvanti, which seems better.

(the sun), they enter again into him (the sun), they look out from him (the sun). He (the sun) is inconceivable, without form, deep, covered, blameless, solid, unfathomable, without qualities, pure, brilliant, enjoying the play of the three qualities, awful, not caused, a master-magician[1], the omniscient, the mighty, immeasurable, without beginning or end, blissful, unborn, wise, indescribable, the creator of all things, the self of all things, the enjoyer of all things, the ruler of all things, the centre of the centre of all things.

2. Indra, the Trish*t*ubh (metre), the Pañ*k*ada*s*a (hymn), the B*ri*hat (song), the summer, the through-going breath (Vyâna), Soma, the Rudras—these rise in the South; they warm, they rain, they praise, they enter again into him, they look out from him. He (the sun) is without end or beginning, unmeasured, unlimited, not to be moved by another, self-dependent, without sign, without form, of endless power, the creator, the maker of light.

3. The Maruts, the *G*agatî (metre), the Saptada*s*a (hymn), the Vairupa (song), the rainy season, the downward breath (apâna), *S*ukra, the Âdityas—these rise in the West; they warm, they rain, they praise, they enter again into him, they look out from him. That is the tranquil, the soundless, fearless, sorrowless, joyful, satisfied, firm, immovable, immortal, eternal, true, the highest abode, bearing the name of Vish*n*u.

4. The Vi*s*ve Devas, the Anush*t*ubh (metre), the Ekavi*m*sa (hymn), the Vairâ*g*a (song), the autumn, the equal breath (samâna), Varu*n*a, the Sâdhyas—these rise in the North; they warm, they rain, they

---

[1] See VII, 11, abhidhyâtur vist*ri*tir iva.

praise, they enter again into him, they look out from him. He is pure within, purifying, undeveloped, tranquil, breathless, selfless, endless.

5. Mitrâ-Varuñau, the Pankti (metre), the Triña-vatrayastrimsa (hymns), the Sâkvara-raivata (songs), the snowy and dewy seasons, the out-going breath (udâna), the Angiras, the Moon—these rise above; they warm, they rain, they praise, they enter again into him, they look out from him—who is called Prañava (Om), the leader, consisting of light, without sleep, old age, death, and sorrow.

6. Sani (Saturn), Rahu and Ketu (the ascending and descending nodes), the serpents, Rakshas, Yakshas, men, birds, sarabhas, elephants, &c.—these rise below; they warm, they rain, they praise, they enter again into him, they look out from him—he who is wise, who keeps things in their right place, the centre of all, the imperishable, the pure, the purifier, the bright, the patient, the tranquil.

7. And he is indeed the Self, smaller (than small) within the heart, kindled like fire, endowed with all forms. Of him is all this food, within him all creatures are woven. That Self is free from sin[1], free from old age, from death and grief, from hunger and thirst, imagining nothing but what it ought to imagine, and desiring nothing but what it ought to desire. He is the highest lord, he is the supreme master of all beings, the guardian of all beings, a boundary keeping all things apart in their right places[2]. He the Self, the lord, is indeed Sambhu, Bhava, Rudra, Pragâpati, the creator of all, Hirañya-

---

[1] See Khând. Up. VIII, 7, 1.

[2] See Khând. Up. VIII, 4, 1, where we find setur vidhritir eshâm lokânâm.

garbha, the true, breath, the swan, the ruler, the eternal, Vish*nu*, Nârâya*na*. And he who abides in the fire, and he who abides in the heart, and he who abides in the sun, they are one and the same. To thee who art this, endowed with all forms, settled in the true ether, be adoration!

8. Now follow the impediments in the way of know-ledge, O King[1]! This is indeed the origin of the net of bewilderment, that one who is worthy of heaven lives with those who are not worthy of heaven. That is it. Though they have been told that there is a grove before them, they cling to a small shrub. And others also who are always merry, always abroad, always begging, always making a living by handi-work; and others who are begging in towns, per-forming sacrifices for those who are not allowed to offer sacrifices, who make themselves the pupils of *S*ûdras, and *S*ûdras who know the sacred books; and others who are malignant, who use bad language, dancers, prize-fighters, travelling mendicants, actors, those who have been degraded in the king's service; and others who for money pretend that they can lay (the evil influences) of Yakshas, Râkshasas, ghosts, goblins, devils, serpents, imps, &c.; and others who falsely wear red dresses[2], earrings, and skulls; and others who wish to entice by the jugglery of false arguments, mere comparisons and paralogisms, the believers in the Veda—with all these he should not

---

[1] This king is not meant for B*ri*hadratha.

[2] This refers to people who claim the privileges and licence of Sannyâsins without having passed through the discipline of the preceding â*s*ramas. As this was one of the chief complaints made against the followers of *S*âkyamuni, it might refer to Buddhists, but it ought to be borne in mind that there were Buddhists before Buddha.

live together. They are clearly thieves, and unworthy of heaven. And thus it is said:

'The world unsettled by the paralogisms of the denial of Self, by false comparisons and arguments, does not know what is the difference between Veda and philosophy[1].'

9. Brihaspati, having become Sukra, brought forth that false knowledge for the safety of Indra and for the destruction of the Asuras. By it they show that good is evil, and that evil is good. They say that we ought to ponder on the (new) law, which upsets the Veda and the other sacred books[2]. Therefore let no one ponder on that false knowledge: it is wrong, it is, as it were, barren. Its reward lasts only as long as the pleasure lasts, as with one who has fallen from his caste. Let that false science not be attempted, for thus it is said:

(1) Widely opposed and divergent are these two, the one known as false knowledge, the other as knowledge. I (Yama) believe Nakiketas to be possessed by a desire of knowledge; even many pleasures do not move thee[3].

(2) He who knows at the same time both the imperfect (sacrifice, &c.) and the perfect knowledge (of the Self), he crosses death by means of the imperfect, and obtains immortality by means of the perfect knowledge[4].

(3) Those who are wrapped up[5] in the midst of

---

[1] If we translate thus, the use of vidyâ for vrithâ vidyâ is unusual; if we follow the commentary, we should have to translate, he does not know the Veda and the other knowledge.

[2] All this may refer to Buddhists, but not by necessity, for there were heretics, such as Brihaspati, long before Sâkyamuni.

[3] See Kath. Up. II, 4.   [4] See Vâg. Up. 11.

[5] Veshtyamânâh, instead of vartamânâh.

imperfect knowledge, fancying themselves alone wise
and learned, they wander about floundering and deceived, like the blind led by the blind[1].

10. The gods and the demons, wishing to know
the Self, went into the presence of Brahman (their
father, Pra*g*âpati)[2]. Having bowed before him, they
said : ' O blessed one, we wish to know the Self,
do thou tell us.' Then, after having pondered a
long while, he thought, these demons are not yet
self-subdued[3]; therefore a very different Self was
told to them (from what was told to the gods). On
that Self these deluded demons take their stand,
clinging to it, destroying the true means of salva-
tion (the Veda), preaching untruth. What is untrue
they see as true, as in jugglery. Therefore, what is
taught in the Vedas, that is true. What is said in
the Vedas, on that the wise keep their stand.
Therefore let a Brâhman not read what is not of
the Veda, or this will be the result.

11. This is indeed the nature of it (the Veda), the
supreme light of the ether which is within the heart.
This is taught as threefold, in the fire, in the sun,
in the breath. This is indeed the nature of it, the
syllable Om, of the ether which is within the heart.
By it (by the Om) that (light) starts, rises, breathes
forth, becomes for ever the means of the worship and
knowledge of Brahman.   That (light, in the shape of

---

[1] See Ka*th*. Up. II, 5.

[2] Cf. *Kh*ând. Up. VIII, 8.

[3] I prefer ayatâtmâna*h*, though it is the easier (sugama) reading,
as compared with anyatâtmâna*h*, those who seek for the Self elsewhere, namely, in the body. It seems to me to refer to those who,
without having subdued the passions of their body, wish to obtain
the knowledge of the Highest Self. Possibly, however, the author
may have intended a climax from anyatâtmâna*h* to anyatamam.

Om), when there is breathing, takes the place of the internal heat, free from all brightness[1]. This is like the action of smoke; for when there is a breath of air, the smoke, first rising to the sky in one column, follows afterwards every bough, envelopes it and takes its shape[2]. It is like throwing salt (into water), like heating ghee[3]. The Veda comes and goes like the dissolving view of a master-magician[4]. And here they quote:

'Why then is it called "like lightning?" Because as soon as it comes forth (as Om) it lights up the whole body. Therefore let a man worship that boundless light by the syllable Om.'

(1) The man in the eye who abides in the right eye, he is Indra, and his wife abides in the left eye[5].

(2) The union of these two takes place in the cavity within the heart, and the ball of blood which is there, that is indeed the vigour and life of these two.

(3) There is a channel going from the heart so far, and fixed in that eye; that is the artery for both of them, being one, divided into two.

---

[1] This seems to be the meaning adopted by the commentator; but may it not be, sending forth brightness?

[2] The simile is not very clear. The light of Brahman is below the sphere of fire in the body. That sphere of fire becoming heated, the light of Brahman becomes manifest. When the fire has been fanned by the wind of sonant breath, then the light of Brahman, embodying itself in the wind and the fire, manifests itself first in the mere sound of Om, but afterwards, checked by throat, palate, &c., it assumes the form of articulate letters, and ends by becoming the Veda in its many branches.

[3] As these are outwardly changed, without losing their nature, thus the light of Brahman, though assuming the different forms of the Veda, remains itself.

[4] See before, VII, 1.

[5] See Brih. Up. IV, 2, 2, 3, where Indra is explained as Indha.

(4) The mind excites the fire of the body, that fire stirs the breath, and the breath, moving in the chest, produces the low sound.

(5) Brought forth by the touch of the fire, as with a churning-stick, it is at first a minim, from the minim it becomes in the throat a double minim; on the tip of the tongue know that it is a treble minim, and, when uttered, they call it the alphabet (στοιχεῖα) [1].

(6) He who sees this, does not see death, nor disease, nor misery, for seeing he sees all (objectively, not as affecting him subjectively); he becomes all everywhere (he becomes Brahman).

(7) There is the person in the eye, there is he who walks as in sleep, he who is sound asleep, and he who is above the sleeper: these are the four conditions (of the Self), and the fourth is greater than all [2].

(8) Brahman with one foot moves in the three, and Brahman with three feet is in the last.

---

[1] A comparison of this verse with *Kh*ând. Up. VII, 26, shows the great freedom with which the wording of these ancient verses was treated.   Instead of—

Na pa*s*yan m*ri*tyum pa*s*yati na roga*m* nota du*h*khatâm,
Sarva*m* hi pa*s*yan pa*s*yati sarvam âpnoti sarva*s*a*h*,

the *Kh*ândogya Up. reads:

Na pa*s*yo m*ri*tyum pa*s*yati na roga*m* nota du*h*khatâm,
Sarva*m* ha pa*s*ya*h* pa*s*yati sarvam âpnoti sarva*s*a*h*.

[2] The conditions here described are sometimes called the Vi*s*va (Vai*s*vânara), Tai*g*asa, Prâ*gña*, and Turîya. In the first state the Self is awake, and enjoys the world; in the second he sees everything as in a dream; in the third the two former states cease, and he is absorbed in sleep; in the fourth he becomes again the pure Self. In the first state the Self has the disguise of a coarse material body; in the second of a subtle material body; in the third its disguise is potential only; in the fourth it has no disguise, either potential or realised.

It is that both the true (in the fourth condition) and the untrue (in the three conditions) may have their desert, that the Great Self (seems to) become two, yes, that he (seems to) become two[1].

---

[1] 'By reason of the experience of the false and the true, the great Soul appears possessed of duality.'   Cowell.

TRANSLITERATION OF ORIENTAL ALPHABETS ADOPTED FOR THE TRANSLATIONS OF THE SACRED BOOKS OF THE EAST.

CONSONANTS.	MISSIONARY ALPHABET. I Class.	II Class.	III Class.	Sanskrit.	Zend.	Pehlevi.	Persian.	Arabic.	Hebrew.	Chinese.
Gutturales.										
1 Tenuis	k	.	.	क	.	.	.	.	.	k
2 „ aspirata	kh	.	.	ख	.	.	.	.	.	kh
3 Media	g	.	.	ग	.	.	.	.	.	.
4 „ aspirata	gh	.	.	घ	.	.	.	.	.	.
5 Gutturo-labialis	q	.	.	.	.	.	.	.	.	.
6 Nasalis	ṅ (ng)	.	.	ङ	.	.	.	.	.	h, hs
7 Spiritus asper	h	.	.	ह	.	.	.	.	.	.
8 „ lenis	'	.	.	.	.	.	.	.	.	.
9 „ asper faucalis	ʿh	.	.	.	.	.	.	.	.	.
10 „ lenis faucalis	ʾh	.	.	.	.	.	.	.	.	.
11 „ asper fricatus	.	ʿh	.	.	.	.	.	.	.	.
12 „ lenis fricatus	.	ʾh	.	.	.	.	.	.	.	.
Gutturales modificatae (palatales, &c.)										
13 Tenuis	.	k	.	च	.	.	.	.	.	k
14 „ aspirata	.	kh	.	छ	.	.	.	.	.	kh
15 Media	.	g	.	ज	.	.	.	.	.	.
16 „ aspirata	.	gh	.	झ	.	.	.	.	.	.
17 „ Nasalis	ñ	.	.	ञ	.	.	.	.	.	.

CONSONANTS (continued).	Missionary Alphabet. I Class.	II Class.	III Class.	Sanskrit.	Zend.	Pehlevi.	Persian.	Arabic.	Hebrew.	Chinese.
18 Semivocalis	y			य	३	ن	ی	ی	י	y
19 Spiritus asper		(ŷ)			init.					
20 ,, lenis		(ĵ)								
21 ,, asper assibilatus		s					‹ج›	‹ج›		
22 ,, lenis assibilatus		z		ज़			ر			z
Dentales.										
23 Tenuis	t			त द			‹ت›	‹ت›	ת ת	t
24 ,, aspirata	th		TH						ת ת	th
25 ,, assibilata				थ ध			‹ث›	‹ث›		
26 Media	d			द ध			‹د›	‹د›	ד ד	
27 ,, aspirata	dh		DH							
28 ,, assibilata				ध ठ						
29 Nasalis	n			न ण			‹ن›	‹ن›	נ ן	n
30 Semivocalis	l	l		ल						l
31 ,, mollis 1										
32 ,, mollis 2			L							
33 Spiritus asper 1	s		s (ʃ)	स	३	৭	‹س›	‹س›	שׁ	s
34 ,, asper 2	z				ৼ	স	ز	ز	שׂ	
35 ,, lenis	z								ס	z
36 ,, asperrimus 1			z (ž)				‹ز›	‹ز›	צ	ʒ, ʒh
37 ,, asperrimus 2			z. (ž)							

Dentales modificatae (linguales, &c.)

No.			Transliteration
38	Tenuis		t
39	„	aspirata	th
40	Media		d
41	„	aspirata	dh
42	Nasalis		n
43	Semivocalis		r
44	„	fricata	r
45	„	diacritica	
46	Spiritus asper		sh
47	„	lenis	zh

Labiales.

No.			Transliteration
48	Tenuis		p
49	„	aspirata	ph
50	Media		b
51	„	aspirata	bh
52	Tenuissima		
53	Nasalis		m
54	Semivocalis		w
55	„	aspirata	hw
56	Spiritus asper		f
57	„	lenis	v
58	Anusvâra		m
59	Visarga		h

VOWELS.	MISSIONARY ALPHABET. I Class.	II Class.	III Class.	Sanskrit.	Zend.	Pehlevi.	Persian.	Arabic.	Hebrew.	Chinese.
1 Neutralis	0									ă
2 Laryngo-palatalis	ĕ									
3 „ labialis	ŏ									
4 Gutturalis brevis	a			𑀅						a
5 „ longa	ā	(a)		𑀆		fin. / init.				â
6 Palatalis brevis	i									i
7 „ longa	ī	(ī)								ī
8 Dentalis brevis	li									
9 „ longa	lī									
10 Lingualis brevis	ri									
11 „ longa	rī									
12 Labialis brevis	u	(u)								u
13 „ longa	ū									ū
14 Gutturo-palatalis brevis	e	(e)			ε(e), ξ(e)					e
15 „ longa	ê (ai)	(ē)								ê
16 Diphthongus gutturo-palatalis	âi	(ai)								âi
17 „ „	ei (ēi)									ei, ēi
18 „ „	oi (ŏu)									
19 Gutturo-labialis brevis	o	(o)								o
20 „ longa	ŏ (au)				(au)					ô
21 Diphthongus gutturo-labialis	âu	(au)								âu
22 „ „	eu (ēu)									
23 „ „	ou (ŏu)									
24 Gutturalis fracta	ä									
25 Palatalis fracta	ï									
26 Labialis fracta	ü									ü
27 Gutturo-labialis fracta	ö									

A CATALOGUE OF SELECTED DOVER BOOKS
IN ALL FIELDS OF INTEREST

A CATALOGUE OF SELECTED DOVER
BOOKS IN ALL FIELDS OF INTEREST

RACKHAM'S COLOR ILLUSTRATIONS FOR WAGNER'S RING. Rackham's finest mature work—all 64 full-color watercolors in a faithful and lush interpretation of the *Ring*. Full-sized plates on coated stock of the paintings used by opera companies for authentic staging of Wagner. Captions aid in following complete Ring cycle. Introduction. 64 illustrations plus vignettes. 72pp. 8⅝ x 11¼. 23779-6 Pa. $6.00

CONTEMPORARY POLISH POSTERS IN FULL COLOR, edited by Joseph Czestochowski. 46 full-color examples of brilliant school of Polish graphic design, selected from world's first museum (near Warsaw) dedicated to poster art. Posters on circuses, films, plays, concerts all show cosmopolitan influences, free imagination. Introduction. 48pp. 9⅜ x 12¼. 23780-X Pa. $6.00

GRAPHIC WORKS OF EDVARD MUNCH, Edvard Munch. 90 haunting, evocative prints by first major Expressionist artist and one of the greatest graphic artists of his time: *The Scream, Anxiety, Death Chamber, The Kiss, Madonna,* etc. Introduction by Alfred Werner. 90pp. 9 x 12. 23765-6 Pa. $5.00

THE GOLDEN AGE OF THE POSTER, Hayward and Blanche Cirker. 70 extraordinary posters in full colors, from Maitres de l'Affiche, Mucha, Lautrec, Bradley, Cheret, Beardsley, many others. Total of 78pp. 9⅜ x 12¼. 22753-7 Pa. $5.95

THE NOTEBOOKS OF LEONARDO DA VINCI, edited by J. P. Richter. Extracts from manuscripts reveal great genius; on painting, sculpture, anatomy, sciences, geography, etc. Both Italian and English. 186 ms. pages reproduced, plus 500 additional drawings, including studies for *Last Supper*, Sforza monument, etc. 860pp. 7⅞ x 10¾. (Available in U.S. only) 22572-0, 22573-9 Pa., Two-vol. set $15.90

THE CODEX NUTTALL, as first edited by Zelia Nuttall. Only inexpensive edition, in full color, of a pre-Columbian Mexican (Mixtec) book. 88 color plates show kings, gods, heroes, temples, sacrifices. New explanatory, historical introduction by Arthur G. Miller. 96pp. 11⅜ x 8½. (Available in U.S. only) 23168-2 Pa. $7.95

UNE SEMAINE DE BONTÉ, A SURREALISTIC NOVEL IN COLLAGE, Max Ernst. Masterpiece created out of 19th-century periodical illustrations, explores worlds of terror and surprise. Some consider this Ernst's greatest work. 208pp. 8⅛ x 11. 23252-2 Pa. $6.00

DRAWINGS OF WILLIAM BLAKE, William Blake. 92 plates from Book of Job, *Divine Comedy, Paradise Lost,* visionary heads, mythological figures, Laocoon, etc. Selection, introduction, commentary by Sir Geoffrey Keynes. 178pp. 8⅛ x 11.   22303-5 Pa. $4.00

ENGRAVINGS OF HOGARTH, William Hogarth. 101 of Hogarth's greatest works: *Rake's Progress, Harlot's Progress, Illustrations for Hudibras, Before and After, Beer Street and Gin Lane,* many more. Full commentary. 256pp. 11 x 13¾.   22479-1 Pa. $12.95

DAUMIER: 120 GREAT LITHOGRAPHS, Honore Daumier. Wide-ranging collection of lithographs by the greatest caricaturist of the 19th century. Concentrates on eternally popular series on lawyers, on married life, on liberated women, etc. Selection, introduction, and notes on plates by Charles F. Ramus. Total of 158pp. 9⅜ x 12¼.   23512-2 Pa. $6.00

DRAWINGS OF MUCHA, Alphonse Maria Mucha. Work reveals draftsman of highest caliber: studies for famous posters and paintings, renderings for book illustrations and ads, etc. 70 works, 9 in color; including 6 items not drawings. Introduction. List of illustrations. 72pp. 9⅜ x 12¼. (Available in U.S. only)   23672-2 Pa. $4.00

GIOVANNI BATTISTA PIRANESI: DRAWINGS IN THE PIERPONT MORGAN LIBRARY, Giovanni Battista Piranesi. For first time ever all of Morgan Library's collection, world's largest. 167 illustrations of rare Piranesi drawings—archeological, architectural, decorative and visionary. Essay, detailed list of drawings, chronology, captions. Edited by Felice Stampfle. 144pp. 9⅜ x 12¼.   23714-1 Pa. $7.50

NEW YORK ETCHINGS (1905-1949), John Sloan. All of important American artist's N.Y. life etchings. 67 works include some of his best art; also lively historical record—Greenwich Village, tenement scenes. Edited by Sloan's widow. Introduction and captions. 79pp. 8⅜ x 11¼.
                                                    23651-X Pa. $4.00

CHINESE PAINTING AND CALLIGRAPHY: A PICTORIAL SURVEY, Wan-go Weng. 69 fine examples from John M. Crawford's matchless private collection: landscapes, birds, flowers, human figures, etc., plus calligraphy. Every basic form included: hanging scrolls, handscrolls, album leaves, fans, etc. 109 illustrations. Introduction. Captions. 192pp. 8⅞ x 11¾.
                                                    23707-9 Pa. $7.95

DRAWINGS OF REMBRANDT, edited by Seymour Slive. Updated Lippmann, Hofstede de Groot edition, with definitive scholarly apparatus. All portraits, biblical sketches, landscapes, nudes, Oriental figures, classical studies, together with selection of work by followers. 550 illustrations. Total of 630pp. 9⅛ x 12¼.   21485-0, 21486-9 Pa., Two-vol. set $15.00

THE DISASTERS OF WAR, Francisco Goya. 83 etchings record horrors of Napoleonic wars in Spain and war in general. Reprint of 1st edition, plus 3 additional plates. Introduction by Philip Hofer. 97pp. 9⅜ x 8¼.
                                                    21872-4 Pa. $4.00

THE SENSE OF BEAUTY, George Santayana. Masterfully written discussion of nature of beauty, materials of beauty, form, expression; art, literature, social sciences all involved. 168pp. 5⅜ x 8½. 20238-0 Pa. $3.00

ON THE IMPROVEMENT OF THE UNDERSTANDING, Benedict Spinoza. Also contains *Ethics, Correspondence*, all in excellent R. Elwes translation. Basic works on entry to philosophy, pantheism, exchange of ideas with great contemporaries. 402pp. 5⅜ x 8½. 20250-X Pa. $4.50

THE TRAGIC SENSE OF LIFE, Miguel de Unamuno. Acknowledged masterpiece of existential literature, one of most important books of 20th century. Introduction by Madariaga. 367pp. 5⅜ x 8½. 20257-7 Pa. $4.50

THE GUIDE FOR THE PERPLEXED, Moses Maimonides. Great classic of medieval Judaism attempts to reconcile revealed religion (Pentateuch, commentaries) with Aristotelian philosophy. Important historically, still relevant in problems. Unabridged Friedlander translation. Total of 473pp. 5⅜ x 8½. 20351-4 Pa. $6.00

THE I CHING (THE BOOK OF CHANGES), translated by James Legge. Complete translation of basic text plus appendices by Confucius, and Chinese commentary of most penetrating divination manual ever prepared. Indispensable to study of early Oriental civilizations, to modern inquiring reader. 448pp. 5⅜ x 8½. 21062-6 Pa. $5.00

THE EGYPTIAN BOOK OF THE DEAD, E. A. Wallis Budge. Complete reproduction of Ani's papyrus, finest ever found. Full hieroglyphic text, interlinear transliteration, word for word translation, smooth translation. Basic work, for Egyptology, for modern study of psychic matters. Total of 533pp. 6½ x 9¼. (Available in U.S. only) 21866-X Pa. $5.95

THE GODS OF THE EGYPTIANS, E. A. Wallis Budge. Never excelled for richness, fullness: all gods, goddesses, demons, mythical figures of Ancient Egypt; their legends, rites, incarnations, variations, powers, etc. Many hieroglyphic texts cited. Over 225 illustrations, plus 6 color plates. Total of 988pp. 6⅛ x 9¼. (Available in U.S. only) 22055-9, 22056-7 Pa., Two-vol. set $16.00

THE STANDARD BOOK OF QUILT MAKING AND COLLECTING, Marguerite Ickis. Full information, full-sized patterns for making 46 traditional quilts, also 150 other patterns. Quilted cloths, lame, satin quilts, etc. 483 illustrations. 273pp. 6⅞ x 9⅝. 20582-7 Pa. $4.95

CORAL GARDENS AND THEIR MAGIC, Bronsilaw Malinowski. Classic study of the methods of tilling the soil and of agricultural rites in the Trobriand Islands of Melanesia. Author is one of the most important figures in the field of modern social anthropology. 143 illustrations. Indexes. Total of 911pp. of text. 5⅝ x 8¼. (Available in U.S. only) 23597-1 Pa. $12.95

THE AMERICAN SENATOR, Anthony Trollope. Little known, long unavailable Trollope novel on a grand scale. Here are humorous comment on American vs. English culture, and stunning portrayal of a heroine/villainess. Superb evocation of Victorian village life. 561pp. 5⅜ x 8½.
23801-6 Pa. $6.00

WAS IT MURDER? James Hilton. The author of *Lost Horizon* and *Goodbye, Mr. Chips* wrote one detective novel (under a pen-name) which was quickly forgotten and virtually lost, even at the height of Hilton's fame. This edition brings it back—a finely crafted public school puzzle resplendent with Hilton's stylish atmosphere. A thoroughly English thriller by the creator of Shangri-la. 252pp. 5⅜ x 8. (Available in U.S. only)
23774-5 Pa. $3.00

CENTRAL PARK: A PHOTOGRAPHIC GUIDE, Victor Laredo and Henry Hope Reed. 121 superb photographs show dramatic views of Central Park: Bethesda Fountain, Cleopatra's Needle, Sheep Meadow, the Blockhouse, plus people engaged in many park activities: ice skating, bike riding, etc. Captions by former Curator of Central Park, Henry Hope Reed, provide historical view, changes, etc. Also photos of N.Y. landmarks on park's periphery. 96pp. 8½ x 11. 23750-8 Pa. $4.50

NANTUCKET IN THE NINETEENTH CENTURY, Clay Lancaster. 180 rare photographs, stereographs, maps, drawings and floor plans recreate unique American island society. Authentic scenes of shipwreck, lighthouses, streets, homes are arranged in geographic sequence to provide walking-tour guide to old Nantucket existing today. Introduction, captions. 160pp. 8⅞ x 11¾. 23747-8 Pa. $6.95

STONE AND MAN: A PHOTOGRAPHIC EXPLORATION, Andreas Feininger. 106 photographs by *Life* photographer Feininger portray man's deep passion for stone through the ages. Stonehenge-like megaliths, fortified towns, sculpted marble and crumbling tenements show textures, beauties, fascination. 128pp. 9¼ x 10¾. 23756-7 Pa. $5.95

CIRCLES, A MATHEMATICAL VIEW, D. Pedoe. Fundamental aspects of college geometry, non-Euclidean geometry, and other branches of mathematics: representing circle by point. Poincare model, isoperimetric property, etc. Stimulating recreational reading. 66 figures. 96pp. 5⅝ x 8¼.
63698-4 Pa. $2.75

THE DISCOVERY OF NEPTUNE, Morton Grosser. Dramatic scientific history of the investigations leading up to the actual discovery of the eighth planet of our solar system. Lucid, well-researched book by well-known historian of science. 172pp. 5⅜ x 8½. 23726-5 Pa. $3.50

THE DEVIL'S DICTIONARY. Ambrose Bierce. Barbed, bitter, brilliant witticisms in the form of a dictionary. Best, most ferocious satire America has produced. 145pp. 5⅜ x 8½. 20487-1 Pa. $2.25

CATALOGUE OF DOVER BOOKS

HISTORY OF BACTERIOLOGY, William Bulloch. The only comprehensive history of bacteriology from the beginnings through the 19th century. Special emphasis is given to biography-Leeuwenhoek, etc. Brief accounts of 350 bacteriologists form a separate section. No clearer, fuller study, suitable to scientists and general readers, has yet been written. 52 illustrations. 448pp. 5⅝ x 8¼. 23761-3 Pa. $6.50

THE COMPLETE NONSENSE OF EDWARD LEAR, Edward Lear. All nonsense limericks, zany alphabets, Owl and Pussycat, songs, nonsense botany, etc., illustrated by Lear. Total of 321pp. 5⅜ x 8½. (Available in U.S. only) 20167-8 Pa. $3.95

INGENIOUS MATHEMATICAL PROBLEMS AND METHODS, Louis A. Graham. Sophisticated material from Graham *Dial*, applied and pure; stresses solution methods. Logic, number theory, networks, inversions, etc. 237pp. 5⅜ x 8½. 20545-2 Pa. $4.50

BEST MATHEMATICAL PUZZLES OF SAM LOYD, edited by Martin Gardner. Bizarre, original, whimsical puzzles by America's greatest puzzler. From fabulously rare *Cyclopedia*, including famous 14-15 puzzles, the Horse of a Different Color, 115 more. Elementary math. 150 illustrations. 167pp. 5⅜ x 8½. 20498-7 Pa. $2.75

THE BASIS OF COMBINATION IN CHESS, J. du Mont. Easy-to-follow, instructive book on elements of combination play, with chapters on each piece and every powerful combination team—two knights, bishop and knight, rook and bishop, etc. 250 diagrams. 218pp. 5⅜ x 8½. (Available in U.S. only) 23644-7 Pa. $3.50

MODERN CHESS STRATEGY, Ludek Pachman. The use of the queen, the active king, exchanges, pawn play, the center, weak squares, etc. Section on rook alone worth price of the book. Stress on the moderns. Often considered the most important book on strategy. 314pp. 5⅜ x 8½. 20290-9 Pa. $4.50

LASKER'S MANUAL OF CHESS, Dr. Emanuel Lasker. Great world champion offers very thorough coverage of all aspects of chess. Combinations, position play, openings, end game, aesthetics of chess, philosophy of struggle, much more. Filled with analyzed games. 390pp. 5⅜ x 8½. 20640-8 Pa. $5.00

500 MASTER GAMES OF CHESS, S. Tartakower, J. du Mont. Vast collection of great chess games from 1798-1938, with much material nowhere else readily available. Fully annoted, arranged by opening for easier study. 664pp. 5⅜ x 8½. 23208-5 Pa. $7.50

A GUIDE TO CHESS ENDINGS, Dr. Max Euwe, David Hooper. One of the finest modern works on chess endings. Thorough analysis of the most frequently encountered endings by former world champion. 331 examples, each with diagram. 248pp. 5⅜ x 8½. 23332-4 Pa. $3.75

THE EARLY WORK OF AUBREY BEARDSLEY, Aubrey Beardsley. 157 plates, 2 in color: *Manon Lescaut, Madame Bovary, Morte Darthur, Salome,* other. Introduction by H. Marillier. 182pp. 8⅛ x 11. 21816-3 Pa. $4.50

THE LATER WORK OF AUBREY BEARDSLEY, Aubrey Beardsley. Exotic masterpieces of full maturity: *Venus and Tannhauser, Lysistrata, Rape of the Lock, Volpone,* Savoy material, etc. 174 plates, 2 in color. 186pp. 8⅛ x 11. 21817-1 Pa. $5.95

THOMAS NAST'S CHRISTMAS DRAWINGS, Thomas Nast. Almost all Christmas drawings by creator of image of Santa Claus as we know it, and one of America's foremost illustrators and political cartoonists. 66 illustrations. 3 illustrations in color on covers. 96pp. 8⅜ x 11¼. 23660-9 Pa. $3.50

THE DORÉ ILLUSTRATIONS FOR DANTE'S DIVINE COMEDY, Gustave Doré. All 135 plates from Inferno, Purgatory, Paradise; fantastic tortures, infernal landscapes, celestial wonders. Each plate with appropriate (translated) verses. 141pp. 9 x 12. 23231-X Pa. $4.50

DORÉ'S ILLUSTRATIONS FOR RABELAIS, Gustave Doré. 252 striking illustrations of *Gargantua and Pantagruel* books by foremost 19th-century illustrator. Including 60 plates, 192 delightful smaller illustrations. 153pp. 9 x 12. 23656-0 Pa. $5.00

LONDON: A PILGRIMAGE, Gustave Doré, Blanchard Jerrold. Squalor, riches, misery, beauty of mid-Victorian metropolis; 55 wonderful plates, 125 other illustrations, full social, cultural text by Jerrold. 191pp. of text. 9⅜ x 12¼. 22306-X Pa. $7.00

THE RIME OF THE ANCIENT MARINER, Gustave Doré, S. T. Coleridge. Dore's finest work, 34 plates capture moods, subtleties of poem. Full text. Introduction by Millicent Rose. 77pp. 9¼ x 12. 22305-1 Pa. $3.50

THE DORE BIBLE ILLUSTRATIONS, Gustave Doré. All wonderful, detailed plates: Adam and Eve, Flood, Babylon, Life of Jesus, etc. Brief King James text with each plate. Introduction by Millicent Rose. 241 plates. 241pp. 9 x 12. 23004-X Pa. $6.00

THE COMPLETE ENGRAVINGS, ETCHINGS AND DRYPOINTS OF ALBRECHT DURER. "Knight, Death and Devil"; "Melencolia," and more—all Dürer's known works in all three media, including 6 works formerly attributed to him. 120 plates. 235pp. 8⅜ x 11¼. 22851-7 Pa. $6.50

MECHANICK EXERCISES ON THE WHOLE ART OF PRINTING, Joseph Moxon. First complete book (1683-4) ever written about typography, a compendium of everything known about printing at the latter part of 17th century. Reprint of 2nd (1962) Oxford Univ. Press edition. 74 illustrations. Total of 550pp. 6⅛ x 9¼. 23617-X Pa. $7.95

THE ANATOMY OF THE HORSE, George Stubbs. Often considered the great masterpiece of animal anatomy. Full reproduction of 1766 edition, plus prospectus; original text and modernized text. 36 plates. Introduction by Eleanor Garvey. 121pp. 11 x 14¾. 23402-9 Pa. $6.00

BRIDGMAN'S LIFE DRAWING, George B. Bridgman. More than 500 illustrative drawings and text teach you to abstract the body into its major masses, use light and shade, proportion; as well as specific areas of anatomy, of which Bridgman is master. 192pp. 6½ x 9¼. (Available in U.S. only) 22710-3 Pa. $3.50

ART NOUVEAU DESIGNS IN COLOR, Alphonse Mucha, Maurice Verneuil, Georges Auriol. Full-color reproduction of *Combinaisons ornementales* (c. 1900) by Art Nouveau masters. Floral, animal, geometric, interlacings, swashes—borders, frames, spots—all incredibly beautiful. 60 plates, hundreds of designs. 9⅜ x 8-1/16. 22885-1 Pa. $4.00

FULL-COLOR FLORAL DESIGNS IN THE ART NOUVEAU STYLE, E. A. Seguy. 166 motifs, on 40 plates, from *Les fleurs et leurs applications decoratives* (1902): borders, circular designs, repeats, allovers, "spots." All in authentic Art Nouveau colors. 48pp. 9⅜ x 12¼. 23439-8 Pa. $5.00

A DIDEROT PICTORIAL ENCYCLOPEDIA OF TRADES AND IN-DUSTRY, edited by Charles C. Gillispie. 485 most interesting plates from the great French Encyclopedia of the 18th century show hundreds of working figures, artifacts, process, land and cityscapes; glassmaking, papermaking, metal extraction, construction, weaving, making furniture, clothing, wigs, dozens of other activities. Plates fully explained. 920pp. 9 x 12. 22284-5, 22285-3 Clothbd., Two-vol. set $40.00

HANDBOOK OF EARLY ADVERTISING ART, Clarence P. Hornung. Largest collection of copyright-free early and antique advertising art ever compiled. Over 6,000 illustrations, from Franklin's time to the 1890's for special effects, novelty. Valuable source, almost inexhaustible.
Pictorial Volume. Agriculture, the zodiac, animals, autos, birds, Christmas, fire engines, flowers, trees, musical instruments, ships, games and sports, much more. Arranged by subject matter and use. 237 plates. 288pp. 9 x 12. 20122-8 Clothbd. $14..50

Typographical Volume. Roman and Gothic faces ranging from 10 point to 300 point, "Barnum," German and Old English faces, script, logotypes, scrolls and flourishes, 1115 ornamental initials, 67 complete alphabets, more. 310 plates. 320pp. 9 x 12. 20123-6 Clothbd. $15.00

CALLIGRAPHY (CALLIGRAPHIA LATINA), J. G. Schwandner. High point of 18th-century ornamental calligraphy. Very ornate initials, scrolls, borders, cherubs, birds, lettered examples. 172pp. 9 x 13. 20475-8 Pa. $7.00

THE DEPRESSION YEARS AS PHOTOGRAPHED BY ARTHUR ROTH-STEIN, Arthur Rothstein. First collection devoted entirely to the work of outstanding 1930s photographer: famous dust storm photo, ragged children, unemployed, etc. 120 photographs. Captions. 119pp. 9¼ x 10¾.
23590-4 Pa. $5.00

CAMERA WORK: A PICTORIAL GUIDE, Alfred Stieglitz. All 559 illus-trations and plates from the most important periodical in the history of art photography, Camera Work (1903-17). Presented four to a page, re-duced in size but still clear, in strict chronological order, with complete captions. Three indexes. Glossary. Bibliography. 176pp. 8⅜ x 11¼.
23591-2 Pa. $6.95

ALVIN LANGDON COBURN, PHOTOGRAPHER, Alvin L. Coburn. Re-vealing autobiography by one of greatest photographers of 20th century gives insider's version of Photo-Secession, plus comments on his own work. 77 photographs by Coburn. Edited by Helmut and Alison Gernsheim. 160pp. 8⅛ x 11.
23685-4 Pa. $6.00

NEW YORK IN THE FORTIES, Andreas Feininger. 162 brilliant photo-graphs by the well-known photographer, formerly with Life magazine, show commuters, shoppers, Times Square at night, Harlem nightclub, Lower East Side, etc. Introduction and full captions by John von Hartz. 181pp. 9¼ x 10¾.
23585-8 Pa. $6.95

GREAT NEWS PHOTOS AND THE STORIES BEHIND THEM, John Faber. Dramatic volume of 140 great news photos, 1855 through 1976, and revealing stories behind them, with both historical and technical in-formation. Hindenburg disaster, shooting of Oswald, nomination of Jimmy Carter, etc. 160pp. 8¼ x 11.
23667-6 Pa. $5.00

THE ART OF THE CINEMATOGRAPHER, Leonard Maltin. Survey of American cinematography history and anecdotal interviews with 5 masters—Arthur Miller, Hal Mohr, Hal Rosson, Lucien Ballard, and Conrad Hall. Very large selection of behind-the-scenes production photos. 105 photo-graphs. Filmographies. Index. Originally Behind the Camera. 144pp. 8¼ x 11.
23686-2 Pa. $5.00

DESIGNS FOR THE THREE-CORNERED HAT (LE TRICORNE), Pablo Picasso. 32 fabulously rare drawings—including 31 color illustrations of costumes and accessories—for 1919 production of famous ballet. Edited by Parmenia Migel, who has written new introduction. 48pp. 9⅜ x 12¼. (Available in U.S. only)
23709-5 Pa. $5.00

NOTES OF A FILM DIRECTOR, Sergei Eisenstein. Greatest Russian filmmaker explains montage, making of Alexander Nevsky, aesthetics; com-ments on self, associates, great rivals (Chaplin), similar material. 78 illus-trations. 240pp. 5⅜ x 8½.
22392-2 Pa. $4.50

HOLLYWOOD GLAMOUR PORTRAITS, edited by John Kobal. 145 photos capture the stars from 1926-49, the high point in portrait photography. Gable, Harlow, Bogart, Bacall, Hedy Lamarr, Marlene Dietrich, Robert Montgomery, Marlon Brando, Veronica Lake; 94 stars in all. Full background on photographers, technical aspects, much more. Total of 160pp. 8⅜ x 11¼.   23352-9 Pa. $6.00

THE NEW YORK STAGE: FAMOUS PRODUCTIONS IN PHOTO-GRAPHS, edited by Stanley Appelbaum. 148 photographs from Museum of City of New York show 142 plays, 1883-1939. *Peter Pan, The Front Page, Dead End, Our Town,* O'Neill, hundreds of actors and actresses, etc. Full indexes. 154pp. 9½ x 10.   23241-7 Pa. $6.00

DIALOGUES CONCERNING TWO NEW SCIENCES, Galileo Galilei. Encompassing 30 years of experiment and thought, these dialogues deal with geometric demonstrations of fracture of solid bodies, cohesion, leverage, speed of light and sound, pendulums, falling bodies, accelerated motion, etc. 300pp. 5⅜ x 8½.   60099-8 Pa. $4.00

THE GREAT OPERA STARS IN HISTORIC PHOTOGRAPHS, edited by James Camner. 343 portraits from the 1850s to the 1940s: Tamburini, Mario, Caliapin, Jeritza, Melchior, Melba, Patti, Pinza, Schipa, Caruso, Farrar, Steber, Gobbi, and many more—270 performers in all. Index. 199pp. 8⅜ x 11¼.   23575-0 Pa. $7.50

J. S. BACH, Albert Schweitzer. Great full-length study of Bach, life, background to music, music, by foremost modern scholar. Ernest Newman translation. 650 musical examples. Total of 928pp. 5⅜ x 8½. (Available in U.S. only)   21631-4, 21632-2 Pa., Two-vol. set $11.00

COMPLETE PIANO SONATAS, Ludwig van Beethoven. All sonatas in the fine Schenker edition, with fingering, analytical material. One of best modern editions. Total of 615pp. 9 x 12. (Available in U.S. only)
                              23134-8, 23135-6 Pa., Two-vol. set $15.50

KEYBOARD MUSIC, J. S. Bach. Bach-Gesellschaft edition. For harpsichord, piano, other keyboard instruments. English Suites, French Suites, Six Partitas, Goldberg Variations, Two-Part Inventions, Three-Part Sinfonias. 312pp. 8⅛ x 11. (Available in U.S. only)   22360-4 Pa. $6.95

FOUR SYMPHONIES IN FULL SCORE, Franz Schubert. Schubert's four most popular symphonies: No. 4 in C Minor ("Tragic"); No. 5 in B-flat Major; No. 8 in B Minor ("Unfinished"); No. 9 in C Major ("Great"). Breitkopf & Hartel edition. Study score. 261pp. 9⅜ x 12¼.
                                                    23681-1 Pa. $6.50

THE AUTHENTIC GILBERT & SULLIVAN SONGBOOK, W. S. Gilbert, A. S. Sullivan. Largest selection available; 92 songs, uncut, original keys, in piano rendering approved by Sullivan. Favorites and lesser-known fine numbers. Edited with plot synopses by James Spero. 3 illustrations. 399pp. 9 x 12.   23482-7 Pa. $9.95

CATALOGUE OF DOVER BOOKS

AMERICAN ANTIQUE FURNITURE, Edgar G. Miller, Jr. The basic coverage of all American furniture before 1840: chapters per item chronologically cover all types of furniture, with more than 2100 photos. Total of 1106pp. 7⅞ x 10¾. 21599-7, 21600-4 Pa., Two-vol. set $17.90

ILLUSTRATED GUIDE TO SHAKER FURNITURE, Robert Meader. Director, Shaker Museum, Old Chatham, presents up-to-date coverage of all furniture and appurtenances, with much on local styles not available elsewhere. 235 photos. 146pp. 9 x 12. 22819-3 Pa. $6.00

ORIENTAL RUGS, ANTIQUE AND MODERN, Walter A. Hawley. Persia, Turkey, Caucasus, Central Asia, China, other traditions. Best general survey of all aspects: styles and periods, manufacture, uses, symbols and their interpretation, and identification. 96 illustrations, 11 in color. 320pp. 6⅛ x 9¼. 22366-3 Pa. $6.95

CHINESE POTTERY AND PORCELAIN, R. L. Hobson. Detailed descriptions and analyses by former Keeper of the Department of Oriental Antiquities and Ethnography at the British Museum. Covers hundreds of pieces from primitive times to 1915. Still the standard text for most periods. 136 plates, 40 in full color. Total of 750pp. 5⅜ x 8½.

23253-0 Pa. $10.00

THE WARES OF THE MING DYNASTY, R. L. Hobson. Foremost scholar examines and illustrates many varieties of Ming (1368-1644). Famous blue and white, polychrome, lesser-known styles and shapes. 117 illustrations, 9 full color, of outstanding pieces. Total of 263pp. 6⅛ x 9¼. (Available in U.S. only) 23652-8 Pa. $6.00

Prices subject to change without notice.

Available at your book dealer or write for free catalogue to Dept. GI, Dover Publications, Inc., 180 Varick St., N.Y., N.Y. 10014. Dover publishes more than 175 books each year on science, elementary and advanced mathematics, biology, music, art, literary history, social sciences and other areas.